Dario Fo and Franca Rame

Dario Fo
AND
Franca Rame

Harlequins of the Revolution

Joseph Farrell

Methuen

Published by Methuen 2001

1 3 5 7 9 10 8 6 4 2

This edition published in Great Britain in 2001 by
Methuen Publishing Ltd
215 Vauxhall Bridge Road, London SW1V 1EJ

Methuen Publishing Limited Reg. No. 3543167

A CIP catalogue record for this book is available
from the British Library

ISBN 0 413 70910 8

Designed by Helen Ewing

Printed and bound in Great Britain by
Creative Print and Design (Wales), Ebbw Vale

For Maureen,
for taking away the shadows

Contents

Preface

On a recent visit to the home of Dario Fo and Franca Rame in Milan, I discovered Dario in conversation, of a sort, with three actors from Sri Lanka. None of the three Sri Lankans spoke Italian, but one of them was making efforts to express himself in English, which was somewhat futile, since Dario has no knowledge of the language. The four were communicating by means of surprisingly random and ill-focused gestures and by looking at production photographs of Dario in various roles. The visitors listened intently and uncomprehendingly as Dario expatiated on the problems of Italian theatre and Italian politics in the early seventies, and he listened with an expression which suggested that the spirit was willing as they told him how much he was revered in their country. He got the idea that they admired *Accidental Death of an Anarchist* and thought they might be seeking permission to stage *Can't Pay? Won't Pay!*, but had not understood that they were saying that these two plays had already been produced and that the depiction of a dissident mysteriously killed in police custody, or the description of people driven by desperation to take the law into their own hands had struck a chord with them.

The following week, I was in Rome listening to Dario's international agent, Flavia Tolnay, speak of plays by Dario and Franca then being staged in various parts of Europe. There had been a production of *Can't Pay? Won't Pay!* which had been panned by critics in London, but a version of *Sex? Yes! Don't Mind If I Do!* was in the fourth year of a run in Madrid, while *Female Monologues* was opening in Stockholm. There was also talk of a production of the *Devil in Drag* by a youth offshoot of the Royal National Theatre, and the Comédie-Française had been in contact about a new work. The growth areas were Brazil and Turkey, who had just discovered Dario Fo. Impresarios there were queueing up to secure rights for works first performed in Italy two decades previously. Why these two countries, she wondered?

This international interest is, in one sense, depressing for a biographer.

A separate study could be made of the reputation of Dario Fo and Franca Rame in many countries in the world. Franca has shown herself to be an astonishing archivist, who has collected everything written about them in every language of every country they have visited since they first worked together. The mass of material is impressive, and overwhelming. There are articles on their work not only in European languages such as English, French and Catalan, but also in Asian languages like Chinese, Japanese and Farsi. Who could digest them all?

It is plainly impossible for any one work to do justice to this level of international interest. Even inside Italy, Dario and Franca have been active in many fields and have touched the lives of many unexpected people. Apart from theatre, they have been involved in many of the political campaigns which have rocked Italy during three turbulent decades, not merely as observers but as participants. Their views and their actions have been influential. Their plays were an important reference point during the years of militant left-wing activity which followed 1968. In the eighties, Franca's monologues reflected and influenced the emergence of feminism, and latterly they have turned their attention to contemporary problems relating to ecology and the environment.

There is a further challenge. Any biography of either Franca or Dario will inevitably become, whatever the initial intentions of the biographer, a joint biography. Franca has complained on several occasions of being written out of the script, or of being reduced to the status of pedestal under the monument which is Dario. The two have not invariably seen eye to eye on theatre and politics and there have been differences in personal affairs, but theirs has been a deep, lasting and fruitful collaboration. Unpicking the contribution of the one or the other is a difficult and probably pointless task. The best that can be done is to keep the dual nature of their work in view.

This biography has set itself three aims. It attempts to execute the prime duty of the biographer, which is to chronicle what its subjects have done and what has been done to them. Next, since theirs has been a life dedicated to theatre, it tries to illustrate the nature of their achievement and the specific nature of the theatrical principles which have motivated them. There is no body of systematic theoretical writings by Fo to stand alongside those of Brecht or Stanislavsky, but it is possible to extract from the various talks, workshops and demonstrations given in many countries a vision of theatre which is as coherent and challenging as anything offered by the others. Finally, their theatre has been, as they have consistently maintained, profoundly political. The topics of many plays, especially in the sixties and seventies, were taken from the headlines of the day. They used box-office income to subsidize movements and causes they supported, and were themselves frequently to be found demonstrating on the streets or in occupied factories. It has been my intention to try and define the political problems and movements in Italy during times of great instability and uncertainty. In addition, there is a new task facing critics of Fo and Rame's theatre. As with Brecht, there is more to their theatre than politics. Fo belongs to a tradition born centuries before a stone was thrown in Paris in 1968, and which will outlast any political demonstration. The task is to determine how he altered that tradition.

There are many people to whom I am indebted for help on this biography. My principal debt is to Franca Rame for her patience and willingness to spend time with me, answering questions. I am grateful to Dario Fo for many conversations, and to Emilio Tadini, Flavia Tolnay, Bianca Fo Garambois, Walter Valeri, Ron Jenkins, Piero Sciotto, Paolo Puppa, Marilyn Suckle, Vittorio Franceschi, Tony Mitchell, Chris Cairns, Nanni Ricordi, Ed Emery and others who preferred not to be named. I owe a special debt of gratitude to Antonio Scuderi for reading through the text and offering many helpful suggestions. I cannot quantify my debt to Maureen.

Chapter 1

Childhood and War

Dario Fo was born in the village of San Giano near Lake Maggiore on 24 March 1926, four years after Mussolini's march on Rome. The stout anti-Fascism of his immediate family left an enduring mark, but the centuries-old culture of his birthplace made a deeper, more lasting impact. 'I am quite certain,' he wrote,

> that everything has its origins in the place you are born. For my part, I was born in a ... village of smugglers and poachers, two trades for which you need, in addition to a generous helping of courage, a great deal of imagination. It is well known that anyone who uses imagination to break the law will always have a lot left over for his own enjoyment and that of his closest friends.[1]

His father, Felice Fo, was a stationmaster, and his mother, Pina Rota, was a woman of peasant stock; and neither of them was given to law-breaking. On his mother's side, Dario found an abundance of that whimsical imagination and creative flair he regarded as his principal inheritance from his boyhood on the lake. The Rotas had lived in Monferrato in Piedmont until Dario's great-grandfather, Giuseppe, moved the family to Sartirana, in southern Lombardy. Only one aspect of Giuseppe's talents has lingered in the family memory: he could read and write in an age of mass illiteracy, and used these skills to compose commemorative eulogies or optimistic madrigals at funerals or weddings. The payment helped keep bread on the table. Sartirana was the chosen destination because it lay in the heart of Italy's rice-growing area, and the Rotas were peasants who intended to stick to their traditional way of life. Rice-growing was crippling, back-breaking work, requiring the mainly female employees to work bent double, with water up to their knees, but at least it offered some form of guaranteed income. Dario's grandmother, Maria, born in 1876, was required to leave home each day before dawn to walk three hours to the fields. It was thankless labour, and any woman who straightened up to relieve the pressure on her spine was liable to feel the supervisor's rod on her back, 'the same as they did with cows or oxen'. By the time Pina started work in the same fields, the rod was no longer in use but the women were still treated 'like beasts. I used to work ten to twelve hours a day when I was only ten,' she wrote, 'bending down in water that came up over my knees, with leeches clinging to my legs.'[2]

The family prospered, after a fashion, thanks to Pina's father, who was given the name Luigi at baptism but was invariably known as Bristin. He was born in 1860, and his hard work and ingenuity enabled him to rise to the status of *perdapè*, a dialect word which translates, approximately if unhelpfully, as 'lost foot'. To make a living from the land, a *perdapè* laboured 'from the stars to the stars', every day of the week, even on Sundays, with such exertion that his feet risked taking root in the soil. In the complex hierarchy of peasant life, he occupied an intermediate position between the normally absentee landowner from whom he rented his land and the casual workers who were taken on when needed. The various grades of peasant lived cheek by jowl on a *cascina*, a collective farmstead. Houses, stables, barns, pigsties and stalls for sheep, goats and cattle were huddled one alongside the other, while the central space was occupied by a compost heap and drinking trough. There were around one hundred people in the *cascina* inhabited by Dario's grandparents. Bristin and his wife Maria had seven children who survived infancy, Pina, Dario's mother, born in 1903, being the sixth. She was a sickly child, prone to all the illnesses that periodically struck the children of the area, so she derived little benefit from the garlic necklace she was made to wear to ward off disease.

It is Bristin who emerges as the dominant figure in her recollections of her girlhood, and as the central influence on Dario as a boy. A man of superabundant energy and initiative who combined the peasant's down-to-earth competence with an irrepressible imagination of his own, he made his mark on all who met him. The traditional methods of agriculture and the modesty of subsistence farming were not for him. He expanded his smallholding and experimented with systems for grafting and cross-pollinating apples and pears or plums and apricots in an attempt to produce new varieties of fruit. The results were sufficiently impressive to cause the university botanists in Padua to invite him, a mere peasant, to share the results of his research with them.

These achievements drew the respect of his contemporaries, but his real fame among them was due to his quixotic imagination, his malicious wit, his biting sarcasm, his ability as a teller of tales and his taste for rumbustious fun. The nickname 'Bristin', a local term for pepper seed, the part of the plant which burns and stings the tongue, was conferred in recognition of these qualities. 'When my father told stories about his own family, he put on the story-teller voice, which was solemn, with breaks for comic comments. We listened to him in astonishment,' wrote Pina. These monologues were acted rather than recounted, but what impressed her, and later Dario, was his ability to change key, to instil in his listeners a sense of fear or awe and then deftly switch the mood to deflating or liberating humour. Pina was especially impressed by the gruesome tale of the monks of Monferrato, a community of holy men who disapproved of the late-night drinking habits of the townsfolk but who, instead of limiting themselves to prayers and sermons, took to frightening revellers by climbing up the belfry and projecting weird, ghostlike shadows on to the walls of the village houses. The terrified drinkers assumed their village was viewed by God as a new Sodom and Gomorrah and, fearing a visitation by the Almighty, resolved to stay at home after nightfall. Business at the inns suffered until a tavernowner discovered that the shadows were not signs of divine displeasure but of vengeful malice by the monks. The enraged population marched on the monastery, locked the monks in the belfry and set fire to it, leaving them to roast. The story had a happy ending, since the frantic ringing of the bells brought rescuers from nearby, but thereafter the roistering and revelling resumed, while the monks were left to their chanting in the cloister. Bristin was an atheist, who took delight in anti-clerical jibes, and doubtless this added spice to the tale.[3]

He had no shame over being a peasant, even if he displayed his caste's ambiguous relationship with the land. For him, peasants were the dispossessed of the earth and working the land meant 'spitting sweat and blood', but he also believed that 'the only real gold was to be had from the land' and that there was a dignity and rightness to such labours. He was enraged when his sons and sons-in-law left the country for the city, one after the other. Pina was anxious to follow them. Dario later wrote that his mother described Sartirana as a paradise, adding that he, too, remembered it that way, and perhaps he did, but the view of the *cascina* and the village she expressed in her autobiographical *The Country of the Frogs* is decidedly disenchanted. The reference to the frogs is double-edged. Frogs were one of the plagues of ancient Egypt and she complained, unsurprisingly, of having to live surrounded by the croaking of frogs which even invaded the houses; but frogs were also a delicacy for those who could not afford meat. Chicken was the food of the masters.

The first meeting of Dario's parents is enveloped in a pleasing air of

Latin romance. Pina's eldest sister, Clementina, was engaged to one Luigi, a member of the extended Fo clan, and the guests at the wedding included Luigi's cousin, Felice Fo. As in the best love stories, Pina and Felice were immediately attracted to each other, but there was an obstacle on true love's smooth path: Pina was already engaged. It was not acceptable for young ladies to break promises of marriage, and when she announced her new love the ex-fiancé reacted as was expected of a man whose honour had been offended. He turned up in the *cascina* with a gun, demanding satisfaction and firing in all directions. Pina managed to hide and the man was calmed down before blood was spilled. Felice and Pina were married in 1925.

By coincidence, the Fos, too, could trace their ancestry back to Monferrato, although family historians speculate that the name was originally Genoese. Fo is not a particularly common name in any part of Italy and indeed Dario's sister, Bianca, claimed that they can always trace some family link with any other Fo they come across. Felice's father, Luigi, led the family migration from Piedmont to Lombardy in the late nineteenth century, with one branch settling in Sartirana and the rest moving up towards Lake Maggiore. They were more open to new technologies than the Rotas, and Luigi found employment with the Italian railways. He married Teresa Barzaghini, and they had three daughters and two sons, of whom Felice, born in 1898, was the youngest. Felice followed his father into the railways, although at the more elevated level of stationmaster.

Employment as a stationmaster was highly desirable in pre-war Italy. D. H. Lawrence wrote that life for an Italian stationmaster was one long conversation interrupted by a telephone call, but Felice took his job with greater seriousness. 'Our degree of poverty can be established in relation to the activity of my father, a stationmaster with the National Railways,' Dario wrote. The family was able to live comfortably, experiencing neither the extremes of wealth nor of poverty. Felice seems to have possessed no suit apart from his railway uniform, a striking red jacket and dark trousers which Pina cleaned every night, but in that he cut an imposing figure. Some pundits have read a great deal into the fact that he performed with amateur dramatic societies. While still in his mother's arms, Dario remembers being taken to see his father on stage in 'a cruel Ibsen play' featuring parents out to rid themselves of their child. His main reaction was dismay at seeing another child using his rocking-horse on stage. Felice was also given to going around the house declaiming, in a loud, resonant voice, verses from Giosuè Carducci, Italy's nineteenth-century Nobel Prize-winning poet, and from *Divina Commedia*.

The marriage was a happy one, but the two were very different personalities. 'My mother', wrote Dario, 'was full of fantasy and irony. My father less so, because he worked very hard and studied. He was self-taught.'[4] Pina was plainly a woman of spirit, of open affections, wide-ranging imagination and boundless creativity. She had little formal education, but shared with Bristin a restless curiosity. She inherited her father's nickname and many of his talents, including a flair for story-telling. Felice, on the other hand, was a man of serious manners and serious mind, and showed his gravitas by a tendency to wear his worries on his sleeve. The world was to be made aware that the problems of bringing up a young family were burdensome, especially on an inadequate income. For Bianca, he was a gentle, amiable man, but Dario remembers a harsher side to his nature.

> My father was severe, a bit like the tyrannical fathers described in the tear-jerking novels of other times. Like my grandfather, he was capable of extraordinary openness with his grandchildren, but he was very hard on his own children. He shouted a lot and at times raised his hands, even if he did regret it ten seconds later. I can still see one scene where my father slapped and kicked my brother because he had gone to steal fruit in the countryside.

Such experiences, and recollections of friends turning up at school covered with bruises or a broken nose, left Dario with an abiding horror of all forms of physical brutality. Later, he and Franca Rame would agree that no form of physical punishment would ever be employed towards their own son.[5]

Felice was a socialist, although not an active party member, and the family are still convinced that the Fascist apparatchiks made him pay by denying him a fixed posting. He and Pina were forced to live a nomadic existence in Lombardy as Felice was moved first to San Giano, where Dario was born, then to Luino, where Fulvio was born in 1928 and Bianca in 1931, then to Voghera, then Oleggio, and finally, in 1936, to Porto Valtraglia, on the shores of Lake Maggiore. Even though he was ten when they arrived there, this is the village which Dario regards as his childhood home.

Porto Valtraglia, a small town of around 1,000 souls, lies halfway up Lake Maggiore on the eastern side, not far from the Swiss border. Nestling between the mountains and the waters, it was and is an idyllic spot which has become a fabled place in Dario's private mythology. The lake was the heart of the world for him as a boy. In spring, the landscape is bright and lively, and in autumn, grave and peaceful. Dario never became a writer who excelled in poetic descriptive prose, but the colours and atmosphere of the landscape around Lake Maggiore appear in many of his paintings. Already, in his boyhood, he demonstrated that ease with the paintbrush which has never deserted him. In his earliest canvases, he depicted valleys, villages and farms of his native region with astonishing vividness and precision.

In Porto Valtraglia, Felice rented an art-nouveau villa, known locally as the *palazzetto*, which was surrounded by a garden stretching down to the lake. Grapes, apples, plums and other fruits and vegetables grew there, but workmen helped with the cultivation of the plants, so the children did not experience the grinding toil which was the lot of the peasant children in the neighbourhood. Near their house stood the villas of the *signori* from Milan, who came there in the summer to escape the heat of the city. Already, as a boy, Dario displayed spirit and imagination. Anecdotes abound. One summer, he built a boat, summoned the children of the neighbourhood for a ceremonial launch and turned up in a white uniform. Regrettably, the naval engineering was not of the required standard, for the craft capsized on its first outing. The *palazzetto* had a little tower, with a window opening on to the garden, and in summer-time Dario, Fulvio and Bianca converted the tower into a puppet theatre. Dario carved the puppets which represented devils, Russian princes or Pulcinella. The three children set up chairs in the garden and asked the infant spectators to make a payment towards the purchase of materials for future enterprises. The inspiration for such shows came partly from the touring puppet theatres which did the rounds of the villages on the lake. Dario and Fulvio went along as frequently as they could and learned by heart several of the standard dialogues. The circus was another occasional visitor. The children would be blacked up by the circus owners and sent round the village dressed in mock-African outfits to drum up interest. Bianca used one incident for a children's story she later published, with illustrations by Dario. In it, Dario disappeared when the circus arrived in town, but turned up in the big top that evening on an elephant's back, in the guise of an African boy.

Political events cast a shadow, but not one of sufficient strength to darken their lives. The opposition of Felice and Bristin to Mussolini and the Fascist regime was purely private. 'Capitalism, Vatican and Fascism – there's the great secret of the Trinity revealed,' was one of Bristin's slogans,[6] but Fascism and anti-Fascism intruded relatively little into domestic life. The parents did what was necessary to keep peace, for example, sending the children to the Fascist youth organization, the *balilla*. When he was sixteen, Dario won an art prize from a Fascist Youth organization for a portrait of

Fulvio.[7] Bianca once came rushing home from school in fear after listening to a denunciation in the classroom of the terrible creatures who were called socialists, and being subjected to mockery in the yard by other children who claimed her father was such a one. Felice diplomatically denied it.

'I had a happy childhood,' said Dario, 'even not counting the fact that I lived in a splendid place, on Lake Maggiore. I used to go to school on skis, just imagine what a joy that was. In spring, I walked there through fields of flowers.'[8] Any amateur psychologist hoping to locate some trauma or wound arising from family circumstances or relationships in Dario or his brother and sister will be disappointed. The nearest approach to any such feeling is the mild annoyance expressed by Bianca over the favoured treatment accorded Dario by Pina. His mother encouraged his youthful creativity and fostered the talents she believed he had, but she may also have been more protective towards him because of an already evident tendency towards absent-mindedness. In another story, Bianca retold a favourite family tale of Dario being sent out to buy butter and returning much later without the butter but with the body of a lizard whose colours had caught his imagination. 'He had always a pencil or a brush in his hand,' recalls Bianca, 'always sketching out some face, figure, tree or house.' His mother's pride was strained when Dario's distracted artistic bent led him to use a nail to scratch wild scenes on the wooden bedstead.

Porto Valtraglia was unlike the other fishing communities which lined Lake Maggiore. Like them, the principal legal occupation was fishing and the main illegal source of income was smuggling, but Porto Valtraglia also boasted a glassworks, an industry which gave this small town an unexpectedly cosmopolitan stamp. The owners of the factory had recruited their workers from all over Europe, from Flanders, France, Germany and Slovenia, so Dario's schoolfriends had a range of exotic names and something of a dual culture. 'It was an absurd, paradoxical place,' he wrote, 'which came to life by night, so much so that the nickname of the inhabitants was "half-mouse", in other words, "bat". Many of the men had to do night-shifts, so the town was alive, with its bars and restaurants always full of people going to and coming from work.' He made the strange boast that Porto Valtraglia had the highest proportion of madmen in Italy. 'They had a special ambulance to transport people from the town to the asylum,' he recalled, bizarrely.

Dario's grandmother, Maria, died in 1938, too early to leave the children anything other than a vague memory of a quiet woman with a soft voice, but Bristin continued to enthral them. After the death of his wife, he sold up but resisted all attempts to have him leave the land. When the Fo children went to visit him in Sartirana, he joined boisterously and vivaciously in their games, and more than once constructed precarious rafts on which, to Pina's consternation, he took them cruising on the region's small canals. Before Bristin's retirement, Dario often accompanied him on his rounds to the nearby villages and farmsteads to sell his produce. Their arrival would cause outbursts of excited expectation, as Bristin publicized his wares with his extemporized tales and extravagant flights of fancy. He spread local news and peddled outrageous gossip, illustrating sexual exploits and misdemeanours with leeks and courgettes. 'Tragedy in Sarzana' was one typical opening gambit. 'He came out on to the balcony in his underwear, dragging his naked wife behind him. "She's a whore," he announced to the crowd. Meanwhile, her faithless friend was racing down the side stairs, but he slipped and broke his leg. You can find him in hospital at Carrara, room 32. Bring him flowers, he deserves them.'[9] Dario later paid Bristin the highest compliment in his repertory by referring to him as 'the first Ruzzante' he had known, associating him with the sixteenth-century actor-author who was to become Dario's supreme theatrical model and inspiration.

Bristin was typical of the *fabulatore*, or story-teller, a familiar figure in Porto Valtraglia and the one who made the deepest contribution to Dario's development. Years later in his official speech to the Royal Academy in Stockholm on his acceptance of the Nobel Prize, he recalled his debt to the men who had fashioned from their own experience, or from their own fantasy, stories they retold for fun or for profit. There were still travelling, professional story-tellers in the region, but the *fabulatori* who particularly fascinated Dario were the local fishermen who spun their yarns as they repaired their nets, or the glassworkers who recounted their narratives while blowing glass.

These stories had no savour of humdrum realism. They were hyperbolic tales spiced with whimsy, in which the grotesque and the absurd, observation and surreal wit, mordant satire and resigned nonchalance mingled together. They transported the audience into a fantasy dimension which somehow overlapped with the world inhabited by the narrator and the listener. Although seemingly a retelling of real events, the list of improbable characters included an enthusiastic fisherman who cast his line so far it fell on the opposite bank of the lake, causing him to haul in a church and congregation; giant snails which terrified their hunters; and women who got drunk in the taverns and returned home to beat up their husbands. There was one long tale, retold during the Nobel Prize speech in Stockholm, dealing with the village of Caldè as it slipped into the lake. The villagers, too stubborn to admit what was happening before their eyes, went under with the village but carried on life under water as though they were exposed to nothing more unusual than a general dampening of the climate. Stories from the Bible or mythology could be adapted and turned on their head. At night, when the three children were in their bedroom, Dario retold these stories to his brother and sister, with improvised additions and comment of his own. Like the Brontë sisters in Yorkshire, the Fo children inhabited their own private fantasy land, peopled by extravagant villagers from far-off lands and by lakeside monsters, creatures of the air and princelings from the east.

The experience of listening to these men left an enduring mark.

> Having grown up in a village where every man is a character, where every character is in search of a tale to tell, I was able to enter the theatre with a baggage which was unusual and, even more, alive, up-to-date and true. True in the way that stories invented by true men are true.[10]

The teller of tales provided him with his first model in theatre, and the art of the *fabulatore* even lay behind mature works such as *Mistero buffo* or *The Tale of a Tiger*. Whimsy had its limits, since Fo believed that the fantasy of the *fabulatore* often concealed a vein of anger.

> Simplicity was their keynote . . . but beneath these absurd tales their bitterness was concealed. It was the bitterness, which perhaps few picked up, of a disappointed people, expressed in an acid satire aimed at the official world. I suddenly discovered both a new, genuine culture and the creative force of those who have always been defined as 'simpletons' or 'ignorant'. They have always been the pariahs of official culture.[11]

Dario was to remain a teller of tales, imbued with the popular approach. The technique of tempering grotesque whimsy with the acid of irony was not the least of his gifts from Porto Valtraglia.

At that time, Italian children were only required by law to attend primary school, but in 1940, when he was fourteen, the family decided Dario was showing evidence of unusual promise and should be enabled to continue his education. The decision meant a daily departure at five o'clock in the morning and a round trip of five hours to Milan. The school chosen was the Brera *liceo*, part of the renowned educational–artistic complex which includes the National Library, the famous art gallery and the Accademia where he would later enrol as an art student. From this point, even if his writing would never be of a sort which would make him a Milanese writer in the way Dickens was a London writer or Balzac a Parisian writer, Dario's growth and development have been inextricably linked with the history of the city.

In 1940, Italy entered the war. Detachments of the Italian army served on the Russian front, as well as in Greece, Albania and North Africa, but in the early stages, for the inhabitants of Lombardy at least, it was a phoney war, fought in far-off lands of which they knew little. This situation changed with the Allied landing in Sicily in July 1943. That month, Mussolini was overthrown by the Grand Council in Rome and was briefly imprisoned before being freed by a German detachment. General Badoglio assumed power in Rome, and the advance of the British and American armies up the Italian peninsula split the country in two, with the South under Allied control and the North ruled, at least in principle, by Mussolini. Il Duce made Salò on Lake Garda the capital of his last regime, a *de facto* Nazi satellite state known dismissively by its opponents as the 'Little Republic'. The situation became more complex when Badoglio declared an Armistice on 8 September 1943. Two Italies now faced each other in a state of civil war. The Little Republic of Salò had its own military and bureaucratic apparatus, and Fascism still had its sympathizers. Armed Resistance groups, whose targets were both the Nazi invader and the Fascist militia, sprang up all over the North.

Since the 1980s, this period of Resistance, Liberation, Allied invasion and Nazi occupation has become a no-man's-land in which rival schools of historians lob grenades and explosives at each other. Once it was an article of faith that the Resistance forces were made up of idealistic knights, while the Salò militia was composed of killers and thugs, but the efforts of revisionist historians in recent times have been directed at establishing the moral equivalence between the two sides. Bad memory, bad faith, guilty conscience, ideological preconceptions and sheer opportunism have helped blur distinctions. Inevitably, Dario Fo has become caught up in these complex political and moral debates, as in his youth he was entangled in the anarchy of those confused and bloody times.

Lombardy, including both Sartirana and Lake Maggiore, was in a territory ruled by Salò and became one of the main arenas of civil war. Bombardments by the Allies were frequent, although Porto Valtraglia itself was never struck. The glassworks were converted into a barracks for the Seventh Infantry regiment, while the Fo house was requisitioned. Bianca had to be moved from her room to make way for a colonel who was billeted with them. Other members of the family faced dangers of their own. Beniamino, Dario's uncle, was in uniform, in the air force, which he had joined before the war out of an interest in aviation engineering. After the Armistice, he was one of some 600,000 Italian soldiers arrested and deported to Germany. His expertise in engineering, which was useful to the German war effort, saved him. The rest of the family engaged in support for partisan groups. Bristin, a sprightly eighty-three-year-old in 1943, was now living with his daughter, Tina, whose house was near the woods along the Po where many escaped Allied prisoners of war were in hiding. He and his son, Nino, brought them food and Nino helped organize escape parties to Switzerland. When the Fascists came to arrest Nino, Bristin caused a diversion which allowed his son to make his escape across the roof-tops.[12] Felice was one of the leading lights in the local CLN – Committee for National Liberation – and he, too, guided parties of escaped British and American prisoners of war across the border into Switzerland. In spite of the presence of the Fascist militia, the garden of the Fo house in Porto Valtraglia was used by the partisans to conceal fuel. This could have created mayhem, but the stocks were never discovered.

There has, however, been considerable mystery and confusion over Dario's own activities at this period, not helped by the varying accounts he has given at different times. The decisions he took in those chaotic, muddled and murderous months have, fairly or unfairly, returned to dog him all his life, and smears by opponents who suggested that he had supported Fascism led to his raising an action for slander in 1978.

In spite of his visceral anti-Fascism, Dario did not, unlike such writers as Elio Vittorini or Italo Calvino, join the partisans or take any direct part in the Resistance. He was not alone in this lack of crispness, and even those who took what was later judged the most acceptable course agonized in the post-war period over their motivations. Calvino, in particular, refused to have his choice seen as dictated by principled idealism. In his novel, *The Path to the Spiders' Nests*, the greatest work of fiction on that period, he dismissed all talk of heroism and highlighted the confusion and uncertainty of his protagonists. In spite of the praise bestowed on it on first publication in 1947, Calvino was dissatisfied with it, and for the 1964 edition he wrote a new introduction.

> For many of my contemporaries, it had been solely a question of luck which
> determined which side they should fight on: for many of them, the sides sud-
> denly changed over, so that soldiers on Mussolini's Fascist Republic became

11

partisans and vice versa. They shot or were shot at on either side; only death signalled an end to their choices.[13]

Luck, or ill-luck, intervened for Dario when in the spring of 1944, aged eighteen, he received call-up papers from the Republic of Salò. He joined up. Later, he wrote a *aide-memoire*[14] on the dilemmas facing him. 'There was no possibility of joining the partisan groups,' he wrote. 'All the groups existing in the zone had been destroyed in recent round-ups, or had withdrawn across the border into Switzerland.' Even those most reluctant to pass judgement on an eighteen-year-old boy must find the explanation strange. Guerrilla war was raging around him, and he tells us his own father was fully committed. To Chiara Valentini, a journalist who has followed his career closely and who is author of a biography of his early life, he added: 'There were two alternatives. Either I presented myself, or I fled to Switzerland.'[15] When interviewed in November 2000 by the *Corriere della Sera* on the publication of a work by Roberto Vivarelli, who had joined the Salò forces out of conviction, Dario said that, unlike Vivarelli, his hope was simply 'to hide away, to come home with my skin intact'.[16] He highlighted to Valentini his father's close involvement with escape groups as making it impossible for him to flee, and suggested that his decision to join was determined by a request from the partisans for inside information. Had he failed to present himself for military service as required, the family house would have been, at the very least, searched, and the operations of his father and the group he was leading put in jeopardy. The consequences could have been much worse. The penalty for anyone trying to escape the draft was death, and during this brutal period of the war in Italy, summary execution, mass slaughter and deportation were commonplace.

Dario adopted what he regarded as delaying tactics. 'Some of my contemporaries had found a way out by enlisting with the anti-aircraft artillery in Varese. This division did not have so much as one cannon, so that immediately after enlisting, these boys were given a month's leave and returned home.' The ruse did not work for him. When he reported to Varese, he discovered that the story about the lack of equipment was a bluff and the new recruits were due to be posted to Germany. The company was moved in cattle trucks to Mestre, where they were issued with German uniforms, then to Monza, where they were kept in a compound while awaiting transfer. Here they were harangued by Mussolini in person, who told them of their good fortune in being chosen for a glorious destiny. They understood they were to take up anti-aircraft operations inside Germany, since the Reich's own manpower had been reduced by the RAF bombing campaign.

The news got back to his home in Porto Valtraglia, where Bianca remembers their frantic mother screaming that she had to go to Monza to see her son before he was dispatched abroad. Dario managed to get a reassuring message to his family, carried to the village by a blind man. The scribbled note read: '*Calma, mamma!* Nobody's leaving.'

In the unpromising surroundings of his barracks, Dario managed to put on his first farce. Unsurprisingly, not a scrap of it has remained except in the second-hand recollections of his mother, who was told that it dealt with a servant who drove his master mad, only to be driven to insanity in his turn by the same master. Pina received, by some means, a photograph of the event, with Dario in the part of the servant.

Shortly afterwards, Dario deserted and spent some time lying low, initially in the mountains. He had forged identity papers with him, so felt able to go to Milan. In Piazzale Loreto, the very square where, a few months later, the corpses of Mussolini and Clara Petacci would be strung up, he was stopped by Fascist officers carrying out a routine check. The false papers duped the guards, and Dario was allowed to go, but the experience left him terrified. In the meantime, Felice had been arrested, and Dario, in his own account, was anxious to avoid any action which might imperil him. He decided to re-enlist. On 10 November 1944, he joined the Folgore parachute division, one of the most notorious of all Fascist forces, in Tradate, not far from his home village. He was given an office job and never took part in the increasingly brutal 'hunt and destroy' missions which the Fascist militia were mounting against the partisans. After two months on the base, he deserted once again. On this occasion, he says, he attempted to make contact with the Lazzarini group, a powerful guerrilla force, but was unsuccessful. For a time, he holed up in various spots in the valleys and mountain caves near his own home, but later found refuge 'in the attic of a colleague of my father, a retired stationmaster'. On more than one occasion, he narrowly escaped capture, so his final judgement that that period was 'an appalling adventure, seven months of fear and horror that seemed as long as seven years' is unsurprising. His overall view is similar to Calvino's: 'we were', he wrote, 'permanent deserters, terrified, disoriented young men. Men in flight, enlisted by deceit, trapped by violence. The greater part of the Salò army was made up of people like us, with no banner, concerned with one thing only: to survive.'[17] The war in Italy ended on 25 April 1945.

Even if his life had been in danger, Fo had not fought in the ranks of the Resistance, as did many others of his generation. He had not been a combatant. Photographs produced during the 1980 libel case show him not in the company of partisans but in the uniform of Mussolini's Little Republic. The Resistance, however, became for him the great myth of liberation, featuring constantly in his plays, particularly those written in the sixties and seventies, after his break with commercial theatre. Dario subscribed fully to the idea, widely held on the left, that the Resistance and the Liberation represented not only victory over dictatorship but the betrayed revolution, the unfulfilled dream of realizing the Italian road to socialism, the denial of the one opportunity Italy gave itself for renewal and purification. 'Remember and relive the Resistance' was the slogan that would ring out in his post-1968 theatre. One of his best and most moving songs, 'Six Minutes to Dawn', depicts the last moments of a partisan about to face the firing squad. The guards and the priest arrive, but when an officer offers a cigarette, the condemned man initially refuses, then accepts only because of the hurt expression on the face of the officer who is about to carry out the execution.

> On the eighth of September I fled
> I ended my time as a soldier
> To my village I returned
> Where they called me deserter
> Loaded on a train
> I fled once more
> I went to the mountains, but yesterday
> They seized me as a rebel.[18]

Dario has had to endure a whispering campaign about his failure to fight with the partisans in the closing months of the war, and particularly by the unqualified description of him as a *repubblichino*, that is, an adherent of the 'Little Republic' of Salò. The historian and ex-Fascist Giorgio Pisanò, who became member of parliament with the neo-Fascist MSI, the Italian Social Movement, published several volumes entitled *Histories of the Civil War in Italy* in the mid-1960s, in which he took a polemical look at the story of Fo's tangled involvement with the Salò forces. Many influential people had interests in discrediting him, so the suggestion in the book that Dario had skeletons in his cupboard was enthusiastically taken up and questions were asked in the Italian parliament. His outraged self-defence then and later was weakened in the eyes of some by the fact that he had not chosen to speak of the matter spontaneously, but had stayed silent until the matter was revealed by hostile critics.

If his involvement in the Resistance had been marginal, Dario shared in all the exhilaration and unrestrained optimism of the Liberation. Italians are fond of depicting themselves as being, by virtue of a culture which combines a Catholic sense of the imperfectibility of humankind with direct experience of much of the worst history can offer, immune to the waves of hopefulness which affect other nations. In reality, few peoples are so prone to bouts of collective optimism or so ready to place their hopes in clay-footed messiahs as are the Italians. It has been Fo's fortune to live through several such waves of public enthusiasm, and to have emerged from the disappointment which succeeded them with his appetite for life undiminished and his Utopianism – his most fundamental trait – unimpaired. No man has ever believed less in original sin.

In 1945, Dario, still only nineteen, put on his first art exhibition in Bergamo. The paintings are realist in style, and some of the more notable include a landscape with unmoving trees picked out against hills, the drawing of a boy pulling on football boots and a self-portrait of a brooding, unsmiling Fo looking defiantly at the spectator. There was a remarkable maturity and confidence to the works displayed, and certainly no sign of any gloom or self-doubt.

Italy itself had no sense of being a defeated country, nor even a country liberated by outsiders, but viewed itself as a land freed by its own sacrifices and struggles. In spite of material privations, there was a sense of elation and determination at large, particularly among those who were young, resourceful, plucky, self-confident, or merely conceited and anxious to seize the day. Primo Levi, on returning to Turin from Auschwitz, was astounded at the 'extreme vitality' shown by his fellow citizens and regretted that he could not share it since 'they were victorious, and I was not'.[19] That sense of being victorious in war and capable of constructing an equally victorious peace was especially strong in Milan and the North, where those who had participated in the Resistance were clustered. The established habits of previous times had been shown to be inadequate, indeed the cause of national disaster and humiliation, so the young found themselves facing not merely the challenge of rebuilding cities but the invigorating task of creating a civilization afresh. Laws were to be redrafted, political institutions reformed, industry rebuilt, economic relations rethought, the relations between classes reshaped and the pillars of a new civil society erected. As Carlo Levi, author of *When Christ Stopped at Eboli,* wrote at the time, 'something deeper has changed in men's souls, something which it is difficult to define, but which is expressed unconsciously in every act, every word, every gesture: the very vision of the world, the sense of the relationship of people with one another, with things, with society'.[20]

Dario responded to that mood. He resumed commuting to Milan, now accompanied by Fulvio, who was studying accountancy at the Bocconi University, and Bianca, who was attending the Brera *liceo*. Dario himself was in attendance at two institutions. Unsure of his future, he enrolled at the Accademia Brera as an art student and at the Politecnico to study architecture. To while away the time during the lengthy toing and froing, the three Fos took to performing recitals and monologues on the train. Dario was eclectic in his tastes, and not unduly demanding of his audience, who had not requested this form of disturbance. Some of the material was written by himself, but he also performed sketches by the humorist Achille Campanile, or by the Neapolitan comic actor Totò, whose work he had always loved and on whom, much later, he wrote an admiring essay. This high-spirited display on a train was not yet a sign of some systematic interest in theatre or ambition to be an actor or playwright. The reopened theatres in Milan commanded the attention of the bohemian young, but painting was still Dario's principal passion.

In 1949, Pina decided that this daily travelling was unduly stressful, and moved to Milan to set up home there. The family found a little house on the outskirts of a city still recovering from the devastation of war. At the back of their house lay the rubble of houses destroyed in the air raids, while the front looked on to the new, nine-storey blocks being thrown up to replace them. Money continued to be a problem. Felice retired from the railway, but stayed on in Porto Valtraglia, where he opened a little business to supplement his pension and help support the family. The rest pitched in as best they could. Pina took in some work as a seamstress. Ever thrifty and inventive, she managed to make from the one blanket a reversible overcoat which could be a male garment for Fulvio or, turned inside out, a more feminine item which Bianca could wear. Dario earned some cash by designing stalls and executing frescos at the Milan Fiera. He sold some canvases and, more eccentrically, made extra cash by sketching cadavers for the theses of medical students. Felice came down to Milan twice a week to visit the new house. The family lived in happy disorder, but felt obliged to rush around replacing door handles, repairing wiring and adjusting carpets each time he was due.

The previous occupants had left a piano, and perhaps by itself this was sufficient to ensure that the Fo house became the favoured meeting place for friends and acquaintances. Jazz had been declared unwholesome by the Fascist regime but was accepted joyously by the new Italy. Fulvio learned to play some numbers on the piano, and Dario imitated the most popular blues and jazz singers. As described by Bianca, the home is reminiscent of the artists' attic in *La Bohème*, with her in the role of Mimì.

> Little by little, our house became the meeting place of all our friends, and there were many of them, painters, poets, actors. We would sit around the sawdust-fired stove, which gave off more smoke than heat, and there were endless discussions about this or that painter, about new forms of theatre or cinema. They spoke of Sartre and existentialism. Emilio Tadini declaimed Garcia Lorca, while every evening Dario would reinvent history and recount stories of poor Cain, or of Samson and Delilah. I was always silent, listening rapt. I could not speak like them.[21]

For the intelligentsia in that climate, to be Communist was merely a matter of good manners and *bon ton*. They took Antonio Gramsci to their hearts. Mussolini had imprisoned Gramsci, Italy's leading Marxist philosopher, and banned his writings, but his *Prison Notebooks* now became available. Any attempt to put flesh on the theatrical poetics of Dario Fo must begin with Gramsci, whose main contribution was to switch the emphasis of Marxist theory away from economics to culture itself. The building of socialism was not a matter for political activity alone, indeed could only be attempted once civil society was reformed. This assertion amounted to a root-and-branch review of classical Marxism, in which cultural activities were no more than a projection on to a 'superstructure' of tensions and contradictions which existed on the basic, that is, economic, substructure of society. Gramsci included culture in his analysis of the power structures in society, since for him it was a means by which privileged élites maintained their authority. In Gramscian terms, culture is a pre-rational complex of ideas, values and assumptions, or a dimension of consciousness which shapes human life as powerfully as any physical or economic force. Fo's early familiarity with Gramscian theories caused him to see cultural change, which could be worked by theatre, as an indispensable tool for the decolonization of the mind, of the will, of the imagination.

One other aspect of Gramsci's thought was of decisive importance to Dario. In Gramsci's analysis, a popular culture reflecting the experiences of the subaltern classes existed side by side with the high, aesthetic culture of the patrician and educated classes. It had, however, been the fate of popular culture to be systematically ignored and derided, or, when it showed some vitality, annexed to the higher culture. In calling for a re-evaluation of popular culture, Gramsci set the intellectual parameters within which Fo later worked. Gramsci's beliefs gave him justification for giving higher priority to the theatrical forms, principally farce, to which he was drawn by innate talent, and for jettisoning the hierarchy which awarded pride of place to tragedy and comedy. In addition, Gramsci called on intellectuals to create not only a new future but also a new past. 'The past is a complex thing, a mixture of dead and alive, in which the choice cannot be made arbitrarily, a priori, by an individual or by a political tendency,' as Gramsci wrote. The past had to be claimed, or reclaimed, as Fo would do with his plays.

These and other topics occasioned rowdy debates among the student body in places like the Bar Giamaica, where they congregated. Dario's circle of friends included future painters, like Emilio Tadini, who later became president of the Brera, sculptors like Alik Cavaliere, musicians like Fiorenzo Carpi, who worked with Fo on many shows, as well as future actors and writers. Fo met up with De Chirico, the futurist Carrà, as well as the new generation of film-makers, including Gillo Pontecorvo, Vittorio De Sica, Carlo Lizzani and Federico Fellini. *Politecnico*, the review edited by the novelist Elio Vittorini, another habitué of the Bar Giamaica, was both an encyclopedia which updated Italians on new thinking in other countries and the main forum for left-wing intellectual debate. Unlike many others in his circle, Dario did not join the Communist Party, but his ideas were in line with theirs.

> Everybody found their way to the Brera; we were all in favour of general change, in art as in politics. We paid no heed to the party, who told us to stick to being artists and to stay in our own place. Today it is hard to imagine what Milan was in those days and how a painter, as I wanted to be, felt himself involved in all forms of expression, from stories which appeared in *Politecnico* to neo-realist cinema.

Almost as an afterthought, he added, 'I gave little thought to the theatre, but theatre pulled us all in.'[22]

It was only gradually that the pull of theatre became irresistible. 'My principal interest was painting. I wanted to be a painter,' he repeated.[23] He continued to pick up prizes. In 1946, he won a prize at the Brera and used the money to go with Tadini to Paris for the first time and familiarize himself with the work of Ferdinand Léger. In 1949, a still life by Fo took first prize at the Triennale in Melzo. For all their protestations of poverty, the group had sufficient means to allow them some mobility, and could, on an impulse, go to Venice or Turin to see an important exhibition.

The Young Turks had no doubts that history was on their side and that the future was theirs to reshape as they wished. The old forms of thought and performance, controlled by a hostile, alien force called the 'bourgeoisie', needed, they were convinced, to be swept away. Baiting the bourgeoisie had the advantage over other forms of political activity that it required no training and overlapped with the expression of youthful high spirits. Paolo Grassi, who was to be one of the founders of Milan's Piccolo theatre, organized groups to visit theatres, but not to study established masters. The members unabashedly called themselves 'whistlers', although the Italian term *fischiatori* also suggests 'booers' or 'jeerers'. Dario enlisted with alacrity. They travelled to venues where plays by old-guard authors, or featuring actors or directors compromised by association with the Fascist regime, were in performance. At sensitive moments, the 'whistlers' rose from their seats and hurled abuse at stalls and stage. Grassi wrote of a particularly lively evening at the Teatro Nuovo in Milan, during the romantic comedy, *Twelve Red Roses* by Aldo de Benedetti, who was judged to have shown undue tolerance towards the *bien pensant*, 'let sleeping dogs lie' mentality which Fascism encouraged in drama. One actress, believed to have been the mistress of a high-ranking Fascist official, was a target for special abuse. That same evening, Vittorio Gassman, later to star both in Italian theatre and Hollywood cinema, leaped on to a chair, declaiming that theatre must mature or die. In the ensuing mêlée, Grassi was heard to denounce the then respected actor Renzo Ricci as 'a worthless old ham'. At a later society soirée, Emilio Tadini concealed himself in a large plant-pot and jumped out as the canapés were being served, screaming, 'Bourgeois! We will bury you!'

Pranks and stunts of the sort tolerated, or endured, in university towns all over Europe for centuries acquired political overtones for that generation. Dario was the Puckish mischief-maker-in-chief. One winter, there was an unusually heavy fall of snow, forcing the city council to take on extra staff. A certain salary was agreed and Dario and his friends were among those employed. The teams spent the morning clearing the roads, only to discover that the council intended reneging on the agreed payment. In protest, the team spent the afternoon replacing the snow on the roads. Alik Cavaliere was the inspiration for another stunt. To make a few lire, an unemployed man had set himself up as guardian of bicycles near the Brera. One day, Cavaliere saw him being booked by the police, who demanded that the bicycles be removed forthwith. Dario and Cavaliere went to his aid. The Brera was being restored at that time, allowing the two to clamber up an extemporized scaffolding bridge between two buildings. From there, they hauled the bicycles up by rope, one by one, leaving them dangling in an elaborate pattern across the façade of the Accademia.

The group's most celebrated escapade involved spreading word that Pablo Picasso himself was about to visit Milan. They persuaded friendly journalists to carry the story in their papers and tickets were sold for a reception to welcome the great artist to Milan. A janitor from the Brera, who apparently had some resemblance to Picasso, was put on the Paris express a couple of stations up the line and was met at Milan's central station by a crowd, including both false and genuine photographers. He was showered with bouquets by Fo's group but, complaining of exhaustion, refused to say anything to the waiting journalists. That evening, substantial numbers of ticketholders turned up for the soirée. 'Picasso' failed to arrive at the appointed time and the festivities continued with a motor bike circulating among the tables and the arrival of a stretcher carrying the injured body of a critic supposedly hostile to Picasso. Dario and his friends moved among the guests, stopping to debate trends in art with painters whose work was fashionable with Milan society, and to tell them how far behind the times they were. Somewhere along the way, what began as an elaborate hoax was transformed into a futurist act of anti-bourgeois scorn, whose object was not enjoyment but exposure of pretension and conformism.

In the midst of this extra-curricular activity, Dario tired of his architecture studies, and in 1949, his final year and the year his mother moved to the city, he abandoned his course. His infinitely tolerant parents continued to support him. He had gained substantial experience in architects' studios and on building sites, but the path architects were following bored and repelled him. His tolerance of the humdrum would never be high, and on this occasion his impatience was mingled with disgust at the neo-brutalist, high-rise architecture commissioned by the municipal authorities and with the misspending of the millions made available for post-war reconstruction. Minimum cost and maximum profit were the order of the day. Such poverty of vision and willingness to cram people into little boxes were a far cry from the dreams for the future he had sketched out in debates in the Bar Giamaica. Dario fell into a nervous depression and dropped out of college, even though he had almost completed his course.

He none the less never regretted his study of architecture, which, like his knowledge of art, enriched his perspective on theatre. In 1984, he wrote:

Even today when I plan a project, when I write, I think in terms of 'plane and elevation', two fundamental architectural terms, two dimensions often used in reference to painting as well: that which is viewed from above and in front of us, as well as the 'opening' and perspective. When I write a play, even before I think of the lines, I imagine the physical space, the space where the actors and audience are situated. In completing a work, it is unusual for me to be uncertain over where the actors enter or exit, or to have to think about it afterwards.[24]

Whatever he believed at the time, his study of art and architecture were to have their real value for his work in theatre, which was beginning to command his attention.

Chapter 2

First Ventures in Theatre

Sheer exuberance of personality rather than some radical dissatisfaction with the *status quo* was the impulse which carried Dario towards theatre. Whether he was travelling on the train or painting in the Brera, there was no way of stemming the flow of fantastic tales. With his companions at the Brera, he improvised scenes and sketches which were played around the Accademia, and he put on small sketches in village halls with his brother and sister. In 1948, he created a longer, satirical work – *The Tresa Divides Us* – which he presented in Luino in the aftermath of the left's electoral defeat in April that year. Everyone agreed that the result of the first democratic elections since the fall of Fascism, with the Christian Democrats assuming power and the Communists retiring into isolated opposition, represented a watershed in the affairs of the fledgeling republic, but there was no consensus on the evaluation of the outcome. Borges wrote that Europe could be divided between those who believed Waterloo was a victory and those for whom it was a defeat. For Dario, April 1948 was a defeat which brought to an end the exhilarated optimism of the Liberation. The issue in *The Tresa Divides Us* is the ownership of milk produced by a cow which wanders between two communities, one 'red', or Communist, and the other 'white', or Christian Democrat. The cow belongs to the people on one side of the river but feeds on the grass on the other. The action, in a foretaste of those elements of rumbustious fantasy which were always to enliven Fo's work, was brightened by a Garibaldi encased in plaster, a motor cycle which careered around the audience and an angel, played by Dario Fo, who descended from a tower to denounce bigotry.

This buccaneering dilettantism constituted a cheerful apprenticeship, but Dario's friends encouraged him to make a move towards professional theatre. There were others in Milan whose ideas on the role of theatre in the construction of the new order were much more developed than Dario's. 'If we are not mistaken' – and the suggestion that they could be mistaken was self-evidently laughable – 'every civilization develops by a process of bringing one group, in all its variety and multiplicity, close to another and integrating them' ran the manifesto of the theatrical company, established by Giorgio Strehler and Paolo Grassi which became the Piccolo Teatro. In January 1947, the Milan City Council had allocated an ex-cinema, used as torture chamber by the Gestapo during the German occupation, to the new group for use as a theatre. The Piccolo was Italy's first *teatro stabile*, or fixed theatre, where '*stabile*' served to distinguish it from the touring companies which ever since *commedia dell'arte* had been the backbone of theatrical life in Italy. In the jargon imported from France, theatre was to be viewed as a 'public service', on a par with transport or education. Theatre was indispensable to the well-being of the body politic.

Grassi took charge of the administration and Strehler of artistic policy. Strehler's position at the Piccolo was of enormous importance to the development of Italian theatre, not merely because of the quality of his productions over succeeding decades, but because it guaranteed the pre-eminence of the theatrical director, still resented by many as a late and unnecessary foreign intrusion into Italian ways. The objective of the new company was to play not to an exclusive élite but to a group who would be the vanguard of a new, more informed mass audience of the future. 'The theatre will remain what it has always been in the deepest intentions of its founders – a place where a community, freely gathered together, reveals itself to itself, where the community listens to words which it will accept or reject.' The emerging Christian Democrat regime was not slow to react. The first scheduled production, Machiavelli's *La Mandragola*, was banned on the grounds that it featured the violation of the secrecy of the confessional and was replaced by Gorky's *Lower Depths*. The choice of a Communist work was deliberately provocative, and it is curious that the council raised no objection. The production, and the official veto, secured the Piccolo's position as rallying point for the new, left-leaning intelligentsia.

Strehler was Dario's first master. The two men, while always expressing admiration for each other's achievements, would frequently veer apart and hurl public execrations at each other over the coming decades, but at this time Dario attended the Piccolo frequently, watching from the wings during both performances and rehearsals. Strehler provided him with an introduction to the craft and profession of theatre-making, but Dario had no wish to develop in the image and likeness of Strehler or of the Piccolo. Strehler and Grassi were dedicated to providing a radical reinterpretation of the classics, but Dario, while he had no precisely formulated aesthetic starting-point, had an instinctive, albeit still unformed, view of his own talents and his own direction. He knew he was a story-teller in the rough-and-tumble, popular tradition, and sought out those who produced the same style of theatre. His decisive breakthrough came in the town of Intra in 1950, when he went to meet Franco Parenti, then at the height of his fame as a stage actor and radio performer of sketches featuring the character Anacleto the Gasman. Anacleto was something of a rebel, an outsider with an anarchic outlook perpetually at odds with the society he inhabited. Parenti was plainly endowed with an unusual generosity of spirit. He must have been accustomed to dealing with hosts of hopefuls turning up with armfuls of scripts, but when Dario arrived at his house asking to be given a chance to show his mettle, he readily agreed. When he saw Dario in action at the microphone, Parenti was impressed both by the surreal inventiveness of the tales and by the freshness and conviction of his performance style. He wrote that, however raw Dario was, 'he had an already formed personality . . . with a definite way of seeing things, of understanding, of delivering judgements'.[1] On the evening of their first meeting, the two went along the lakeside for a stroll. For Dario, it was his introduction to the world he wished to inhabit, while for Parenti the meeting was an encounter with a talent which would enrich his own professional life. Dario recounted other tales from his repertory and Parenti promised to use his influence to introduce him to others who could help him.

Parenti took him on tour to theatres and halls around Milan, sometimes run by unscrupulous managements and frequented by an audience who made few concessions to performers, young or old, who did not meet their standards. He also secured Dario a radio audition. Dario was brought in cold to an audition room where the producers were seated, bored and unsmiling, almost defying the candidates to make them laugh. His first instinct was to turn tail, but he persisted and was encouraged when he detected the outlines of a smile on the face of one member of the panel.[2] He was given a commission for a series of twelve humorous monologues, to be broadcast over the 1950–1 season. The monologues were collected under the title *Poer nano*, and were staged at the Odeon in Milan in 1952 as part of a variety show.

Poer nano is a dialect expression common in Lombardy, corresponding approximately to 'poor sod'. While there is little advantage in subjecting juvenilia to overinterpretation, all the distinguishing marks of Fo's work are already present. Tragic figures are viewed through the prism of a comic vision that sees the heroic in the commonplace and the commonplace in the heroic. The tales as a whole display a taste, which Dario would never lose, for the grotesque, the absurd, the satirical, the paradoxical and the ironic. Delight in viewing the world from the perspective of the underdog would become a staple of his theatre. Performance and writing were combined from the outset. Then, as later, he had little interest in publication. When *Poer nano* was eventually published in 1976, it was in a revised, comic-strip form, prepared by his son, Jacopo, who did the drawings.

The 'poor sod' is closely related to Chaplin's tramp in his mixture of pathos and guile. The hero is the underling, the downtrodden victim of misfortune or oppression. Dario here gives the first glimpse of his basic comic technique, which is the overturning of conventions, expectations and roles; the character receiving pity is the one who had conventionally been seen as a villain or tyrant. The biblical Cain, who would always be a favourite of Fo's, appears not as murderous bully but as a good-hearted, goofy, ill-at-ease adolescent overshadowed by Abel, his dazzlingly talented and good-looking brother. Samson is transformed into a conceited cretin who stands in front of his mirror every morning, asking who is the strongest in the kingdom, Noah into a benign but weak father figure with too much fondness for wine, even God emerges as an absent-minded old buffer. The story of Goliath, a lonely giant who is forced by politics to fight David, his only friend, is brought up to date to incorporate jibes against war, especially 'short wars which then last a decade'.

Three of the tales, 'Hamlet', 'Othello' and 'Romeo and Juliet', were based on Shakespeare, with the tragedy transformed into comedy. This Hamlet could not care less about his late father. The events in Elsinore are recounted by a friend who is surprised when he ends up in a place called a theatre, where a group of vulgar voyeurs gawk at Hamlet and Ophelia, who try to find a bit of privacy to conduct their love affair. To the dismay of the narrator, these unwelcome onlookers refuse to get out of their seats to stop the fighting and brawling. Juliet, who has a preference for 'difficult loves', causes problems for both sets of parents with her offensive manner. This becomes too much for Romeo's father, who gives her such a severe slap that she dies, causing poor Romeo to kill himself. Othello makes his entrance singing a blues number, and complaining of the lack of black faces among the angels on the altarpieces of Venice. This Othello is childish, prone to tantrums and so given to tears that he ends up with a collection of hand-kerchiefs. He kills Desdemona out of pique because she had not kept his things in order, only to discover later that Iago was the guilty party.

Christopher Columbus, later to feature in *Isabella, Three Caravels and a*

Con-Man and *Johan Padan*, makes his first appearance here as spoiled brat who annoys his parents and neighbours by his demands for a hundred lire to enable him to go to America. In his home village he played tricks with eggs, but it all goes wrong when he uses an egg to explain a point to Queen Isabella, lets it fall, stains the queen's dress and is chased from the royal presence. Another monologue features Verdi's Rigoletto, as the first example of that central figure in Fo's work, the *giullare*, or jester. Already, this key character faces the dilemma of being either court entertainer, and hence the plaything of authority, or the voice of the people.

The success of these radio and theatre performances led to an invitation for Fo to appear in cabaret and revues. In 1951, he took part in *Seven Days in Milan*, a summer revue. During the run, he met Franca Rame, also appearing in the same bill. The subsequent personal and professional lives of these two are inseparable.

Franca was born into a family which as a matter of routine produced the popular theatre which Dario was later to write and perform as a matter of intellectual conviction. The Rames were a family company of touring actors in northern Italy who could trace their ancestry back to the seventeenth century, and who performed a style of improvised drama which had its roots in the *commedia dell'arte*.[3] Originally the family were puppeteers who produced the entire paraphernalia of their trade. Some items belonging to the company are now on display in La Scala museum. Since they lived on their daily takings, they had to be attentive to the signs of the times. In the early twentieth century, the menace came from the encroachment on to their territory of a new invention called cinema. At a family council around 1920, the Rames decided that the popularity of moving pictures represented a switch in public taste that it would be futile to oppose or ignore. Other family troupes attempted to incorporate short films into their shows, while others again viewed the new technology as a passing fad. Grandfather Pio Rame was of that mind, but his sons Tommaso and Domenico, the father of Franca, were resolute modernizers.

The family moved into what they termed *teatro di persona* – people, rather than puppet, theatre. It was a bold move, but they decided to stay as close to their previous area of expertise as possible. They transferred all the devices, tricks of the trade and even the plotlines they had accumulated in more than a century of glove and string puppet-theatre into their new craft. The scenery had to be modified, costumes prepared and once that had been done, the family considered themselves equipped. They had a friend, a scene-painter at La Scala, who managed to acquire costumes no longer needed for opera for them. It was their boast that, unlike other troupes of strolling players, they were not mere charlatans who turned up in a town, set up an extemporized stage in the main square, took the money and moved on. They converted some public hall or cinema and insisted on fitting it out it with a stage, scenery, props and backcloth. The backdrops were their pride and joy, and on more than one occasion Franca has had the experience of being a guest in a house belonging to the well-heeled bour-geoisie of Milan and seeing a tapestry hanging on the wall which had started life as a prop in their shows.

On switching from puppetry to acting, they did not consider retraining, but then they had never trained. The family drew on inherited skills, on instinct and observation, on an apprenticeship which began at birth. Stanislavsky, who wrote that actors were required to make the performing space their home, would have envied the easy domesticity of the Rames on stage, but he might have been horrified by their relaxed relationship to character and their nonchalance over identifying motive or understanding the wells of action. Much later, Franca would scandalize an audience of actors in Scandinavia who asked how she prepared for a part. 'I read it through and go on stage,' she replied. Rame family theatre was theatre of improvisation, which did not mean free invention day by day. The family members had consigned to memory a range of dialogues and exchanges relating to situations which might arise in several different plays. Round the table at dinner one evening, Dario coaxed the family to play variations on the boy-meets-girl theme, such as 'she is in love but is too proud to say so', 'he is in love but is tongue-tied', 'the two meet but are conscious of being watched'. Each individual took on the required role then and there. The appropriate lines were thrown back and forth between the risotto and meat courses, each seemingly fresh and spontaneous but ready for use when the need arose on stage.

On other occasions, improvisational skills of a different order were needed. When the run of six performances from the established repertoire was completed but the family felt there was sufficient interest to allow them to prolong their stay in a particular place, Domenico would summon the family to a meeting and explain to them the plot of a book he had been reading. Alternatively, especially in a town they had not visited before, they would enquire about local legends, about miracles associated with the local patron saint or episodes in the history of the area. Domenico would then allocate parts, explain exactly what was expected to each member of the family-cum-company, prepare an outline plot detailing the essential action and giving the various entrances and exits. The outline was pinned up in the wings, and the family would take their cue from it between entries and exits. Rehearsals were kept to a bare minimum, because a troupe like theirs could not afford the luxury of unprofitable time. The adaptation unfolded spontaneously on stage.

Such companies were not unknown in other countries, but whereas elsewhere they were a pleasing sideline, they were the quintessence of the Italian tradition. Many historians of Italian theatre have puzzled over why a theatre of such vibrancy could have produced so few playwrights. Only Goldoni and Pirandello have an undisputed place in the classical European repertoire, with De Filippo and Fo claiming a place among the moderns. One of the reasons for this scarcity is surely that companies who operated like the Rame family were actor-centred. The writer was a redundant figure and the director simply unknown. Domenico Rame could stand as a representative man of Italian theatre. He was a performer–organizer who could have played with the Andreini family in the sixteenth century at the birth of *commedia dell'arte*, who could have appeared with the Comédie Italienne in Paris in the days of Molière and would have undergone a period of crisis in the eighteenth century when Carlo Goldoni introduced his reforms.

The Rame family, not Strehler or the *teatro stabile*, provided the model Dario would follow in the late sixties. Art did not figure in their outlook. The Rames were professionals, as sure of their place in a community as the bakers or butchers. Franca followed the family profession unthinkingly. She once said that 'if my father's job had been shoe-making, I would have set out to make shoes'.[4] In meeting Franca and her family, Dario had his first encounter with much of what would characterize his own theatre, especially post-1968. For him, as for Domenico Rame, the actor would always be the central figure in the process of theatrical creation. Unlike Domenico, Dario was a writer whose plays could be performed by others, whereas Domenico's scripts were written for that evening's performance, not for posterity. He had no truck with the effete conceit that he was writing only to please himself. The only standard of success he would recognize was audience approval.

The Rames might occasionally use established scripts, but they cheerfully modified them for their own purposes, in accordance with the tastes of the community for whom they played. One of the most popular items in their repertoire was a version of *Romeo and Juliet*. They knew their audiences would not cope with a straight translation of Shakespeare's verse, so they produced their own adaptation, refashioning the plot without parody, making it accessible and emphasizing narrative momentum. They played tear-jerking melodrama and knockabout farce, but also produced lives of Galileo and Giordano Bruno, adapted stories from the Bible (as Dario had heard the *fabulatori* do) and staged versions of Chekhov, Ibsen and even modern authors like Gabriele D'Annunzio. Popular culture, as Dario Fo would later grudgingly admit, was intricately bound up with the official culture. They were both islands in the same sea, washed by the same tides and obliged to cope with the same flotsam and jetsam swept up on their beaches. The Rame family acted as mediators between two slants of mind, but for them popular culture was not the downstairs, philistine version of concepts elaborated by its upstairs counterpart. They exploited high culture, even if they also scoffed at it.

Anyone who married into the family was expected to learn the trade. Franca's mother, Emilia Baldini, came from a family who were not exactly well off but regarded themselves as being a cut above itinerant players. Her father was an engineer in Bobbio, a town in Lombardy which was on the Rame circuit. At eighteen, Emilia was already at work as a primary schoolteacher when she met up with Domenico, twenty years her senior. Initially, he was unsure of this girl from a different world and his doubts were more than shared by the Baldinis, who were not enamoured of the prospect of their daughter marrying an actor. Emilia was a young lady of spirit and would brook no resistance. She and Domenico were married in 1924 and Emilia threw herself into her new life. Like Franca after her, she became the company administrator, learned to sew, helped mend costumes and prepare scenery. Even more remarkably, she became the company's leading actress, taking on the roles of Juliet or Tosca according to the requirements of the touring programme.

In spite of the Baldinis' objections, the Rame family were not rootless bohemians living in caravans. Their regular touring schedule took them no further afield than Lombardy and Piedmont, and normally they performed only from Sunday until Thursday, when they returned to their home in Varese. When they were away for longer periods, they rented a house as a base and travelled from there to the communities in the vicinity. On Sunday, the company would split into two and do a total of four performances, usually with the assistance of other professional actors or amateur members of local drama clubs. Both the families of Domenico and of his brother Tommaso lived on the earnings of the company, but they made a good living. Emilia and Domenico were able to purchase a house on the coast, as well as a flat in Milan.

Franca, the youngest of a family of three girls and one boy, was born on 18 July 1929, in Parabiago, in the province of Milan, where the family happened to be performing. She made her first appearance on stage eight days later in the part of Genevieve of Brabant, a child of the woods. From then on, she took the parts appropriate to her age. Being the youngest, she had the advantage of having seen her sisters in the same roles, but it was her mother who took it upon herself to teach her parts. When she was three, her mother decided she should be acting and taught her the lines 'mouth to mouth', as the expression was. This apprenticeship has made her an actress almost unique in today's profession. For her, improvisation is natural and undemanding. She speaks witheringly of actors who are incapable of thinking on stage, who listen only to the rhythms of speech of fellow actors while waiting for their cue, and who are incapable of adjusting if something goes wrong. She was delighted at the panic that came into Dario's eyes when, during a performance of *He Had Two Pistols and White and Black Eyes*, she forgot her lines and began to improvise. The stagehands began making frantic signals that they would pull down the curtains, but she continued until she chanced on the right word. Dario learned improvisation from her. She is quite bereft of the nerves and fears which even seasoned actors feel before their first entrance. One awed colleague said that he noticed that every actor standing in the wings would feel their hands either freeze or turn clammy with perspiration and that several of them had developed a superstitious rite of touching Franca's hands, which were always at their normal temperature, before going on stage.

Being on stage with members of the family playing parts foreign to their nature could be a confusing experience for a child. In an autobiography which she started but abandoned after a few pages, Franca recalls one such event:

My mother, who always took the important decisions, decided that I should take the part of the second angel, supporting my sister Pia who was the first angel, in the *Passion of Our Lord*, Act V, Garden of Gethsemane. 'Repent, Judas, you traitor. You have sold your Lord for thirty pieces of silver. Repent, Repent,' I was to shout from time to time. The part was not long, and my mother made me repeat it over and over again as she peeled potatoes. I had had no rehearsal. I only knew that I had to follow my sister on stage and that at an agreed signal from my mother I was to scream 'Repent, Judas', and so on. What I did not know was that Judas was played by Uncle Tommaso, a man whom I had always seen as calm, smiling, who told me beautiful stories, and was always great fun. To see him there with a nasty black wig on his head, shouting out in despair 'May the crows tear out my innards, may the eagles pull out my eyes!' had a terrible effect on me. I swear I could have spoken, but it did not seem right to make things worse for him. What was going on? In little steps, the way angels do, I went up to him, put my arm round his neck and hugged him. My sister fell silent and from the wings my mother was making signs which held promise of nothing good. Uncle Tommaso lost the place for no more than three seconds, before beginning 'God, thou art good! To this dreadful sinner you send the final comfort, a little angel . . . ' With a scream he rushed off-stage in search of a tree to hang himself. I do not know if it was a fear of being told off or a sense of duty which urged me on, but I shouted out 'He is hanging himself. He has not repented!' From then on, there were always two angels in the *Passion of the Lord*, one of whom gave Judas a hug to demonstrate the greatness of God. And to send the audience home in tears.[5]

The German occupation of Italy created difficulties for travelling players. At the age of fifteen, Franca underwent the terrifying experience of being hauled from the classroom to answer questions about her first boyfriend, who had disappeared. The guards suspected, rightly, that she knew he had left to join the partisans, but her air of innocence convinced them otherwise. On another occasion, after a performance in Masnago, the family were rounded up by the SS, together with others who happened to be on the street at the wrong time, and kept in custody all night in a courtyard. Only later did they discover that they had been held as hostages against the success of a Nazi raid. If the raid had gone badly, they would have been shot.

When Franca was eighteen, her father had a stroke which left him paralysed on one side. It was impossible to continue as the family had done for generations, but the main concern was not the abandonment of tradition but what to do with Franca. She had not been notably successful at school, which was hardly surprising since she had often been working until late at night and had to sleep on top of a trunk in the dressing-room. Her sisters were in more secure positions, but Franca presented an intractable problem until someone suggested that she enter nursing. The fact that she had a neurotic fear of blood was not viewed as an insuperable problem. The thinking was that she would be able to do home visits and if she were able to establish a round of thirty daily injections, her future was assured. Nursing college it would be.

Under prevailing arrangements, a student nurse was admitted to the training centre for a probationary period of two months. Franca's background as an actress was held against her and she had one especially vicious supervisor who used to rub her finger over Franca's cheeks each morning in an attempt to detect some trace of make-up, a sure sign of reprehensible activities. Franca recalls those months as a period of unending humiliation, and it may be significant that a hospital is adopted as a symbol of the police state in at least two of Dario's early plays. In the television series *Canzonissima*, she retold the story of the bullying supervisor and received a letter of apology from the woman. In her 1990s one-woman piece, *Sex? Yes! Don't Mind If I Do!*, she transferred into comedy the intense embarrassment she felt when a man, whose private parts she had been requested to hold while the doctor conducted an examination, had an erection. On the expiry of her two-month probationary period, she was, to no one's surprise, told she was unsuited for the nursing profession. This period of depression coincided with Dario's over his decision to abandon architecture.

She had set her face against any return to the stage. All her life, she has claimed that she has no love for acting or the theatre. However, her stated aversion towards the stage was regarded in family circles as a girlish affectation, so she was sent to do auditions with a 'primary company', as her family referred to the big city companies. Her experience and her talents did her no harm, but the Milanese impresarios were only interested in her looks. A young blonde with a perfect profile, seductive smile and soft eyes was a guaranteed draw. She was taken on with alacrity, and for one of her first parts was required to appear in an underdress. Her mother was in the stalls and was so shocked that she sent Franca an anonymous letter, in her own handwriting, saying that she was an admirer of this emerging actress, but that since she was so talented, she had no need to stoop to that kind of display. Franca was next hired for the show *Seven Days in Milan*, by an impresario who was married to her sister. She had only one line to speak. This was the revue in which Dario was also cast.

He claims to have seen her photograph in the house of a friend, and to have been immediately attracted. During the run, he was too intimidated by this stunningly good-looking woman, who was always surrounded by hosts of admirers, to make an approach. He drew portraits of her, with which he covered the walls at home. When Bianca first met Franca, she recognized her immediately from the sketches she had seen. Franca claims to have grown increasingly irritated by this 'gauche, lanky, thin and somewhat ugly boy' who kept staring at her but never made any move. Dario regarded himself as the ugly duckling who could never arouse her interest. As he wrote later for a women's magazine,

> It wasn't that I hadn't noticed her. That would have been impossible. Franca was so pretty that all the men went wild over her. Anyway, she had a boyfriend, and was always pursued by hosts of men prepared to go to any lengths. I didn't want to enter the lists. I said to myself, with all those bees buzzing around her, she won't even see me. In addition, I didn't want to get caught up in the cyclone that was Franca, with all those pyrotechnics and confusion, or that jealousy and theatricality. I was working like a madman; I didn't want to think of her. I thought to myself – halt, danger, get out, flee, don't even look back or you'll turn into a pillar of salt.[6]

And so it was that Franca made the first move, and with appropriate drama. They were performing in the Cinema Colosseo in Milan in 1952, and backstage she grabbed him by the lapels, pinned him against the wall and gave him a long, passionate kiss until he was breathless. Bernard Shaw insisted that it is always women who decide who their partners will be, even if they normally allow the male the illusion of believing himself the hunter. Dario Fo could have had no such illusion. The two started seeing each other regularly and, to the dismay of other cast members, making arrangements on stage for what they would do later that evening. 'When I was courting Franca, we were both poor. We used to cross Milan at night from the theatre where we were working to the house where she lived. I made her laugh all the way. I would jump and dance on the tramway, or stop and invent fantastic stories. We seemed younger than we were.' Their careers, however, required periods of separation and this created difficulties and break-ups.

> Before we finally got married, this gorgeous bitch had left me, a couple of times. Once it seemed it was for good. She had become famous. They called her the Italian Rita Hayworth. Visconti wanted her in one of his films. Someone else had written a script for her in one of those variety shows where she would be garlanded with feathers. And she left me. And I cried. I had to wait until we got back together in *A Poke in the Eye* to win her back.[7]

In June 1954, they were married. Franca insisted on a grand religious ceremony at the Basilica of Saint Ambrose in Milan.

Their partnership has often been fraught, but personally and professionally the two of them have come to rely on each other so deeply that it is simply meaningless to wonder what would have happened if, in some parallel universe, the pair had operated separately. Together, they have come to create one of the great theatres of our time. Initially, Dario was slow to recognize the extent of her contribution to their joint work, and in a curious dedication to his early collection of his *Ballads and Songs*, he wrote: 'If you permit, comrades/ I this serenade/ wish to make to my partner:/ yes, to Franca, /to her who so many times/ has remained in the shadows/ to provide the accompaniment/ to suggest to us the words . . . ' When the book was reprinted in 1976, this dedication was dropped, since by then Dario had come to acknowledge that Franca had given more than 'accompaniment' and that there was no cause for her to remain in the shadows.

Chapter 3

The Absurd at Work

Having appeared on radio, performed in theatre and exhibited his paintings, in 1953 Dario recorded his first song, a brittle, ironic number entitled
'The Moon is a Lightbulb'. The lyrics were his, the music composed by a
friend from the Brera, Fiorenzo Carpi, and the feelings expressed in a
whimsical–absurdist style wholly in keeping with the *Poer nano* stories.
'The Moon is a Lightbulb' happily guyed the sentimental motifs of popular
music of the time, touchingly recounting the torments of a spurned lover
as he paces the street below the house where his unfaithful love, Lina, is
entertaining Nino, a wealthy barber. His torments do not stem from a broken heart or unrequited passion but from the fact that the number 38 tram
has already gone and the 28 has been taken off, leaving the tortured soul
facing a long walk home. To make matters worse, his feet are hurting.
Romantic clichés of the moon and stars as the comfort of unhappy lovers
are also stood on their head.

> The moon is a lightbulb attached to the ceiling
> The stars are lemons dragged across the puddles
> And, Lina, I walk backwards and forwards on the pavement
> And my feet are sore, sore, sore, Lina.[1]

Dario's own recording had little success, but the song became a hit two
years later when it was reissued by Enzo Jannacci, a popular singer-songwriter in Italy. In the 1950s, music, both Italian and imported, was already
beginning to occupy a central place in popular culture. In the heady days
after the Liberation, American music meant blues and jazz, but by the early
fifties this was being replaced by mawkish, commercialized Tin Pan Alley
products. Italy spawned its own crooners and vocalists who aped what was
being done across the Atlantic, but there was a cult following in the cities
for music of a more subversive, unconventional kind. Dario, who had a
ready flair for ironic ballads with a whimsical narrative, was able to meet
this demand. 'The Moon is a Lightbulb' was followed by other numbers,

such as 'I Saw a King', which features a monarch in tears on horseback but asks for sympathy for the horse, and the more famous 'He Had a Black Taxi', an updated version of the Cain and Abel story, with Abel as a taxi driver and Cain a tyre thief. The tyre which Eve gives Abel as a Christmas present is stolen by Cain, leading to Abel's sad demise.

Dario was not the only writer attracted by the music industry. Italo Calvino wrote some wry pieces for a group called Cantacronache, while Umberto Eco and the poet Franco Fortini also wrote lyrics. Domenico Modugno, who had a worldwide success with 'Volare', and the singer-song-writers Paolo Conte, Giorgio Gaber and Enzo Jannacci, who all emerged in the mid-fifties, were part of the same trend. Their success was in some respects a reaction against the domination of the market by American singers, but was also due to the encouragement offered by the Ricordi music company. Ricordi itself was a venerable, long-established family firm which had published the music of Verdi and Puccini, but Nanni Ricordi, the unconventional scion of a respectable dynasty, set up a subsidiary dedicated to providing music to appeal to a generation which viewed itself as in rebellion against its parents' ways. Nanni Ricordi became a firm friend of Dario and Franca, and would be involved with them on various fronts over the coming decades. In the fifties, his studio in Milan became the meeting place for the new creative spirits of Milan, not only singers and lyricists.

As a singer, Dario may have a limited range but his strong, idiosyncratic voice, which has character rather than melody, more than compensates. He has the presence, intonation and personality of a Charles Aznavour, and in this genre deficiencies can be glossed over as expressions of a distinctive style rather than as indications of limited vocal gifts. The number of songs authored by him is extensive but most were conceived not as single numbers but as part of a show. It is something of a quirk that the plays which have travelled best have been those without music, leaving many of his admirers outside Italy unaware that the majority of his theatrical works have been built on a mixture of song and dialogue.

At this time, although he made many recordings of his own, his songs were brought to a mass public by other singers, particularly Jannacci, whose own compositions and humour were similar to Fo's. The two met courtesy of Ricordi. Jannacci had written a surreal song entitled 'The Dog With the Hair', which features a dog of unusual vanity who spends his time peering at himself in shop windows and endlessly adjusting his hair-styles. The dog goes into a shop to ask for three cigarettes, but is ignored by the shop assistants, unaccustomed to dealing with a dog with hair. Nothing more happens. Jannacci sang this piece at an audition with RAI radio but was dismissed with a wave of the hand. Some months later, in the Ricordi studio, Dario burst in on him and said: 'You're the guy with the hair.' Initially Jannacci thought this stranger was making slighting comments about his hair-style, but then realized that the reference was to the dog in the song. "Come home with me," continued Dario. "You must learn." He took me back to his place and made me listen to a song of his, which turned out to be "The Moon is a Lightbulb".[2] The two became firm friends and were to collaborate on many ventures.

There are links between Dario's songs and the French *chanson*, which was in vogue in the early 1950s. Singers such as Georges Brassens or Juliette Greco found an audience which included both devotees of light music and adherents of existentialism, surrealism or the 'absurd'. Songs of Greco's featuring armed tanks filled with penguins and ducks would once have been consigned to the category of nonsense compositions, but at the time were viewed as expressing a philosophical outlook similar to Ionesco's or Adamov's. Some of Dario's early songs are redolent of that absurdist mood, while others, notably those written in Milanese dialect for theatrical productions by Giorgio Strehler, are in folk-song mode. Dario and Strehler collaborated on some of these songs, while others were written by Dario alone, but the authorship was concealed since Strehler wished to pass the numbers off as anonymous. 'He wanted to let it be believed that we had collected popular songs from a city which had never in fact existed. There did exist tunes and pieces like "Porta Romana", "El Barbisin", "La Balilla" which had been sung in taverns and which we collected.'[3]

Song was integral to the revues produced by the company Dario set up in 1953 with Franco Parenti and Giustino Durano, an actor he had met while doing *Seven Days* in Milan. The new group, in a somewhat heavy parody of a popular comedy group called *The Hunchbacks*, dubbed themselves *The Uprights* and chose a genre close to music-hall or cabaret. There is not, as Umberto Eco once wrote somewhat wistfully, a tradition of cabaret in Italy to compare with Berlin in the twenties or Paris in the belle époque. The reasons Eco proposed for this absence were related to a lack of trust in democracy. 'Italian customs have remained Bourbon. Cabaret exists because it can speak badly of the authorities, and the authorities in Italy are not to be touched. The absence of cabaret in a country means that, in spite of appearances, liberty is allowed but not licence. And democracy thrives on licence.'[4]

Dario, having already displayed comic flair and irreverent talent in conventional revue, was ready to provide that licence. His new troupe negotiated the lease of the Piccolo for the summer months when the theatre was normally closed. All three members of the group were to collaborate on the script, although in the event the writing was done by Fo and Parenti. Fiorenzo Carpi, who had been appointed the Piccolo's musical director, composed the music. Franca was a member of the cast. The title, *A Poke in the Eye*, was taken from a satirical column in *L'Unità*, the Communist daily. Somewhat oddly, Dario always denied that the show should be classified as cabaret, preferring to emphasize the satirical element and to place the work in the variety tradition, as *avanspettacolo*, an equivalent of the British or American 'curtain-raiser'.

> I've never done cabaret, but rather a form of theatre linked to popular traditions . . . When we did *A Poke in the Eye* with the Piccolo Teatro, the ambience was not that of cabaret – the space itself, 700 seats, a stage twelve to thirteen yards wide, a complete set, the number of people acting (there were twelve of us), and finally the concept of the piece which was not a string of sketches but had a logical continuity of its own . . . *A Poke in the Eye* was based on a history whose origins go back to the goliardic tradition, but mixed with elements of *commedia dell'arte* and modified by my experience with the theatre of Strehler who, at that time, was truly revolutionary. It had little to do with the French or German tradition in cabaret. That is, it was something better than cabaret which forces one to adopt a certain unnatural format: a café performance requires a very private and intimate form of speaking. With us, everything was expanded, the action, the amount of physical expression inherent in our way of acting, a pantomime learned not from the traditions of the white mime, but from *commedia dell'arte* . . . Moreover, there was a popular element which consisted of the story-teller's visual narration, and this we used explicitly and directly.[5]

Dario has a tendency to impose, retrospectively, a seamless unity on his work. In spite of these later protestations, his first shows had much in common with the Parisian cabaret he had seen at first hand in the French capital. If he had not had the chance, as he put it, to experience the twin poles of Paris and Milan in the immediate post-war years, he would have been a different person.[6] Although Italian medieval performance and *commedia dell'arte* would be the principal influences on him for most of his career, in the 1950s it was French cabaret and boulevard farce which provided his principal inspiration.

Fo differed from Eco's belief that the authorities in Italy could not be touched. 'Italy prefers the *canzonetta* (the ditty)', wrote Eco. 'The mandolin and the moon are the themes of our *folkgeist*. It appeals to the sensibilities but does not undermine them, or demand that they be overturned. There is nothing unpredictable.' Fo was determined to be unpredictable. *A Poke in the Eye* was eventually tagged an anti-revue. If the approach was satirical, it was not yet the blazing, violent flame of later years, but a flickering little light, still in need of tending. The impact was akin to Gilbert and Sullivan's gentle satire on the House of Lords in *Iolanthe*, not Karl Kraus's savage, frustrated rage in *Last Days of Humanity*. All three members of the company were Communist sympathizers, but the script was less a venture into current affairs than an attempt to dismantle the myths of history, to jeer at accepted wisdom, to laugh at the shibboleths of the tribe. Censorship made it difficult to deal with political matters, but at that juncture, with Fascism a recent memory, the work of re-evaluating national myths had an essential cathartic function. Fascist oratory and the Fascist education system had glorified all Italian achievements, real or imaginary, to produce a public version of history and a private cast of mind which were narrow, introverted and self-satisfied. Dario was out to puncture that conceit.

He was still learning his craft. He designed costumes and scenery, and received all-round support from Strehler, who even designed the lighting scheme, and from Jacques Lecoq, who supervised the rehearsals and became *de facto* director. Lecoq, the leading exponent and teacher of mime for his generation, had arrived in Italy in 1948 to work with Gianfranco De Bosio's university troupe in Padua on their productions of Brecht and Ruzzante. In 1951, he moved to Milan at the invitation of Strehler and Grassi to set up a drama school at the Piccolo. In Lecoq's account, the Fo–Durano–Parenti company 'revived the radical spirit of Italian satire, both through the political commitment they showed and the physical language they used'.[7]

The radical element might not be as strong as Lecoq suggests, but his own contribution in imparting a 'physical language' was decisive in shaping Dario's stagecraft. Lecoq in his turn was intrigued by the natural talent he detected inside Dario's awkward body. Fo's grin was toothy, his nose jutted out like a small promontory, his arms dangled, his legs were seemingly out of proportion to his trunk and his gait was gangling and tumbling, as though he moved on short stilts. Lecoq helped him convert these oddities into assets. He worked on his voice, helping Dario acquire that range of laughs and onomatopoeic vocalizations which have been indispensable to his monologues and have enabled him to reproduce everything from storms at sea to tigers licking wounds. Lecoq also, as one critic has observed, helped with 'the gags, the moon-faced expressions which will often indicate the exact opposite of what the words will express, something which has remained one of Fo's favourite procedures'.[8]

In later life, Dario came to disagree with Lecoq's general approach to mime, which he criticized as too abstract and too indifferent to the uses to which mime techniques could be put. Fo distanced himself from teachings which could be applied equally by the oppressed or oppressor, and which were not integrated into some wider system of belief, political or otherwise. In rehearsals at the Piccolo, however, he was happy to be educated in technique alone.

The twenty-one sketches which make up *A Poke in the Eye* examine aspects of history from classical to contemporary times, with the captains and the kings debunked and the conventional viewpoint overturned. Production photographs of the opening scene, set in Egypt, show the cast striking the customary rigid poses depicted on Egyptian tomb drawings and caricatured by generations of comedians, but the text, plainly inspired by Brecht's poem 'To the Worker-Reader', asks who built the pyramids – the Pharaoh whose name it carries, or the nameless slaves who transported the stones across the desert? In another sketch, Napoleon and Nelson squabble like two boys in a playground over their future glory as measured in the number of soldiers they will leave dead when the battles are done. Nelson ends by claiming his reputation will be greater and his death the more glorious, since he will be buried with pomp and splendour while Napoleon will die on a remote island, a prisoner with stomach pains. Napoleon retorts that that death is of no importance 'since Manzoni will come . . . he will write a fine poem about me . . . and that way I will pass to posterity!' Posterity, on the other hand, will take no interest in the nameless soldier played by Fo himself in a sketch set on the plains of Troy. This soldier has the bright idea of ending the whole business by manufacturing a giant horse, but he gives all the credit for the invention to the decidedly dim but aristocratic Ulysses. The standpoint is that of the Good Soldier Schweik, the slightly baffled, unremarkable Everyman who remains unawed and unimpressed by his betters. Already Fo was experimenting with a dialectic between history and the present day. In future works, he would mount a sortie into history either to find metaphors for contemporary conditions, or to reconquer spaces in the past which he considered had been wrongly ceded to the victors.

The show was a success and went on tour to several Italian cities. Its black humour caught the mood of at least the left-leaning part of the public, but it was well received by critics of right-wing papers as well. There were warning signs of a more hostile response from the political and religious authorities. The theatre in Trieste refused to host the company unless they agreed to cuts, the bishop in Vicenza insisted that the police pull down the company's posters, and in various centres the show was denounced by zealous parish priests. The real tussles with the censorship still lay ahead, but the defenders of the *status quo* had already identified Fo as an adversary.

Following the success of their first ventures, the authors prepared a new show, *Madhouse for the Sane*, again using the satirical cabaret format. Lecoq and Fiorenzo Carpi were fully involved. The new work opened at the Piccolo in June 1954, once again in the unwanted summer season. Franca, who was pregnant, did not appear on this occasion. The new work portrayed twenty-four hours in the life of an unidentified city with a close resemblance to Milan. The element of the absurd caused the Nobel Prize-winning poet, Salvatore Quasimodo, then working as theatre reviewer, to make the acute comment that the production contained not only 'an unnoticed return to *commedia dell'arte*' but also traces of 'decadent, surreal French poetry'.

The prevailing tone was ironic rather than surrealistic, and the focus of the satire was this time on contemporary subjects and politicians in office. Individual sketches ridiculed the situation in Italy at a time when the Cold War was at its height and clerical domination on the increase at home. A magazine editor and publisher are shown in discussion with a journalist eager to explain his most recent articles. The editor is indignant at the suggestion that he should actually read the pieces before publication, since his job only requires him to count how often the terms 'nation', 'cradle of civilization' or 'liberty' occur. The portrayal of Cabinet deliberations is hardly more flattering. The ministers discuss the state of Italy in grandiloquent terms, but cannot help noting that the roads, which under the monarchy were the best in Europe, are now badly in need of repair. One minister deplores the abdication of the king, since it had once been the patriotic practice of the inhabitants of villages to repair roads when a royal visit was imminent. Could we not learn from Russia, suggests another; an idea which causes dismay until he clarifies that the reference is to Tsarist Russia.

A range of excited proposals are put forward. When Isadora Duncan or Sarah Bernhardt paid a visit to a town, people would throw coats or furs on the roads to conceal their real state, so could not the road problem be solved by dispatching attractive women on semi-official visits? A housing problem? Unpaid prison labour could be pressed into service, and instead of providing training for prisoners the solution might be to jail building workers. Agricultural unrest? In Britain, they sent the queen to trouble spots, and America had just appointed Clare Booth Luce as ambassador to Italy. She attained notoriety by calling on the Italian government to take determined steps to root out Communism, so perhaps Mrs Booth Luce could be persuaded, for the good of Italy, to take on an out-and-out regal role?

Before being staged, the work was massacred by the censors. Censorship of theatre and cinema had been established by the pre-Fascist Liberal government, and maintained both by Mussolini and by his Christian Democrat successors. In the 1950s, authors were required to submit their scripts in advance to an Undersecretary of State, who happened to be Giulio Andreotti, then a young Christian Democrat politician and subsequently six times prime minister of Italy. The application of censorship laws has always delighted connoisseurs of the far reaches of bureaucratic insanity, and Italy was no exception. Sartre's theatre was outlawed, but so too was Machiavelli's *La Mandragola*. Falstaff could appear in *Henry IV*, but only after certain lines were cut. The innocuous Ealing comedy *Kind Hearts and Coronets* lay awaiting approval for many years because one of the female ancestors of the murderous aristocrat, played by Alec Guinness, had married an Italian. Distribution in Italy was permitted only when the offending character was made Spanish. There is no record of Generalisimo Franco's response. This slapstick masked the heavy hand of the growing clerical–political domination of Italian cultural life. National censorship was only half the story. The Church at local and national level imposed its own standards, with each parish issuing a list of approved and disapproved films and plays. There were various categories of refusal, and Fo and Rame became accustomed to having their work included among those which the Catholic faithful were most strongly advised to avoid.

Madhouse for the Sane was sent back from Rome covered in red ink, so the staged version was only a pale copy of the original script. Franca recalls that the stalls were filled with little men with little torches, peering at the script in the dark to make sure there were no deviations from the approved version. It was to become a familiar experience. The work had a successful summer in Milan, but was less appreciated in the smaller centres to which it toured. After the run, the main figures in the company were unable to agree on the next move, and split up. Durano returned to conventional revue, while Parenti and Lecoq set up their own troupe to put on new work. Dario had no objection to this aim in the abstract, but had strong reservations over their most favoured new writer, Eugène Ionesco. In the event, the Parenti and Lecoq company had a short life, for all the money they had made in the revues was lost with their productions of *The Chairs* and *The Bald Prima Donna*.⁹ Ionesco has remained a *bête noire* for Dario. On any occasion he was asked about the break-up of the Fo–Durano–Parenti company, he explained it by referring to Parenti's admiration for Ionesco, as though that were justification enough. Dario was distrustful of the avant-garde in all its manifestations, and considered himself vindicated by the increasingly rightist positions Ionesco adopted. Ironically, when he staged his one-act farces a couple of years later, he would see himself described regularly as the 'Italian Ionesco'.

If Fo associated Parenti's split with Ionesco, Parenti blamed the break on Dario's desire to move into a new medium, film.¹⁰ Italian cinema at the time was at its most buoyant and influential. The neo-realism of the immediate post-war years had given it an international lustre, and the willingness of directors like De Sica, Visconti and Rossellini to use film to focus on such topics as the Resistance, internal immigration, urban poverty and unemployment made cinema, not theatre, the main forum for discussion of national issues. In the early fifties a new wave which included directors like Pietro Germi and Ettore Scola brought *commedia all'italiana* to the screen, and opened up new vistas. In 1955, not long after the birth of their son Jacopo on 31 March, Dario and Franca moved to Rome to work in cinema. For a time, they lived close to Roberto Rossellini and Ingrid Bergman, who were then being doorstepped by journalists and photographers anxious to report on the scandalous liaison, begun during the filming of *Stromboli*, which had led to them setting up home together even although they were both married to other people. Dario hoped to find openings both as scriptwriter and actor, and brought with him a film script in which he attempted, like Jacques Tati, to employ age-old clowning techniques to express a sense of human disorientation in a society which had become too complex, too mechanized, too incomprehensible, too fast. Tati had also, with *Monsieur Hulot*, developed for himself the comic character of the simple man who just manages to survive but causes mayhem with his inability to abide by rules. Fo had already devised such a character in the *Poer nano* monologues, although this figure inhabited a timeless zone, not a techno-logical society. Similarly, in *Madhouse for the Sane*, he had created a comic panorama of scenes and incidents in a cityscape no longer made in the image and likeness of man.

The script of *Lo svitato*, which could perhaps be rendered as *Screwball*, brought together all these elements. The central figure, Achille, showed Dario's preference for characters who could be given their head rather than ones with too tightly defined a role, but in the cinema industry Dario was in the anomalous position of having a reputation sufficient to compel the film-makers to take his proposals seriously, but insufficient to justify him being given a position of directorial control. The expertise he had acquired in the theatre, he was continually told, was of no value in the cinema, which had its own rules and conventions. Dario found himself imprisoned in bureaucracy. He contacted the producer Nello Santi and his Galatea Films company, as well as the director Carlo Lizzani, a friend from student days. Lizzani had already directed a couple of successful films, including *Chronicles of Poor Lovers* (1948), based on the novel by the realist writer, Vasco Pratolini, and *Achtung! Banditi!* (1953), an account of the Resistance, but he had no experience of comedy. The professionals agreed that Fo's script was interesting, promising, showed his enormous ability and would, in due course, after reworking, make a good film. In all, five scriptwriters were brought in to do the retouching and rewriting. These were not mere hacks. Furio Scarpelli, in particular, went on to write the scripts for several of the most important Italian comedies of later years, but the combined talents of these ill-matched cooks, each adding their own ingredients, produced an odd broth. Fo, to his own later regret, felt obliged to give way to the greater experience and knowledge of his collaborators, although no one can now say whether or not his original script would have worked on the set. Nello Santi later described the result as representing 'six authors in search of a film'.

The film was shot in Milan and released in autumn 1956. The debt to Tati was obvious, although Achille was also the first of the many modern Harlequins Dario was to play. Achille was somewhat dim but gifted with a higher naïveté and gullibility which allowed him to survive in circum-stances which would have crushed more intelligent men. He falls for a gangster's moll and it takes him time to realize that there is another girl, played by Franca, who is in love with him. His home is a crumbling build-ing long abandoned by all other tenants and surrounded by cranes and demolition machines, all waiting to raze it to the ground and replace it with some soulless box. Achille is involved in a variety of bizarre mishaps, including a Keystone Cops chase, pursued by a pack of grim and ferocious dogs through city streets jammed with cars and lorries. There are hints of protest against uncontrolled building work which was to dehumanize the city, and suggestions that this wild place is unsuitable for human habitation, but the film was judged a failure both as a comedy and as a vehicle of protest. It was mauled by critics and was no great success with the public.

The failure left a profound mark on Dario and Franca. With just a touch of poetic licence, Franca described the film as 'the greatest failure in the history of the cinema', but she continued to believe that Dario's original script had a vivacity and imaginative force which was destroyed in the rewrites. She believed that all could have been remedied had they had the resources to buy back the film and reshoot some of the sequences. Fo never reconciled himself to the flop and laid the blame elsewhere, principally on the critics. Tati had not made an enormous impact when his films were first shown in Italy, and Fo believed that his was a film without context. 'Faced with the response to this film I realized how much joy there is in Italy in destroying. Of course there were some mistakes, but there are other pieces which have been reprinted and bought by cinema museums.'[11] Years later, he could repeat audience figures in various cinemas in Rome, recite box-office takings in an experimental cinema in Milan and could even remember the acclaim which greeted the film at a festival in Florence and during the four brief days when it was given a screening in Rome. He remains convinced that this local success could have been the prelude to wider recognition had the film not been taken off because the management had contractual obligations with other companies. He was also appalled by the powerlessness of actors and writers in cinema, both in the creation and the eventual distribution of the work. In theatre, he would always work with companies where, in principle, everyone had some say, and where he himself had some control over the work he produced.

In spite of this disappointment, Dario still nurtured an ambition to succeed in cinema. The couple remained in Rome until 1958, and Dario was taken on as gagman by Carlo Ponti and Dino De Laurentiis, the leading producers of the day. He submitted to the rigours and tedium of endless rounds of meetings and discussions, and made a contribution as scriptwriter to various unremarkable films with titles like *Souvenir d'Italie*, which came out in 1957, *Rascel Fifi*, released later the same year, and *A Woman Born in March*, which reached the cinemas a year later. Franca played some minor roles in several other films, and appeared in theatre in a Feydeau farce, *Don't Go Round in the Nude.* One evening, the Sicilian novelist Leonardo Sciascia was in the audience and was struck, as he recalled years later in *The Knight and Death*, by the incongruity between the suggestive title and the thick housecoat which the censors required Franca to wear.

It was an unhappy, unfulfilling time. Franca found little satisfaction in the film parts which she accepted to help pay the bills, and encouraged Dario to start writing for the theatre again. In the free time he had from looking after Jacopo while Franca was working on the set, he produced a series of one-act farces. They vowed to have no more to do with a *métier* they decided was not for them. Their life would be devoted to theatre. Dario made no further appearances on screen until the 1990s, and then only in minor roles as a favour to friends. Dario and Franca remain the only actors of any established reputation in the post-war years who have made their names exclusively in theatre.

As with his study of architecture, Dario has tried to draw some advantage from his exposure to film-making techniques, but the return from those years was scant. A benevolent critic might agree that in the comedies which he wrote during his so-called 'bourgeois period' in the early sixties there are traces of cinematic techniques in the slick switch of scene, in the sharp cuts from sequence to sequence, in the development of momentum and pace in his plots, but this is meagre booty from three years of routine and unproductive labour. When, in his 1987 book *The Tricks of the Trade*, he spoke of cinema and of how he had learned from it the fundamental value of montage and situation, the directors to whom he referred were Eisenstein and Pabst, not the people he had worked with in Rome.

It was time to return to Milan. Dario and Franca contacted Paolo Grassi about the availability of the Piccolo, but once again were offered only the less prestigious summer season. They accepted and sold up in Rome. The Fo–Rame company made its début on 6 June 1958, with four farces under the overall title *Thieves, Mannequins and Naked Women.* Spectators were continually tantalized by the promise of naked women in this phase of Fo's output, but nudity was limited to words on the hoardings. One of the plays in the original programme was the Feydeau farce *Don't Go Round in the Nude*, but this was replaced during the run by a new play of Fo's, *Bodies in the Post and Women in the Nude.* This play was the first of Fo's to be televised, but the censors insisted that the second part of the title be cut. Nudity, this time male, featured in another title, *One Was Nude and One*

THE ABSURD AT WORK

Wore Tails, while the remaining titles were more chaste: *House-Painters Have No Memories* and *The Virtuous Burglar.* The programme was such a success with audiences that its run was extended into the winter, where it alternated with *Comica finale,* another programme of four farces by Dario. This second programme was premièred at the Stabile in Turin, where the director was Gianfranco De Bosio, the man who had invited Lecoq to Italy. Perhaps De Bosio had another plan. He was among the group who had rediscovered and rehabilitated the Renaissance actor-author, Ruzzante, who was already Dario's model and idol. De Bosio wanted Dario to perform Ruzzante, but the time was not right. Dario was intent on making his own name and establishing himself as a writer and actor, and had no time for performing the works of other writers. He had debts to Ruzzante which he would pay, but not yet.

In the meantime, his debts were to the Rame family, since the second programme of farces were based on scripts from the Rame archive. As he would do repeatedly throughout his career, he selected material which he then rewrote, updated, modified and reinvented according to his own tastes and needs. The two programmes that season, *Mannequins* and *Comica finale,* represent twin aptitudes and contrasting attitudes to tradition. In the first, Dario operates as a writer of his own time and gives free rein to his own inventiveness, and in the second he displays a willingness to plunder and to operate inside a tradition. All the works can be classified as farces. If he had suffered from critical ill-timing with the release of *Lo svitato* before Tati became an icon, he enjoyed a piece of critical good fortune with the staging of his first one-act plays. In the fifties, when Beckett, Adamov and Ionesco in France had found farce the most appropriate means of expressing the senselessness and absurdity of life, this once-despised genre basked in high critical esteem. Dario modified techniques of farce according to his needs at different phases of his life, but from the outset he was happy to crusade in favour of farce as such. 'I want to rehabilitate farce. Theatre critics have adopted the habit of saying that an unsuccessful comedy "declines into farce". Now, in my view, farce is a most noble – and modern – genre of theatre.' He admired the clockwork precision of the French *farceurs,* their speed of movement, the unending switch of situation, the carefully phased chains of revelation, the nonchalant insouciance of the characters as they heedlessly pursued a logic which was clear to them but preposterous to anyone watching. His farces had more in common with the rumbustious boulevard variety of the nineteenth century than with the dark, existential farce of the twentieth. He had read

Feydeau, Labiche and Courteline, and came to ridicule society with the tools they provided. Far from standing in rage before the metaphysical emptiness of the cosmos, like Beckett or Ionesco, he encouraged in his audience an attitude of amusement at the arrangements of social life. This distinction between the metaphysical and the social was not fully realized in the 1950s, when, in spite of having broken with Franco Parenti over Ionesco, Dario now found himself viewed as the Italian exponent of the absurd and as an importer of Parisian philosophy and Parisian dramatic innovation.

Fo had no yen for that particular garland. There may be a point at which the surreal and the absurd can overlap with the merely burlesque, a point at which Gilbert and Sullivan can be made to seem Kafkaesque, but in their origin and their objective they are as distinct as wasteland and Wonderland. Whereas the absurd was a metaphor for the enduring absence of all metaphysical order for the writers of twentieth-century farce, absurd situations when presented by the light-hearted *farceurs* of nineteenth-century Paris represented a state of merely temporary chaos. Feydeau made himself lord of misrule for a day, but he was, as his third acts make clear, the most conformist of writers. Dario had no comparable interest either in a mystical emptiness or in dénouements which reinforce the social *status quo*.

Satire is not the dominant force in the pieces that make up *Thieves, Mannequins and Naked Women*. The first farce, *House-Painters Have No Memories*, is set in a brothel, and offers the titillation of scantily clad prostitutes prancing across the stage and gathering round the figure of the bordello-owner's husband, frozen into a state of immobility by an injection which has the power to paralyse but not kill. It could be remarked that there are a number of stock characters and stock situations which will recur constantly in Fo's theatre. He had, in purely theatrical terms, a fondness for prostitutes, who will appear later as comic figures, as golden-hearted bearers of temperate values, as representatives of freedom from the oppression of routine or even purveyors of political wisdom. Similarly, the transforming injection would be a device he employed on many occasions. In this play, the injection has a purely comic function, administered by mistake to one of two house-painters, who is then immobilized. The husband, not having received his daily dose, comes round and denounces his wife for paralysing him since he was too attractive to the other occupants of the house. All ends happily when the wife is injected and immobilized, leaving her husband and the painters to live in bliss with the frolicsome girls. This is as undemanding a romp as vaudeville could offer.

The most successful piece remains *The Virtuous Burglar*, later given an off-Broadway production, gaining the honour of being the first Fo work to be performed in English. The play juxtaposes the moral code of the burglar and his wife, who are sexually faithful but indifferent to property rights, with the practice of the house-owners, who are rigid believers in property but faithless hypocrites in sexual matters. The burglar breaks into a well-to-do apartment but is disturbed by a phone call from his wife, asking him wheedlingly to bring her a little present. No sooner has he appeased her than the house-owner and his mistress arrive. The burglar takes refuge in a grandfather clock, where he overhears the husband attempt to entice the woman into the bedroom. The attempted seduction is disturbed by a further phone call from the burglar's wife, which causes the couple to fear that their liaison has been discovered and the burglar's wife to believe that her husband is engaged in an affair of his own. The plot has so many twists and turns and the various situations are so rapidly established and dismantled that the one-act format is strained to its limits. Although there is no final resolution to this imbroglio, there is certainly no comfort for the bourgeoisie. Inversion of society's standard is the stock-in-trade of all comedy, and here the burglar is the positive hero. He emerges as the honest-to-God labouring man who expects a fair day's pay for a fair day's work. The burglar and his wife are faithful to each other, unlike the middle-class couple who indulge in casual but concealed infidelities. Hypocrisy has been one of theatre's favourite targets, but Fo gives the subject a mild class edge.

Fo's frame of reference is society, and he never strays on to the adjoining Beckettian wasteland where displaced individuals trade jokes while waiting for Godot or God. There are echoes of such conversations in *One Was Nude and One Wore Tails*, but they have the ring of pastiche or parody. The naked man in a dustbin cannot fail to recall Beckett's *Endgame*, while the two roadsweeps with a philosophical bent are reminiscent of the tramps in *Waiting for Godot*. The chatter between the two as they set to work covers such topics as the possibility of attaining truth and happiness, the nature of madness, the validity of yoga as a means of fulfilment, the Platonic view of the absolute, and the likelihood of the Pope's knowing where God resides, but their flow is interrupted by a distraught woman and a naked man. His confinement in a dustbin has an earthy explanation since it is revealed that he is an ambassador who had to exit quickly from his lover's bed. The tone is whimsical and jocular, and the plot develops according to a series of mistaken identities. The roadsweeper spots a flower-seller still dressed in an evening suit which he needed to sell bouquets in a night-club. He purchases the suit for the ambassador but ends up wearing it himself and being treated like a lord. So, who is then the gentleman, the distressed Don Juan or the street-cleaner decked out in elegant attire? Behind the temporarily upside-down situation lies the tentative notion that possibly the world could be more fairly and equally ordered according to merit, but the laughter is genial and Fo is still less than a firebrand.

With the other four-farce programme, *Comica finale*, tradition is vividly and exhilaratingly made flesh. Dario has transformed the Rames' original pieces, sometimes retaining only single characters, but preserves the spirit of the source material. The recreated past is a fantasy age, with no connections or lessons for the present. *When You Are Poor You Will Be King* presents the kind of inversion which Mikhail Bakhtin, then unknown in Italy, identified as the core of the carnival spirit. Four youths poke fun at a poor man who entertains the illusion that once he has squandered all he possesses he will ascend a throne. *Marcolfa*, named after a stock character from Italian comedy, follows the adventures of a serving girl of that name, famed for her ugliness, but discovered to have unsuspected charms when she is rumoured to have won the lottery, while *The Three Lads* unfolds in a fairy-tale atmosphere. The three lads are called to the castle to defend it, but find themselves objects of attention for the daughters of the lord, who had forbidden them from seeing other men.

Oscar Wilde once described *The Importance of Being Earnest* as a play 'about butterflies, for butterflies'. The same description could be applied to these largely escapist farces. Contemporary critics were impressed by Fo's natural clowning abilities, his impeccable timing and his improvisational skills. The two programmes commanded a great deal of critical attention, most of it positive, and the theatres were packed at a time of the year when, according to received wisdom, people had other things on their minds. By the end of the run of the two programmes, Dario was a well-established, if slightly puzzling, figure in theatre. He had appeared in revues, in film, in farce, and had asserted himself as a writer in all these genres. It was now commonplace to say that he was a phenomenon. But of what sort?

Chapter 4

Being Bourgeois

Pinball machines caused much excitement in Italy in the late 1950s. Dario was addicted to them, and in moments of tension or vacuity found undemanding relaxation in mindlessly flicking balls up and down the table, around plastic obstacles and into little holes. However, in the Italy of the 'economic miracle', everything was scrutinized for its symbolic meaning and potential moral menace, so the pinball machine was, like the jukebox, the teenager, Hollywood films and Coca-Cola, deemed to be part of the new Americanized pop culture, and caused such alarm in pulpits and boardrooms that the Ministry for the Interior proposed to ban it altogether. It was, in the words of an official communiqué, guilty of 'creating an atmosphere favourable to crime, taking up hours which could be devoted to work and study and causing the waste of money'.[1] In this context, Fo's decision to give the title *Archangels Don't Play Pinball* to his first full-length play had the double advantage of being both fashionable and polemical.

Dario and Franca had now become 'personalities', whose tastes, views and lifestyle were assumed to be of interest to the public at large. For readers of glossy magazines, Franca took on the role expected of fashionable actresses. She was happy to be photographed encased in furs, tight skirts, close-fitting jumpers or in staged *déshabillé*, seducing the camera and the reader with a girlish pout. Dario let the world know that he was a supporter of Inter Milan, that his favourite food was risotto, that if he suffered from homesickness while abroad, a plate of pasta helped but rice would not serve this purpose because he would not trust anyone else to cook risotto as it should be done. The ideal revolutionary couple, as they would become, were at this time the envied model for a consumer society: he was talented, witty, intelligent and politely radical; she was talented, youthful, pretty; and both were evidently destined for even greater success.

Dario developed, or had thrust upon him, the image of a scoffing but jovial bohemian rather than that of an enraged iconoclast. In the guise of the clown, he played and cavorted at the margins of society, exposing absurdities, jeering, sticking out his tongue, delivering derisive witticisms or satirical shafts, making himself a nuisance to the authorities, breaking a few windows but without pulling down temples or overturning altars. There was something very traditional and expected about his role at this time. The circus clown knows the rules as clearly as the court fool, and both know that to go too far is to risk the whip. Dario's overriding urge was to make his own way and to have his own voice heard in theatre. He adopted the leftist positions held by many writers and artists, voting Communist, deploring the Christian Democrat rule, favouring divorce and advocating an increase in state ownership of industry. If his position was dissident, it could still be incorporated within the system. In a 1954 interview, he stated that the writers with whom he felt most affinity were Shaw and Chekhov. The choice of Chekhov, who was later to become a *bête-noire* as the very incarnation of bourgeois drama, was surprising, but the resemblances to Shaw at this period are clear. Both were inconvenient voices, determined to upset the *status quo*, but both accepted, at least for a time, the ease of a role as licensed entertainer-cum-oracle in society.

In January 1959, Dario made his first appearance on television in a comedy, *Five Lire Pieces*, and his celebrity was further increased by his starring role in a series of television commercials. Television advertising and programming were both in their infancy and the directors of RAI, the public broadcasting authority, thought they could check the intrusiveness and power of the advertisers by clustering all their ads on a mini-programme called *Carosello*. The other programmes in those days of strict political and clerical control were so dull that *Carosello* was soon the most popular work on the screen. A mildly humorous approach wrapped in a narrative framework was the order of the day, and Dario suited this purpose. That toothy smile, that India-rubber face, those eyes which seemed to widen to the dimensions of a screen, that range of odd gaits, that perfectly timed delivery boosted the sales of products from pasta and mineral water to petrol. The stories Dario acted out stretched the two-minute format to straining point. In ads for Agip, the Italian oil company, he appeared in the guise of the detective Joe La Volpe, a parody Philip Marlowe, who slouched about in a bowler hat and ill-fitting suit with a revolver bulging under the jacket. The makers of commercials for Recoaro, the mineral water firm, chose a more absurdist approach. Dario and his partner, both zany carpet-fitters, would go into the house of some awkward housewife, only to grow exasperated with her demands and end up tossing her out of a window. 'Let's freshen up our ideas' went the refrain. 'Yes, but what with? – Recoaro.' For the same brand, Dario created the figure of the garrulous Signor Presenti, who talked and talked until his fictional listeners felt in need of refreshment with mineral water. He was also employed by Barilla, the pasta manufacturers, as a braggart who bored listeners at the bar with his accounts of fantastic exploits, only to be finally shown up as a windbag.

These were essentially side-shows, and Dario itched to return to the theatre. The opportunity came with an approach in early 1959 by an impresario, known familiarly as 'Papa', who managed the Odeon theatre in Milan. Papa had the shrewdness and acumen, as well as the philistinism, of his breed, and having seen Fo on stage realized immediately that there were commercial prospects to be exploited. He offered him a deal which gave Fo artistic control of a space of his own. The style and content, be it satirical or conformist, comic or tragic, did not matter to the proprietor, provided they put bottoms on seats. The Fo–Rame company was rearranged, with Dario as writer and lead actor, Franca as first actress, her sister Pia as wardrobe mistress and her brother Enrico as administrator, while Carpi was retained as musical director. From 1959 to 1968, excepting only 1962, when they were involved with television, Dario turned out a play a year, always a comedy, always with music, generally for the Odeon, and always categorized, with hindsight, as 'bourgeois'.

Fo's 'bourgeois period' in theatre corresponded to the age of the 'economic miracle' in Italy. For Fo, this period, with nuances and qualifications, runs from *Archangels Don't Play Pinball* in 1959 to his break with commercial theatre in 1968, while in the case of the nation itself, the boom lasted from around 1958 to the slump whose effects began to be felt in 1963–4. Against all the prophecies made by the left in the aftermath of the 1948 election, capitalism was working, the country was being transformed and wealth was trickling down. The new affluence was symbolized by the Vespa, the scooter which carried Gregory Peck and Audrey Hepburn around the streets of the Eternal City in *Roman Holiday*, and by Fiat's economy car, the Seicento. It was not a time of great ideological disputes. When the ferociously anti-Communist American ambassador, Clare Booth Luce, complained of the dominance of the Communist trade unionists on the Fiat workers' councils, the workers obediently voted them off. Historians have identified a certain wry symbol of the times in the shape of a Communist trade unionist at Fiat who tried to whip up interest in elections to the factory councils, only to discover that his own members were more interested in brandishing the coupons giving them special terms for the purchase of the Seicento. Purchasing power was all. Fo himself performed in these years in the company restaurant of Rinascente, a department store with branches in most major cities.[2]

The tag 'bourgeois' was a polemical one applied by critics and does scant justice to the actual content of Fo's works at this time. Certainly Dario was no revolutionary, nor could the works from this period be termed 'political' in the sense Brecht or Meyerhold used the term, but his comedies sat at an awkward angle to the expectations of a middle-class audience in search of a 'good night out'. They were bourgeois in the sense that they were played in commercial or 'bourgeois' venues, but in the 1950s there were no other venues.[3] The plays produced by the Fo–Rame company were not judged innocuous by the censors of the day, and on various occasions it was touch and go whether the show would be given authorization. Approval for *Archangels* was officially withdrawn by the Ministry on account of the number of ad libs for which approval had not been sought. With the 1960 work, *He Had Two Pistols and White and Black Eyes*, the authorities ordered so many cuts that initially the company decided it would not be worthwhile to proceed. Eventually, they chose to go ahead with the original script and risk the consequences: the censors backed down. For *Isabella, Three Caravels and a Con-Man*, Dario was the subject of a report to the prosecution services because of a remark considered defamatory to the armed services, and actually received a challenge to a duel from an ex-cavalry officer. That situation was defused when Dario picked up the gauntlet but specified that the duel had to take place bare-footed, under the laws of Thailandese wrestling, of which he claimed to be national champion.[4] His opponent withdrew. One production had to be suspended because of a bomb threat, and at the end of another in Rome, Dario and Franca were attacked by a group of neo-Fascists. The zealous censors were such regular visitors that the view from the stage of torches shining on copies of the script resembled fireflies at night in the countryside.

The new works were termed comedies rather than farces, but the distinction is at times imperceptible. There is assumed to be a greater sophistication to comedy than farce, but these comedies are a chain of farcical situations rather than one overarching plot. 'The choice of writing a comedy involves the choice of a more complex structure than that of farce. While the farce is based from beginning to end on a theatrical mechanism based on a single device, comedy has a structure articulated according to the storyline, and so the devices can be multiple,' wrote Dario. The characters have a quality of Puckish naughtiness which makes them, at least in part, descendants of the Harlequin of *commedia dell'arte*, and gives the impression that even the more stuffy among them could at any moment pull off his shirt and tie to reveal the lozenged costume. If they raise a glass to their mouth, they are as liable to squirt the wine over the face of their neighbour as to sip it politely. Dario's comedies do not provide an unravelling in the final act of situations set up in the early sections of the play, but a series of stops and starts and fresh beginnings, only some of which are resolved. His genius lies in his unrestrained inventiveness, not in his ability to channel his creativity into structured plot.

A Fo text is never complete. He will modify it in rehearsals, alter it during the run or rewrite it in response to audience reactions. At times, he succumbs to the temptation to concentrate on the detail or the individual scene and to incorporate, even at the expense of the coherence of the whole, all manner of visual jokes or gags, especially when they have some association with *commedia dell'arte*. At this stage in Fo's writing, Franca was, by her own admission, too overawed by Dario's energy and inventiveness to make what would become critical contributions.

Dario, who always writes at speed, produced *Archangels Don't Play Pinball* in twenty days. The main players are a group of young hooligans or petty criminals who live on the margins of society in some urban setting. Never before had Fo devised characters from a specified social grouping rather than from an abstract, almost metaphysical background.[5] This is not a work of social protest. The lads are jolly scoundrels who cheat bakers out of cakes and bread, but their actions do not invite judgement. Among them is one whose real name is Weather, and whose Christian name could be Serene, Cloudy or Turbulent, but who is known as Lanky. This character, written by Dario for himself to play, was a cousin germane of Achille of *Lo svitato*, and was first of the many *faux-naïf* characters who people Fo's theatre. His apparent simplicity is a mask behind which there lurks not an intelligence but a cunning and pluck that will show up pretence and sham in society.

His friends gull Lanky into believing that a beautiful, wealthy Albanian woman has fallen in love with him and wants to marry him. The woman turns out to be a local prostitute, known ironically as Angela, but the 'wedding', with a phoney Coptic priest officiating, goes ahead. When the two are left alone, the dialogue between them takes on an unexpectedly gentle and lyrical tone. Such moments of emotion are rare in Dario's theatre, and perhaps these passages can be seen as a reflection of the relationship between Dario and Franca. He is the least autobiographical of writers, and intimacy or personal relationships are not his *forte*. He is not a poet of the emotional side of the human psyche and is immune to any fascination with the manifold strategies which Jack uses in novels and plays to entice Jill into bed. There is no shortage of married couples in his works, but only with *Open Couple*, the other idiosyncratically autobiographical work in his canon, is the success or failure of the marriage the focus of attention.

The couple split up when Lanky informs her that he must go to Rome to claim a pension due to him for a wound he received to his *osso sacro*, or sacrum, a bone which, with its odd name and embarrassing position, has always been a favourite of Dario's. The pension claim takes Lanky into a ministry, and allows Fo to satirize the workings of bureaucracy. There is something of expressionist absurdity in this scene of bureaucrats working like robots on a factory line, but it is another of those scenes which finds its worth only in performance. The words are secondary, and even the stage directions are banal. To his dismay, Lanky finds that he has been registered as a bloodhound. The official registration is his only proof of existence, and since the form says 'bloodhound', Lanky must take on the characteristics and lifestyle fitting a bloodhound.

A plot with such an abundance of twists and changes of direction can leave the audience dizzy, and critics were still unsure of what to make of Dario's puzzling talent. His histrionic gifts were undisputed, but the theatre magazine *Sipario*, when publishing the script of *Archangels*, gave voice to the criticism which was to dog Fo throughout his career. It was an enjoyable work, of course, excellent on stage, brilliantly acted, but did it have any value when set down on paper?

> Farce rediscovers here – after references to reality which are anything but random – all its congenial slapstick and knockabout. It would be pointless, in an attempt to avoid losing the 'best', to look for the rest on the pages of the script; by the 'best', we mean the bare-fisted struggle in which Dario Fo the actor and Dario Fo the author engage on stage to gain the upper hand in the show. Is it right to publish in *Sipario* a play which (precisely because of the genre to which it belongs) cannot boast sufficient literary autonomy? Let the reader judge, but let him judge by giving to the speeches of Lanky – it is an undemanding effort of the imagination – the intonations, the pauses, the accents, the absurd flurries, the stutters and the malicious cadences of the actor Dario Fo.[6]

The 1960–1 theatrical season saw Fo at the same venue with a more complex work, *He Had Two Pistols and White and Black Eyes*, a fable which reflects and distorts society with the devastatingly malicious wit of a

Jonathan Swift or John Gay. Dario played both the leading roles, those of a priest who has lost his memory and of a bandit on the run. The opening scene unfolds in a psychiatric hospital 'which resembles the cloister of a monastery', run by doctors and nurses dressed in the conventional white coats but topped by white capes embellished with the red cross of the Knights of Malta.[7] The mental hospital managed by clerics provides an unsettlingly acerbic image of an Italy ruled by the Christian Democrat Party, and allows Fo to introduce a favourite device of presenting the supposed madman as the representative of sanity. In a society which is corrupt and insane, the lord of misrule is the only legislator who can be trusted. Fo told his Danish translator Bent Holm that at this stage of his life he wrote largely according to instinct, but agreed that he was already drawn to that dramatic reversal of roles which Mikhail Bakhtin identified as the essence of carnival. Where the Italian constitution reads that 'Italy is a republic founded on work', the crooks' trade union in the play wanted the statute altered to read 'a republic founded on work and theft'. They put in a claim for a percentage of all theft, 'except for those committed inside ministries'.

The public response to the play was gratifying. Official figures showed that the Fo–Rame company was attracting audiences far in excess of those attending the works of any other theatrical company in Italy. According to an unbreakable law of criticism, every plaudit induces an equal and opposite censure, so reviewers were already suggesting that the attractions of the *beau monde* and increasing prosperity had begun to blunt Fo's satirical purpose. Whatever the reason, the next season's play, *He Who Loses a Foot is Lucky in Love*, premièred on 8 September 1961, received some of the most hostile notices Fo was ever to draw. The left-wing press, especially the Communist daily, *L'Unità*, was especially severe. In the play, Dario transfers the Apollo and Daphne myth to the Milan of his own time, and attempts to interweave a love story with criticism of construction companies involved in wholesale fraud. The criticism is not sustained, and in the attempt to build on the myth, the plot itself comes to resemble one of those ramshackle manor houses where each successive generation has added an extension. Barbs from the left were not sufficient to enhance Dario and Franca's standing with the establishment. The attack on corruption in business only extended the circle of their enemies.

Dario's theatre was beginning to win him an international reputation. Yugoslavia was the first country to stage a translation of one of his plays, but Scandinavia was also enthusiastic. By 1962, his work had been presented in three theatres in Stockholm, and two in Helsinki, as well as in

Denmark and Norway. Danish television presented *He Had Two Pistols and White and Black Eyes*, while other works were staged in Holland and Poland. As with a volcanic eruption, all the authorities in Italy could do was move as many people as possible away from the area likely to be affected. Apart from commercials, Dario and Franca were kept off the television screens – not a difficult feat in a country where broadcasting was run by government placemen.

However, by 1962, the membership of the ruling establishment was widening due to the change in government alliance known as the 'opening to the left'. Pope John XXIII was on the papal throne, the modernizing Vatican Council was in session, the liberalizing trends which marked the 1960s were already making their impact and the Christian Democrat Party was suffering from public irritation with the scandals in which it was involved. Under Fernando Tambroni, they tried to bolster their declining position by establishing a coalition with the neo-Fascist right, but this manoeuvre led to rioting all over the peninsula and the attempt was abandoned. Amintore Fanfani, then identified with the party's reforming wing, spearheaded a drive to the left, aimed at prising the socialists away from their alliance with the Communists. After an extended courtship, a centre-left government, with Fanfani at the helm, was formed in February 1962.

Dario was among the opponents of a move which he saw as neutering the socialists and giving new legitimacy to their Christian Democrat enemies, but for him the outcome was beneficial. In the first year of the new government, the law requiring pre-emptive censorship was rescinded, although it became clear in due course that this gesture was equivalent to the sixteenth-century legislation which legalized deer-hunting in the royal forests when there were no deer left to hunt. Theatre had a diminished value in an age when primacy in public entertainment, and in the expression of attitudes and beliefs, had passed to the newer media. In any case, the Italian authorities, as Fo was to discover, retained sufficient control to deal with any troublesome thespian who looked likely to pose a threat. Local police chiefs retained the power to examine the content of works in performance, and to take measures against anything which posed a threat to 'morals, good customs and public order'.

On assuming political power, socialists were allowed to share not only government office but also what Italians cynically termed 'sub-government', that is, the right of appointment to the many quangos, boards and commissions, as well as banks and nationalized companies, which were involved in the governance of the republic. One of these was RAI, and in the early stages the socialist appointees let in gusts of fresh air. In the same year, 1962, RAI opened a second channel, RAI2, a minority channel in every sense. Since few existing licence-holders had sets equipped to receive its programmes, RAI2 could be used as a ghetto for experimental programming or controversial works.

Dario and Franca were among the first to be invited to appear on the new channel, and five of the earlier one-act farces were transmitted. Dario directed the plays himself, receiving payment of three million lire, which was then a generous payment. The response was enthusiastic, and the couple were invited by RAI2 to present a mini-series of the variety show, *Who's Seen It?* The show opened with a mock occupation of the studios by supposedly dissatisfied viewers, aiming to instal comedians whose work was more in keeping with their own, iconoclastic taste. The various sketches presented are said to have been unconventional, and the series is said to have stirred the waters of television variety with its irreverent parodies of other shows. No one now can judge, since RAI later destroyed all copies of the programmes.

Emboldened, RAI next invited Dario and Franca to take charge of *Canzonissima* ('The Big Song'), the station's highly popular variety show, transmitted at prime time on the first channel. Conceived as an accompaniment to the national lottery, this programme had risen in popularity with the growth of the pop-music industry. The format had been altered after the first series to give the show a competitive edge. Each week, a different genre of song was featured, with the singer who received most votes from the audience at home going on to the final, where one overall winner was chosen. There were thirteen programmes in all.

Initially, Franca and Dario were sceptical and unenthusiastic. After the failure of their venture into film, they had devoted themselves to theatre and had been successful in building up their own audience. The first episode of *Canzonissima* was scheduled for October, which would mean missing a whole season and breaking faith with their public. In addition, *Canzonissima* was escapist entertainment, in which relentless light-heartedness and light-headedness were prized. Television was not their *métier*, and they were unsure of what level of autonomy they would be afforded. On the other hand, it was not as though Italian theatre had been an arena of unrestricted liberty for them. The presence of prowling censors had been fatiguing, while their own experiences with *Who's Seen It?* had been positive. Provided they could reach a firm agreement that they would control the content of the programmes, and that they would be at liberty to reshape it, they decided to accept.

The Director-General of RAI2 was Sergio Pugliese, whom Franca describes as open-minded and cultured. Schedules for all twelve programmes, excluding the final one, were drawn up and submitted to him for discussion. Dario was prepared to defer to Pugliese's expertise in his own professional field, but he was determined that *Canzonissima* would rise above mindless giggles, chatter and sing-song. He insisted on the right to take a satirical look at contemporary Italy. This was accepted, and the format and outline scripts were agreed with the broadcasting authorities.

The resultant programmes, a compromise between conflicting demands, sound uncomfortable from today's standpoint, but accurate assessment is not possible since RAI erased these tapes too. The scripts are extant, as are the volumes of newspaper comment which followed the first and each successive programme. Choruses of high-kicking, scantily clad, sequinned dancing girls preceded mordant sketches on aspects of public life in Italy: a monologue by Fo was followed by close-ups of some idol of the moment singing his or her newest number on the pains of teenage passion. Yet the theme tune composed by Dario, with its mockery not of the powerful and wealthy but of those who allow themselves to be gulled and tranquillized by the desire of goods and gadgets, set a satirical tone.

> Oh people of the miracle
> Economic miracle,
> Magnificent people,
> Champions of liberty [. . .]
> He who sings is a free man,
> Free of all thought
> He who sings is already content
> With what he does not have.
> Come now, let us sing,
> Let us have done with thinking [. . .]
> Let us hear the orphans sing,
> And the weeping widows,
> And striking workers
> Let them all join in the song . . .[8]

Tired executives had not expected to while away their evenings listening to Fo pouring scorn on Italy's much vaunted 'economic miracle'. They were disconcerted by his focus on the losers in the economic process and by efforts to prick the vanity and vacuousness of those who regarded themselves as winners. In one sketch, a deferential worker in awe of his employer thanks him for the scents he spreads in the air with his factory chimneys, for the light he puts into bulbs and for his kindness in increasing the worker's pay packet – the actual packet, not the money inside it. 'Give to Caesar what is Caesar's' is taken as the motto of the employer, whose name is Caesar. In a lengthy monologue, Dario described the plight of two Venetians arrested in Germany for having shot at sparrows, a delicacy in northern Italian cuisine. Having expatiated on the decency of Germans as defenders of little birds, he wonders what was the name of that park where swallows were killed after the accidental release of gas . . . Buchenwald, was it? The subsequent song contrasts a decent people who kill birds with a people who spare birds but declare war on creatures who live on the ground.

The greatest satisfaction for any satirist is to see from the bitterness and rancour of his opponents that his darts have found their target. Dario must have been a contented man in the succeeding weeks. In Franca's words, 'War was declared on us by the right.' The press inveighed against the free-dom afforded to the Communist Fo to command the air waves. Methodical leaks informed newspaper readers of the concern felt in the upper echelons of RAI. The tempo was raised as the weeks went by. The Parliamentary Commission of Vigilance met in special session, and issued a communiqué saying that viewers expected relaxing entertainment, not politics. The Italian armed forces, a notoriously sensitive body of men, expressed out-rage at a scene which poked fun at the uniforms they had worn during the war. The Liberal Party leader weighed in to opine that satire only served to exacerbate, not alleviate, problems. In the face of this pressure, the overall agreement covering all episodes was set aside and it was decreed that each one must be subject to rigorous internal scrutiny. A dispute between the managements in Milan, where the programmes were made, and Rome, where the RAI executive was based, added to the difficulties. The scripts were re-examined. Dario was asked to remove words like 'orphanage' because it had inappropriate connotations in modern Italy, 'bed' since it had all kinds of promiscuous overtones, and even 'liberty', since it might lead to revolution. His sketch on Cain and Abel, was red-pencilled, although it had been performed on radio years previously, presumably on grounds of blasphemy. The director of the channel, Giuseppe Piccioni, later a senator, made a personal visit to the Fo flat in Milan where, according to Franca, he went down on his knees in front of the astonished couple to beg them to tone down their work. It is only fair to add that he denies this.

In spite of this sniffing over the scripts, there were points which still caused offence. In one programme, a woman played by Franca sent someone out to buy a watermelon, with the advice to choose one which was good and red. A sharp-eyed reviewer spotted a subversive message in the preference for something red. That had to be a veiled message to the comrades, surely? In this climate, even rational people become capable of the most bizarre excesses, as happened to two valiant priests who denounced Fo in their parish magazine over a blasphemy they had detected in an anti-romantic love song, 'The Boil'. The song, with tender pathos, outlines the plight of a young man who detects a boil under his earlobe and, knowing that his girlfriend cannot stand such things, fears that their relationship is at an end. The alleged blasphemy was not apparent to the naked eye, but Fo took the charge sufficiently seriously to raise a legal action. The penitent clerics admitted they had got it all wrong, and backed down.[9]

The quality of the programmes suffered as a result of the interference of the censors, but there was no lessening of satirical attacks on sinister bodies no one else had the courage to name. That year, one of the Mafia's many internecine wars was under way in Sicily, but it was taboo even to admit in public that there was such a body as the Mafia. On *Canzonissima*, Dario ridiculed the mob, and in reply received a letter, stained with drops of human blood, containing the words 'those who strike at the Mafia, die by the Mafia'. In an act of bravado, they stuck it up on the wall of their house, but reacted with more sobriety when their son, Jacopo, then aged six, was also subject to threats. For six months, Jacopo was escorted everywhere, to school and swing-parks, by police officers.

Unsurprisingly, audience ratings were climbing week by week. Some individual episodes were weak, but the series became the stuff of legends. It is still possible to meet taxi-drivers in Rome who will tell you that the programmes were a financial disaster for them. During transmission, they say, no one was on the streets. The crunch came in episode eleven, with a sketch depicting a building contractor in a state of sham self-loathing over the apparent death of an employee who had fallen from badly erected scaffolding. To ward off criticism, the contractor feigns despair and promises improvement, but on learning that the worker's injuries were actually slight, he returns to his old cynical ways and threatens to punch any worker stupid enough to slip. The directors of RAI totally refused to sanction the broadcast of this sketch, particularly since there was a strike in the building industry at that time. Dario retorted with an ultimatum of his own: no sketch, no show. The interminable round of consultations lasted a full week, but neither side would budge. Lawyers were consulted. The advice given to Dario and Franca was to abide by their contractual obligations, turn up as normal at the scheduled time and make the standard preparations for the show just in case the management backed down. On Saturday evening, they went to the studios, donned their costumes, hovered in the studio wings complete with make-up, still not knowing whether the programme would go ahead or not. Only when they heard the continuity announcer state that 'as of this evening, Dario Fo and Franca Rame have decided to leave *Canzonissima*' was the situation clarified. They put on their coats and went out into the night where, as the news spread, their progress along the street became a triumphal procession.

The fracas was headline news in Italy the following day. Leader columns debated the freedom of the air waves, the conduct of the RAI, the intrusiveness of politicians and the comic talents of Dario Fo. Dario and Franca were pictured seated on their sofa, with Franca wearing an expression of ferocious indignation. They came out of the whole fiasco well. Most commentators considered that they had been shabbily treated and had behaved with dignity. Each side sued the other and the case dragged on through the Italian courts for over a decade. Initially, Dario and Franca won and were awarded damages, but this was overturned on appeal, then further reversed, until finally the case went against the couple, who were compelled to pay high, but not ruinous, compensation.

The whole shambles secured their place in the public mind. There could not now be a person in Italy unaware of who they were. Previously, Dario had enjoyed a vogue as a writer and actor in theatre, but television bestowed fame in the full modern sense of the word – recognition in the streets, forfeiture of privacy, subjection to gossip, entry into public consciousness, attribution of glamour, conferment of an image and full public identifiability. The two were now 'personalities' or 'celebrities', with all the ambiguity that status confers, and their later careers are inseparable from that defining moment. They were barred from the television screens until 1976, when a further shift in Italian politics brought the Communist Party into a government alliance and permitted their return. In the meantime, having excluded themselves from cinema, they concentrated on theatre alone.

Canzonissima went on after the two walked out. The comic Walter Chiari took over as presenter, the competition to choose the best song was won by a number entitled 'Quando, quando, quando', and the regime did not totter. The affair dispelled such traces of innocence as remained in Dario and

Franca. The cynicism of the powers that be and their tenacity in the defence of self-interest took them both aback. The censors had backed down when Dario rejected demands for substantial cuts in *Archangels Don't Play Pinball*, but were intransigent when, on the new, popular medium of television, he threatened to make full use of the power of such direct address to a mass public. Dario and Franca returned to theatre, the medium they knew best, convinced that such direct address to a mass public could be subversive, and determined to make theatre the vehicle for that appeal.

Echoes of the *Canzonissima* affair rumble through the next play, *Isabella, Three Caravels and a Con-Man*, premièred at the Odeon in September 1963. The Isabella in question is the Most Catholic Queen of Spain, and the con-man is Christopher Columbus, making a return visit after his brief appearance in *Poer Nano*. Columbus, who requires royal patronage to realize his monomania for sailing to the Indies, has of necessity turned himself into a courtier who haunts the royal palace, where he is treated with condescension and impatience by his betters. There is a self-deprecating, satirical autobiographical undertow to this depiction of Columbus, whose dilemma reflects that of Fo in the corridors of RAI. In interviews prior to the production, he repeated that this was a serious farce, whose aim was to expose the compromises made by those leftist intellectuals who, after the 'opening to the left', were tempted to make their accommodations with the establishment. With his relish for irony, Fo revived the play on his return to television in 1977.

To add to the multi-layered complexity and polyphonic diversity of this work, Dario also pitted himself against Brecht. Giorgio Strehler had that year chosen to put on *The Life of Galileo* at the Piccolo, and for a time the two productions were in performance in theatres within walking distance of each other. Both works turn to history to debate the present, both subject celebrated figures to critical scrutiny, and both employ to the full devices and approaches characteristic of their respective authors. As a dramatist, Brecht presents himself as an iconoclast and non-conformist nuisance who uses the stage as a quasi-scientific, unemotional forum for debate. Fo, too, views himself as a breaker of conventions, but his theatre also includes elements of sheer mischief as well as of irony. Brecht's Galileo, perhaps in spite of his author's intentions, attains some aura of heroism, while Fo's Columbus is continually undermined by the sheer absurdity of all that surrounds him. The desire to arouse laughter is part of the tactic of subversion which is the essence of Dario's drama, but he cannot resist a gag for its own sake. When the heavily pregnant Isabella stretches herself out on a sofa in the centre of a room where Columbus and the learned men are debating the shape of the planet Earth, her grotesquely swollen belly is casually and nonchalantly employed by them as a globe to illustrate the routes that could be followed by ships moving around its circumference. The passage reveals nothing about Columbus, but it lightens the atmosphere and heightens the comedy.

The basic structure is the tried and tested play-within-a-play. The first sounds heard are of nails being hammered in to a gallows where an actor is to be executed for the crime of performing a work which seems to be *La Celestina*, by Fernando de Rojas. It is carnival, a feast which permits the temporary dethroning of bishops, the replacement of reason by folly and the general overturning of established order. Fo was increasingly intrigued by this event.[10] As part of the carnival rites, word comes that sentence has been suspended, but not yet revoked, to allow the actor to perform on the scaffold the drama of Christopher Columbus. In the words of a guard, this freedom is granted 'so that it can be seen that in our country anyone can do what he likes on the scaffold; there is no censorship on this stage'. There are two audiences – the crowd on stage and the spectators in the stalls – and several time-frames, with the condemned actor referring back to the Catholic Spain of Ferdinand and Isabella and forward to the Catholic Spain of Franco, which is itself a metaphor for Christian Democrat-controlled Italy. Dario was plainly still smarting from his treatment at the hands of the authorities, but was equally outraged at his own gullibility and at the complacency of others like him who had allowed themselves to be manipulated. Official annual statistics revealed that *Isabella* was the most popular production of the season.

Seventh: Thou Shalt Steal a Little Less, written for the 1964–5 season, sold out in the Odeon, causing him to hire the Puccini theatre to extend its run in Milan. The subsequent tour of Italy throughout winter of 1964 and spring 1965 took in fifty-one venues, so that, according to official figures, over 200,000 spectators paid to see the show. There are elements of fantasy in the new work, but not a fantasy designed to create an elfland where problems can be smoothed away. This is *1984* or *Brave New World* rewritten for the Mad Hatter's tea party, for underlying the new play is a real rage against an Italy mired in sleaze and corruption. Once again, the image of an ecclesiastical mental institution is employed to depict the nation, but this time the citizens themselves are subjected to biting sarcasm for their passivity and inertia. The play marks a milestone in the evolution of Franca, who for the first time plays the principal part, the gravedigger, Enea. Instinctively deferential towards the forces of law and order, Enea initially applauds a police charge on strikers, but in the graveyard she meets and forms a relationship with an accountant, who happens to have a mania for collecting and sleeping in coffins. Her consciousness of politics and laws deepens as she undergoes a process which sees her become another of Fo's prostitutes ('it is the only profession which emancipates, elevates, makes you feel someone') before donning a nun's habit. The relationship with the coffin maniac continues even when he has seemingly died. He revives and stumbles on the truth about the scale of corruption perpetrated by the hospital's governing body, but is silenced by surgeons who drill a curious rotating fan into his brain to reduce him to robotic acquiescence. Techniques of farce can scarcely conceal the savage violence of the vision behind it. The closing number, 'The Song of the Italiot', played with frenzied pace by a chorus of asylum inmates, arouses in the audience laughter which is as jarring and brittle as the sound of an open blade dragged along a stone wall.

> We are happy, we are content with the brain we have,
> We have the propeller which makes us follow the flow.
> If they tell us: he's thieving, he's stealing, he's on the fiddle
> We shrug our shoulders and smile like idiots.
> Because we are the ancient Indo-Phoenician race, the Italiots
> We are happy, we are content with the brain we have.[11]

Always Blame the Devil, premièred in September 1965, is set, like the later *Mistero buffo*, in the Middle Ages, an epoch which fascinated Fo. It provided a quarry for metaphors for the present day and was part of his reconstruction of an alternative history of the nameless, the poor, the dispossessed, the huddled masses who had been written out of the official chronicles. The Cathar heretics who find themselves facing imperial forces in thirteenth-century Italy are comparable to the Vietnamese in their war with the Americans, and it requires no leap of imagination to see links between the Cathar 'communards', who preached the abolition of private property, and Italian communists. Fo also believed that the Cathar heresy, or rebellion, represented both political protest and the authentic gospel spirit. The heretics facing execution have had, as the executioner explains, the effrontery to suggest that 'Catholics should apply the gospels to the letter',[12] meaning that the emperor and his court would have to follow a rule of poverty. The religious sentiments dramatized in Fo's works are primarily

66

images for a political and social outlook, but that does not disguise the undercurrent of respect for authentic Christian belief which frequently surfaces in his work.

And all the time, Dario's reputation was growing. He had shows running in fourteen European cities, from Reykjavik to Budapest. In 1966, the Fo–Rame company toured to sixteen countries, from Scandinavia to Israel. The grandly titled *Annuario dell'Istituto del Dramma Italiano*, in its 1969 edition, announced that there were a total of 569 registered playwrights in Italy, although few of them were likely to be known to the general public. The same organ also revealed that of the works performed the previous year, forty-four were written by Eduardo, Titina and Peppino De Filippo, members of the Neapolitan dynasty of actor-authors, while twenty were by Dario Fo.

The category 'registered playwright', which has no equivalent outside Italy, was a cipher for all that enraged Dario in the creeping institutional-ization and taming of theatre by the political establishment. The *teatri stabili* had now lost the vitality which had made them such a revolutionary force in Italian theatre in the post-war years and, more seriously, had effec-tively ceded their independence to the political bosses in local and national government. Appointments were made, as in every other sector of Italian life, on the basis not of competence but of party allegiance. Even the best of directors paid their dues to the system. Giorgio Strehler's work continued to be widely respected, although Fo was no longer among his admirers, but he would not have been able to continue had he not associated himself with the Socialist Party who were uncontested rulers of Milan.

For years, Dario Fo and Eduardo De Filippo had stood, almost alone, outside this system, although now, in the swinging, irreverent sixties, the mood of discontent was spreading. 'Registered playwrights' contained a sub-category of the 'non-performed playwright', a group which drew Dario's withering contempt. Many performed playwrights, who had had their work staged thanks to their deference to the structures of power, also drew his ire, since both groups were guilty of failing to produce plays which linked up with the society of their own time. Dario's preferred models were those who refused an easy accommodation with authority and who offered a challenge to society and grappled with history. 'I have heard the old lament on the crisis facing living authors, and on how only dead authors are performed, but I wonder if we are sure that these living authors are really alive? Rooting about in theatre history in all times, I find that where authors were genuinely tied to the history of their own age, they invariably found an audience to support and encourage them.' In contrast, he suggested a mind experiment in which researchers of the future attempted to reconstruct the history of our times from a selection of comedies and dramas which had been fired up into space. 'They would find nothing but a stream of grand concepts and of words playing blind man's buff without ever finding each other; there would be nothing but characters out of time and bereft of all sense of reality. Nobody could ever manage to guess when or by whom those works had been written. Days, nights, months, eras – all without context.'[13]

Dario was now worried that, although he viewed himself as a trespasser on an alien habitat approximately defined as 'bourgeois', he was being made too welcome. His humour, wit and taste for madcap jollity wrong-footed his audiences, but as a satirist his aim was to unsettle and irritate them. He was growing uneasy about the comfortable, well-heeled people who were flocking to see his work, and who exited chuckling and laughing in evident delight. Had he missed his mark? He found a focus for his unease in one anonymous, fur-coated lady whom he espied in the foyer before and after a performance of *Isabella*. Her dress and demeanour singled her out as a member of the wealthy middle class, and if she of all people was not ill at ease, something was going wrong.

He felt the need for a new context for his own work. In the course of a trial for witchcraft in *Always Blame the Devil*, the judge discovers that the accusers are communards, and invites them to sing their hymn to him. The prisoners are bemused by the request, but the judge tells them: 'Make the people sing, said the poet, and you will see their soul. I am very interested in seeing this soul.'[14] This judicial view on traditional or folk music was one to which Fo became converted after his contacts with NCI, the Nuovo Canzoniere Italiano.

The NCI was established in 1962 to conduct research into popular history, folk culture and protest movements as these were expressed in song. They organized concerts, produced a learned periodical, cut several records and later established a research centre. Their first show carried the title *The Other Italy: A Selection of Italian Popular and Protest Songs, Old and New*, so it was only a matter of time before they and Dario attracted each other's attention. The NCI attained national notoriety in 1964 with *Bella ciao!*, a programme of popular and Resistance songs performed at the Spoleto Festival. They had agreed to submit all their material to the festival managers, but at the last minute the lead singer lost her voce and her replacement sang an anti-war number from World War I, 'O Gorizia', which had not received approval. It contained a line about 'treacherous gentlemen officers, who had always wanted war'. The delicate sensibilities of Italy's armed forces were offended and they sued.

Nanni Ricordi, now NCI's manager, arranged a meeting at which Dario was invited to participate in the show which became *Ci ragiono e canto* ('I Think It Over and Sing About It').[15] The group were conscious of their own lack of theatrical experience, but they were afflicted by an ideological rigidity typical of the sixties and determined not to be accused of the capital sin of 'selling out'. It is hard to imagine a less promising starting-point, and indeed the production process was marred by both personal animosities and the group's protectiveness towards material they had gathered. The resultant tensions were expressed in ideological terms. Ideology, and its leering twin, jargon, now enter the Fo–Rame story. Certain of the arguments in the late sixties and seventies which caused cooperation to founder and friendships to splinter were conducted in a sub-Marxist jargon which is now as impenetrable as the disputations of medieval monks.

The agreement was that Fo would direct the NCI in their stage production of the material they had collected, but actually ceding control proved tricky for the group. Factions were formed, with Fo and Ricordi finding themselves on the opposite side from Roberto Leydi, the show's author. Leydi left to join the Piccolo, a move regarded by others in the NCI as 'going over to enemy's side of the barricade'.[16] His departure did not resolve all disputes over production values and styles. Fo wanted to introduce movement and choreography in accordance with the visual requirements of the stage, but the NCI were chary of anything which smacked of trivialization. He was accused of tending towards the 'grotesque' style, while the NCI wanted performance to be dictated by the rhythms and meanings of the songs. Fo countered that what was taken as grotesque was an attempt to establish some correlation between the rhythms of the songs and the work which they accompanied. Some NCI members were outraged when Dario wrote some musical numbers of his own which he wanted to pass off as original pieces. An open letter, dotted with self-important italics, was circulated among the group.

> It is right not to present the songs according to a visual aesthetic; it is right to use a *historicizing* presentation of them; but beware lest once they have been spruced up in that way, they lose that fire which comes from the fact that *they are also a presence in the contemporary popular-peasant world*: contemporaneity becomes the most important element of the process of theatrical historicization, and this is the source of the provocative violence

which the traditional popular heritage, together with the social song, brings with it.[17]

Fo was never moved by any undue reverence for the historical authenticity of material when he believed its immediate theatrical impact could be enhanced by rewriting. His productions were always defiantly impure. The author of the letter, Gianfranco De Bosio, resigned from the production but took a menacing seat in the back stalls throughout the period of the rehearsals.

The final work was staged in 1964, and televised with many members of the original cast in 1977. The material is varied, including work songs, protest songs, nursery rhymes, cradle songs, love songs, political songs and anti-war songs as well as traditional folksongs from all regions of Italy. The production was moderately successful. 'The show perhaps was not what we would have wanted, and certainly was not what Fo would have wanted. It was in essence a difficult collaboration, but it did undoubtedly lead to a stimulating show.'[18] Probably that was the only judgement possible. The collaboration, however tense, forced Dario to deepen his notions of popular culture.[19] All sides were indebted to Gramsci, but the NCI group had engaged in more thorough, systematic, empirical research than Dario had ever considered until that point. They believed, as they wrote in the programme, that they were dealing 'not with a culture so much as with a civilization' and one which was 'equipped with a great capacity for defence of its own values and for resistance in the face of the dominant culture'. Not all leftist theorists were convinced by this notion, and in the ensuing debate, a dissenting voice was raised for the Communist Party, the PCI, by Achille Occhetto, later party leader. The PCI, like its French counterpart, was never entirely happy with the notion of popular culture. Occhetto was concerned that this division of cultures would implicitly exclude the working class from the treasures of mainstream Western culture, relegating them permanently to a lower spiritual division.

The immediate concern of the NCI itself, however, was with the cost of lighting, scenery and costumes, which far exceeded estimates. When the extent of the deficit incurred by *Ci ragiono e canto* became clear, Nanni Ricordi handed in his resignation. He formed close links with the Fo–Rame company and became administrator of the theatrical cooperatives they established some years later. His contacts, both with the world of finance and with the upper echelons of the PCI, were invaluable. One of the musicians, Paolo Ciarchi, also left to join the Fo–Rame troupe. Some members of the NCI, notably Michele L. Straniero, later wrote about Fo with a ferocity of feeling which the passing of time did not serve to abate.[20] The group itself was shaken to its foundations, and although there were two subsequent programmes of song given the same title, *Ci ragiono e canto*, and produced by Fo in 1969 and 1973, the NCI was not involved.

Chapter 5

Viva la Rivoluzione!

Dario's travels in late 1966 took him both to eastern Europe and Castro's Cuba, a Mecca for left-wing activists. He returned from Havana fired with enthusiasm not only for the vigour and enthusiasm Cuban companies displayed but also, temporarily, by what he had seen of the local version of 'poor theatre'. Its willingness to engage with issues of the day resonated with Fo, but he differed in his production values. Stage design was one of the skills he brought to the theatre, and even when his company was later involved in touring from village to village, he refused to compromise on scenery and stage furniture. His vision of theatre, political or otherwise, required the whole paraphernalia of costumes, artistically designed sets, elaborate lighting effects and props.

The 1960s in Europe were a period when a multitude of self-serving sins in theatre could be concealed under the labels of experimentation, happening or avant-garde. Dario, whose own interests were in the development of a line of theatre which had mass appeal, for the most part steered clear of such trends. However, he invariably offered generous support to fellow practitioners of whatever stamp, especially when they encountered problems with censorship. When the American radical, innovative director Julian Beck toured Italy with his troupe, Living Theatre, in 1966, they hired the Durini theatre in Milan for their own style of happening, or 'Free Theatre', but it was too strong meat for the theatre's aristocratic owner, who summoned the police and had them turned out. Dario championed their cause and was responsible for having the company invited to the Parma Festival to stage their *Antigone*. Whether this enhanced the standing of Living Theatre with the authorities is debatable, since when they returned to Italy in 1969 with *Paradise Now*, they were denounced for obscenity, refused an extension of the permits they had negotiated, escorted to the border by the police and expelled. Dario also became friendly with Eugenio Barba, the Italian avant-garde director who had established his Odin Teatret in Jutland. Barba's vision of non-narrative theatre, his desire to establish a semi-monastic community of actor-devotees was diametrically opposed to Fo's notion of theatre, but the two shared a vision of actor-centred theatre, and Fo was impressed by Barba's attempts at achieving a primacy for the body in theatre.

Dario's own position in commercial theatre was increasingly uneasy, but he performed twice more on the mainstream stage before breaking away. In January 1967, he produced, in the same Durini theatre from which the Living Theatre had been expelled, *Sunday Parade*, a version of a work by the French playwright Georges Michel. Only very rarely has Fo worked on the script of another author, and on such occasions his tendency has been to dismantle the original and produce what is better described as a parallel work than as a translation. *A Sunday Stroll* was received coolly. The impression was that Dario was marking time.

Some of his best-known songs were composed for a one-man show later that year starring Enzo Jannacci and entitled simply *22 Songs*. These numbers included 'Veronica', the song of the girl who liked music which was symphonic but played on the fisarmonic and whose love was anything but platonic, and 'The Priest Liprando', the ballad of a medieval cleric who was forced to undergo trial by ordeal after denouncing his bishop for simony. Jannacci, like the NCI, wanted help with tempo, movement on stage and self-presentation, and he and Dario worked together in rehearsal for two highly intensive days.[1] The show went well, without the rancour which had marked the NCI experience.

Dario's major work in 1967 was *Toss the Lady Out*, premièred at Milan's Teatro Manzoni in September. This free-wheeling play, which for once exploited the liberty of the sixties 'happening', is commonly given as the last in Fo's 'bourgeois period', although there is nothing bourgeois about its politics, an onslaught on consumerism and the American intervention in Vietnam. By 1967, Fo was plainly chafing at the bit. He needed to find a new form of theatre, but he bypassed the contemporary avant-garde in favour of the less-trodden paths of theatre history. Clowns began to interest him, as they had Mayakovsky, whose influence on him was also on the increase. He made contact with the Colombaioni Brothers, two clowns who belonged to a well-established circus dynasty, and devised his new play to incorporate their abilities. *Toss the Lady Out* was set in a circus big top, and all the parts were played by clowns or in the style of clowns. The actors in the company, including Dario, spent the months of rehearsals learning a new trade, walking on their hands, cartwheeling, employing falsetto tones of voice or plunging with the appearance of nonchalance into tanks of water. Franca mastered the techniques of the trapeze artist.

In his discussion of clowns, Fo again displayed his tendency to stretch history. The clown was transformed into a cousin germane of the stock characters of *commedia dell'arte*.

> In our own days, the clown has become a figure whose job is to keep children happy. He is synonymous with puerile simple-mindedness, with picture-postcard ingenuousness and with pure sentimentality. Today's clown has lost both his ancient capacity to shock and his political–moral commitment. In other times, the clown used satire as a vehicle against violence, cruelty, hypocrisy and injustice. Centuries ago, he was an obscene, diabolic figure; in the cathedrals of the Middle Ages, on the capitals and the friezes above the entrances, there can still be seen representations of comic buffoons in provocative couplings with animals, mermaids or harpies, grinning broadly as they show off their organs.
>
> The clown's origins are very remote, and certainly clowns were already in existence before the advent of *commedia dell'arte*. It could be said that the characters of *commedia* were born of an obscene marriage between female jesters on the one hand and storytellers and clowns on the other, and that, after this act of incest, *commedia* spawned hosts of other clowns.[2]

The clown was given the status of forerunner of Harlequin, but in the show the fact that he was primarily an actor was to be kept in full view; the characters were known simply as Clown Dario, Clown Franca, Clown Valerio, etc. While the performance constituted a declaration of affection for the scorned practitioners of a derided craft, the attacks on America over its conduct of the Vietnam War were boisterous. *Toss the Lady Out* can scarcely be regarded as a play, but the looseness of the circus format suited Fo perfectly. Some of his sketches were traditional, playful pieces of knock-about for its own sake, while others cocked a political snook at specific targets. The circus itself was one representation of America, as was the circus-owner, the Old Lady, now dying, noisily and angrily, on the large bed which occupied part of the performing area. The passing of her inheritance to a younger woman, also played by Franca, signified the transition from an old to a new America that the accession of the Kennedy dynasty repre-sented for many. Fo was not an admirer of Kennedy, but in the midst of deliberately grotesque imagery he devised an unexpectedly poignant depic-tion of the assassination at Dallas. The blonde circus-owner was seated astride a trapeze, wearing a straw hat decorated like a target board, and when she was shot, her body fell silently backwards, swinging lifelessly to and fro. It only lasted a moment. Fo showed more enthusiasm for the various conspiracy theories, mocking the trajectory of the magic bullet which supposedly killed Kennedy and wounded Governor Connolly.

Toss the Lady Out was the last production of the Fo–Rame company, which then dissolved. Dario and Franca made the decision that they had to break completely with commercial, or 'bourgeois', theatre. Whatever success he may have had in integrating satire and politics into bourgeois comedy, Dario felt that the company was, both in its structure and stage policy, no longer the appropriate vehicle for changed times or for the political vision he wished to propose. In the sixties, writers were urged, when they needed urging, to conform to the idea of commitment enunciated by Jean-Paul Sartre, to mount the barricades, identify with the proletarian cause or participate in pouring scorn on the bourgeoisie. Delicate members of the intelligentsia in New York, London, Paris and Rome found it necessary to consort with ferocious, and genuine, revolutionaries and could be heard opining that only an art based on the New Left or on Marxism as reinterpreted by Herbert Marcuse had any integrity or aesthetic justification. The revival of Marxism among well-heeled young people has puzzled historians and commentators, such as Eric Hobsbawm, who advanced the theory that Marxism provided the only alternative ideology to materialism and consumerism. Whatever the explanation, Marxism mingled with anarchism was the ideology preached, chanted and scribbled on walls by the students who took to the streets in Paris in May 1968, and by their Italian counterparts in the 'hot autumn' of strikes and demonstrations which shook Milan and Rome in 1969. No section of society was more affected by the new mood than the artists, writers and creative spirits of the time.

The movement of 1968 was in a very real sense a cultural revolution, but whereas in China Mao forced cultural operators into the factories and fields to experience proletarian life, in the West the ambition was to take cultural activities to the factories. No previous radical movement had ever been more self-consciously theatrical. It is tempting, in retrospect, to see some Punch-and-Judy symbolism in the fact that the students who in Paris 1968 were proclaiming the end of the bourgeois order gathered in the Odéon theatre. In its August–September number that year, *Sipario*, the theatre periodical, issued a questionnaire to theatre workers to ascertain whether, in view of the student demonstrations and the strikes in factories as well as the general sense of malaise in the world of culture, 1968 should be regarded as year zero for Italian theatre? Eduardo De Filippo gave a waspish reply, saying that it had always been the task of theatre to hold up a mirror to society, but people's success in deciphering the images they received varied with their own abilities. There were those who were ahead of the times, those who were in step with their times and those who would always be years, perhaps centuries, behind, he said.

Dario was determined to be ahead, while official, commercial or bourgeois Italian theatre was, by the unanimous consent of the brightest and best, centuries behind. January saw an ill-focused strike by actors, although it was never clear who they were striking against, and the issue of imprecise promises by the government brought them back into line. The novelist Dacia Maraini set up her own, feminist theatre company in Centocelle, a housing estate on the outskirts of Rome to which she was guided by the Communist Party, anxious to assist her search for a 'popular audience'. She later came to wonder if such an entity existed, and said that most of her experience of 'decentralizing' consisted of a search for this mythical creature. She ended up in a converted garage which had been occupied by a karate school, while the local population, who had been happy with karate and were sceptical of the beneficial claims made for culture, looked on.

The *teatri stabili* which had been the hope of the post-war generation were now viewed as ossified structures, dominated by grey bureaucrats and ineffable politicians. Gianfranco De Bosio shook the dust off his feet as he resigned from the city theatre in Turin, as did Giuliano Scabia in Genoa. Giorgio Strehler was in a more exposed position.

> One morning, hearing voices outside the window, he looked out and saw a band of students shouting slogans and carrying banners and red flags. 'They're at it early, I thought. I wonder who they've got it in for?' He soon found out. 'They had it in for me; the banners and shouts left no doubt. Down with the tyrant of the Piccolo! Down with the baron of the stage! Get rid of the monster! Get off your throne!' Strehler . . . held a public meeting at the Piccolo with the demonstrators alongside the theatre staff and technicians. Then he took one of the marchers into his office, pointed to his armchair – the infamous throne – told him he could have it, and left.[3]

Strehler set up a new, decentralized company, Gruppo Teatro e Azione, designed to explore political issues, but the company itself played only established theatres. This policy did not impress Fo, who was also determined to forge a new repertoire of popular, political theatre but wanted to play to a new audience in alternative venues. It was an aspiration shared with many playwrights and performers in many countries. In Holland, the Het Werkteater, in Britain, 7:84, and in Italy the Teatro Due of Parma all declared an intention of taking theatre to the places where working-class people would feel at home, and performing plays on issues which mattered to them. Fo expressed his own aspiration in a formula he was to repeat on many occasions: 'We were tired of being the *giullari* of the bourgeoisie, on whom our criticisms had now the effect of an Alka-Seltzer, so we decided to become the *giullari* of the proletariat.'

There was a certain rich irony, missed at the time, in the use of a term Fo had borrowed from medieval history as he set out to create revolutionary theatre for today. The *giullare* was the strolling player of the Middle Ages, the all-round entertainer who moved from piazza to piazza to entertain an audience in its own idiom and in accordance with its own vision of the world. It is not easy to find a satisfactory translation in English. Etymologically, the word has the same roots as 'juggler', but its connotations are wider. The figure has much in common with the minstrel, or the Shakespearean fool. Perhaps the word 'busker' would pass muster, but the term 'jester,' provided it is not taken as the court jester, comes closest, and will be adopted here. The figure makes his first appearance in *Archangels Don't Play Pinball*, when Lanky tells Blondie that his trade is to have people make a fool of him. 'Do you remember who the *giullare* was?' he asks. When she replies that he made kings laugh, Lanky agrees but adds that since there are no more kings, he is happy to make his friends in the bar laugh.[4]

In 1968 Dario Fo set out to be the jester for his own times, the spokesman for Everyman. Historically, he believed, the jester was a representative of a popular culture, who shaped and gave voice to the discontents of ordinary people. His was the comedy not of escapism but of transmuted anger and dissatisfaction. This view of the jester is disputed by various academic authorities, who see him as a more neutral, less ideologically motivated figure, but this is to miss the point. Revolutionary rhetoric is not the currency of the stand-up comedian in music-hall, but his much-vaunted rapport with his audience conceals an instinctive identity of outlook, perhaps even of class. He plays to an audience in the stalls according to professional rather than political criteria, but expresses by his wit their scorn for toffs, idlers or social parasites, as well as for lords and masters. Fo viewed the jester as the articulate representative of a non-articulate culture, voicing deep feelings of injustice. His own comedy is based, in another of his own formulae, on a combination of 'laughter with anger'. It can be merciless laughter. Fo recognized no boundaries of taste when he set out to flay the politicians or churchmen. Any idiosyncrasy of dress, defect of speech, oddity of behaviour or even sexual tendency which could serve to make a man of power ridiculous, and therefore less awesome, was grist to his mill. When deriding the Christian Democrat Mariano Rumor, for example, he made reference to the Roman habit of describing him as 'the liar', but also pointed out that the Romans used the feminine form. Rumor may or may not have been homosexual, and Fo has no homophobic tendencies, but if that description served the purpose, he would use it. Humour is pitiless and, as the jester, Fo can be coruscating.

The attractions of the jester figure were varied and paradoxical. The jester was essentially a one-man performer, and it must seem curious that Fo declared himself a reincarnation of the jester at precisely the moment when he was planning to establish a cooperative. At some level, he must have known that a cooperative structure of performance, if not necessarily of management, would stifle and crush his own talents. His desire to behave in accordance with egalitarian ideals was at odds with his urge to find an outlet and expression for his genius as actor. Fo declared himself a Marxist, if an idiosyncratic and unsystematic one, and the jester represented a compromise between political ideology and theatrical aspiration. The performance style associated with the jester left Dario the unshackled freedom of the Victorian actor-manager. The jester belongs to an established canon and illustrates one other paradox in Fo. While revolutionary in politics, he is traditionalist, indeed conservative and even reactionary, in theatre. Tradition is his habitat.

But in 1968, politics were all. Sections of public opinion in Italy, including many who viewed the prospect with horror, were convinced that the old order was about to be swept away in some onrush of popular enthusiasm. For Dario, the late sixties were, after the Liberation, the second such moment of public exhilaration he had known in his lifetime. He and Franca determined to forge a new kind of theatre in a new kind of troupe. Together with others, they set up Nuova Scena, which, it declared, would be 'at the service of the revolutionary forces not so as to reform the bourgeois state, but to favour the growth of a real revolutionary process which could bring the working class to power'. The new company was established as a cooperative, to be run according to the principles of the socialist pioneers, with each member having one vote on all matters affecting the affairs of the association. Democratic assemblies would be held when needed, in the belief that after the full and frank expression of views, majority decisions would be respected. Each member was to draw the same salary, although that did not mean that they would all have the same income. A writer would retain his right to royalties as well as to the standard pay he would receive for his work as performer, or for whatever other function he carried out. The money to buy the props, vans and other company good was advanced by Dario and Franca, but as a loan. Most of it was repaid from takings over the two years the group remained together.

The new company was not a Mark 2 version of the Fo–Rame outfit, but took in other actors and writers. Fo made contact with the Theatre of October, run by Nuccio Ambrosino, a gifted young director who had produced various shows in Milan. He in his turn sought out the actor-author, Vittorio Franceschi, who could have been Fo's theatrical twin. Franceschi was then thirty-two and, like Fo, had started out as writer-cum-performer in satirical cabaret. He had gone on to write his own plays and in 1968 was in Trieste where the local theatre had performed two of his works. The previous year had seen him at the centre of a rumpus over an anti-war piece which had aroused the ire of ex-servicemen's associations. He too joined the new cooperative.

Theatre of October wanted to retain its own name and identity, so Nuova Scena became an umbrella organization with, at least initially, two sub-groups, or souls. One was the October company, with Franceschi performing and touring with them, and the other consisted of Dario and Franca plus other actors performing works by Dario. Legally, Nuova Scena constituted itself as a club, since this status would afford them, it was believed, immunity from censorship laws and freedom from interference from police or magistrates. Its cultural politics were set out in one of its publicity brochures:

> theatre, like all other means of expression, has always belonged to the ruling class, which makes use of it as an instrument of ideological and political pressure. The structures of theatre – architecture and site of the buildings, performance times, ticket prices – exclude popular audiences from participation, while that theatre itself, in its choice of script and language, offers exclusively bourgeois-style products; it speaks to the society which supports it. Nuova Scena was born to replace this theatre with one which will establish an active and critical relationship with popular audiences and which, without concealment, operating on the basis of the political choice it has made, defines itself as an instrument of struggle for socialism.

This explicit political purpose made for a complex relationship with the Italian Communist party, the PCI. The New Left everywhere in Europe believed that the established Communist parties were bureaucratic and reformist and guilty of abandoning their revolutionary ideals. Nuova Scena may have agreed with much of this criticism, but members took a pragmatic view of the potential for changing the course of PCI development. Franca had been a member of the Communist Party for some time, and although her allegiance was faltering, she kept the party card until 1970. Dario, who had an innate distrust of all organizations, never joined, but both viewed the members of the party as their natural constituency. For this reason, Nuova Scena, who held established commercial theatres in contempt and aspired to build an 'alternative circuit', concluded that this circuit should be provided by 'houses of the people' and community centres run by ARCI, the Italian Recreational and Cultural Association, a body close to the PCI.

The ubiquitous Nanni Ricordi was secretary of ARCI in Milan, and he and Dario met Achille Occhetto, the PCI spokesman for cultural affairs, who agreed that ARCI provided the ideal forum. Ricordi moved to Nuova Scena, becoming its administrator. In ARCI, the recreational side of its activities had long since taken precedence over its cultural remit. Dario was fond of recalling that many of the centres had emblazoned above the portals a slogan which ran: 'If you want to give charity to a poor man, give him five pennies – three for bread and two for culture.'[5] In the same interview, Fo explained that culture:

> did not mean simply knowing how to read and write, but also to produce, to express your own creativity, starting with your own conception of the world. The grave responsibility of the parties of the traditional left lies in the fact of not having put themselves at the service of the creativity of the people, which is extraordinary, enormous. The principal fact of the Chinese cultural revolution is that it believed in the people, in its force of creativity and production, and above all in having goaded intellectuals to participate in a political life beyond their own artistic life, to enter into the class struggle.
>
> With us, the influence of [Italian Communist leader] Togliatti destroyed this relationship between intellectuals and the popular masses. Togliatti showed himself to be an aristocrat. He was a professor and had maintained a bourgeois attitude toward culture. He considered intellectuals as people who should produce works, without ever involving themselves in politics. Politics was for politicians . . . In Italy, among 'men of culture' often given as examples, many were guilty of betrayal, had no dignity. Take Visconti, who today works for the Fascist industrialist Rusconi, or Pasolini and various other intellectuals who have sold out to the right or to Social Democracy.

In addition to the inner core of actors and stagehands, membership of Nuova Scena was open. Subscription fees were set at a price between 1,500 to 1,700 lire, which entitled members to attend one show by Fo plus two others staged by the company. Where there was no established ARCI centre in a town, Nuova Scena was dependent on the enthusiasm of volunteers and supporters to adapt cinemas, halls, sports centres or disused theatres, or to create totally extemporized performance spaces. Local members were also responsible for such pre-publicity as was issued. Whatever the space, Dario always insisted that there be some form of recognizable, properly equipped stage. He refused to countenance the suggestion that in political theatre, purely ideological values should have pre-eminence and the poetics of theatre could be viewed as secondary.

> When we arrived to put on a play at the 'houses of the people', we would turn up with a lorry packed with materials, and would spend the whole day creating a special stage. We would put up the lights, perhaps as many as forty or fifty reflectors, because we said that the people, with television, or in ordinary theatres, if they go there, are used to a particular sort of presentation . . . we must avoid at all costs giving them the impression that we are offering 'minor theatre', something tossed together, a theatre which is not up to using those means which, consciously or unconsciously, they are used to.[6]

Frequently the cast had no changing rooms, and had to make do with an overturned trunk. The entertainment followed an unchanging format – two acts of the scripted play followed by a 'third act': discussion with the audience. Mere agit-prop was taboo, although Fo ended up developing a new genre which could be termed didactic farce. In Britain, playwright John McGrath, whose militant comedy written for 7:84 had much in common with Fo's theatre, entitled the manifesto for his theatre *A Good Night Out*. Fo shared McGrath's objective of providing entertainment plus politics and of creating a carnival atmosphere. Laughter, Dario wrote, is both the enemy of catharsis, which is to be avoided at all costs in a theatre which has a critical function, and a release of tension, a liberation from the humdrum, a venture into the dimension of imagination and fantasy, a form of escape, if not of escapism, which audiences are entitled to expect in theatre. 'What do you mean by a show?' he asked himself. 'A show means enjoyment. Enjoyment is obtained by technical means, by stage devices which can be quite complex, as well as by the technical and ideological preparation of the actors.'[7]

If Fo's decision to establish a cooperative was in keeping with the spirit of 1968, the choice of touring theatre was a return to the roots of Italian theatre, the theatre from which Franca Rame had emerged. The success of Nuova Scena was due in part to the fact that *Canzonissima* had made Franca and Dario stars, but also to the fact that the company revived memories of a theatre common in Italy within living memory. Fo and his red guards were following in the footsteps of the touring players who had been the backbone of the Italian tradition, who had made theatre from *commedia dell'arte* onwards, and whose last representatives were companies like the Rame family. Prices were kept low, but production and travelling costs meant that every show would play at a loss unless it attracted a mass audience. One of the few critics who took an interest in the new project reported with astonishment that he saw families who had never before been to the theatre arriving an hour early and remaining for debates which sometimes went on until three in the morning. 'Dario's first question at these debates was always: how many of you have never been to the theatre before? There was invariably a large show of hands.'

During the 1968–9 season, Theatre of October presented a work entitled *Given That*, an attack on consumerism. Fo's own troupe performed a new large-scale pageant piece, *Grand Pantomime with Puppets Large and Medium*, and, later in the season, *I Think Things Over and Sing About Them, No 2*, which was not a revival but a completely new show. In spite of the proletarian rhetoric which surrounded *Grand Pantomime*, its style and content linked it with the 'bourgeois' *Toss Out the Lady*. Grand pageantry incorporating music and dance was intercut with episodes of slapstick and knockabout. The eleven actors and three actresses were dressed in neutral costumes, which allowed them to switch parts rapidly, but wore masks which 'allude to *commedia dell'arte*'. Instead of using clowns as in his previous play, Fo hit on the idea, later borrowed by the French director Ariane Mnouchkine, of using puppets to enlarge the cast. The approach was that of the medieval morality play, and the target was those revisionist writers and political leaders of the left who had betrayed the heritage of both the Resistance and socialism. A monstrous, deliberately grotesque puppet, with outsize rubber lips, wrapped in mock-medieval clothes, towered over proceedings. Stage directions specify that it must be 'over three metres high' and that it must be seen as 'a clear allegory of Fascism'. From its belly emerge equally allegorical figures representing Bourgeoisie, Capital, the General, the Bishop, the King and the Queen and their court. Opposing them is another puppet, a Dragon, with one actor supporting the head over his shoulders, and four other actors under the body of the beast, representing 'the Proletariat in struggle'. If the large puppet is an act of deference to the Italian carnival tradition, the dragon is drawn from Chinese sources. The dragon's arrival initially causes consternation among the establishment figures, but in modern society political rebellion can be stymied by sexual seduction. The Bourgeoisie figure is a voluptuous young girl with generous breasts, who is encouraged by Capital and Monarchy to strip for the good of the nation. The dragon roars and sighs, and eventually the leader of the proletariat is seduced and neutralized by the charms of the Bourgeoisie. The tranquillization of a rebellious proletariat is completed by the seductive pleasures of football, television and pop songs, leading a member of the proletariat to quote 'the old proverb: the television's on, the revolution's off'.

The first season went well. The company gave some 370 performances in all, in a total of 125 centres, some of which were factories occupied by striking workers. In August 1968, they played in the occupied steelworks in Brescia. The matter was reported to the local magistrate, who two years later charged Franca and Dario with trespass and infringing the rights of the owner, the first of many summonses they would receive. According to figures released by the ministry, the total number of spectators attending performances amounted to 240,000, of whom 90 per cent claimed never to have been previously to a theatre. These audience figures are all the more remarkable considering that the same source gave attendance figures for all theatres in Italy as 3,000,000. ARCI locally and nationally was impressed, and there was little in the plays to disturb friendly relations with the PCI.

Nevertheless, there was already friction inside the company. The idealists were coming face to face with the harsh theorem which lies at the basis of conservative politics: the belief, however formulated, that not all people are equal and not all are good. Shaw once wrote that any revolutionary movement will attract both those for whom the world is not good enough and those who are not good enough for the world. The first squabbles were over equality, an article of faith inside Nuova Scena. All actors in a given performance were listed in alphabetical order, a small thing in itself, but Dario and Franca had also ceded the leading roles to less charismatic, less talented and sometimes completely inexperienced members of the company. Gains for equality were outweighed by theatrical losses. Talent and training were needed to carry the burden of the performance, particularly in a theatre like Fo's, where the distance between script and performance is minimal and where acting skills are essential. There was also a clash between audience expectations and internal philosophy. Audiences, however enthusiastically they proclaimed their allegiance to the ideals outlined by the actors in the debates, were attracted by the fame and notoriety of Dario Fo and Franca Rame and were disappointed to find them taking such a low profile.

The internal assemblies became interminable. The members of the company were invariably loquacious, articulate and self-opinionated, and had a command of a jargon which could, like all jargons, replace thought. Others looked on in despair at this turn of events. At an assembly in March 1969, Vittorio Franceschi recognized that they had all paid a high price in terms of 'physical exhaustion, psychological wear and tear and economic sacrifices' but he reminded the assembly that the audiences 'did not deserve our internal dissensions'.[8] Nuccio Ambrosino's group were the most alienated. They were dubious about the decision to stage *I Think Things Over and Sing About Them*, which they judged insufficiently revolutionary and militant for the needs of the moment. A further source of strife at the end of the first season was over the future shape of the cooperative. Shows had been presented under the apparent formula: Nuova Scena presents Dario Fo, or Nuova Scena presents Theatre of October in . . . The various elements of Nuova Scena performed on successive evenings in the same venues and, however much they doubted it at the time, the other groupings benefited from the drawing power of Fo and Rame on the first evening. Dario, with the agreement of Franceschi, believed the time had come for the cooperative to be wholly united and the subsidiary identities to be abolished. Theatre of October wanted to maintain its autonomy and title. 'For me, Dario is fine as he is. I think it's right that he puts on his own shows with anyone he wants and in the way he wants. On the other hand, I do not want other methods, other work requirements to be snubbed or undervalued, much less castrated,' Ambrosino told the assembly.[9] The internal conflicts proved incapable of resolution, and in the first of many internal schisms Ambrosino and his troupe parted company with Fo and the others.

ARCI was still keen to maintain the collaboration, but wanted a fuller programme. The agreement was that in the following season Nuova Scena would present five works. In accordance with the cooperative principle, the task of preparing these scripts was shared out. Dario would write three, Vittorio Franceschi one, while the final work would be a collage of songs and sketches assembled and written by several younger members of the group. With this decided, the group broke up for the summer. However imminent the revolution, it would have to wait for *ferragosto* and the annual seaside holiday.

Tanned and refreshed, the company reassembled in the late summer of

1969 to prepare for the autumn season, or campaign. All sides in an increasingly divided company were agreed that they had to respond to the deepening political crisis in Italy in 1969, a year which marked the beginning of that state of turmoil which was to last for over a decade. That autumn passed into history as the 'hot autumn' of student 'contestation' and trade-union militancy. If the students made the headlines, the workers had the real clout, but for a time at least the two groups made common cause. Industrial contracts were due to be renegotiated, but the demands made by new grass-roots organizations were not merely for higher pay and renewed contracts of the same type, but also for improved conditions, for greater attention to safety at work and for salaries which were, as the new jargon had it, 'autonomous', that is, unrelated to business profitability or national economic conditions. Disputes, sit-ins, factory occupations, strikes, demonstrations involving private- and public-sector workers spilled from the workplace on to the streets in all the major cities of Italy. Clashes with the police became commonplace. In October, in Turin, Fiat workers smashed the vehicles standing on the assembly lines. In the same month, a demonstrator was killed, apparently by a police bullet, in Pisa. The disputes widened in scope. In November, a crowd estimated at 25,000 gathered outside the headquarters of RAI in Milan. On 19 November, a police officer in Milan was killed in a brawl which followed a meeting during a strike for improved housing.

In this new climate, the established parties of the left found themselves outflanked by new, extra-parliamentary formations. The PCI had initially been relaxed about these groupings, in spite of being denounced vociferously for their pains, but their position hardened during 1969. In accordance with Mao's writings, if not his practice, a thousand flowers bloomed on the Italian left. The groups which were to dominate the extreme left over the next decade, and which would play no small part in the lives of Franca and Dario, made their appearance. The most significant were Potere Operaio (Worker Power), Avanguardia Operaia (Worker Avant-garde), and, the most important of all, Lotta Continua (Continuous Struggle). The latter produced a journal of the same name, whose first number appeared in Milan in November 1969.

Not all Italian intellectuals were enthralled by the new youthful movements. Pier Paolo Pasolini wrote a poem denouncing the students and sided with the police on the grounds that the students were the pampered children of affluent bourgeois parents, while the policemen were the sons of working-class people, often from the poorer South. The poem aroused heated discussion, and the poet Roberto Sanesi wrote a counterblast accusing Pasolini of vulgar demagoguery. Leonardo Sciascia, with that acute disillusion which is the cultural heritage of the Sicilian, satirized in his novel *The Context* the new chic, patrician left as nothing more than the *bien-pensant* conformism of the well-heeled. Fo embraced the new ideology with the enthusiasm of the young Wordsworth hailing the French Revolution, and was hailed in turn as the movement's spokesman.

The divisions of Italy were deeper and of a different kind from those becoming apparent in other Western societies in those troubled years. If the rise of a revolutionary left had parallels elsewhere in Europe and North America, the resurgence and mobilization of violent neo-Fascist movements with historical roots in Mussolini's regime and with covert links to the ministries run by Christian Democrat politicians was unique to Italy. The 'reds' and the 'blacks', who even had distinctive uniforms of denims and parkas for the leftists and boots and gloves for the rightists, clashed in the universities and on the streets. These youthful right-wing formations were a minor irritant compared to the adult version behind the explosions and terrorist attacks which first occurred in 1969. When the suggestion was first advanced that this right-wing terrorism was officially defended and even sponsored by sinister forces inside the ministries of Rome and the barracks of police and army officers, it was dismissed as left-wing paranoia, but the careful work of investigative journalists such as Camilla Cederna and Philip Willem has established the political complicity and guilt beyond all reasonable doubt.[10]

The first terrorist acts occurred in January 1969, and while they were milk and honey compared to what was to follow, they mark the point when terrorism became part of the fabric of Italian society. The aim of the neo-Fascist 'strategy of tension' was to create widespread panic which would lead to demands for a 'strong man' to restore the golden days of Fascism. The Greek colonels had recently come to power, and many feared, with reason, that their *coup d'état* was a model for a future *putsch* in Italy. This fear dominated left thinking, and obsessed Giangiacomo Feltrinelli, the millionaire publisher, who in the summer of 1969 formed the first of the underground leftist groups, GAP, a name originally used by a partisan group in the Resistance. Feltrinelli, who had an enormous capacity for self-aggrandisement and self-deception, went into hiding, although no one was actually searching for him. Myriad left-wing terror groups, the Red Brigades and Front Line being the most important, began to emerge. Their immediate origins lay in the 1968 movement, although some saw their deeper origins in a culture termed 'Catho-Communism', which linked the equal and opposing absolutisms of Catholicism and Marxism. Fo set his face unflinchingly against the use of the gun in politics, whether by the left or the right. Preaching revolution was one thing, but advocating bloodshed was another. His position was delicate and precarious. In the decade following 1969, he was on the crest of a wave but also astride a tiger. He had been denouncing reformism and revisionism, and was in every respect perfectly at ease with the political positions occupied by the revolutionary left, but shied away from the advocacy of violence.

The 'revolution' he preached did not require definition. Utopianism is the poetic twin of naivety, and if Fo was never naïve, he was certainly Utopian. Marxism was one, transient form of his enduring Utopianism. His principal political motivation was horror of injustice, exploitation and every manifestation of man's inhumanity to man. Socialism is an elastic term, and Dario is not given to systematic formulations. He has worked as tirelessly as Voltaire against individual miscarriages of justice, and has carried the same passion into the public arena. He is also one of nature's dissidents, who would, as certainly as André Chenier under the French Revolution, or Mayakovsky or Essenin under Bolshevism, have been consumed by any successful revolution of whatever hue. If the man he most frequently quoted was Mao, his *alter ego* was Mayakovsky, who maintained his ironic distance from the Bolsheviks once they were in power. Fo is a man of the 'decency' George Orwell sought in writers who occupied themselves with politics, though he did completely suspend all use of his ironic faculties in regard to Mao.

For the vast, amorphous, disenchanted, dissident but unswervingly radical movement, often known simply as the Movement, Fo became an inspiration. 'Struggle' was a key component of the jargon for those years when the rhetoric of class warfare was routinely used by innocuous individuals. Perhaps, in the post-play discussions, Dario became more of an oracle than any man should. Certainly both Vittorio Franceschi and Nanni Ricordi, neither of whom were middle-of-the-road liberals, came to think so, but audiences from Palermo to Trieste demanded his views on all manner of subject.

Before taking to the road for the 1969–70 season, the assembly had to approve the scripts. Fo and Franceschi had their promised scripts written. Franceschi's was entitled *A Dream of the Left*, an account of a young bourgeois who plays the part of the revolutionary militant for a season, only to scuttle back to his family and class when the stakes become too high. The other group had found the temptations of the beach too alluring, or the task too difficult, and were not able to deliver their text. With only ten days left if the agreement with ARCI was to be respected, the task was pressing. The assembly entrusted Franceschi with the task of cobbling together a performable text.

He decided to return to the kind of cabaret work with which he had begun his career. Writing various pieces himself and coordinating the work of others, he produced *MTM*, a series of songs and documentary pieces on the lives and experiences of working people in an industrial society. The finished work had to be submitted to the assembly, where one of his songs was subject to criticism which crystallized emerging problems. Franceschi had heard a news item about a young employee who had thrown himself under a high-speed train. Inquiries into the suicide revealed that he had been suffering from nervous exhaustion after being threatened with redundancy. On a similar train, Franceschi had been struck by the sight of butterflies which seemed to flock around the last carriages and appeared to follow the train over extended distances. He introduced this imagery into his song, but was reprimanded in assembly by one comrade who demanded to know what butterflies had to do with the tragedy of an exploited member of the working class. Was the poetic tone appropriate for a song designed to stir up feelings of anger? After anxious debate, the song was approved, and the show staged in the form in which Franceschi had submitted it, but the temptation of overt agit-prop for members of the company remained strong. Fortunately, Fo had unearthed a quote from Mao which said that actors should not use the stage as a political platform, otherwise they risked doing a disservice to both theatre and politics. There was no appeal against the authority of Mao.

Two of Dario's plays, *Chain Me Up and Still I'll Smash Everything* and *The Worker Knows 300 Words, the Boss 1,000, That's Why He's the Boss*, were approved without dissent. There was some perplexity over the relevance of the medieval setting of the third, the one-man *Mistero buffo*, but he got his way. To meet the demands placed on them, the company split into three. The first was headed by Franceschi and produced his two works; the second was headed by Franca Rame and staged the two works written for the company cast, and the third consisted of Dario alone with *Mistero buffo*, probably his best-known and finest work.

Mistero buffo was premièred at Sestre Levante on 1 October 1969, although there had been a try-out production at Milan University during a student sit-in. Dario has subsequently performed the work, which exists in varying versions in all available media, in all five continents. Among his plays, only *Accidental Death of an Anarchist* has had comparable international success. With *Mistero buffo*, he fused his gifts as actor and author, revived historic popular theatre as a living force and found a subtlety of political expression he never again attained, while providing himself with a vehicle for his own unique stage talents. Initially, Dario planned to do the plays in the conventional style with several actors, but it simply did not work. The pieces had to be done by a single performer-jester, moving into and out of part, doubling as story-teller and as the cast of characters who people the tale. The initial text has been expanded over the years with new sketches, scenes, monologues and extensive introductory material. One critic has calculated that if Fo were to perform all the material he has collected under the heading of *Mistero buffo*, the performance would last a full day and night.

The work consists of a series of scenes and sketches adapted, sometimes substantially, from biblical and medieval tales retold by jesters. Dario had been combing ecclesiastical and theatre archives in Italy and in Czechoslovakia, Poland and Yugoslavia for jester material.[11] He had uncovered a series of sketches but was uncertain how best to stage them for modern audiences. A philologically accurate version which could delight only the dry-as-dust experts did not appeal, so he gave himself freedom to rewrite, and this in turn has led to debates on the piece's historical authenticity. He has been accused of what could be termed reverse plagiarism, that is, of taking imperfect archival fragments as cues for the creation of new work which was then presented as a faithful translation of some lost comic jewel.[12] There is some truth in the accusation, although whether it matters is another question. On the first outing, Dario illustrated the performance with slides of medieval frescos and paintings, but discovered himself short of some images. No problem for a man of his talents. He spent the next day executing the images in the required style, photographed them himself and used the slides the following night as a reproduction of the work of an unknown master from the Dark Ages. There is no known medieval version of some of the better-known pieces, such as 'Boniface VIII', or 'The Birth of the Jester'. At most there are a couple of lines which have been elaborated and worked by Dario in the appropriate style. Behaviour of this kind has given experts a field day, but most people will view such polemics as the modern equivalent of the Swiftian dispute over the appropriate way to crack a boiled egg. Those who gingerly tap the rounded end and meticulously peel away the cracked shell to reveal the white and yolk view with disdain their more crass colleagues who blithely chop off the top and tuck in. Fo may be ranked with both at different moments. He is as fastidious as a professor at the Sorbonne in his researches, but he has a sense of living stagecraft which is not part of that professor's armoury.

His erudition is formidable, even if the Middle Ages he presents on stage are as imaginary as Thomas Chatterton's. Ideologically, his imperative is to take sides and line up with one kind of history and one social class. His reading of the medieval texts led him to the conclusion that the jesters had inserted the protests of the poor and deprived inside these apparently religious texts. When the satirical protest was lacking, Dario wrote it in. He has repeatedly drawn attention to the interweaving of social and theological themes in performance pieces produced by medieval Christianity and to the positioning of gargoyles alongside pious statues on the façades of medieval cathedrals. By temperament, Fo is at one with the sculptor of gargoyles. Unfortunately, not all his new comrades were of the same mind, and in the superdemocratic, ultra-leftist atmosphere of the Nuova Scena assemblies, he found it difficult to persuade them of the sense of his new enterprise.

> Speaking of religion, as did the jesters, I intended to speak about politics, while also making a play out of it. I came to religious theatre almost as a polemical reaction to the comrades I was working with, who, with considerable superficiality, branded the people's religious problem as a distortion with no cultural or political significance. The people's relationship with the divine, with the problem of God, with their own religion, with the religiosity of things is a problem which, regrettably, Marxists have never understood and have dodged.[13]

It may be that there is a greater ambiguity in Fo over Christian belief than his own pronouncements on the subject allow. His principal scorn was reserved for institutional religion, but he also claimed to be a non-believer, with no interest in religion itself. However, the subtext conflicts with his public statements. Christ is the final arbiter of what is decent and good, and Fo was drawn to Christian ethics and the person of Christ to an extent that appalled stern Marxists. Perhaps on this point his critics inside Nuova Scena saw more clearly than Dario himself. Two decades later, some Catholic writers would call attention to the pull of the transcendental in Fo, and even the Vatican would thank him for keeping religious themes in the public eye. But that lay in the future. In 1969, newspapers linked with the Church reacted with horror to this secularizing of Christ and Bible stories.

Fo provided grist for their mills. Talking of 'The Raising of Lazarus', he described the underlying situation as:

> the miracle seen as a conjuring trick and not as some victory of the spirit over death in the tragic and generous schemes of God. The approach is proclaimed from the very outset with the arrival of one of the characters in the graveyard. He asks the attendant if this is the place where the raising of Lazarus will take place. There and then the attendant fixes an admission fee for those who intend to spectate, and you can almost see him punching the tickets![14]

Christ is similarly humanized in 'The Marriage Feast at Cana', or even turned into a Bacchus-like, jolly god. A decidedly killjoy archangel, the sort of person who became dominant in the puritan traditions, and a merry drunkard vie with each other to recount the story of the changing of the water into wine. This Christ is no paladin of repression but an exponent of liberation and even gratification. 'Drink, good people, be happy, get drunk, don't save it till later, enjoy yourselves . . . !'[15]

While *Mistero buffo* was offending the Vatican and the Christian Democrat Party, the plays performed by Franca were upsetting the Communist Party. *Chain Me Up and I'll Still Smash Everything*, a portmanteau title for two one-acters, was written, as was to happen frequently in subsequent years, in response to a request made in discussions after shows. *The Boss's Funeral* took as its topic injuries and deaths at work. A butcher comes on stage carrying a knife and a goat which he is about to slaughter, meaning to shake the audience from their inertia by inviting them to question their distaste for the shedding of animal blood as against their indifference to industrial accidents. The work never satisfied audiences or the company and after a tepid reception in Florence, it was withdrawn. The companion piece, *The Loom*, irritated the PCI, and its anti-party bias was heightened when it was rewritten in 1972 as *Order! by GOOOOOOOOD*. On tour in Emilia-Romagna, the PCI heartland, audiences had raised the problem of the exploitation of domestic piece-workers, and Dario wrote this play on the basis of the information provided. Husband and wife are both loyal Communists, but are trapped in a cycle of domestic drudgery which obliges them to produce a certain number of items per week. The villain of the piece is a party official who is also employed to go from house to house to collect the domestic work. In the later version, feminism was more of a force, so the girl is given a live-in boyfriend who belongs to an ultra-left faction, and who is very sympathetically portrayed, while one of Fo's virtuous prostitutes helps all concerned to see their way through their political and personal dilemmas. In both versions, the mother is accidentally knocked unconscious by the father, who is driven to despair and smashes the looms, and in her delirium the mother has dreams of a more militant, less revisionist Communist Party.

The real storm with the PCI broke over the accompanying play, *The Worker Knows 300 Words, The Boss 1,000, That's Why He's The Boss*. The title was taken from a book of letters written by pupils, *Letters to a Teacher*, but it chimed in with Fo's convictions. The action unfolds in an ARCI circle similar to the one used for performance. While the members are transforming the library into a billiards room, the books fall open allowing the characters to emerge and act out their drama. Gramsci appears to debate popular culture, while a Soviet official from the Stalinist era, dressed provocatively in the uniform of a Francoist official, conducts a show trial against the Czech Communist Resistance leader, Rudolf Slansky. Even more irritatingly for the PCI, Fo twinned American military activity in Vietnam with Soviet aggression in Czechoslovakia, denounced the 'historic compromise' between the PCI and the Christian Democrats by having the Communist mayor of Bologna waltz with the cardinal of the city, and finally brought on Mayakovsky, here clearly Fo's spokesman, to defend his policy of performing to factory workers against an apparatchik who says such exhibitions are against party rules.

Giannino Galloni, the official theatre critic of *L'Unità*, the PCI daily, wrote a broadly favourable review, but he had misread the runes. The review was suppressed and he resigned in indignation. In the officially sanctioned substitute column, Fo was held guilty of 'errors of evaluation and perspective which are to be condemned'. The editor, Maurizio Ferrara, although he tried to cool the dispute in the columns of his own paper, told an interviewer from *Panorama* that the work was an out-and-out attack on both the PCI and the Soviet Union. Giorgio Napolitano, an intellectual and theorist on the PCI executive, later Italy's Minister for the Interior in the late 1990s, accused the work of 'crude, sentimental *qualunquismo*', where *qualunquismo* is a virtually untranslatable but gross offence which involves encouraging indifference and generalized hostility to all matters political. The debates in the northern cities were lively affairs, and Fo discovered that he had alienated large swathes of the organized left.

To add to their troubles, Franca and Dario heard while on tour in Sicily that they had lost the latest round in the *Canzonissima* affair, which was still lumbering through the courts. The verdict in the lower court had gone in their favour, with RAI ordered to pay 7,200,000 lire to Dario and 3,600,000 to Franca for breach of contract. This was overturned by the High Court, which sent the case back for reconsideration. Meanwhile, at every stop on the tour itself, they had to face hostile questions from PCI die-hards. Carlo Pagliarini, the PCI official who had negotiated the Nuova Scena–ARCI agreement, was now seriously worried by the feedback he was receiving from local bodies. He was present one evening in Sestre Levante, when Franca Rame burst into tears while responding to him. The overall strain, the sheer physical effort and as well as her disappointment at the attitude of the PCI, of which she was still a member, were taking their toll. The following day she fainted during her performance of the Mayakovsky scene and had to be rushed to hospital. Initially it was feared she was suffering from a coronary, but eventually she was diagnosed as suffering from nervous exhaustion. She had to be replaced for the remainder of the tour.

Internal relations within the group were again fractious. The composition of the company had changed following the decision of Nanni Ricordi to admit new recruits dubbed 'the politicals', people from the new ultra-left who, although unencumbered with theatrical skills or experience, were regarded as capable of ensuring that the comrades did not stray. Their presence was resented by those, like Franceschi, who feared a slide into overt propaganda or agit-prop. The group still included many idealists, like the future novelist Daniele Del Giudice, who cheerfully carried props and played minor roles, as well as various eccentrics. Several members recall a Trotskyite hairdresser who declared he had joined so as to be able to touch Dario Fo. The dissensions were often bitter. Assemblies remained in session until seven in the morning, and there are accounts of tears and temper as well as of constructive debate. The survivors of those days all now adopt the same tone of nostalgic melancholy. They will insist that the good times, the companionship of shared ideals and the delight in the welcome they received in many places were strong forces in their lives, but they talk obsessively of the bad times, of the bickering, cliques and manoeuvrings.

In any community, it is not the major issues which wreak havoc. Inside Nuova Scena, personal relations began to suffer and, as happens in any marital breakdown, the worst interpretations were put on all gestures. Dario has never been capable of handling money, and indeed rarely carries any with him, so he would on occasions invite people for a drink only to discover that he had no cash to pay. He was branded 'mean', which is untrue. Franca, who has a keen business mind, was manager for the company and the family. She is capable of limitless generosity, but this liberality was construed in some quarters as an attempt to extend power and win votes for assembly decisions. Technicians in the company voiced discontent of a non-ideological nature on discovering they were working longer hours than required by a commercial contract, for lower pay.

Gossip had it that an inner troika of Dario Fo, Franca Rame and Nanni Ricordi was in real control. Dario was losing any respect for the PCI and its traditions, and was moving towards the newer extra-parliamentary groups. Although technically ARCI was independent of the PCI, a cooling of relations with the party inevitably had implications for collaboration with the sister cultural body. Dario was prepared to jettison the ARCI link, rather than soften his criticisms of the PCI. He also, while wishing to continue touring, came to feel that the company's objectives would be more easily met if they had a home base in Milan. Endless touring is tiring, especially when there was no fixed point where an administration could be housed, where rehearsals could be held and where productions could be premièred and finessed before the tour began. Some members were worried about the cost of a theatre in the city; others again wanted to separate these two initiatives, to find a base but to continue touring the ARCI venues. Having laboured to establish a national alternative circuit, the prospect of rejecting it seemed madness to them. Meanwhile, ARCI itself was wavering. Several circles wanted to withdraw all performance facilities, and when the central executive of ARCI convened a meeting, eight out of eleven threatened to resign if the facilities afforded Fo were renewed. The most frequent accusation was of breach of trust. By January 1970, Nuova Scena were told they would not be welcome unless changes were made.

Nanni Ricordi found the group a Milan base, a workshop, Il Capannone, in via Colletta, a working-class district of the city. An unpretentious, curved-roof, prefabricated building, concealed from the street in a backyard behind a row of high-rise flats, it was no better or worse than the buildings Peter Brook was using in Paris. The acquisition of this property resolved one problem, but plans had still to be laid for next season. Dario had written a version of the play which would become *Accidental Death of an Anarchist*, while Franceschi had scripted a work on compulsory schooling entitled *Class Diary*. The plays were read to the assembly, which was open to outsiders. Accounts differ, but it appears that Dario's play did not require much discussion; non-approval was simply unthinkable. Franceschi's play was viewed favourably, but both Fo and Ricordi voiced doubts, principally on its failure to display adequate class consciousness. In a vote, it was decided that only Fo's play would be staged. For Franceschi, this was the last straw. When the company voted on continued collaboration with ARCI, a majority were in favour, with Dario, Franca and Nanni in a minority. The minority decided to withdraw from Nuova Scena and to set up a new cooperative. Nuova Scena continued to tour ARCI centres until the 1973–4 season, and is still in existence as a producing company. But its days as a revolutionary cadre were over.

Chapter 6

On the Road Again

The split in Nuova Scena was a schism rather than an apostasy, and Dario and Franca emerged with their beliefs in the cooperative ideal and revolutionary socialism intact. In October 1970, together with Nanni Ricordi and Paolo Ciarchi, who had composed the music for Nuova Scena, they set up a new group, La Comune, a name which recalled the 1870 Commune in Paris but had associations with the sixties-style commune and 'summers of love'. Regrettably, the new cooperative was to be no more a prolonged love-in than its predecessor.

The establishment of La Comune represents the second disruption in Dario's career. After the 1968 break with commercial theatre came the 1970 break with the PCI and the alternative circuit provided by ARCI. Dario, in search of an alternative to the alternative, now threw in his lot with the Movement. The new company was once again based on open membership and nationwide autonomous circles. On legal advice, the private club status was retained. Policy was to be determined by free votes in assemblies, although past experience had led Dario and Franca to abandon local autonomy and opt for a centralized secretariat charged with implementing decisions and overseeing administration. At its peak, the cooperative boasted some 150 circles, which provided the basis of a fresh 'alternative circuit', separate both from commercial theatre and from spaces managed by ARCI.

Fo was determined from the outset that La Comune would not become identified with any single one of the burgeoning extra-parliamentary left groups. Freud wrote scathingly of the 'narcissism of tiny distinctions', and it is often the case in politics that two alignments whose differences are imperceptible to outsiders are divided by a ferocity of mutual contempt greater than that which divides them from declared enemies. This was the case in those days with the bewildering array of groups of Maoists, Trotskyists, Leninists, anarchists, situationists and the like, all dedicated to achieving the red revolution. This sectarianism exasperated Dario, who

96

hoped that La Comune could provide a rallying point for all leftist tendencies. As a document drawn up in 1970 had it, 'our aim is to put our work at the service of the class movement; being at the service of the movement does not mean placing ourselves in a pre-prepared dish, but contributing to the movement as such, having a presence, changing with it, with its struggles and its real needs'.[1] Theatre-makers were viewed not as independent artists but as spear-carriers in a proletarian army, while theatre itself operated not as a purveyor of rest and recreation but as a mechanism for challenging received ideas, offering an alternative vision of the world and resisting the encroachment into the people's imagination of alien concepts peddled by a hostile media.

The theatrical collective was only one branch of the cooperative, and when conversion work was completed on the Capannone, they found they had spare capacity for offices for the many causes with which La Comune involved itself. Franca emerged perhaps even more strongly than Dario as a political figure and as the focal point for both theatrical and wider political activities. Publishing pamphlets was a thriving business in itself. The scripts of Dario's plays were often submerged in prefaces and postfaces made up of weighty analyses of social and political trends, of indications of the imminence of the revolution or of meticulously researched chronologies of recent events. Performances were still followed, and occasionally preceded, by debates.

Fo's writing in this period was more obviously didactic and more tied to the headlines of the day than previously. The first piece presented in the Capannone, *I Would Rather Die Tonight if I Had To Think It Had All Been In Vain*, premièred in October 1970, turned out to be an under-dramatized work which challenged the double standards that allowed the Italian Resistance to be regarded as a heroic liberation struggle and the Palestinian guerrilla war as a terrorist campaign. Dario had been researching the experiences of Italian partisans when King Hussein launched his offensive against Palestinians resident in Jordan.

> The play was a result of a discussion on the Amman massacre. Some comrades came to us because they thought that something had to be done. We gathered writings and documents on the partisan struggles, and other comrades and political groups helped us out. The play developed from performance to performance. In fourteen performances, it changed completely because new material was added all the time.[2]

Readings were interspersed with songs, but in spite of the lack of rehearsal time, the play attracted more than 6,000 spectators in Milan alone, and the Capannone found its place in the theatrical topography of the city.

During the run, Dario was already collecting material for *Accidental Death of an Anarchist*. The principal propaganda function of his theatre, as he conceived it, was to provide 'counter-information', to debunk misleading accounts whispered by government sources to compliant journalists. There was much that was mysterious and obscure in the Italy of those days. The strife between the 'opposing extremisms' of right and left was marked by a growing level of violence and rising tally of deaths, but the suspicion on the left – well founded, as it transpired – was that the neo-Fascist underground was backed by prominent figures in ministries, the armed forces and the upper echelons of the police. The rightist 'strategy of tension' was wreaking havoc and slaughter, but no one was ever brought to book for these crimes. The first act in that strategy was played out at Piazza Fontana, in Milan.

Five bombs were planted in Milan and Rome on 12 December 1969, one of which failed to ignite. The three in Rome caused minor injury and damage, but the bomb in the Banca Nazionale dell'Agricoltura in Piazza Fontana left sixteen people dead and over ninety injured. Before proper inquiries were under way, responsibility was laid by the police at the door of anarchist groups. Pietro Valpreda in Rome and Pino Pinelli in Milan were immediately arrested and publicly identified as perpetrators of the outrage. There is something quaintly old-fashioned in the attribution of responsibility for this first bomb outrage to anarchists rather than to revolutionary Marxists, as though the investigators had been digging out memories of childhood tales of atrocities. 'Monster' was the word used even by *L'Unità* for both Valpreda and Pinelli. The police officer who arrested and interrogated Pinelli was Luigi Calabresi, a man loathed by the left.

The whole affair was, and remains, as murky as any which stained Italian public life in those years, but the central fact was that the Italian public was invited to believe that they were exposed to danger from a clique of psychopathic madmen acting in the name of left-wing ideology. More careful inquiries over time made it clear that the perpetrators were neo-Fascists whose guilt was to be the subject of tortured and protracted court hearings, but those revelations lay in the future. Pinelli was held in the police station in Milan, where he was subjected to interrogation and perhaps torture until around midnight on the night of 15–16 December, when his body crashed on to the courtyard below. It later transpired that an ambulance had been called before the fall was registered. Initially, the death was presented as the suicidal gesture of a man consumed with guilt, but there were signs of blows on the body, and Calabresi had already acquired the nickname 'Inspector Parachute' for his fondness for making suspects perch precariously on window ledges during interrogation. The Pinelli case became a *cause célèbre*. There were various hypotheses formed by investigative journalists: that Pinelli had died under brutal treatment; that he had been pushed; or even that he had accidentally fallen from an unstable position. The conviction, fostered in no small measure by Dario's play, gained currency that the state and its officials carried responsibility both for the initial bombing and the killing of Pinelli.

The past career of Commissario Calabresi was investigated. He had been deeply involved with the CIA, as well as with the Italian General De Lorenzo, who had attempted a *coup d'état* in 1964. He was known to have been responsible for the dubious convictions of trade unionists and left-wing activists. His involvement with American intelligence services was made public, so for the left he quickly filled the position of monster which had been foisted on to Pinelli and Valpreda by the press. He was hounded mercilessly and unremittingly by the daily *Lotta Continua* and it appears that the witty but brittle cartoons the paper published undermined his increasingly fragile nervous equilibrium. One particularly vicious cartoon showed a suspect presenting himself with a parachute strapped to his back at a door marked Luigi Calabresi. Another, with the caption 'A good boy, good husband, father of one' has Calabresi quietly playing at home with his daughter. The discordant element in this picture of domestic bliss is that the toy is a guillotine. Calabresi felt isolated, but under pressure from his superiors raised an action for libel against *Lotta Continua* and its editor, Pio Baldelli. The trial began on 9 October 1970, but the defence lawyers deftly transformed the hearing into an inquest into the death of Pinelli, with Calabresi in the dock.

In December, *Accidental Death of an Anarchist*, based on the Pinelli case, opened in the Capannone in Milan. In it, Dario unleashes a supposed madman with a talent for disguise on the successive accounts which the police offered to explain Pinelli's death. The play has enjoyed enormous success worldwide, but it may surprise those who have relished its wit, imaginativeness, humorous extravagance and comic rhythms that it is based on fact and is even a drama *à clef*, with most of the characters having a counterpart easily identified from news bulletins at the time. The 'second commissario' dresses in the polo-neck sweaters which Calabresi habitually wore, while the woman journalist is clearly the writer Camilla Cederna, who had done so much to demolish the official story. The only intruder in this identity parade of the usual suspects is the madman, played by Fo himself. The character, who has long antecedents in the Italian tradition, may be viewed as a modern-dress Harlequin. His madness, itself a common enough device in Fo's theatre, is madness with method, an outlet for the earthiness, guile and low cunning showed by the classic Harlequin. He is gifted with a wit, perspicacity, divine insouciance and fearlessness denied those of conventionally sound mind. He enjoys a fool's licence to blurt out truths which the authorities would prefer to suppress, but in an upside-down world, where the worldly wise have made their peace with a society of unreason policed by violence, the madman is the only arbiter of decency and reason.

No play by Dario Fo ever reaches a definitive form while still in performance, but this work was designed to change daily so as to incorporate material which had emerged at that day's hearing. The trial itself did not reach a conclusion, since on 17 May 1972 Calabresi was himself gunned down outside his house. Outside family circles, there was little mourning. *Lotta Continua* was openly exultant, while La Comune stated, somewhat callously, in a postface written for the Einaudi edition of *Accidental Death*, that the trial was suspended following the 'non-accidental death of the actor'. At the time, no party or group claimed responsibility. It was believed in some quarters that Calabresi, who was showing signs of crumbling under the weight of isolation and public scorn, had been eliminated by elements of the Italian secret services. In 1988, Adriano Sofri, who had been one of the leading spirits in *Lotta Continua*, and two of his comrades were arrested and charged with the murder. This act brought the Calabresi case back into the headlines and brought Fo back into the affair, this time to defend Sofri's innocence.

If the play is a counter-enquiry into official responsibility for the massacre in Piazza Fontana, for the unjust detention of Valpreda and the killing of Pinelli in police custody, the theatrical format is Fo's unique style of farce. The refusal to arouse mere pity for an individual rather than a more all-embracing scorn and anger against all men in government was intrinsic to Fo's poetic and to his choice of farce as a genre, but there is a nonchalant boldness here which goes beyond theatrical convention. Fo's farce is both serious and guffawing, and on this occasion no one could doubt his claim that his farce was an outgrowth of a tragic vision. The police station where the tragic events unfold is an updated version of the 'blasted heath', with the tale recounted by Lear's Fool. His jeering at painful events allows the underlying tragedy to remain in the mind, but the laughter is not the nihilistic variety which suggests that all life is senseless and all systems equal, but an uncomfortable laughter followed by anger, and hence, in Fo's view, by action and hope. As he said in one of the post-performance discussions:

> We do popular theatre. Not populist theatre. Popular theatre has always made use of the grotesque, of farce – farce is an invention of the people – to develop its most dramatic themes. We could produce hundreds of examples, but anyone who has seen *Mistero buffo* will realize that even to tell the story of Christ, the people do not use the dramatic method favoured by the aristocracy, the one which aims to grab you by the throat or the guts, but tries to get there by a moment of violent laughter. Because laughter truly does remain at the back of the mind among the ferocious dregs which cannot be scraped away. Because laughter helps avoid one of the greatest of dangers, which is catharsis. That is to say, when people cry, they liberate themselves from pain.[3]

An outpouring of tragic grief was a response which would not survive contact with fresh air on the streets when the play was over. Some deeper reflection was called for, some reflection which would be triggered by, but would not end in, laughter. The task was to reveal 'the reactionary nature of a state which was not "born of the Resistance", but was a continuation of the old Fascist state, with a few demagogic flourishes'. More immediately, the goal was

> to win the battle for the liberation of Valpreda and the other arrested comrades and to single out those who were really responsible for the killings, both at operational and tactical level. In this general framework, which placed a heavy responsibility on all revolutionary militants and on all sincere democrats, *Accidental Death of an Anarchist*, a grotesque farce on a tragic farce, had its part to play.[4]

Judges, policemen, bureaucratic functionaries, bishops and army officers all emerge badly from Fo's satire. Although he specifies that the action must unfold in 'an unremarkable office in the central police station', the device of having a madman-impersonator as his central character allows him to expand the range of his targets. The madman had passed himself off as a psychiatrist, but in the police station he plays judge, bishop and police officer in his efforts to point to the complicity of all sections of the Italian establishment in the crime and its cover-up. The mechanism of farce is unleashed when the arrested madman finds a folder on a desk referring to the case of the anarchist and carrying the name of the judge due to arrive from Rome to conduct an inquiry into police conduct. He transforms himself into that judge and initiates his own inquiry. The political tempo is stepped up, but the dramatic impact lessened, with the introduction of the female investigative journalist. However effective this character may be from a political viewpoint, the unrelenting seriousness of her part makes it appear that she has strayed in from another play. She is too obviously the didactic mouthpiece, the speaker of the unmediated truths the authorities wish to conceal.

In addition to a myriad of incidental changes which he introduced during the run, Fo toyed with two different endings, neither totally satisfactory. In the first version, the madman secures a tape-recording of the conversations, brandishes a bomb which had been concealed in a drawer, handcuffs the others to a clothes-hanger and flees. There is an explosion, the journalist frees herself and reports that a crowd is gathering around what appears to be a body in the courtyard below. A man played by the same actor as the madman makes his entrance, identifies himself as the real investigating magistrate from Rome and opens an investigation which takes the form of a discussion with the audience. Later, Fo amended this and had the work end with a declaration from the madman that the release of the tapes would unleash not revolution but scandal, 'the manure of social democracy', and that finally the Italians would become a social democracy, like the British or the Americans and realize that 'we are in the shit up to our necks, which is why we walk with our heads high!'

Neither of these endings was used in the first British adaptation of the play by Gavin Richards for his Belt and Braces troupe. The play was initially produced on the London Fringe in the 1978–9 season, but was such a success that it was transferred to the West End in 1980. Richards modified the play substantially, cutting out the role of the bishop and even inserting a sneering reference, spoken by the journalist, to Dario Fo's failure to give meatier roles to women. In place of Fo's single ending, Richards devised two alternative endings, one which had the journalist rush out, leaving the police and magistrate tied up while the bomb goes off, and a second in which she is duped into handing over the key to the inspector, who promptly escapes, leaving her to her fate. Fo attended the première in London and was outraged by the alterations and the switch in spirit which, as he saw it, reduced the play to mere farce while ignoring the deeper tragedy inherent in the work. It took all the efforts of Stuart Hood, who became editor of the English translations, to persuade him that Richards had made a genuine move across cultures, substituting the British music-hall tradition for the Italian tradition of *commedia dell'arte*. Whatever its deficiencies, the Richards version remains one of the few which preserved the vigour and comedy of the original without losing its political fervour.

Fo's judgements on most foreign productions of *Accidental Death* have been harsh.

> This exercise of the grotesque, of paradox, of madness could stand on its own even without the political discourse, so much so that certain directors (God break them on the wheel!), in their concern to achieve pure entertainment, have removed all indications of realistic conflict and have exaggerated the comedy to the point of making it pure clowning. They have ended up with a kind of surreal *pochade* where people are left rolling in the aisles, only to leave the theatre unburdened by any indignation or disturbing thought. This was the operation they conducted on Broadway, at the Belasco theatre, where the political element was literally murdered. The theatrical situation still worked, so the critic of the *New York Times* was able to write: 'In this play there are two murders; the first and most obvious is that of the play.'[5]

Accidental Death would not be the first work of mordant political satire to be relaunched, or neutered, as a jolly exercise of fantasy. Jonathan Swift, whose *Modest Proposal* Fo regarded as one of the supreme examples of acerbic satire, wrote *Gulliver's Travels* as a scornful denunciation of political shenanigans, but lived to see it treasured as a children's tale. Some directors have staged *Accidental Death* in the same spirit. More commonly, it has become the all-purpose protest play, used in different countries to satirize authorities and mobilize opinion against some abuse of power in that society. British adapters incorporated references to establishment spy scandals involving Anthony Blunt, and later to miscarriages of justice involving Irishmen wrongly imprisoned for crimes they did not commit. In Japan, it was used by environmentalists to attack the extension of Tokyo airport, while in Germany it became a vehicle to denounce abuses of prison regimes. Marco Ferreri wanted to adapt the play for the cinema, but when the matter was put to the vote in a Comune assembly, the majority were against. Such permission would only be granted once there was a chain of 'alternative cinemas' to match the alternative circuit of theatres La Comune was striving to establish. Dario went along with the majority, but later regretted it.[6] Unsurprisingly, *Accidental Death* was the object of more than forty official actions and complaints, a higher total than any other single play by Fo.

While on tour, the company received bomb threats and had to endure petty problems created by the police and magistrates. In Bologna, they were refused permission to perform in the grand Duse theatre, but attracted an audience of six thousand in the sports arena. The title was altered to include a reference to the death of the publisher, Giangiacomo Feltrinelli, whose body was found beneath an electricity pylon on 15 March 1972. Close by were various sticks of dynamite, and the official sources concluded that Feltrinelli killed himself accidentally while attempting to cut the electricity supply to Milan. This verdict was derided by Fo at the time, but later revelations about Feltrinelli made it appear likely that, on this occasion, the official version was nearer to the truth.

Fo returned to the developments surrounding the Pinelli and Feltrinelli cases in *Bang! Bang! Who's There? The Police!*, premièred in December 1972. The armed forces, who had been absent from Fo's life for some time, decided that this was the moment to reappear and raised their now familiar action for contempt. The published version with its lengthy, detailed chronology of events surrounding the Piazza Fontana bombing, thumbnail sketches of the protagonists and magistrates' reports on right-wing terrorism was a political pamphlet rather than a playscript. The work itself was written in seven days and plainly found a resonance among Fo's audiences in those dark days. The actors wore no costumes and read their lines from behind desks in an office inside the Ministry for the Interior. By opening night, Calabresi, who had been appointed to investigate the Feltrinelli crime, had himself been assassinated. In the play, his death is imputed to 'Machiavelli'. The work has an Orwellian atmosphere, with anonymous, Big Brother figures conversing about events relating to terrorism which are obscure to the man in the street but clear to those who have manipulated everything.

The attacks on established parties of both left and right made the organization of touring schedules tricky. The company was routinely refused permission to perform in towns with a Communist town council, and *L'Unità* refused to carry publicity. Dario further alienated the established left-wing parties with *All Together! All United! Excuse Me, Isn't That the Boss?*, premièred in Varese in March 1971. Where had the left in Italy gone wrong, where were the roots of the drift away from revolutionary socialism, he asked? The play carried the subtitle *Workers' Struggles 1911–22*, the period between the war in Libya and Mussolini's March on Rome.

Unusually for Fo, there were no farcical or grotesque elements in the tale, which was dramatized from the perspective of Antonia, a seamstress who had no interest in politics until her husband was killed by Fascist thugs. Her own political education begins there, and in due course she avenges his death by killing his assassin. Any interpretation of this act as support for 1970s terrorism is nullified by Antonia's immediate regret for this impulsive gesture, since she realizes that she has 'killed the dog, not its owner'. Dario directed but did not appear on stage, leaving Franca, who gives the best of herself in dramatic roles, with the lead role in the play. All reviews agree on the quality of her performance, both in bringing to life the flashbacks to the factory occupations in Turin in 1920 and in tracing the inner development of Antonia. The Socialist and Communist parties were united in expressions of outrage, the former because their historic leaders were derided, the latter because, probably rightly, they saw the attack on socialist moderation yesterday as an assault on Communist compromise today. The film producer, Carlo Ponti was enthusiastic about the work, and negotiations were opened with a view to securing the rights for a film in which his wife, Sofia Loren, would have played the main role, but the discussions were inconclusive.

Being lead actress was only one of Franca's roles within the company. The burden of general administration fell largely on her shoulders, particularly after Nanni Ricordi resigned in 1971 to pursue his own interests in the family business. Dario and Franca's home became an extension of La Comune office or a general debating chamber where friends and comrades met to discuss company policy and the questions of the day. Privacy, never a particularly strong concept in any part of Italy, was now denied them. Franca found the day-to-day stress of being a wife and mother as well as an actress and general factotum of the company excessive. Dario, whatever views he later formed of male responsibilities in the abstract, never succeeded in acquiring an ability to assist in his own home. The exception was cooking, where he found as much pleasure in preparing risotto as he did in painting. When writing, he was capable of periods of the most intense, exclusive concentration, sitting at his desk for long hours at a stretch, not eating and scarcely sleeping, but he was indifferent to matters around him. When he was on his own, he would leave mail not only unanswered but unopened. Money was a special problem. On several occasions, taxi-drivers came to the door to ask for the refund of a fare for conveying a penniless Dario across the city. When Franca offered them the cash, she frequently found that she had also to refund the money they had lent him to buy himself dinner in a trattoria.

Franca had another role thrust upon her. La Comune decided to turn its attention once more on the plight of the Palestinian people, but opted for a documentary format. Somewhat to her dismay, Franca was elected to go to Lebanon to recruit some flesh-and-blood Palestinians. Late in 1971, she arrived in Beirut, to be greeted by a customs officer who assumed from her dress that she was a prostitute hired by some wealthy client. After some delay, she was admitted to the country, where she toured the camps and invited a group of ten refugees back to Italy. The format of *Fedayeen*, presented at the Capannone in January 1972, was rudimentary. Franca appeared on stage with the Palestinians, who told their story in narrative and song. Later, the company, who found themselves cold-shouldered by the Italian left and even picketed by Palestinian students loyal to the main Palestinian organization, Al Fatah, admitted they had behaved rashly. The ideology of *Fedayeen* was based on the critique made by the extremist Popular Front for the Liberation of Palestine, and La Comune had decided that Al Fatah was an establishment party, guilty of acts of deviation and compromise similar to those committed by the Italian Communists. They were embarrassed by pamphlets handed out at the door accusing them of aiding a Zionist game of divide and rule.

Official police and government files on both Dario and Franca were already bulging. In June 1971, Dario received a summons from a judge in Brescia for entering an occupied factory in 1968 to perform for striking workers. Franca ran into problems when she went to renew her passport to allow her to take up an invitation to perform in France. Initially, the officer was relaxed, asking only if there was any outstanding legal business to be cleared up, and when she replied that there was only the *Canzonissima* case, he promised her a new passport within weeks. When she returned, she found the officer barely visible behind a mountain of paperwork referring to the various cases under investigation by magistrates the length and breadth of Italy. To have a passport issued, she would need to request permission from each and every one. Meanwhile, both were convinced that their phones were being tapped and that they themselves were being followed by policemen. At times, the situation had overtones of black comedy. When they made two phone calls in quick succession, they could hear agents in some office discussing the first before they were connected for the second. At other times, the phone would ring and their entire conversation would be played back to them. Franca recalls once having a puncture on the way to the airport. She was on her own and waited until the officers who were tailing her drew up. Being not entirely bereft of gallantry, they got out, changed the tyre, bid her *buon viaggio* and got back into their own car to follow her. On another occasion, when attending a trial, she got into conversation with a 'charming young man'. When the verdict was announced, she was about to raise her clenched fist, when she felt him grip her tightly by the wrist and hold her arm down. 'That would cause you trouble,' he whispered, telling her he had been appointed to keep an eye on her.

There were definite limits to the comedy. The 'years of lead', as the age of terrorism became known, were now under way. The Red Brigades had made their first appearance with an action at the Sit-Siemens factory in August 1970, while news filtered out of an attempted neo-Fascist *coup d'état* led by the 'black prince', Junio Valerio Borghese, in December. The Prefect of Milan, Libero Mazza, sent a much debated report to the Ministry for the Interior, in which he calculated that there were around 20,000 members of ultra-left groups in Milan, to which had to be added an unspecified number of adherents of the ultra-right.[7] The police employed *agents provocateurs*, infiltrators and spies to maintain surveillance on left-wing groups, including La Comune. The magistrate Guido Viola, who was in charge of investigations into left-wing terrorism, regarded Dario and Franca as suspects. Viola ordered the prosecution of Dario for the poster advertising *Bang! Bang! Who's There? The Police!*, an ink drawing of a man, woman and child with blotches round their head, presumably taken to indicate blood. The poster was confiscated and removed from circulation.

The terrorist campaign plainly caused havoc in society, but in an unexpected way it polluted the atmosphere for the left, even the revolutionary left, where Dario and Franca positioned themselves. It drove the PCI into an even closer union with the Christian Democrats, but it also caused a certain tentativeness in left-wing circles, who saw support for their cause ebbing away with each successive outrage. Such was the suspicion of Dario and Franca in official circles that, years later, in 1998, when the crisis had passed, an official report revealed that some magistrates in the seventies had entertained the belief that Dario was the *éminence grise* behind the Red Brigades. In fact, neither he nor Franca had any truck with terror or violence, and spoke out determinedly and forthrightly against the cult of death which terrorism represented. On the other hand, a belief in revolution involved a certain cult of violence, and more than once their plays ended with them spraying imaginary bullets from an imaginary gun over the audience. In that climate, innocent souls who would normally recoil at the sight of a bleeding nose could be seen happily chanted blood-curdling slogans and revelling in fantasy violence. One slogan which had great currency at gatherings, including those of La Comune, was the cry 'Never Again Without The Gun', shouted in unison and accompanied by raised fists and yells.

La Comune was a sprawling network of organizations, and certainly included among its members some who were at least sympathetic to terrorism, perhaps some responsible for terrorist acts and others who were drawn into terrorism through contacts they made there. This, by his own account, was the case with Mauro Borromeo, an ex-administrator in the Catholic University of Milan, arrested in 1981 for involvement with Autonomia Operaia. As he explained, the turning-point in his personal odyssey was the bombing at Piazza Fontana, but his account of his gradual drift into terrorist circles was spiced with bitter criticism of Dario and Franca:

> I began to attend Dario Fo's plays, and I appreciated both his talents and political beliefs, but I ended up taking a critical view of certain attitudes of his and of Franca's. For instance, even if in the context of La Comune they preached the rights of communist equality, in reality when on tour they always lodged in the best hotels, leaving the technicians and electricians to fend for themselves on their 5,000 lire per diem allowance. The Fo couple too, demagogically, took their 5,000 per day, but contrary to the anti-commercial ethic which had inspired the foundation of La Comune, they kept the entire income from the sale of scripts and recordings. It was at that time that I first heard of Red Aid. It was not merely a red charity which gave material help to prisoners and their families, but it had wider, deeper and unofficial functions. Specifically, it concerned itself with finding lodging for people who were being sought by the police ...[8]

Borromeo was speaking after his arrest, and with an element of special pleading. He claimed that his group had operated inside the framework of Red Aid, and that 'practically unaware of what was happening, operating in conditions of clandestinity or semi-clandestinity', he had found himself engaged in finding safe houses for terrorists on the run. Red Aid itself had other, more peaceful, objectives.

It was Franca who, in 1972, set up Red Aid to work for prisoners' rights, to campaign for decent prison conditions and to provide practical support for detainees and their families, including legal advice, chains of comfort letters and food parcels. The organization was established when, after a performance at the Capannone, Franca was approached by a woman who had been a baby-sitter for Jacopo years before. The son of a friend had been arrested in Florence following demonstrations at a meeting addressed by Giorgio Almirante, leader of the neo-Fascist MSI. She asked Franca if she could help in any way to alleviate the conditions the boy was facing in jail. Franca made an appeal from the stage, suggesting that some people might like to send a postcard or a postal order for 1,000 lire. That evening, seven people came forward. Within three months, Red Aid had some 10,000 adherents, and over the years of its existence offered assistance to around 1,000 prisoners. Franca was the organization's administrator, spokesperson and public face, but, as Günter Grass found in Germany, it is impossible to advocate humane treatment or understanding of groups regarded by public opinion as satanic without attracting opprobrium. Franca's own public profile and image now changed radically. She was already widely viewed as La Pasionaria of the New Left, but her work with Red Aid made her both the most loved and the most loathed woman in Italy. In her own eyes, she was an Elizabeth Fry and Red Aid a human-rights campaign. For police, magistrates and sections of the press, she was a Rasputin or Mephistopheles, as well as apologist for terrorism. She became, even more than Dario, public enemy number one. She explained the objectives of Red Aid in a 1980 interview:

> Let's say it was a kind of welfare activity. A prisoner who needed it received a small monthly cheque, perhaps a parcel, books and letters, often hundreds of letters. Then there was the work of counter-information, to demolish frame-ups, like the 'state massacre', or the Valpreda case. In the early stages, we only concerned ourselves with the 'politicals', but they themselves pointed out that this was unfair, and so we gave the same attention to the 'ordinary prisoners'.[9]

Franca found the work exhausting but also strangely exhilarating. Having repeatedly said that she was an actress by accident and that she would have preferred some career in social service, she now found a sense of mission. This was, she said, the most 'grandiose' work she had been involved with. The Red Aid network was always somewhat ramshackle, but in the first place, since the police were indifferent to the plight of families of terrorist suspects, it arranged for families to be informed of the arrest and whereabouts of their son or daughter. The one-act play which Franca later performed, *A Mother*, was based on her contact with a woman who learned from television of the arrest of her son. The dispatch of prisoners to jails far from home became increasingly common when the anti-terrorist unit under General Carlo Alberto Dalla Chiesa established special prisons in remote spots. Franca revealed herself to be a highly efficient bureaucrat, keeping track of prisoners all over the peninsula and labori-ously making cyclostyled copies of circulars to keep members in touch with each other. Later, the word 'militant' was added to the title of the organization, but the humanitarian aspect remained uppermost.

Initially, Red Aid concerned itself with political prisoners arrested on demonstrations or sit-ins, but with the heightening of the terror campaign the nature of the crimes with which its clients were charged soon changed. They were not misunderstood lads from poor backgrounds, or the victims of miscarriages of justice. They had declared war on the state and were in some cases guilty of horrific acts of violence. The slightly twee phrase 'misguided comrades' gained circulation among those who wished to dis-sociate themselves from terrorism but not totally from the terrorists themselves, especially when they were exposed to maltreatment. Franca campaigned for the human rights of the prisoners, irrespective of their crimes. 'I used to say to myself: I am not in agreement with what they do, but they are in jail, things are bad for them, because in jail things are indeed bad, and they will "pay" for what they have done. It is up to the court to judge, but meantime I must defend their right to be treated like men and not like beasts.'[10]

The Italian state replied to the terrorist threat with treatment that would, in an international context, have contravened the Geneva Convention. Stories of sensory deprivation, psychological bullying and petty vexations of the sort which saw short-sighted prisoners denied the use of their spec-tacles, were rife, but there were also tales of systematic beatings and torture, of prisoners left tied to benches for days, of starvation diets. Franca wrote a letter of protest to the President of the Republic:

> The letters, the stories, the dramas which have come to our attention all tell the same sort of tale – misery, despair, ignorance – and they cannot leave you indifferent. They are dreadful stories, of real torture, terrible stories not tol-erated by the Constitution. There are some people who have preferred to die by swallowing fragments of blades, nails, spoon handles, or by garroting themselves rather than continue to live that life . . .
>
> There is one prisoner with his back broken by a prison guard following a revolt (we have the documents), another who had a testicle removed (it was no longer any use to him, since they had crushed it underfoot! We have the

documents). Another had his arm broken with an iron bar, an arm which no one put in plaster.

It calcified by itself. In time it ankylosed. (We have the documents.)[11]

Alberto Franceschini, one of the founders of the Red Brigades, wrote in his autobiography[12] of his despair after being removed to Asinara, a special prison in Sardinia, locked up in a hut in the scorching heat without water and finally being given, at eleven at night, a few rolls which were too hard even to be bitten. Towards midday the following day, he heard some confusion outside and the door opened to reveal Franca Rame whom he had known in the early days of the student movement. When Franceschini began to recount his experiences, the prison governor, Luigi Cardullo, hustled Franca away, on the grounds that she had no authorization to speak with Franceschini. Only rarely was Franca permitted to make such visits, since, as Judge Viola revealed, there was a ministerial decree in force that all requests from her were to be routinely refused. Postal orders she dispatched to prisoners were, illegally, rejected and returned to her. Lawyers associated with Red Aid were victims of mysterious burglaries where nothing of value was stolen but correspondence was rifled; on other occasions, their doors were broken down and furniture smashed. *Agents provocateurs* were again active, and Franca sometimes received suspiciously generous donations, which she returned or handed over to the police, believing that they could be dirty money from drug dealings or kidnapping. Once, she received a parcel of false identity papers, with an accompanying note explaining that they would be of assistance to people on the run. Red Aid was not involved in offering assistance to fugitives from justice. Franca suspected that the parcel was a crude trap and took it immediately to the police. It was no doubt a coincidence that her home was visited by policemen later that very day.

La Comune now found itself subjected to harassment which affected its theatrical work. According to its own calculations, it played to some 700,000 people in a year, and had a membership of 27,000 in Milan alone. In 1972, sales of playscripts reached 60,000. Since the company eschewed the conventional theatre circuit, it often converted cinemas into temporary theatres, so the authorities hit on the ruse of refusing permission for such temporary conversions, or of threatening the cinema owner with the withdrawal of his projection licence. Since this meant bankruptcy, many owners, unsurprisingly, reneged on deals they had already struck. In addition, several police chiefs insisted on having officers present throughout performances or even rehearsals in case there were threats to public order. Dario refused to perform in the presence of the police, believing that the club status of La Comune gave it immunity from legal provisions regarding censorship.

The owner of the Capannone decided that he too had had enough and in July 1972 served the company with notice to quit. He had no complaints over their tenantship, had received regular payments of rent and had seen his property improved, but he was under pressure and concluded the game was not worth the candle. The group went quietly. The premises are now in use as a car workshop, but the people in the bars in the neighbourhood still reminisce fondly about the bustle and excitement when they too went to theatre. The company signed a lease with the Pier Lombardo theatre (now called the Franco Parenti theatre, after Fo's early partner), but after it was signed, the management changed its mind.

The next problem concerned two senior magistrates, Guido Viola of Milan and Mario Sossi in Genoa, both of whom had taken an undue interest in everything involving Dario and Franca. They had indeed distinguished themselves by their zeal in seeing red conspiracies everywhere, and for initiating prosecutions which were subsequently rejected by the Appeal Court. Sossi's attention was drawn to a doctoral thesis on prison conditions written by a student in Pavia, Irene Invernizzi, who was a member of La Comune. In Sossi's view, the work could be viewed as an invitation to revolt, or as incitement to escape. In his inquiries, he examined letters written by prisoners but intercepted by the prison authorities which made reference to Red Aid. An article appeared in the Genoese daily, *Il Secolo XIX*, written by Mario Massai, saying that Sossi had ordered an official inquiry, an essential preliminary to full legal proceedings, into Dario Fo and his relationship with the Red Brigades. There were hints of some connection between a spate of riots in Italian jails and the activities of Fo and Rame, with the implication that the real aim of Red Aid was to establish a network of revolutionaries inside the prisons.

In October 1972, Dario was in Stockholm attending a session of the Russell Tribunal on the continued imprisonment of Pietro Valpreda, and on his return to Milan he was greeted by Franca and a journalist from *L'Unità*, who told him of these developments and of the likelihood that Sossi was about to transfer the case to Viola in Milan. Dario called a press conference the following day on the steps of the High Court in Milan, where he denounced the proceedings as 'fourth-rate farce', and launched into what reporters present described as a devastatingly funny piece of mimicry of the two magistrates. The two had no need to be either 'actors or authors by profession', as they enjoyed those advantages which, according to Voltaire, made magistrates the most fortunate of performers. The show they put on under the guise of justice was essentially contrived to serve private interests, leaving them free of the need to win the favour of any audience, or even of public authorities. Several papers carried the story, with Ibio Paolucci writing in *L'Unità* of previous 'grotesque initiatives' by Sossi.

Sossi raised a criminal, not civil, action for defamation against Fo and *L'Unità*. The law's delays meant that it was January 1974 before the case came to court, but then it had to be further postponed for the most dramatic of reasons. On 18 April, Sossi was kidnapped by a Red Brigade detachment headed by Alberto Franceschini. Even in a country becoming hardened to killings, knee-cappings, bank raids and planned violence, the seizure of Sossi caused a sensation. In his autobiography, Franceschini admits that the group would have killed Sossi had it been necessary. During his captivity, Sossi's wife wrote to the Pope and the president asking for their intervention, and the Red Brigades replied with a communiqué saying that he would be executed unless members of the 22 October group, who had been put on trial in Genoa on Sossi's orders, were released. Franca had taken a special interest in this group, and was in attendance in court every day. The authorities held firm, but it appears that, once they were holed up with their hostage, some version of the Stockholm syndrome took over, and acts of violence against a somewhat pathetic figure became unthinkable. Sossi was released unharmed after thirty-five days.

The kidnap, as was made clear by the bulletins issued by the terrorists on his seizure, was related to his political stance and to his zeal in seeking lengthy sentences for terrorists. It was not related to Sossi's disputes with Dario or Franca, and Franceschini makes no mention of Fo in his account of the interrogations. However, on his release, Sossi returned to his attacks on Fo with two contradictory accounts. He reported that the Red Brigades had referred to Fo with derision, but simultaneously made half-hearted suggestions that Fo was indeed the real leader of the entire underground movement. He said he had come under pressure to drop the case, and then later in the trial said that this pressure made it essential for him, in the interests of justice, to proceed with it, even though he would have preferred to abandon it. The kidnap made an enormous impression on Italian public opinion, and the possibility that Fo and Rame were indeed manipulators of terrorism was raised in various publications. Sossi was the hero of the hour. At the re-opening of the trial, he appeared surrounded by guards and plain-clothes officers.

In the dock on charges of libel were Fo, Paolucci and Romolo Galimberti, editor of the *L'Unità*. Fo's defence was that he was replying to an outrageous provocation by Sossi, as reported in *Il Secolo XIX*. Called to give evidence, the journalist Mario Massai first said that he had got the story that Dario was under suspicion directly from Sossi, then said that he had come to this conclusion after conversations with other magistrates. He added that the offending article was not his, but was written by two other journalists, who stated in court that they had no memory of the events. There was also ambiguity over whether or not Sossi had issued a denial when he saw the story in print. At one point, he claimed he did not think it worthwhile, but later said he had issued a denial, but no one paid any heed. The final verdict was worthy of Solomon. Dario was acquitted since he had been put in a situation of 'putative provocation', which seemed to mean that he believed the newspaper story was true and had responded as any decent man would. Massai came in for harsh words, but the unfortunate journalists from *L'Unità* were found guilty, although the fines imposed on them were light. How a journalist can be guilty of slander in reporting events or remarks which are themselves deemed free of all taint will remain an enigma for those unencumbered with legal qualifications.

In the midst of all this, Dario and Franca were evicted from their home. The proprietor objected to their views on Palestine and wanted them out. The press of the time carried various fetching photographs of Franca seated on suitcases, surrounded by armchairs and sideboards, in front of the house which had been theirs. Poverty was not the issue. They had a second house in Cernobbio on Lake Como, but finding a home in the city was now awkward. This troublesome duo were not welcome neighbours for the douce bourgeoisie of Milan.

Chapter 7

1973: *Annus Horribilis*

The year 1973 was on all fronts an *annus horribilis* for Dario and Franca. Problems were already developing inside the company as well as from the usual suspects outside it, so it is scarcely surprising that several associates recall that at this period of embittered isolation, Dario was prone to extreme mood swings from exhilaration to depression and gnawing worry. He gave expression to these feelings in an unusually forthright interview in February, venting his spleen on people in the world of politics and theatre.[1] The duo of ex-friends who ran the Piccolo theatre were objects of special scorn. He slammed Giorgio Strehler for his expressions of jeering surprise over what he had termed Dario's decision to play for a bourgeois audience in non-bourgeois sites, and Paolo Grassi for his part in having him banned from the Chamber of Labour circuit. The lack of recognition in official circles was plainly beginning to irk him, so although normally free of all trace of braggadocio, he complained of being celebrated abroad but ignored at home and even suggested that in the prevailing political vacuum created by the rightward shift of the PCI, he *was* the opposition in Italy. The preferential treatment accorded Pier Paolo Pasolini in the Communist press rankled.

> He is supposed to be a left-wing director. I write about domestic labour, about riots in prison, but for the PCI I do not exist. They are very good at praising signor Pasolini, who chooses to do Boccaccio, in other words a reactionary writer in his own time who attacked the Ciompi rising, a workers' revolt. To make his *Decameron* acceptable, Pasolini inserts gratuitous pornography in keeping with the bourgeois pederastic tastes which he finds pleasing.

For Fo, Pasolini became the very model of the *bien-pensant*, well-heeled, salon radical. The two held sharply differing views on popular culture, on political theatre, on the use of dialect, but the savagery with which each expressed his animus towards the other cannot to be explained by mere politics. Later that year, at a time when Dario required public support, Pasolini would reply in kind.

La Comune had been searching for a home since their eviction from the Capannone, and found a seemingly willing partner in the owner of the Rossini cinema, but after agreeing a deal with them, he raised the rent. This was accepted, but the police intervened to remind the proprietor of the terms of his cinema licence, so he withdrew altogether. In exasperation, La Comune occupied the building. To ward off any police action, the cast – then performing, ironically enough, *Bang! Bang! Who's There? The Police!* – slept in the building.

Bombs were discovered under theatres where La Comune were performing, and the couple's house in Cernobbio was set ablaze. Threatening letters arrived frequently, though the couple tried to treat them lightly. One particularly sinister missive, delivered by a group calling themselves Italian Executioners, was pinned to the living-room wall. The caption, over a cartoon of a hanged man, read: 'Red Pig, This Will Be Your End!' The level of surveillance on them had increased and Franca and Dario both remember a van which circled menacingly around their house. This was nothing compared to the outrage perpetrated on Franca in March. It was not merely the inhuman savagery of the deed itself which was chilling, but the fact, later proven beyond all conceivable doubt, that the attack was premeditated and planned by officials inside the Italian police forces.

On 9 March, Franca made an appointment by telephone with her hairdresser, and at 6.30 she left the Rossini cinema for the salon. As she was walking on via Nirone, near her own home and near a *carabinieri* station, she was seized from behind by several men, one of whom pointed a gun at her back. The human mind is prone to entertain the most incongruous thoughts at moments of greatest crisis and Franca later recalled that as she was being bundled into a van her mind raced to the Costas Gavras film *Z*. 'Oh God,' she thought, 'it's just like Greece here. Now they're kidnapping me and then they're going to kill me.' Lest there be any doubt about the political motivation of the attack, they jeered at her work in the theatre and at the activities of Red Aid. She was tossed on to the floor and held down by her captors who over the next couple of hours systematically tortured, beat, slashed and then raped her as they drove the vehicle around Milan. The men stubbed out cigarettes on her neck, cut her breasts with razor blades, stripped, slapped, punched and kicked her, and while one of the men held her down, at least three raped her. Franca thinks she may have fainted, causing the group to grow alarmed in case they had killed her. She remembers the man at her back complaining that he had not been allowed to rape her too, but they had been driving for some hours and the others were now desperate to dump her immediately. They threw her ripped clothes around her and pushed her on to a street near the Sforza castle. She staggered around for some time before getting to a phone and calling Dario. He rushed to the spot and found her bleeding, bruised, dazed and weeping convulsively.

Back home, she said she had been assaulted but did not reveal the full heinousness of the ordeal. It would be years before she could tell even Dario that she had been raped. When word of the assault got out, people descended on the Rossini cinema to express their outrage and anger, and all over Italy in the following days, the fragmented left came together for demonstrations of sympathy. Dario made a lengthy statement to *Paese Sera* outlining the horror Franca had endured, but saying that it was part of the campaign of violence the working class was enduring in that phase of repression and reaction.

Ironically, the magistrate put in charge of investigations was the same Guido Viola who was already leading the prosecution against them in other cases. He visited Franca, expressed sympathy, but his inquiries made no headway and some years later he notified her that he was shelving the case due to lack of evidence. Twenty-five years later, in 1998, when Italy's internal conflicts had been settled and the award of the Nobel Prize had consolidated Fo and Rame's position as international celebrities, the full background to the case was revealed, not by some excitable left-wing ideologue, but by a sober judge, Guido Salvini. Salvini had been asked to conduct a fresh inquiry into the responsibilities of neo-Fascist groups for the series of unsolved outrages from Piazza Fontana onwards, and was directed to focus especially on possible connivance between police forces and right-wing terrorists. His report ran to 60,000 pages, divided into ninety-two volumes, based on over 400 interrogation sessions. Only two pages were dedicated to Franca Rame, but they established that the rape was, as the phrase had it, a 'state rape' and that the attack had been not only condoned but commissioned by high-ranking officials in the *carabinieri*. It was implied, but not proven, that authorization might have come from higher up, from the Ministry for the Interior or for Defence.

The judge's conclusion vindicated what Fo and Rame alleged at the time. The fact that the attackers had such precise information on her movements was puzzling, as was the fact that the *carabinieri* had not seen a thing even although the assault took place near their barracks. Shortly afterwards, a bug was found in their telephone at home. Jacopo, who was then almost eighteen, took the attack on his mother particularly hard, and had to be dissuaded from joining one of the terrorist groups involved in the 'armed struggle'. Franca found it difficult in the extreme to cope with her suffering and with the endless flashbacks which pursued her. Once, Jacopo put on a piece of pop music on a record player at home, but this simple act reminded her that her torturers had been playing music in the van to drown out her screams.

> I could not sleep unless Dario was there, or unless Jacopo, who was not yet 18, cradled my head on his chest. I had no longer the same face; it was as if the blood, life itself had drained out of me. My hands were constantly shaking. I never went out, and when Dario persuaded me to go with him to a meeting in Pavia, people came up to him and asked how Franca was, when was he going to bring Franca, and I was there at his side, but no one recognized me. When I started to go out, I had to have someone with me. Once I threw myself into the arms of a traffic policeman, because I was sure I was being followed.[2]

Nevertheless, by May, Franca felt able to resume work, aided by Dario and Lanfranco Binni, a member of the company who also became Dario's Boswell. *No More of These Fascists!*, a multi-media piece using video and recordings, recounted the experiences of partisan women. It was premièred in Lancenigo, with Franca performing various parts, but when she came to the episode of a female Resistance fighter beaten up by Fascist thugs, she broke down and had to interrupt the performance. The following month, she helped workers from the Fiat factory in Turin put together a play of their own based on the experiences of a family who had migrated from the South.

Franca dealt with her own experience publicly two years later by writing a one-woman play, entitled starkly *The Rape*. In this case, there was no question of co-authorship: this work is indelibly and unmistakably Franca's. She wrote it in one sudden, unstoppable spasm of emotional power, showed it to Dario, who read it, fell silent, then embraced her. He was still ignorant, supposedly, of the sexual violence perpetrated on his wife. 'Probably he already knew, but I had finally managed, even if only on a piece of paper, to tell him.'[3] At a time when violence against women was more openly discussed, Franca felt an obligation to women to stage the piece and encourage debate about rape, but the courage always deserted her. In Lucca, in 1978, she finally found the strength to go through with it, but even then some concealment was needed. In post-performance discussions she maintained the subterfuge that the inspiration had come from an article in the women's periodical *Quotidiano donna*. There was hardly a word of her own, she claimed. She held to this fiction until November 1987, when she told the truth after performing the monologue on a Sunday afternoon television show, *Fantastico*.

There is no concealment in the writing, no ambiguity, no comedy, no grotesque, no retreat from the bitter, flint-hard truth.

> The blade they used to slit open my sweater is waved in front of my face a couple of times. I can't tell whether they've slashed me or not . . .
>
> 'Move your hips, whore . . . you're supposed to be giving me a good time!'
> Blood's trickling down my cheeks into my ears.
> Now it's the third one.
> It's disgusting to feel a man inside you like this . . . enjoying himself, grunting like a wild beast.[4]

Plainly, a work like this, as regards both writing and performance, is drawn from inner sources beyond conventional considerations of the art of the stage, but it remains a remarkable transcription of a pain beyond most people's imagining. Dario too wrote, or improvised, a piece on rape, but in his own style, with anger contained and shaped inside the grotesque. The difference in approach is instructive. His sketch, *The English Lawyer*, featured a medieval law-officer who defends a nobleman charged with rape by throwing the blame on to the girl. Fo employs *grammelot*, one of his favourite comic and satiric devices. Originally used, in his account, by the actors of *commedia dell'arte* in Paris to evade the attentions of the censors, *grammelot* is nonsense speech made to sound authentic by being delivered in the tones and accents of a particular language. In this monologue, Fo harangues an imaginary jury in mock-English cadences and inflexions, throwing in occasional genuine words to reinforce the illusion. In the prologue, however, he lets the mask of comedy slip. He had read, he said, a report of four men attacking and raping one woman, and although a lifelong opponent of capital punishment, he wonders whether it might be justified in certain cases. (He decides it is not.)

The case had been officially closed, but after Franca's 1987 broadcast it emerged that a neo-Fascist, Angelo Izzo, had told a court in Bologna of the collusion between right-wing terror groups and the Pastrengo division of the police. Izzo, already in jail for crimes of rape against two women, one of whom died, said the attack on Franca was aimed to intimidate her and warn her off the Red Aid work. He gave the name of one of the assailants, Angelo Angeli, and reported a startling conversation between two generals, Vito Miceli, then in charge of the secret services, and Giovanni Battista Palumbo, of the Pastrengo division. Miceli suggested that Palumbo should sever his links with the National Front, an extremist right-wing organization, while Palumbo retorted by reproaching Miceli for having coerced him into organizing illegal acts against Fo and Rame. Izzo was not believed and the magistrate declined to reopen investigations, but in 1998, Judge Guido Salvini confirmed Izzo's allegations in full. These inquiries revealed that the rape of Franca had been planned in the police stations of Milan, with the execution of the plan entrusted to thugs operating in the urban swamplands where common criminality and neo-Fascist terrorism met. Nicolò Bozzi, a *carabiniere* officer who later rose to the rank of general, gave an account of General Palumbo in line with Izzo's. When Bozzi informed his superior of the rape on Franca, he remembered vividly Palumbo's reaction. 'High time,' he said. Bozzi added that the news was 'greeted in the police offices with euphoria, the commander was celebrating as though he had pulled off some splendid operation'.[5]

In the hubbub created by the Salvini report, Franca spoke of what may have been another attempt at an apology. Years after the rape,

> the one who held me down started to phone me, telling me that he had become a decent man, that he wanted to meet me. I screamed in terror and slammed the phone down. Once, in the morning, a car blocked mine and a man came up to me to tell, 'I'm the one', but I made off in desperation, without even seeing his face.[6]

He, whoever he was, had nothing more to fear. Twenty-five years had elapsed between the crime and the publication of the report, which meant that under the Statute of Limitations, no prosecution could be mounted.

For all this private trauma, La Comune seemed to outsiders to be growing in self-confidence and prophetic dogmatism. According to the introduction to the third version of *I Think Things Over and Sing About Them*, which opened under Dario's direction in Genoa in February 1973, the task was no longer

> merely the recovery of the cultural values of the people . . . but *also* – and it is here that there has been in our eyes a substantial step forward in the production values inside the theatre collective – the indication of the alternative, not only stated at the ideological level (communism as strategic objective) but now present in the experience of the struggle.[7]

It may have been a step forward, and it may have seemed outwardly confident, but this was to be the last production of the cooperative. The same combination of ideological, professional and personal conflicts which had led to the break-up of Nuova Scena was creating tensions inside La Comune. The deterioration in relations and the atmosphere of growing distrust manifested themselves in the drafting of lengthy documents, night-long arguments over obscure ideological points, the summoning of interminable meetings and the endless clustering of factions in bars and foyers. The failure of socialism in one company was not an exhilarating spectacle. Those who thought that these tussles and squabbles could be resolved by an injection of the protein of ideology were mistaken. At stake were bruised feelings, basic emotions and primitive resentments that lay too deep for tracts. One unusually fanciful image gained currency during the crisis. La Comune was likened to a penny-farthing bicycle, but was this inequality – inequality being the cardinal sin of a Marxist–Maoist cooperative – of wheel size to be corrected by reducing the size of the penny or by expanding the farthing? The suggestion that the large wheel be reduced was advanced in all seriousness in assembly, although the means by which this could be achieved were not made clear. Franca countered with the proposition that surgeons and nurses could be regarded as equal, but that did not mean that a nurse should be left to perform operations. The distribution of labour and the employment of differing skills could be maintained, she suggested, without damaging the fundamental principle of equality of rights. Increasingly it appeared that the role of professionalism, or nature's unequal distribution of talent, created difficulties to which classical Marxism could provide no answer. La Comune was rich in stage-struck enthusiasts who could not accept the attribution of secondary roles in the process of writing and acting. The fact that reviews spoke of Dario and Franca, and not of the sterling efforts of the others, rankled. Routine matters, like instructions given by Dario as director to one member to enter stage left, caused ructions, which had to settled by an ad-hoc assembly. 'It is important not to confuse democracy with democraticism,' said Dario. 'Perhaps that is one of the biggest mistakes Franca and I have made.'[8] But once again the nature of the mistake is not clarified by the terminology. Franca added later, 'The dominant force in our collective had been a sort of damaging cult of democracy, which was the prime cause of so much dissent, so many conflicts and separations. Determined not to be star players, Dario and I committed the opposite error, in other words we had in fact left our collective without any real direction.'[9]

Many of the factions and groups operating inside the Movement had their own motives for fomenting trouble. Earlier socialists had given priority to education, but the distinguishing features of post-68 political activity was the tenacious belief in culture as the architecture of society. If culture could be revolutionized, the pillars of capitalism would crumble. Every groupuscule dedicated itself not only to pamphleteering, agitation and demonstrations but also to the establishment of a network for the diffusion of a new, radical culture. It seemed to strategic executives of various groups that La Comune, properly infiltrated and directed, provided a ready-made vehicle for this kind of work. Its leaflets already carried slogans declaring it to be 'For A Revolutionary Culture, and Against the Bosses' Culture'. Dario was the main prize, and he shared the belief in the revolutionary potential of culture:

> And here it is worthwhile to recall – even at the cost of repeating ourselves and seeming tiresome – but only to certain advocates of the 'the only hope is with the gun' line – what Mao had to say: 'No culture, no revolution . . . A man without culture will never be a real revolutionary. At the most he will be a rebel. A man without culture is like an empty sack. In the wind of the revolution, that sack will be inflated and will seem full and powerful, but when it rains, and it often rains in the revolution, you will find that sack soaking at your feet, to trip you up.'[10]

He was disconcerted when Lotta Continua set up October circles as its own national circuit of political–cultural clubs. Several members left La Comune to join up with the new body, a move Dario Fo denounced as 'sectarian' in a 1972 document circulated around the company with the title 'Our tasks on the Cultural Front'. He complained that the competition between La Comune and the new body

> takes place not on a political but on an economic level. The October circles give the impression of a commercial activity pure and simple. They are justified by the comrades of Lotta Continua themselves as a branch of the group, entrusted with the task of collecting funds for the newspaper or other activities of the group.
>
> Following this logic, you could 'hire' authors who 'have a following' and who bring in cash, like Pasolini and other members of the bourgeois cultural world . . . the comrades of Lotta Continua display an attitude of mean manipulativeness vis à vis cultural work. Showing films or organizing recitals of songs takes on the prime function of making money . . .[11]

The broadly supportive Milan circle produced a paper of its own in March 1973, snappily entitled 'For a Revolutionary Culture at the Service of the Class Struggle Under the Guidance of the Workers' Vanguards'.[12] It traced in tedious detail the evolution of the group, identifying a first phase when it was no more than an extension of the theatre company, followed by a second phase when it developed its autonomous political life and faced the problem of 'mass intervention in communities, in factories, in schools'. If the theatrical collective was now only one branch of a broader organization, Dario saw his autonomy threatened. This problem of liberty of action was aggravated when Avanguardia Operaia, another of the legion of Marxist movements of the extreme left, started manouevring to reduce La Comune to the status of a branch of their movement. Harsh words flew. Dario and Franca refused to forfeit their right to write and act as they saw fit, and resisted all attempts to reduce the theatre collective to a platform for one group. For their pains, they found themselves accused of heinous and incomprehensible deviations such as 'bureaucraticism' and 'adventurism'.

This fresh dispute needed fresh jargon. Dario and Franca declined to move from being 'militants at the service of the working class' to being 'artists of the left'. The distinction was an elusive one, but an artist of the left was ultimately a servant of a party line, or a hired pen. To be viewed as 'artists of the left', wrote Franca, meant 'accepting compromises, being prone to opportunism, losing all rigour not only as regards the writing of scripts but also, and especially, as regards collective and individual behaviour, both externally and internally'.[13] Neither would countenance this demotion or loss of say over strictly political or artistic matters. In that topsy-turvy world, Dario found himself fighting the same battle for autonomy and against censorship he had waged with the executive at RAI during the *Canzonissima* fracas. As well as being involved in an ideological struggle, Dario was also engaged in a battle to win for himself the conditions in which his own talent could flourish. His model remained Mayakovsky, who retained the jester's freedom to mock and to appeal to a sense of humanity which the Bolshevik commissars lost after 1917.

Dario was now facing a third split. After the break with commercial theatre in 1968 and with Nuova Scena and the PCI in 1970, he was now cutting adrift from elements of the Movement. This time it was not of his choosing, and at a final assembly of the cooperative in July 1973, in the Milan circle, Franca and Dario remained silent but came out deflated. Franca, who was still recovering from her own ordeal, resigned first, followed by Dario. The split was rancorous and poisonous, marked by petty acts of uncomradely dishonesty. It was discovered that one member, who had access to the bank accounts, had been giving herself and her husband a rise, even although the assembly had turned down the request. The company accounts were looted. Two signatures, that of Franca and another member, were needed on company cheques, and statutes laid down that no cheque could be for more than one million lire. On the day after the split, Franca had a phone call from the bank to say that the other signatory was coming to the bank every hour, to withdraw sums of one million lire. 'Let her,' said Franca. Since Dario and Franca took the decision to leave, they abandoned their rights to company property. All the props, stage equipment and costumes which had been accumulated in the course of their life in theatre were lost. During the debate, they formed the impression that Avanguardia Operaia sided with the faction which would command the reflectors and lights. Even the van remained with the rump of the company. It was found abandoned and rusting about a year later.

Officially, Paolo Ciarchi, the group's musician, took over as president and La Comune remained in being, although not for long, but on this occasion Dario and Franca decided that they too wished to maintain the company name, which they modified to 'Theatrical Collective La Comune Directed by Dario Fo'. The other Comune publicly expelled people like Lanfranco Binni for incomprehensible sins such as 'a vocation to scissionism'.[14] When Dario's company resumed performing, the other faction rushed to inform the left-wing press of his dubious right to the company title. They did admit that Dario was indeed still formally a member of La Comune 'inasmuch as he is not expelled', but was 'not centralized to it'.[15] With the break-up of La Comune, unlike the splintering of Nuova Scena, a watershed had been reached. Dario and Franca had been forced to the rueful conclusion that the cooperative was not a viable structure in theatre, and that plays could not be mounted if all decisions were devolved to assemblies. La Comune had hardly been a United Artists in the first place, and it may of course be that this disparity of talent was not something which could be incorporated within an egalitarian ideology. In London at about the same time, Kenneth Halliwell was hacking Joe Orton to death because he could not breathe in his shadow, but could not flee it either. In Milan, no axes were wielded and no human flesh was torn, but the emotional havoc was immense.

That summer, there were other problems which pursued Dario. In June, the Ministry for Entertainment chose to issue a circular which, although not mentioning him by name, was dubbed by the media the Dario Fo Law. Its small print stated that theatrical subsidies would be made only to companies 'who perform in public places or in places open to the public, and to which the public can have access by the acquisition of a regular ticket'. It was a classic sting. Fo could not play in public places as defined by the law and was now being refused a subsidy to perform in the private spaces willing to host him. At the same time, the *Canzonissima* affair made a reappearance. The Appeal Court decided Dario and Franca were after all responsible for the disruption of the programme, and ordered them to pay 26 million lire damages.

Dario retreated to his villa in Cernobbio on Lake Como. He was now forty-seven, at what should have been the peak of his creative career, but he found himself isolated. He has never found it difficult to occupy his time. When not working, he can absorb himself in the most diverse activities, from watching B-movies on television to painting, cooking risotto or indulging his interest in cycling races or Formula One motor racing. More than one admirer has been disconcerted to be invited home after a performance only to have his expectations of stimulating conversation on life and theatre dashed by the spectacle of Dario slumped happily and vacantly in front of a television screen, surfing mindlessly through the channels. He conserves his energy for essential activities. That summer he spent some time working on a collection of puppets he had been assembling pell-mell.

Both Dario and Franca felt they had been cheated and wronged, that they had made sacrifices of their own talents and resources only to be met with malicious misrepresentation and querulous disapprobation. Political quarrels with opponents were expected, but wounds left by squabbles with former friends or comrades were deep and hurtful. Since his début, Dario had constructed and dismantled companies, had attracted and discarded successive audiences, be they bourgeois, Communist activists or New-Left militants. Perhaps there was a fundamental clash between his politics, with the primacy of democracy and equality they entailed, and his theatrical talents, which required selfish self-assertion. Leaving aside the special case of Franca, he had not been able to form a lasting professional or artistic relationship with the various actors who had joined his companies. He aroused in his colleagues either useless adulation or unfocused resentment, so that, although personally endowed with bonhomie and generosity, he had been involved in polemics and disputes all his working life. It is striking how often the less resentful explanations offered by others for the various breaks involve some inchoate expression of the sheer impossibility of inhabiting a shadow as vast as his. During the death throes of La Comune, some gentle spirit with a touch of poetry in his soul complained that 'you cannot live always in the shadow of an oak tree; even the little trees must breathe'.[16] Others spoke in more curmudgeonly and embittered tones.

Now he was once again on his own and unsure of the next step. The cooperative was officially dead. His new company might maintain the name La Comune, but the qualification 'Directed by Dario Fo' was important. The troupe was now a more conventional hire-and-fire company. For some years, he had been writing three major texts for the company per season. Summer was the season when he found most liberty to write, but that summer he wrote no major new work. Sections of the press were openly exultant, and there were sneering articles which suggested he was to be viewed as the flotsam and jetsam of a failed experiment.

There were other personal ramifications to the break-up. Dario and Franca had been planning to live in a kind of commune with friends from La Comune. Land had been bought, division of property made and plans drawn up for seven detached houses in the same compound. With the growth of families and the endless bureaucratic delays, these plans were modified to one large block of flats with a communal area. Dario and Franca offered loans to the others, and when the local people objected to the lack of nursery facilities in the area, offered to incorporate a nursery into the building. This caused dissent, since some of the members worried about the consequent depreciation of value of property and, good socialists as they were, even worried about having their children mix with the locals. When the work was almost completed, some of the others moved in, but the Fos, who were to have had two flats in the complex, delayed. With the breakdown of friendships occasioned by the split, and rising fears occasioned by the neo-Fascist attacks on the two of them, they were told they were no longer welcome. Franca threatened legal proceedings and went into the property to recover some of her belongings. The architect in charge of the scheme accused her of having raided his office and taking keys. He raised an action, at which allegations against her were dismissed, but the couple were awarded only 170 million lire in recompense for 700 million lire they had invested in the project.

In spite of the break-up of the company, Dario and Franca continued to receive appeals for help from trade unions and striking workers. To dramatize specific conflicts on the spot, Dario devised a new sort of improvised 'theatre of intervention', jokingly called a 'field-mass' after the open-air, religious ceremonies celebrated by military chaplains. They performed at a 'march for peace' in the Veneto, appeared in support of an anti-Fascist demonstration in Pavia and put on a sketch in the port town of Marghera near Venice, where some men were on trial, charged with public-order offences committed in the course of a 1969 industrial dispute. In Pescara, where some fifty prisoners were accused of offences committed during a prison riot, the group familiarized themselves with the facts of the case and, while the trial was in progress, made them the subject of an improvised, satirical, deliberately grotesque performance with the title, *God, Fatherland and Prison*.

> The people knew nothing about it, they were uninformed. We gave a theatrical form to what was going on in the trial . . . inventing situations, improvising . . . certainly there was none of the fine rhythm, none of that marvellous balance when voices, lights, timing, cut-and-thrust merge . . . there was very little that could give the satisfaction of 'fine theatre' . . . it was all chopped up with axes . . . but, according to the comrades who were there, who saw the performance as an echo chamber for their political work, this was all right; they said 'more of these plays, even if they are indifferent' – (yes, indifferent, because we were not especially pleased with it ourselves).[17]

The collection of material on the Resistance continued, and both were enchanted by an encounter with a large, effervescent woman known as Mamma Togni. After her husband and son had been slaughtered by the Germans, she interrupted a speech by an official of the Republic of Salò and drove him away from the microphone with a club. A monologue based on her experiences became part of Franca's repertoire.

Prison conditions would have formed the subject of their next work, had Dario not been galvanized by the violent overthrow, on the night of 10–11 September 1973, of Salvador Allende, Marxist President of Chile. Parallels between Chile and Italy had been frequently invoked throughout the 1970s. The Italian Christian Democrats had good relations with their Chilean counterparts, while the PCI was inspired by Allende's success at the polls. However, party officials were dismayed at how casually democracy could be overthrown when it produced results displeasing to local capital or to the Pentagon's ideal geopolitical map. While many of his followers took to the streets in rage, PCI leader Enrico Berlinguer made a more detached analysis and developed a policy known as the 'historic compromise'. In his view, the coup demonstrated that the greatest threat facing a Communist Party after electoral victory was 'isolation in power' and exposure to American intervention. He announced that, irrespective of the majority it might eventually win, the PCI would make an 'historic compromise' by seeking a coalition with its traditional opponents, the Christian Democrats. Dario dissented from this line. The coup reinforced his belief that the support given by moneyed classes to democracy was a sham, and that any attempt by the PCI to win middle-class approval by a rightward drift was both doomed to failure and a dereliction of revolutionary heritage.

Allende's overthrow provided Fo with a passion and a cause which shook him out of his lethargy. In slightly over a month, he produced *The People's War in Chile*, a denunciation of the military aggression in Santiago which also took Chile as a metaphor for Italy. Initially, the play was conceived as an angry monologue to be delivered by Franca in the role of a painted whore, an allegory for the Chilean Christian Democrat Party. This character was retained in the final version, with the whore expressing a gamut of changing convictions, denouncing Allende on his election, hailing the coup, then growing horrified when the military turned on the Christian Democrats and finally begging foreign support for a popular, anti-Fascist front. Dario altered and added as rehearsals proceeded. He expanded the work in length and scope to incorporate the piece on Mamma Togni as well as a collage of monologues and sketches reflecting the experiences of anti-Fascists in Chile and Italy. Among the Chilean and Italian songs in the show, the compositions of the folk-singer Victor Jara, who had his fingers cut off before being murdered in the Santiago football stadium, featured strongly.

The overall style was of the tried and tested variety, except for one new device, or 'provocation', which gave the play a startling, controversial force.[18] During the performance, Dario wore a collar microphone and, in the midst of a denunciation of Pinochet, the audience heard a crackling noise, seemingly interference, come over the line, followed by what appeared to be a policeman's voice ordering patrol cars to take a detour to the north. Fo stopped in mid-phrase, eyes wide in mock consternation, joking with the audience that these policemen had been on his tail for days and now they were even interrupting the performance. The interference became more and more frequent, giving the impression that the patrol cars were bound for the theatre. Someone from the body of the theatre shouted that the telephone lines were down and that the radio had gone dead. Fo attempted to maintain calm, until another voice shouted, in supposed reassurance, that nothing could really be happening since 'this is Italy. It's not as if we are in Greece, or Chile. We have the Communist Party, trade unions here ... a *coup d'état* couldn't happen here.' The door burst open and a uniformed officer strode up on to the stage to announce that the performance was suspended and read out the names of local activists who were to accompany him to the police station for questioning. The intention was that at this point a plant in the audience would start singing the Internazionale, which was to be taken up by the whole audience as an act of defiance, like the exiled French in *Casablanca* breaking into the Marseillaise. The individuals named were to believe that they were enjoying their last moments of freedom before an uncertain future, but in the course of the singing, the police officers were themselves to climb on to the stage, raise their clenched fists in the air and join in the chants. The stage directions recount that 'the audience will remain for a moment astonished, before realizing that they have been duped. The reactions are various and always unpredictable. From here, an extremely lively debate *invariably* develops.'[19]

In fact, Dario's plausible inventiveness created mayhem on a par with Orson Welles's radio version of *War of the Worlds*. One unfortunate lad in Turin swallowed his address book for fear of incriminating comrades; another tried to throw himself out of a window, while yet another had to suffer the humiliation of watching his mother hurl herself, in spite of the efforts of Franca to restrain her, on to the 'police officer', screaming that her son had nothing to do with any extremist organization. The same selfless thespian in uniform was several times threatened with knives. As a theatrical device, the false coup was a stunning success, but Dario was criticized by right and left for going over the top and devising a bluff of undue realism and violence. In some quarters, it was suggested that he had trivialized the seriousness of a real situation in Chile and of a potential threat in Italy. He rejected such accusations scornfully and declared himself satisfied that he had both aroused the active reaction he had sought and had made clear the parallels between Italy and Chile.

In November, the schedule took the company to Sassari, in Sardinia, where they rented the Rex cinema for performances of the Chile play and *Mistero buffo*. The local police chief, Renato Voria, sent a request to see the script of the new play, but was refused. On 8 November, he dispatched some fifty police officers to the performance. Fo refused them entrance but the performance was cancelled and the evening given over to public discussion on police activity. The following day, the police turned up during rehearsals. When Fo once again tried to prevent their entry into the hall, the officer in charge had him arrested. Some of Dario's colleagues seized hold

of him and for a time he was hauled this way and that until the police succeeded in handcuffing him and leading him off to the station. He was
charged with 'resistance and verbal violence to a public official'.

The Italian press corps descended on Sassari, and the story was the lead
in every television news bulletin and made the headlines in most papers. A
photographer was somehow on hand to record the sight of Fo in handcuffs
being led off, somewhat plaintively, to prison. Even those elements of the
PCI which had been distrustful of Fo expressed their outrage at the conduct of the local police. In the town itself, a committee for the release of
Dario Fo was instantly set up and groups marched on the prison to establish a permanent vigil outside the walls. Some marchers reported hearing
the inmates reply with a chorus of 'The Red Flag'. Franca and the other
members of the company joined the picket, converting the demonstration
into a 'happening'. Franca climbed on to the top of a car which had been
requisitioned and performed various pieces, including 'Mamma Togni'. In
her account:

> [Dario] was arrested in the evening. That night there was a demonstration
> for Chile, and the representatives of the various groups, parties and trade
> unions agreed on the times and routes of the protest marches for the fol-
> lowing day. The schools went on strike. There was an enormous procession.
> Some shepherds arrived even from Orgosolo. At the same time, for reasons
> of their own, the bakers too were on strike, and when they saw our demon-
> stration they found out what was going on and they too joined in. The
> march stopped in front of the prison to welcome Dario, who was expected
> to be coming out after the interrogation by the judge. But he never seemed
> to be coming, and so while we were waiting we decided to put on a play. They
> put me on top of a Cinquecento, between the police and the demonstrators;
> the police were lined up at my back, with the people at the front looking at
> me. On this unusual stage, I performed from ten o'clock until a quarter to
> two, with other colleagues taking a turn. We brought the bakers up on stage
> too, to explain their problems; everybody was enthusiastic.[20]

These words were written later, but at the time the outcome was not so
certain. Dario was kept in captivity from 7.30 in the evening on 9
November until 2.30 the following afternoon, during which time he neither
ate nor slept. He later said that when they put the handcuffs on him, the
thought flashed into his mind that the coup really had taken place in Italy,
but that most of the time he was aware of the preposterousness of the
whole episode. The public outcry was such that he had to be released as

quickly as the proprieties of the law would permit, but for all the harlequinade which attended it, the matter was serious enough. An actor in a democratic state had been taken from stage to prison cell for attempting to express views which were permitted on any reading of the constitution. Fo was aware that performers, minstrels, strolling players, tumblers and mountebanks had been subjected throughout history to persecution and repression, and that only in this century had the actor been tamed by being converted into an object of cult in a religion of celebrity. The paradox was that Fo was a danger precisely because of his celebrity. One has to assume that some anonymous enthusiast from the acting profession would have performed unharassed. The further paradox was that the attentions of those same Sardinian police ensured that Dario Fo again became a force in public life.

Since the break-up of La Comune, the smart judgement was that he was a busted flush, that the Movement he had served was now tottering and that Fo would disappear under the growing force of the backlash. Sassari brought Fo back to public attention and he emerged with renewed vigour and self-belief. He was the object of various discussion forums and profiles in newspapers and magazines, most of which were unexpectedly eulogistic. The magazine *Panorama* produced a special supplement in which they asked various ex-collaborators, like Nuccio Ambrosino, or prominent theatre people, such as Giorgio Strehler and Paolo Grassi, to express their views on the event. Whatever blows they had received from Fo in the past, they all weighed in with sincere support. The main exception was Pier Paolo Pasolini, perhaps still smarting from Fo's attack on him earlier in the year. 'My opinion on Dario Fo and his work is so negative that I refuse to speak of him,' he opined, before going on to give the view he had refused to give. 'Fo is a kind of plague on Italian theatre.'[21] It was out of tune with the mood of the moment but a fitting epitaph for a miserable year.

Chapter 8

Occupations

In January 1974, Dario was invited to perform *Mistero buffo* in three venues – Chaillot, Besançon and Paris – in France. A French journalist, dispatched to interview him in Trento, was amazed to discover that although there were no posters announcing where he was performing, her taxi-driver was able to get the information from the first passer-by. Her greetings to Dario were interrupted by a call from the mayor of the next stop on the tour, to inform him that the police had raised objections to the hire of the theatre. 'In Italy,' she wrote, 'Dario Fo is a kind of national phenomenon, a sort of Marxist Maurice Chevalier . . . Even if "little difficulties" prevent people from knowing in advance where he is performing, the most varied crowds people (students, middle class, workers, peasants) flock to see him wherever he performs.'

While in France, Fo met the distinguished actor and director, Jean-Louis Barrault, who had also abandoned conventional theatre in 1968 but who had managed to establish his own permanent theatre, the Lilà, a disused railway station on the outskirts of Paris. The meeting heightened Dario's dissatisfaction with the nomadic life he had been required to live since his eviction from the Capannone, and on his return to Milan he made contact with the city council to enquire about renting one of the city's many empty buildings for use as a theatre. The councillor in charge of council properties was the socialist Carlo Tognoli, an admirer of Fo's work.

The first response was promising. The two men visited various properties, and the choice fell on the disused Palazzina Liberty. The term 'Liberty' had nothing to do with freedom in this case, but was derived from the famous Liberty's shop in London and denoted art nouveau. Built around 1930, it had originally been a central part of the fruit and vegetable market and was left standing in solitary splendour in the middle of a park when the market was transferred to another site. It is a striking building, incorporating those elements of the pseudo-classical which could be reconciled with modernism. The royal crown and the coat of arms of the House of Savoy still stand atop the main entrance, while mosaics depicting a young woman languidly picking oranges in some mythic grove decorate the walls. Narrow columns surmounted by lions' heads and little carved bunches of grapes leave space for grand oriel windows, and the whole is fronted by a long balcony which had never had any practical use until Fo pressed it into service as a stage. By the 1970s, it was in a state of decay and only the intervention of Italy's leading conservation society, Italia Nostra, blocked proposals to have it demolished.

Tognoli and Fo reached an agreement on rent and the keys were handed over. In view of later developments and myths, it is worth emphasizing that the first moves were made in strict accordance with the law of contract. The understanding was that the company would be responsible for the restoration of the building and would oversee the provision of community facilities, including a library, crèche and rooms for meetings and various activities, all in addition to their own theatrical activities. In mid-March, Dario and La Comune Theatrical Collective took possession. However, once Tognoli's initiative was announced to the council, the Christian Democrats reacted with fury. In retrospect, granted Fo's notoriety, it seems curious that Tognoli had not done more to square his coalition partners, but the matter was clearly within his departmental competence and he had secured an excellent deal for the council. Additional revenue was guaranteed, the council would remain owners of the building and the restoration work of an unused architectural jewel would be carried out by La Comune. Had it been anyone else, political agreement would have been a formality, but the Christian Democrats in Milan regarded Fo as an enemy. Massimo De Carolis, the local party leader, declared his outright, indeed, his enraged, opposition to the move. De Carolis was already an important figure within the Christian Democratic Party, the DC, nationally, and would shortly enter parliament.

The council backtracked and, in a hastily convened meeting of 30 March, Dario was ordered to surrender the keys and evacuate the building. He refused, and from that moment the occupation of Palazzina Liberty began. This was the time of occupations, whether by tenants of apartment blocks or by workers of factories, but this case was different. Dario was entitled to believe he had been treated wretchedly. He had behaved with the propriety of a businessman-cum-philanthropist. He had undertaken to pay a fair rent, to restore life to a neglected building and to provide facilities to a run-down area of the city, only to have his good intentions flung rudely back in his face for the meanest and crudest of political motives. Certainly he had, to say the least, done nothing to ingratiate himself with the Christian Democrats, but their conduct now confirmed all he had been saying about the nature of power and the standards of those who exercised it.

The company and its supporters swung into action. They organized a petition and gathered perhaps as many as 20,000 signatures in support. Work was already under way on a building whose only inhabitants were mice and rats. Processions of lorries carted away rubbish of all kinds and members of the group, aided by local people, started cleaning, scrubbing, brushing, painting and repairing. Meetings with residents in the neighbourhood were arranged and, after an early stand-off, local people formed the view that a revitalized Palazzina would be an asset. Several of them turned up with pots of paint they claimed to have found lying uselessly around their houses, while others were craftsmen with valuable skills. Dario, with his architect's training, got to work on plans to transform the interior. Meetings were held each evening to discuss progress, and it was a matter of policy to schedule these meetings at a time convenient for everyone.

On 31 March, the day after the council decision, a Committee for the Popular and Democratic Utilisation of the Palazzina was established. The red flag was unfurled. The first big rally in the surrounding parkland took place on 7 April, drawing a crowd whose size was estimated by various sources at anything between five and fifteen thousand people. Contemporary photographs show Fo, every inch the Roman tribune, standing on the raised balcony performing the 'Lazarus' and 'The Marriage Feast at Cana' from *Mistero buffo*, together with a short extract from Molière. Even for a man accustomed to playing to huge audiences in arenas, it was an astonishing *tour de force*. Those at the back could scarcely see him and certainly could not follow any facial expressions or gestures. The stage was the balcony which ran round the building and he performed without props, costumes or fellow actors, yet held the attention of a vast audience, many of whom were anything but theatregoers. No doubt the general exhilaration of trespassing, of taking part in an act of impudence against the authorities, contributed to the prevailing mood of shared excitement, but this was a day recalled later with delight by those who participated.

It was not all beer and skittles, for Dario demanded that attention be paid to local and national politics. Italy was about to face a referendum on divorce. Legislation legalizing divorce had been passed by parliament but the Christian Democrats, led by Amintore Fanfani, had gathered the signatures needed to force a referendum to repeal the new law. The Communist Party entered the referendum campaign unwillingly, afraid not only of defeat but of a setback for their new strategy of alliance with the Christian Democrats. Fo promised that the Palazzina could be used as headquarters and meeting place for the many groups involved in the pro-divorce side. He satirized the Milanese Christian Democratic Party, but in an oblique way, through an adaptation of the story of Fra Dolcino, the medieval Franciscan dissident who had featured in the earlier *Always Blame the Devil*. It is hard to imagine any other agitator advocating socialist policies by reference to one of the leading heresiarchs of the Middle Ages.

The mass meeting was asked to approve a very bureaucratically worded motion backing the occupation and attacking the council. 'Enough of the illusory, hypocritical promises of the council which seeks only the demolition of the Palazzina, in the same way as the Christian Democrat government allows the destruction of factories and countryside, in accordance with a logic that serves the profits of the boss class.' According to the motion, the Palazzina was to become:

1. A centre for *popular artistic production* open to all.
2. A centre for *cultural and political debate* at the service of the workers.

The Committee proposes the following initiatives:
- Opening of a *school of popular theatre* directed by Dario Fo, open to all young workers and students.
- Formation of *collectives of artistic production*.
- Organization of *plays for children*.
- Works by the *La Comune Theatrical Collective Directed by Dario Fo*, and other theatrical groups from Italy and abroad, who identify themselves with this struggle.
- Projection of *cycles of films and audiovisuals*.
- An *exhibition of popular art* open to workers, students, with the participation of progressive artists who support our programme.
- Cycle of *meetings, debates and conferences* (above all a series of initiatives connected with the *referendum*) and the opening of a *library* for further study of the subjects under discussion.
- Opening of a *nursery* where the children of participants at the plays and other initiatives of the centre can be left, and where the children can play together, be looked after and live collectively.
- A *weekly bulletin of information* on the Palazzina struggle.
- A *national propaganda campaign* on these issues.

Never before had italics been given such an overtly polemical purpose. In the following days, the professional sceptics and cynics of right and left joined in a chorus of syncopated derision. Where is the money to come from? Do not people today prefer soap operas to the frantic pursuit of artistic excellence (popular or otherwise)? Is not Fo a dreamer when he is not a dangerous fanatic? Should we not simply give him enough rope and leave him hang himself? No doubt Fo is a dreamer, a Utopian dreamer with a boundless optimism in the capacities of the human animal, and in this project his Utopian visions had the freest of reins. The Palazzina, according to these schemes, or dreams, was a combination of the Pompidou Centre and the Abbey of Theleme. The Utopian reformers and optimistic visionaries of Europe, that tribe of impatient improvers of man's estate, were leaning over his shoulder as he penned his manifesto for the building. His schemes had a breadth and nobility to rival those of such radical pioneers as William Morris, Robert Owen, John Ruskin or indeed Antonio Gramsci. Like them, he aimed to unleash in the individual a creativity which had been stifled, to encourage the growth of multi-sided talents and to foster joy, happiness and a more glorious world. The individual was to be enhanced as an individual so as to attain the fullest richness of mind available to each. That is not the manifesto of dull politics, and indeed, this project eschewed direct political activity – if one excepts the room left for debates and conferences – in favour of cultural activity. The programme rested on the conviction that education and the cultivated mind were the prerequisites of social change, and that socialism was an attainment of the spirit before it could be a rule of society. The proposal voted on that day had the grandeur of an ideal, even if it provided easy meat for scoffers.

The city council, indifferent to these high-minded utterances, were still intent on having Fo removed. On 10 April they offered to reimburse the company for the work they had done, but the offer was rejected. In off-the-record briefings, council spokespeople made reference to the presence among the occupiers of revolutionary groups who advocated violence, and used Franca's plan to establish Red Aid headquarters in the Palazzina to justify vague and wholly unsubstantiated hints that the building was a den of terrorists or a hiding place for fugitives from justice. The suggestion was whispered that if only Dario and Franca were to separate themselves from the extremists around them, the council would see them accommodated elsewhere in Milan. A deconsecrated church in some working-class area was mentioned, but no one was hoodwinked as to the seriousness of the offer. There followed the kind of harlequinade, dictated by bamboozlement, which often attended the conduct of public affairs in Italy at that time. The council sent a team of workmen to construct a fence around the Palazzina. A crowd of local people gathered to demonstrate and the two sides faced each other with largely good-natured tolerance for a couple of hours until the council employees concluded they were all members of the same working class, downed tools and went home. The council cut off electricity supplies but this was made good by the gift of a generator which provided energy for all the activities of restoration and creation.

Fo performed to another huge crowd on May Day. The park was flooded with people, while stalls selling food, trinkets and pamphlets were arranged inside and outside the building. Various bodies, including the Radical Party, the Proletarian Bookshop, the Manifesto Group, Lotta Continua and Avanguardia Operaia, not to mention several groupings of radical students, came to demonstrate support. Two days later, the council instituted court proceedings, but since the mayor, Aldo Aniasi, failed to appear in person, the hearing was postponed until 17 May. The court duly decided in favour of the council, and Fo was ordered by the magistrate to leave the building. He entered an immediate appeal which was, to general surprise, upheld. The Appeal Court agreed that entry into the Palazzina had been made in accordance with a legal agreement, and held that the council had been unduly cavalier in overturning it. The order compelling La Comune to leave was rescinded. The council counter-appealed. Court cases were to drag on for years, but in the meantime Dario and Franca had possession of their theatre. The police kept the Palazzina under continual surveillance. Fo's lawyer, the Sicilian Giovanni Piscopo, recalls meeting police agents whom he recognized prowling around the Palazzina in disguise. When challenged, they replied that they were having their evening stroll. Others were prepared to employ more brutal means. On 13 June, sticks of dynamite were discovered in a telephone box in the street nearby.

Fo challenged Massimo De Carolis to a public debate. The offer was accepted, provided it took place not in the Palazzina Liberty but before an invited audience in the local Christian Democrat office. There was, as was to be expected, no meeting of minds. De Carolis was an astute politician, confident of his own position and not likely to be cowed by Fo's wit or irony. His case was that Fo had every right in a democracy to full freedom of opinion, but no right to preferential treatment. What was Fo's entitlement to the use of public property when his purpose was to establish a platform from which to express subversive views? Fo retorted that the core of the problem was the role of culture in society. He attacked the Christian

Democrats for having supervised the decline and degradation of cinema and television, and for resorting to censorship when they risked losing the argument. Had the DC sunk to the level of replying to ideas by recourse to (metaphorical) violence? De Carolis rejected the accusation, saying that revolutionaries like Fo had always been spoiled by the system, and concluded that if the Palazzina Liberty were to be given to anyone, it should not be to Fo, who would use it from morning to evening to spit on the Christian Democrats. He was undoubtedly right. Fo had never had any hesitation in biting the few hands which fed him.

Meanwhile, the transformation of the Palazzina was in full swing. The company scoured Milan for seating, but discovered on several occasions that would-be benefactors received phone calls advising them against association with Dario Fo. Undaunted, Fo announced that 'the occupation of the Palazzina Liberty is one of the most important shows we have ever produced'. The Chilean artist Sebastian Matta painted a series of grand murals in his own idiosyncratic style, combining elements of magic realism, allegory, pure fantasy and political spleen. The subject of the cycle was *The Death of the General*, showing the assassination of a warlord. This work adorned the main hall of the Palazzina, and now hangs above Franca's desk in her office.

Dario intended to open the premises with *God, Fatherland and Prison,* a play he had on the stocks, but he decided the moment was not right and it was again postponed. Instead, the Ferrari company of puppeteers, with a workshop on the history of puppets in the morning and a show in the afternoon, became the first company actually to perform in the Palazzina. In the first three months of occupation, twenty-five theatre troupes as well as twenty groups of singers, from Italy and abroad, took the stage. Dario's own first production was one of his few complete flops. Still anxious to establish continuity with popular culture from other periods, he had been reading two dialect poets, the Milanese Carlo Porta and the Roman G. C. Belli. In May, he put on a script which was barely more than a dramatized reading, *Porta and Belli Against Power*, but it pleased no one and was withdrawn after a week.

The promised playgroups and workshops for children were instituted. The Xerox copier, an indispensable instrument of left-wing activity in the era before the photocopier, was installed and bulletins began to be produced in profusion. The inhabitants of the neighbourhood were bombarded with earnest little leaflets, some written in the jargon of the time but others couched in the spirited irony which is Fo's own trademark.

One much appreciated leaflet read: 'After years of being left to enjoy themselves in the Palazzina Liberty, *The Mice Wish to Thank the Christian Democrats for the efforts they have put into preventing the Palazzina being taken away from them and saved from collapse.*' The city fathers looked on aghast as demonstrations followed one after the other in the park around the Palazzina. On 9 June, demonstrators gathered to protest against 'imperialism, Zionism and internal repression in the Middle East'.

In mid-June, the Palazzina hosted a grand, three-day Conference on Culture. According to leaflets distributed in the neighbourhood, discussion was to focus on lessons learned from the take-over of the Palazzina, move on to the role of the intellectual as producer of culture and lead to the identification of common ground on this topic between rival strands of left-wing thinking. It was optimistically promised that the use of abstract or ideological jargon would be outlawed in favour of the examination of practical experience, but since the event drew an impressive number of scholars, researchers, journalists, theatre practitioners, political activists and members of far-left formations, the possibility of prohibiting polysyllabic speech was remote. The event offered Dario, who is more a polemicist than a systematic thinker, an occasion for clarifying to himself his own thinking on popular culture. He thinks as well with a microphone as with a pen in hand, and responds best to the provocations and prompts of debate, leaving it to others to impose structure and form on the views which emerge. His forte is the lively phrase or the unexpected insight enlightened by a combination of wit and lively imagination, but always based on genuine knowledge. His reading has been wide and it provides him with a private library of quotes, many of which have unfortunately never been uttered by the writers to whom they are attributed, but which serve to illustrate the tenor of his own thinking.

Since the break-up of the first version of La Comune, Dario had spent many anxious hours reconsidering the relationship between art and politics, and specifically trying to determine which should have primacy. Socialism and the revolution – he never attempted to define exactly what 'revolution' entailed – constituted the only creed he professed, but all around him he heard voices suggesting that art was *de trop* in the political struggle, or that, in his own phrase, the artists were 'like confetti, or the filling of a cake or the trimmings alongside the main course'.[1] The artist, he feared, was expected to view himself as the clown in motley whose task was to drum up interest and entice the crowd but to move aside when it came to the serious work of propaganda and agitation. Slightly less fearsome was the possibility, which at different times Mayakovsky and Vittorini had rebelled against, that the writer would be required to create according to preordained paradigms, and forfeit autonomy of action. Fo was anxious to establish in his own mind his right to an autonomous space and to demonstrate, at least to himself, the political value of his work as writer and performer. The dangers and benefits of amalgamating political discussion with entertainment had always intrigued him, but the encroachment of self-appointed commissars instinctively appalled him. Fortunately, Lenin and Mao were on hand to lend him support.

> The concern is, and we are reminded of it in downright peremptory terms, to recall Lenin's phrase, a phrase which is too frequently distorted: 'What is art? Art is a small cog in the mechanism of the class struggle.' Well then, this cog has become smaller and smaller in the minds of many comrades of the various groups, to the point where it has become superfluous. In other words, they mean that if you remove this cog, the class struggle will go forward under its own steam. No, when Lenin spoke of the cog, he did not mean it was superfluous. He said that this cog was as important as other larger cogs. Without the cog of culture, without the cog of art, of class art obviously, the machine would not go forward. It may be small, but it is important to understand that it is essential, that it is part of the whole problem of revolution.

Mao was even more helpful.

> Mao says: a man without culture will never be a revolutionary. At most he will be a rebel . . . So, it is clear, without culture there will be no revolution. And what does Mao mean by culture? He means another vision of the world, he means changed relationships between men. He means a particular concept of love between people, one quite different from that which the bourgeoisie expresses, for theirs expresses all the forces of capitalism. Mao insists that *before* the revolution cultural work must begin, that *during* the revolution there must be cultural work and that *after* the revolution cultural work must continue.[2]

There was no appeal against such masters. Art was not a flimsy wrapping designed to make palatable the stern maxims of *Das Kapital*, but an indispensable element of a life devoted to the 'struggle', that other voguish word trotted out at conventions. Dario, however, was still in search of some overall poetic of popular culture and of the kernel of difference between it and the hegemonic culture. Lenin and Mao were of limited use here, but Fo lined up with Sartre, who wrote that bourgeois culture was polluted by a vein of pessimism and distrust, or even contempt, for humanity itself. Bourgeois writers inhabited a cul-de-sac of their own making, and could construct no exit. The cardinal sin of those who gave voice to the angst of the age was an inability to believe in the prospect of change and improvement. As a corrective, Dario appealed to a long tradition stretching back to the Middle Ages of a people's culture which was critical and which cast a satirical eye on the activities of those in power or authority. While it was true that strands of popular culture were vacuous or mindless, he found in authentic popular culture a vitality which outshone the shallow nihilism of the avant-garde. He was delighted to find that Brecht had spoken of 'the sheer happiness of theatre', and even commended Strehler, with whom he was at daggers drawn, for finding the theatrical means of expressing that happiness. 'What does a play mean?' Dario asked. 'A play means enjoyment,' he explained. Theatre was not didacticism, not a lecture on ends and means, but a release of pressure and an occasion for the expression of communal joy. This laid an obligation on the makers of popular theatre to work to the highest standards. The bourgeoisie should not have the best tunes. The slapdash was not acceptable in popular theatre, political theatre or ideological theatre. The enjoyment which theatre offered could be attained only by the 'technical and ideological training of the actors' and by using the best available scenery and the finest lighting and sound equipment. A cultivation of popular values did not excuse a sacrifice of professional standards.

With the ideological framework clear, Dario was able to face certain problems anew, notably that of the 'fourth wall' and of the 'aside', which may not have concerned ideologists but which had been debated in theatre for generations. The link between the 'fourth wall' and the 'aside' was that both assumed a lost immediacy of relationship between stage and stalls. Any aesthetic which constructed barriers between performer and spectator, or which reduced the spectator to a condition of passivity, was anathema to him.

Is the fourth wall only that magic, rectangular space fixed by the framework of the stage, which divides the audience from the performers? No, it is also the footlights which create a particular kind of atmosphere . . . the corpse-like make-up on the actors' faces, their gestures and their habit of emitting sounds in special cadences . . . which put the spectator in the condition of a peeping Tom spying on a story which has nothing to do with him and which is on the other side to the fourth wall.

The construction of a 'fourth wall' was responsible in its turn for the suppression of the 'aside'. The actor who inhabited the closed space of the stage and denied the presence of an audience observing him was deprived of the possibility of turning away from fellow actors and addressing remarks directly to that audience. The premise for Fo's wish to rehabilitate the 'aside' was a wish to do away with all division between the two sides of the footlights. Rather than giving access to the character's hidden fears, the 'aside' was an invitation to the audience to participate and hence to form a community. It also had implications for the style of acting it permitted. 'The aside means that at the moment the actor says something to another actor, he can give an immediate denial, he can do a commentary for the audience. He can *criticize* the character from outside, he can detach himself from the part. In other words, he can act in an epic style.' The use of Brecht's terminology was not accidental. Dario, too, believed that an actor should seek not to identify himself with the character he was playing so much as to *present* that character. 'Presenting means making continual use of the "aside", in other words speaking to the audience, and to be able to speak to the audience the actor must be able to exit from the part, mediate it, present it, indicate it . . . this is the basis of vision of theatre of cinema which is, ideologically, completely different.'[3]

Fo now found himself tussling with the two leading twentieth-century theorists of theatre, Stanislavsky and Brecht. He has never been totally at ease with either. He respected the German playwright as the great precursor and teacher in political theatre, and generally ascribed any disagreements between them to deformations introduced by unintelligent directors or slavish acolytes. Nevertheless, the differences are real, particularly over the value to be ascribed to the popular tradition. Towards Stanislavsky, on the other hand, Fo displays the consistency of unremitting biliousness. The Russian is his great *bête noire*. Dario abominated the entire Stanislavskian approach, which he dismissed polemically, and comprehensively, as 'the worst, most reactionary, conservative, bourgeois position in history'. Stanislavsky's fault, in Fo's interpretation, was to envisage the creation of an intimate, closed theatre, where private traumas or individual affairs of the mind or heart could be scrutinized. Fo's ideal was big, rumbustious, public theatre, where clashes which affected an entire community and its way of life could be aired and dramatized. He abominated a theatre where audiences had the role of eavesdroppers or voyeurs, ogling a spectacle which they had happened upon by chance. Inherent in this concept was the further notion, which Fo rejected even more strongly, that the actor should delve in to his own ego or subconscious or his own store of emotional memories so as to act out dramas which were his alone. If the spectator recognized these traumatic memories of the actor's, that was a bonus for Stanislavsky but not of the essence.

> When we arrived at the need to knock down the fourth wall, or when we got to the point of talking of collective problems, we found ourselves in completely opposing positions over the question of identifying the actor and the character. *I* who am the actor and try to identify, to find inside myself all the odds and ends, all the guts, all my defects, all my qualities so as to dress myself in the character ... this is Stanislavsky ... But for my part I try to create the vision of a community, of a chorus, of a communion. Obviously I try not to talk too much of myself, but of problems which are collective. If I seek out problems which are collective, my speech, my language will be different, will be of necessity epic. That is why all popular theatre is always epic. Because at the bottom there is a clear ideological factor. There is the ideology of the community, of interests, which are social interests, interests of living together, of producing together, of dividing what is obtained.[4]

This outlook is far removed from the commercial imperatives of modern theatre, and perhaps from modern theatre *tout court*. Once again, there is a historical depth to Fo's thought. His ideas of epic acting derived less from Brecht than from the nameless medieval jester-actors who preceded *commedia dell'arte*. 'We also understood', he told his audience in the Palazzina, 'why in medieval theatre the actor tended to present himself alone on stage and construct several characters ... Because only in that way could he produce with his own repetitive presence the epic moment of the performance, of chorality.' The jester was never meant to erase himself and become his character. When required to address his audience directly, he scarcely even had to exit from his part, any more than Fo had had to do in *Mistero buffo*. There is always a touch of aesthetic egoism in Fo. When talking about the stage, popular theatre or even acting techniques, he invariably provides a *raison d'être* for the display of his own skills. By the end of his discourse on popular theatre, Dario had found that Dario Fo the jester was entitled to be always and everywhere Dario Fo, and never, unlike an Olivier, a Barrault or a Gassman, sink his own being behind that of a Lear, an Othello, an Orestes or a Faust.

Discussions of theory were all very well, but work had to go on. In June 1974, within a week of the conference, Dario, Franca and the company were in Brescia where, in late May, Italy's most recent terrorist outrage had occurred. A bomb had been left in a portico, timed to go off when a demonstration by the United Anti-Fascist Committee was passing. Eight people were left dead and over a hundred were injured. The president of the republic and the prime minister were jeered when they visited the town to attend the funeral of the victims. A few days later, members of Dario's Comune organized a 'people's trial' in Milan against the perpetrators of the outrage, calling on eyewitnesses, journalists, lawyers, ex-Resistance fighters and local members of La Comune who had taken photographs of the event. On 21 June, the company moved to the premises of their Brescia branch, and invited those who had participated at the demonstration or who had been sheltering in the portico to recount what they had seen. The company then put together a show which they performed that evening in the main square. Some pieces were reprised from the recent play on Chile, Franca again did her monologue on Mamma Togni and various Chilean and Italian Resistance songs were worked in. The central part of the work consisted of the direct testimony of those who had seen the massacre and who wished to denounce the neo-Fascist groups responsible.

Over the summer of 1974, Dario was engaged in writing the work to which he gave various titles before settling on *Can't Pay? Won't Pay!* As was common practice in these years, Dario drafted the script but then discussed it with colleagues and with the first audiences in factories in Milan. 'Following the debates, we realized there were gaps in the script, scenes which should be played differently. The, genuinely constructive, criticisms made by our comrades convinced us to change and rewrite the finale. This is, in our view, the correct means of creating "collective" theatre.'[5] The seemingly innocuous last sentence carries a polemical sting. Taking soundings from real people who draw on their own experience is the 'correct' means of constructing political theatre, whereas heeding an ideological commissar is not.

The play, a more fully rounded and well-made piece than Fo had written previously, was born of the observation that the principal problem facing working people in the 1970s was not unemployment but inflation. Hourly wage costs rose by 24 per cent in 1970, as employers and government strove to control the dissent unleashed by the 'hot autumn', and economists blamed this rise in on-costs for a drop in investment and for inflationary pressures over the following two years. A modest increase in productivity was registered in 1973–4, but this came to an abrupt end with the oil crisis. Monthly inflation statistics spiralled out of control as interest rates rose to levels not seen in Europe since the Depression of the 1930s. The continual rise in prices played greater havoc with the lives of people on fixed incomes than had a decade of terrorism. Even at the height of the violence and mayhem, it was possible for ordinary people to continue with their day-to-day lives, but unbridled inflation represented a threat of a different order.

Anger at inflation produced a genuinely spontaneous rebellion. Men and, more especially, women took matters into their own hands by embarking on a course of action to which political activists, who had not initiated it and could not control it, gave the dignified name of 'proletarian expropriation', or 'self-reduction'. Baldly stated, people refused to pay increased fares for public transport, higher bills for gas or electricity, higher tariffs in factory canteens and, above all, rising prices for goods in super-markets. Some customers continued to pay the old price, others offered only what they themselves deemed a fair price, while in other cases groups of women simply took what they wanted from supermarket shelves and refused to pay at all. It was, in its own way, a challenge to the system and to the economic *status quo*, but it was a campaign which dismayed all sides of the political spectrum.

Later, it was said, by friendly critics, that Fo had intuitively or magically foreseen this development before it had got under way, and by hostile critics that *Can't Pay? Won't Pay!* was the inspiration for shoplifting. In fact, the first recorded acts of 'proletarian expropriation' pre-dated anything Fo wrote. Instances of non-payment, or 'self-reduction', occurred at a rock concert as early as 1971 when an event in Milan featuring Led Zeppelin led to prolonged and violent clashes between the police and fans demanding free entrance. The fans claimed they had a 'need for music' which no eco-nomic system had a right to deny them and that in demanding entrance without buying a ticket they were taking control of the 'musical product'. The riots led to the banning of all rock concerts in Milan for a period. Newspaper articles at the time report that in some neighbourhoods people took 'collective action' to loot cheese and fruit from supermarkets. In March 1973, Joan Baez went to Rome to do a concert and was asked to play free for the 'proletarians' of La Magliana. Initially she agreed, but then backed down. *Stampa Alternativa* (Alternative Press) organized a protest and handed out leaflets which read: 'Joan Baez said yes to the masters, no to the proletarians. Tonight the police are going to massacre the proletari-ans who want to get in without paying. WE say no to Joan Baez . . . servant of the Yankees.'[6] This situation, with its mixture of popular resentment and street burlesque, could not fail to appeal to Fo.

At the beginning of the summer, in some quarters of Milan and Mestre, there were cases of reduced shopping bills. From these early indications, it was easy to see that if this crisis, pumped up by the ruling class, were to continue at its frantic pace, the proletariat would devise its own appropriate response. We sensed that a new style of struggle was being invented, one that would be organized and become widespread. What we did not foresee was the extent of the counterattack by the boss class, which would, in a very short period of time, reduce the purchasing power of an enormous number of people by 40–50 per cent.[7]

In addition to focusing on a new situation, *Can't pay? Won't Pay!* dramatized those basic human urges he always identified as motivating Harlequin in *commedia dell'arte* or as present in the theatre of Ruzzante. Fo had long been fascinated by how certain street performers and writers of the late Renaissance had devised mechanisms and gags which wrapped the basic appetites for food, shelter and sex inside comic situations and now invited people to see parallels between his own play and

> the old Venetian and Neapolitan popular farces [in which] the basic key is hunger. To resolve the atavistic problem of appetite, the initial, instinctive solution is for everyone to look after no. 1, but this can be switched into a need to act collectively, to organize and to struggle together, not simply to survive but to live in the fullest sense of the term . . .[8]

However, *Can't Pay? Won't Pay!* has more in common with French farce than with *commedia*, and it is no coincidence that Fo termed the new work a 'pochade', a description he had used for *The Virtuous Burglar* in the fifties. The plot has a slickness and deftness which had been absent from his assembly-line products, giving it the quickfire, hurry-scurry of Feydeau, as well as the relentless momentum, breathless busyness and non-stop rhythm farce requires. The action unravels through endless twists and turns, as Fo closes in on the various characters in turn, allowing each to make their contribution to the situation. There was also a greater balance in the writing and characterization than had been evident for some time. Fo played Giovanni, and Franca Antonia, his wife, but these two do not dominate the stage to the exclusion of the others. It would be possible – just – to read the play and wonder which part Fo had written for himself. It is interesting to speculate whether this too is a consequence of the break-up of the old-style Comune. Now that he was directing a standard theatrical troupe, he could count on the experience and skill of his fellow actors.

As a bonus, in this work Fo restrained his tendency towards pulpiteering.

The politics arise from the fantasy of the plot, although that did not make the politics any less dangerous, as the police presence at various points on the tour testified. The play is rooted in the conditions experienced by two working-class couples living in unremarkable city flats. Antonia and Margherita enter burdened with foodstuffs 'liberated' from the local supermarket in the fracas which followed the discovery that prices had been raised overnight: a voice was heard to declaim 'You're fully entitled to pay what is right! This is like a strike, except that in a strike the workers have to give up their pay . . . but this time it's the bosses who'll have to cough up something.'[9] Antonia's exhilaration is tempered by her fear of explaining what she has done to her husband, Giovanni, who, as a stalwart member of the Communist Party, is never willing to deviate from the party line. The PCI in the mid-seventies was more papist than any pope, to employ the Italian expression, and had adopted the puritan ethics of the secular humanists and the law-abiding politics of caution and moderation. Politics aside, Giovanni is the incarnation of the good-hearted, gormless, credulous idiot who has provided entertainment on European stages from the days of Aristophanes or Plautus. 'You can tell him any load of cobblers you like and he'll swallow it,' says Antonia of her husband.

Giovanni and Luigi make up a Laurel and Hardy double act. Giovanni arrives home to find a police raid under way, and is astonished to find himself in conversation with a Maoist constable who recites from the Little Red Book, and whispers that at heart he is in sympathy with the militant direct action of the housewives. The revolution is still far off, and in the meantime a man, especially one from the poor south of Italy, has to eat. The various situations interlock. The women conceal their booty by wrapping it around their stomachs, making them look pregnant. Giovanni hears of the raid on the store and tells Antonia that, unthinkable though it is, if she had been involved in those scenes he would be driven into a homicidal rage. Thereafter, the play proceeds at the pace of a fast-forwarded movie, swinging between two centres of focus. Giovanni is hungry and unwittingly devours cat food; he sees Margherita no longer pregnant and believes a tale that a new device is available for the transplant of unborn babies but fears that his wife, in her candour, may have offered her womb to help out her friend. There is, within the logic of farce, a totally satisfactory stitching together of all these bizarre dangling threads, and even a happy ending when Giovanni sees the error of his blind support for the party.

There was more to the play than was appreciated at the time.

Contemporary critics concentrated, not surprisingly, on the advocacy of 'self-reduction' and the championing of the actions of the housewives in Milan. Only a few mentioned the continued anti-Communist Party satire, and none at all drew attention to the wholly new element, which was the first tentative blossoming of feminism. Franca Rame's thinking about woman's estate had been evolving with the emergence of feminism in Italy and the parts Fo wrote for her reflected this evolution. *Can't Pay? Won't Pay!* is Fo's first feminist play. Antonia takes the initiatives; it is she who denounces the inadequacy of the party both she and her husband had adhered to in the past, and she who develops the fantastic tales needed to gull the police. Certainly, the dilemmas she faces are not those feminist writers were then addressing, nor those which would appear in Franca's own work shortly afterwards, but Antonia shows herself a plucky individualist who has emerged from her husband's shadow to adopt her own independent position. This independence was not what was becoming known as 'separatism'; the independence was a claim for women's rights and autonomy inside the family. Antonia is not Ibsen's Nora, who slams the door on her husband and family and goes off to forge her own destiny alone: no such figure would appear in Franca's theatre. Franca's independent woman will always remain wife, mother and family woman. Similarly, the discussion of the position of women in society in this play assumes an orthodox Marxist perspective. Oppression is a function of class, not gender.

Can't Pay? Won't Pay! was revived at the Palazzina Liberty in 1980, and excerpts of it were broadcast on Italian television as part of *Trasmissione forzata*, a series of variety programmes Dario and Franca co-presented in 1988. It was also the first of Fo's plays to reach the British stage, and thus the first to be subjected to a very British process of transposition, adaptation, cutting and reworking to make it conform to the director's notion of what a British audience can cope with. A translator was asked to prepare what British theatre calls 'a literal translation', and the adaptation was done by Bill Colvill and Rob Walker. Walker was resident director at the Half Moon theatre, and directed the play when it was staged in 1978 under the title *We Can't Pay? We Won't Pay!* In 1981, after *Accidental Death of an Anarchist* proved a hit in the West End, the other play was also given a West End run, under the snappier, and now accepted, English title of *Can't Pay? Won't Pay!* The English version retained, and perhaps even heightened, the comedy, but it never achieved anything deeper than belly laughs. Most of the directors who stage Fo are drawn to him by a meeting of minds over political viewpoints as much as by an admiration of his stagecraft, but they rarely attain the balance between, in Fo's own terminology, laughter and anger, or between tragedy and farce.

The prospect of tragedy striking Dario and Franca was never completely absent. On the night of 21–2 December, a bomb exploded outside the Palazzina Liberty. According to the police, it was an amateurish device, but it caused considerable commotion and shattered windows in the vicinity. Several people sleeping in the park had to be treated for shock. Dario's views still aroused violent responses.

Chapter 9

Politicians Revered and Reviled

There was consternation, accompanied by jeering hilarity in Italy's more effete literary salons, when the news broke in February 1975 that, on the initiative of the Swedish Pen Club, Dario Fo had been nominated for the Nobel Prize for Literature. He himself regarded the nomination as a venture into Never-never Land, and dismissed the proposal:

> You'll never see me in tails; it doesn't suit me. As to bows, I have become famous for my aversion to reverences and genuflections of any kind. This business of the Nobel Prize is really funny. I can just imagine the faces of certain prefects, magistrates and politicians of my acquaintance. There they are, beavering away to shut me up and clap handcuffs on my wrists, and the Swedes pull off a gag like that! Can you imagine how embarrassed they would be if they had to arrest a Nobel Prize-winner!

When he was asked if he would accept the prize if it were offered, he fended off the question with a light witticism:

> It would be really amusing, almost like one of my own comedies. Can you see me in Stockholm? The king summons me, I present myself: 'Good morning, sir, no, I mean king, no, I mean majesty . . . (What the hell am I supposed to say?) There's a prize for me? Thanks, what an honour for my country! By the way, are you aware that in Italy they chase me away from all the places where I go to perform, and that I am involved in a lawsuit with Milan City Council because they don't want to let me have an abandoned building which is due for demolition? But who cares, I have won the prize and I am cheered up . . . Give us a kiss, Your Majesty.' Can you imagine a more grotesque scene? . . .
>
> I do not run any risk of winning the Nobel Prize, for two precise reasons. The first is that the Nobel, like every other prize, has its own political overtones, and so it's highly unlikely that they are going to give it to a pain-in-the-arse like me. The second is that my theatre is not made to pass into history. I write and perform satire linked to the day's

events, to everyday news. They are texts which immediately burn up their contents.[1]

As it happened, comments and objections of this sort would be trotted out and used against him when a renewed nomination was accepted by the Swedish Royal Academy in 1997. In 1975, the award went to Saul Bellow.

Now that the Palazzina Liberty was established as company base, the project of re-establishing a national 'alternative circuit' was effectively abandoned. By the year's end there were 85,000 members of the new Comune in Milan alone. Any other professional or city theatre in Italy would have regarded half that number as a sign of success and popularity. Other companies and campaigners made use of the venue, and in the run-up to the municipal elections of June 1975, left-wing parties used it for meetings and conferences. It was not a place for ambitious people to be seen. At an event in May, Romano Canosa and Antonio Bevere, two magistrates who were members of the left-leaning Democratic Magistracy, announced their doubts about proposed measures on public order. Their speeches were reported and they were reprimanded by their superiors.

Turbulence continued on the streets of Milan. On 15 May, a group of Red Brigade terrorists burst into the office of Massimo De Carolis, Fo's opponent on the city council. He was subjected to summary trial for misdeeds against the people, found guilty and shot in the leg. Given the prevailing savagery of the terrorist campaign, De Carolis was lucky. A month later, Margherita Cagol, known as 'Mara', one of the founders of the Red Brigades, was killed after a shoot-out with policemen who had stumbled on their hide-out while searching in the Monferrato hills for a kidnap victim.

Franca was still the object of newspaper speculation about supposed links with terrorism. According to one rumour whispered by police officers into the ears of sympathetic journalists, witnesses had reported a certain resemblance between Franca Rame and the woman who drove the getaway car on the evening of the kidnapping of judge Mario Sossi back in 1974. The woman had blonde hair, and that obviously clinched the matter. A Milanese daily, *La Notte*, ran a story in May saying that the police were closing in on her over the kidnapping, and even implying that she was the real financier of the Red Brigades. Franca issued a statement denying it and pointing out that on the night in question she had been 500 miles away, performing in public. Although exhausted by endless dealings with the law and lawyers, she raised an action against the journalist and the editor of the paper, which issued an apology.

*

The general election campaign brought Dario back to the television screens for the first time since he had walked out on *Canzonissima* in 1962. The Democratic Party for Proletarian Unity invited him to appear in a party political broadcast. Being broadly sympathetic, he accepted, but made it known that he maintained his independence and was not a member of the party. Although appearing with sober politicians, Fo clowned in his own satirical, grotesque style, mocking opponents but also raising the issues of the moment including arbitrary arrest and questions of law and order. In a reassuring tone, he promised that if the left won, they would be gentle with the Christian Democrats. 'If we win, we will allow them back on to the television screens in thirteen years.' The establishment was piqued. 'Politicians of other parties were outraged,' wrote Dario. 'What's going on? An actor, a song-and-dance man coming here to steal our job, speaking to people in a language they can understand . . . ' Parliament rushed through emergency legislation, forbidding singing or acting on party political broadcasts.[2]

Dario also included in the broadcast excerpts from the play he was preparing, *The Kidnapping of Fanfani*. Amintore Fanfani was one of the founding fathers of Christian Democracy and held the office of prime minister on six occasions. In 1963, he led the 'opening to the left' which brought the Socialist Party into the government coalition with the Christian Democrats, but thereafter made himself the spokesman for all right-wing causes. In the guise of upholder of traditional family and Catholic values, he came forward in the early seventies to lead the campaign against divorce. The prologue to the published version of *The Kidnapping of Fanfani* described him as 'incarnating Fascist corporativism and Catholic neo-corporativism' and identified him as the leader of a tendency inside the Christian Democratic Party which was using the struggle against terrorism as a cover for a sinister campaign of 'pre-emptive militarization of the country . . . and of the imposition of a "Chilean solution" on the workers' movement'. A curiosity of particular interest is an article which had originally appeared in *Il Manifesto* on 29 November 1973, entitled 'Supposing They Kidnapped Fanfani?'

Whether Fo got the idea from the newspaper or not, the fantasy kidnap of the politician was the theme of his play. The writing was completed in eight days and the play, which opened on 5 June 1975, was intended as a contribution to the election campaign. Lacking the finish of *Can't Pay? Won't Pay!*, the new work is a throwback to the off-the-cuff, rough-and-ready burlesque which Fo had performed in previous years. Fanfani is kidnapped at the opening of a charity art exhibition to raise money for Vietnamese children. It transpires that the kidnapping was the work not of the Red Brigades but of the Christian Democrats. The plight of the party is so desperate that their only way of warding off defeat in the forthcoming elections is to appeal for a sympathy vote.

Once unleashed, Fo's inventiveness careers off under its own steam, sparking against rocks and knocking bark off trees. Where he cannot create, he 'borrows'. He once said that every good playwright is a good thief. On this occasion, he stole inspiration from an incident during the kidnapping of J. Paul Getty III when captors clipped off a piece of his ear and sent it to the family. Fanfani's kidnappers report that the press are sceptical about the seizure and that his party colleagues have suggested that one of his ears should be adequate to convince them. Mixing whimsy and malice, Fo has his group find refuge in a convent, where the nuns specialize in abortion. Fanfani is disguised as a woman, and, in an echo of similar situations in earlier plays, has his stomach pumped up until he gives birth to a black-shirted puppet. The exertions are such that Fanfani dies and goes to heaven, where the Madonna, played by Franca, berates him and his party for their crimes. She also prophesies that their days are numbered and that the international working class will shortly spew them and their like out of office. Fanfani awakes to discover that this was all a dream, and this is where the initial version ended. In rehearsal, however, Fo rethought his ending, and introduced a double bluff. Fanfani wakes up alive and on Earth but facing two armed gangsters dispatched by Andreotti, who hopes that Fanfani's kidnap will indeed guarantee victory to the Christian Democrats. As he is dragged off, Fanfani cries out that it is all useless since 'they will have their revolution anyway . . . it will all come true, it will all come true'. Whatever disappointments he may have endured from his comrades, Dario still had no doubt that the revolution was imminent. 'It is on this point that I cannot agree with the parties of the traditional left or with the Communist Party,' wrote Dario. 'I believe in the creativity of the struggles, in the fact that silently, perhaps underground, even in Italy, everything is in readiness for the great clash.'[3]

What captured attention was the brio of the production and the wit of the solutions Fo found to excoriate Fanfani, who was diminished in the most literal sense. The real point of the play was its merciless evisceration of the Christian Democratic Party as a whole, but Fanfani was more than a symbol of the party. Fo had a real personal animus against him. Short of stature, slightly stout and choleric, Fanfani had an off-balance physique which delighted cartoonists. These were not adult observations, but Fo revelled in lampooning his target. His only problem was the technical one of finding a means of exaggerating and reproducing in comic form the physical defects of Fanfani. He delved into *commedia dell'arte* and, in what one critic described as an 'extraordinary case of reincarnation', discovered that there had existed the stock character of a dwarf called Fanfanicchio. To create the dwarf effect, Fo had a plank placed along the stage a few feet from the ground, and put shoes on his hands and a tiny pair of baggy trousers over his arms. His head and that part of his upper body which remained on view made a diminutive human being, whose arms were provided by another actor. It was a *tour de force*, recognized as such even by those – on this occasion, a majority – who did not admire the play. 'It is difficult', writes the critic Franco Quadri, 'to convey by other than a direct statement the monstrous acting skills of Fo as dwarf, weaving his way through dances, scratching his nose with his shoes, launching himself into flight or strolling along the walls, never forgetting [the character's] fixation with law and order or his Napoleonic poses.'[4]

The left made substantial progress at the polls, although the revolution remained on the far side of the horizon. Massimo De Carolis, happily recovered from the terrorist assault, was upset by the outcome of the vote, and was quoted in the *Il Manifesto* on 29 June as saying that 'it is clear that a society in which girls can go around without bras is not likely to produce nuns'. This Delphic comment was the subject of much puzzled and whimsical debate, even if its literal truth was scarcely in dispute. The socialist Aldo Aniasi became mayor of Milan, and at the time things seemed likely to be easier for Fo in his dealings with the council in the still-unresolved dispute over the Palazzina.

The Kidnapping of Fanfani was linked closely to the personnel and issues of political life in Italy, and as such had little appeal abroad. It went on tour in northern Italy, and played to 8,000 people in Turin. Fo used his visit to the city to involve himself in other causes. In July, he paid a visit to the members of an organization calling itself the Gruppo Abele, who were then on hunger strike, to express support for their work in rehabilitating addicts. The visit was the first public demonstration of interest in drugs, an issue which was increasingly to occupy the mental and emotional energy of Dario and Franca in coming years. The group provided meeting places for users and drug-workers but also dissented from the voguish cult of drug consumption in Western society, arraigning not only pushers but poets, singers and intellectuals. They set their sights on the likes of

Timothy Leary, Bob Dylan, the Beatles and the Rolling Stones, as well as the whole beat or hippie culture, not to mention surrealism, Rimbaud, William Burroughs or the brand of Indian mysticism which George Harrison had made popular among Western youth. The use of drugs, they reckoned, was the consequence not only of poverty, drifting hopelessness or unemployment, but also of a cult of drugs which had deep roots in youth culture.

Also in Turin, Dario and Franca were involved in protests in support of the lawyer, Giambattista Lazagna, imprisoned in the town of Fossano. The story of Lazagna was a curious one, even for those baffling times. Under the pseudonym 'Saetta' (arrow), he had attained legendary status as a partisan leader in the later phases of the Resistance. After the war, he set up a legal practice in Genoa, but in March 1972, to general disbelief, he was arrested for supposed association with terrorism. In May, police investigating the activities of Giangiacomo Feltrinelli let it be known that there had been connections between Feltrinelli and Lazagna, although it was never shown that this acquaintanceship was linked to terrorist acts. In September 1974, Lazagna was again arrested as a result of information passed to the police by Silvano Girotto, known as 'Brother Machine-gun'. Of all the exotic fauna which flourished in the undergrowth where terrorists, self-serving criminals, double-dealing informers, mythomaniacs and assorted conspiracy theorists fed each other's diseased fantasies, none was more bizarre than 'Brother Machine-gun'. This man had genuinely been a Franciscan friar but had left the order for South America, where he joined, or claimed to have joined, some guerrilla grouping. He returned to Italy wearing this past as a combatant as if it were a war medal and was able to make the acquaintance of leading figures among terrorists. He turned informer and gave information which led to the arrest of two of the founders of the Red Brigades, Renato Curcio and Alberto Franceschini. Leaflets found in Bergamo alleged links between Girotto, Lazagna and the Red Brigades. This link was expanded in the press to the point where Lazagna was indicated as the evil genius behind the whole left-wing terror movement.

His case was taken up by Franca's Red Aid, but by the time Dario and Franca arrived in Turin, Lazagna had been in jail for nine months. They joined in a march from Turin to Fossano, where pictures show them standing outside the prison with their fists raised, shouting slogans of solidarity with the detainees they regarded as political prisoners. Those inside replied with shouts of gratitude. Dario gave a statement to the press, saying that

Lazagna is a fundamental step in the repression. He is in prison on the basis of a political frame-up which originated with the false accusations made by Girotto. But we are not marching only to demand the immediate release of Lazagna. He is only the tip of the iceberg, because the repression has also struck representatives of Democratic Magistracy, as well as lawyers and workers. Italian democracy cannot allow this game to go on.

Fo remained in the news all throughout that summer. In *Il Giorno*, the columnist Giancarlo Vigorelli published an attack on *The Kidnapping of Fanfani*, but thirty-eight journalists published an open letter protesting against the 'neo-Fascist tone' of the article in question. It was an odd incident in itself, showing how little freedom of speech is respected when it is expressed as freedom for awkward views, but also showing the level of support Fo commanded. Things were easing for him in other respects too. The democratic left had made substantial advances in the 1970s, and the Communist Party held, or at least shared, power in Milan, Turin, Genoa, Rome and Naples. Opinion polls gave the party a commanding lead for the general elections due in 1976. The Socialist Party had representatives on various state holding companies, and one of these, Beniamino Finocchiaro, who was on the board of RAI, chose this moment to wonder whether Dario should be allowed back on to television screens. 'Thirteen years ago, Dario Fo interrupted his participation with *Canzonissima* because the scripts of which he was author had been censored. In the new course of the company, would this be possible? Censorship, I mean. The chairman says not.' The suggestion was not immediately followed up.

In July, Dario and Franca had a meeting in Rome with Jean-Paul Sartre to discuss what must surely rank as one of the great opportunities *manqué* of recent decades. Sartre had been invited by French television to prepare a series of programmes on the history of Europe in the twentieth century. Sartre said that he wanted Fo as his collaborator, and French television raised no objection. Fo, who never understood why Sartre had chosen him, was excited at the prospect. The two shared common left-wing, broadly Marxist beliefs, had both been galvanized by the revival of Marxist thought following the 'events of May' in Paris, 1968, and both were admirers of Mao and the Cultural Revolution. Both, too, had taken up the cause of imprisoned terrorists: Sartre the cause of the Baader-Meinhof group in Mannheim prison in Germany, Fo the cause of many Italian terrorists in Italian jails.

Sartre wanted to begin work immediately, but Dario and Franca were committed to a trip to China in September, so the project was put back to the autumn. Dario told the *Corriere della Sera* that the exact nature and extent of his collaboration had not yet been decided, but that he and Franca would make

> a contribution to the script, will do some pieces, as well as some sketches and some sung extracts. We will meet in Paris in a couple of days, to put the final touches to the plans. However, what interests us is the encounter with Sartre, to whom my generation owes so much. All the great shake-ups, the things which have impacted on reality have come to us from him, so I consider this possible collaboration a great fortune. For me in particular, it could be an incentive to find new models, new formulae since, apart from anything else, the man is so stimulating.[5]

If personal relations with Sartre were relaxed, those with Simone de Beauvoir were much less so. Franca was appalled at de Beauvoir's haughtiness and rudeness on their first encounter.

> In Sartre's house in Paris, the key turned in the lock, and there she was: shopping bag in hand, scarf on head. She threw a 'don't smoke' at Sartre, and withdrew into the kitchen. Sartre, like a naughty child caught stealing the jam, stubbed out his cigarette or cigar. 'Simone,' he muttered. So that's who it was! I was more upset than Dario. Perhaps because I was a woman, I thought I had the right to at least a greeting.[6]

De Beauvoir appeared to believe the project was of little value, but in the event her opinions made no difference, since the project was aborted, seemingly on instructions from the Élysée Palace. General de Gaulle had taken a benevolent view of Sartre, regarding his activities with a tolerant good humour which his successor could not match. Dario and Franca were given to understand by Sartre that Pompidou had vetoed the proposal. This decision must be a matter of regret. It is impossible to imagine what kind of wildly idiosyncratic, truculent, conceivably misshapen and possibly ill-focused history might have emerged from this implausible coupling of unique talents, but the failure of the project must be accounted a loss.

The same could be said of another venture Dario undertook for Sartre. He was highly impressed by Sartre's book *Theatre of Situation*, particularly by the chapter on Beckett's *Waiting for Godot*. He began to translate the work into Italian, but translation rights were refused by Sartre's French publisher. By the time the latter was persuaded to change his mind, Dario was involved with other projects.

*

Sandwiched between these encounters was Dario and Franca's visit to Maoist China. The company comprised Dario, Franca, their son Jacopo and about twenty members of La Comune. Other members of the group included Mario Capanna, a leader of the 1968 student movement who had recently been elected to the Lombard Regional Council for the PdUP, and Hrayr Terzian, a psychiatrist and director of a mental hospital in Verona. 'To know, to understand how the Chinese live and work, you would probably need three lives, while we have only three weeks at our disposal,' said Fo on their departure. 'We can only promise not to waste even one minute of our time.' The group set off on 20 August, following a pre-arranged itinerary which took them to Shanghai, Bejing, Canton, Nanjing, Tien-tsin and Chinan.

From his many references to Mao and Maoism in debates on theatre and politics, it is clear that, for Dario, everything, not merely this or that line of thought or action, could be associated with the Chinese Cultural Revolution. China and the Cultural Revolution was another pleasance where Dario's good-hearted Utopianism flourished. He was not alone in thinking this way in the seventies. Men who are desperate for a solution are easily persuaded because they wish desperately to be persuaded, wrote J. K. Galbraith in *The Age of Uncertainty*. Bolshevism had self-evidently failed, so large swathes of the *bien-pensant* intelligentsia of the West were in thrall to a fantasy of the Great Helmsman. In certain sectors of Western society, China had assumed the status occupied in antiquity by Atlantis. Devotees saw Mao as the anchorite who lived in poverty or the benevolent ascetic who, in the Cultural Revolution, had stepped down from his throne to lead a campaign against deviation, corruption, bureaucracy and even his own regime. Maoism, and the cult of the Little Red Book, provided the underpinnings to the politico-philosophical convictions of the European, especially French and Italian, New Left. Romantic Maoism had become the jargon of a generation.

Fo's case was more complex. The Cultural Revolution was a dogma with him, making it easy for party and people in China to be recipients of transferred loyalty. Dario and Franca went to China in the frame of mind of pilgrims on their way to Santiago de Compostela. When they got there, they saw what they expected to see, they found confirmation of all that they already believed, they accepted what they were told and came home with their faith nourished.

In all these years, we have read a great deal on the subject, we have seen many documentaries, we have attended many debates, many comrades have gone ahead of me and have spoken about it. China is today the highest moment of socialist experience in the world. If in Europe the Cultural Revolution has determined the nature of contestation, in China it had and has an enormous weight, because it is the greatest demonstration there has ever been.

At the time of their visit, China was still shaken by the aftershocks of the Cultural Revolution, while the upper echelons of the party, aware that Mao could not survive much longer, were engaged in jockeying for power. The most recent campaigns launched by the cadres of the party had identified as enemies, however improbable they appeared as bedfellows, the philosopher Confucius and Lin Piao, a party functionary once close to Mao but who, after losing out in a palace *putsch*, had fled and died in a plane crash near the Soviet border. Much more is now known about the career of Mao than could have been known by Franca and Dario at the time of their visit. The portrait which emerges from recent biographies[7] gives Mao rank among the great politician-criminals of the twentieth century, alongside Hitler, Stalin or Pol Pot. In the seventies, however, little was known of the hundreds of thousands who were slaughtered, tortured, maimed, exiled, imprisoned or driven to suicide as a result of his activities, nor of the up to twenty million who died of famine as a result of the campaigns masterminded by Mao and his inner coterie.

This was not the China that Dario and Franca saw. 'Over there they are constructing a new humanity. I know, it has been said many times, now it is almost a cliché, but it is really true. I have been to Russia, to eastern Europe, to Cuba but what I saw in China cannot be compared with the reality of any other country.'[8] Dario Fo watched China from afar, in the spirit in which William Wordsworth, Beethoven or Ugo Foscolo watched the unfolding of the French Revolution. He believed himself in the enviable position of witnessing a major, irreversible shift not merely in society but in the very nature of humanity. Society was being transformed from predatory capitalism to a gentler form of cooperation, bringing closer that state of justice and happiness to which human beings had always aspired. He recounted uncritically the history of the Cultural Revolution as it had been recounted to him.

A university lecturer, who lived through the entire revolution, one evening talked us through the various 'passages' of the revolution. There was nothing random about it; the revolutionary movement was carried forward in a precise way by the Communist Party and by Mao. It all began with some violent criticisms of a film, which featured a character who lived centuries ago, and who was portrayed as a saviour of the fatherland. In reality, he was a leading bourgeois. Mao wrote some important letters, of considerable weight, about the film. Shortly afterwards, a series of articles came out, all signed by a group calling itself 'the three families' in which they advanced some considerations on girls' tresses, on fashion, and they hoped for the return to certain forms of hair style and to all that, in journalistic language, goes under the name of 'colour'. Life, they say, is not only class struggle, but also taste, nostalgia for green days gone. Finally there was the famous comedy, *The Mandarin*, I say famous because it marked the beginning of the cultural revolution.[9]

In the screening of this film and performance of this play, in Dario's account, lay the origins of the Cultural Revolution. There ensued a mass mobilization of between 90 and 150 thousand people from all over China, who converged on Bejing in support of the revolution. So numerous were they that Mao found himself compelled to use a car to inspect them all. Groups from the far left, particularly around the universities, took advantage of the situation created by the mass assemblies, and there were clashes leading to deaths among the workers, who 'did not react'. The Communist Party took a low profile in these encounters, 'unlike other Communist parties, thereby showing its trust in the working class'. In Shanghai, one of the most important centres of railway activity in China, Fo had been told by a fireman 'who spoke as though he were a story-teller' of the resistance the workers put up to the bureaucrats and directors. The central role was played by

> cultural propaganda, that is by cinema, newspapers, great debates in assemblies, theatre, story-tellers. All these means were adopted to make people understand the importance of the fight against revisionism. There were stand-offs between railway workers and some directors, there were clashes, some directors went so far as to block trains and ships. The workers reacted in the only way possible, making propaganda in the packed station at Shanghai, among the thousands of passengers waiting to depart, sometimes even climbing on to the roofs of carriages. Finally they managed to bring to their knees the directors who had been attempting in every way possible to create disorder, difficulties, chaos, anything to impede the advance of the revolutionary movement.[10]

The lack of critical independence Fo displayed in the many interviews he gave on his return is startling. His glowing account of the devotion of the Chinese people for Mao and the Communist Party reads like the life of saint in a devotional manual, but throughout his life, the coruscating satirist dismayed by injustice or abuse of power has been the twin of an idealist in search of some lost purity. If it is the former who is better known through his major works, from *Accidental Death of an Anarchist* to *Free Marino! Marino Is Innocent!*, the latter is always present in the folds of the pages. It is a pity that the Utopian Fo was given fullest voice in a meeting not with some imaginary Shangri-La or El Dorado of his own devising, but with a historical land in which real people lived and suffered. In the China of the Cultural Revolution, he found a society which satisfied his aspirations. Whether it corresponded with the historical China of 1975 is a different matter. Unlike fellow-travellers in Stalinist Russia, he did not justify executions, the imprisonment of dissidents, the state persecution of minorities. He coined no smart slogans about necessary crimes or about cracking eggs to make omelettes. He simply did not see the darker, crueller side.

His disenchanted, satirical stance *vis-à-vis* power wholly deserted him when the holder of power was Mao. Years later, when much more was known about Mao's years in power than in 1975, he still replied when asked by a journalist for an example of a politician with a sense of humour: 'Mao Tse-Tung, crude but with a sense of self-irony.'[11] On his return to Italy, he gave many interviews, and it was clear to him that Maoist China was all that the West could and should be:

> The first thing that struck me was the matter of merchandise. Here, man is an object, a piece of merchandise in fact, who tends to sell himself at the highest possible price at every moment of his life: when he offers his labour, when he is looking for a wife, even when he is getting dressed. With us, there is a sharp division between concepts of good, morality and relationships of production. In China, on the other hand, eating, drinking, getting dressed, principles of morality are all part and parcel of the same thing. There is a profound conception of life which determines everything. There is the new man because there is a new philosophy.[12]

When he was asked if there was much opportunity in China for the expression of dissent, Fo replied in enthusiastic terms about the spread of liberty of speech:

> It seemed to me that there is ample space [for dissent]. You will understand this immediately from the debates, if you are a bit alert. Everyone says exactly what they think. So the bureaucrat and the real revolutionary emerge, the one who would like to apply the principles of Maoism as though they were

pieces on an assembly line and the one who tries to get to grips with the reality. In any case, there is a real confrontation, no blah-blah.

I would like to add that a great stimulus to dissent, to free discussion was provided by the relentless battle being waged in China against the deviations of Lin Piao. His aim was to extend to the limits the cult of personality of Mao, to make him into a charismatic figure so that the role of the party, of the masses was diminished. 'One sentence by Mao is worth ten thousand sentences by everyone else,' Lin Piao believed. And Mao in reply said: 'Nothing is sacred, everything I say can be overturned.' Even the ordinary, stereotyped gesture of raising the Little Red Book, which no one in China does today, was a symptom of not thinking for yourself.

In a meeting with the Jinan Artistic Company, the spokesperson told Fo and La Comune actors that they had once been misled by

> the revisionist line of Liu Shao-chi, and for a time had gone down the wrong path; we did not succeed in satisfying the needs of a socialist society. Through the struggles of the Cultural Revolution and the campaign of criticism against Confucius and Lin Piao, the artists of our company have acquired new vigour and have transformed themselves. Under the direction of the party, they take as a weapon Marxism-Leninism and the thought of Mao Tse Tung and undertake to follow the orientation indicated by Chairman Mao and to put 'art and literature at the service of the workers, of the peasants and of the soldiers'.[13]

This was delicate ground for Dario, who had struggled against state censorship and against the imposition of party line. He replied only that La Comune aimed to be a company run by 'workers, peasants and progressives, by those who moved forward the struggles in Italy. The Chinese Cultural Revolution was the principal reason for our decision.' He also told them that 'the repression under way by the judicial system, by the authorities is extremely violent, and many comrades are being arrested'.[14]

Having been invited principally as a man of theatre, he had meetings with fellow actors and theatre directors in China. Strangely, in none of his first interviews does he mention hearing the tale which would later become *The Tale of a Tiger*, one of his best-known monologues. He and his colleagues acted and sang in many factory canteens, in streets and in private houses. At the Bejing Opera, he performed the *grammelot*, in cod English, of the American technocrat and his failure to build a rocket which could take off from the ground, and extracts from *The Kidnapping of Fanfani*. By his own account, the piece met with great success, and everywhere they went, they were met by people who demanded 'Do us your Fanfani!' The performance was greeted with laughter and questions – 'But is it really true? It can't be! Did he really say those things on the defence of the race? Is he really so sure of himself? Couldn't we invite him to China? That would be funny!' The joke was on Fo when, later that year, the vicissitudes of global politics caused the Chinese authorities to issue an invitation to senator Amintore Fanfani himself, together with Franz Josef Strauss and other representatives of the European right. Fo wrote a humorous piece, telling Fanfani not to be troubled if during visits to schools children came running up to him to see if he was kept moving by some trick device.

Fo had his own beliefs on popular theatre and performance techniques confirmed by the practices he found current in China. 'In Nankin, I saw a worker perform by himself in a square, without mask or make-up, in front of a small crowd. In other words, he was performing a Chinese *Mistero buffo*,' he reported.[15]

> The area around Shanghai is filled with story-tellers who recount new and ancient stories, or tell tales from the newspapers. For instance, there is a jester, alone on the stage, who reproduces, playing all the parts himself, a trip in a tram round the city ring road: what the people say, comments which have nothing to do with politics, the pushing and shoving, discussions about work, salaries, the struggle against Lin Piao. There is one man who believes that Confucius is a party functionary, another who has not understood a word of the recent instructions. All of this is done in a grotesque, exhilarating style, accompanied by rolls of drums which convey the rhythm of the situation, and with the underlying indication that that is the correct line. It is something which reminded me to an extraordinary extent of my work on popular theatre, *Mistero buffo*, for example.[16]

It appeared that on all important points there was a complete identification between the theatre performances and beliefs of Dario Fo in Italy and the practice of his Maoist counterparts in China as sanctioned by the Cultural Revolution.

On his return, Fo became embroiled in controversy with the film director Michelangelo Antonioni, who in 1972 had released the film *Chung Kuo*, for which he had received the assistance of the Chinese authorities. The work was seen by critics as a return to a earlier documentary style which he had abandoned for films such as *Blow-Up* or *Zabriskie Point*, although Antonioni himself preferred to describe his work as 'travel notes'. The voice-over is largely descriptive of what the camera records, with little attempt at analysis or contextualization of a society or culture which Antonioni, as he readily admitted, lacked the knowledge to penetrate in any depth. The film had aroused the indignation of the Chinese, and Fo on his return made himself spokesman for their discontent. The core of the dispute concerned the possibility of understanding Chinese culture given its profound divergences from Western ideas and assumptions, and the interpretation of the political conduct and turn of mind of Chinese people.

'Rather than phoney, Antonioni's China was escapist, he limited himself to providing local colour on things without explaining them. And in China, this is easy, granted that everything is uncovered, exposed to daylight,'[17] wrote Dario, who had made use of extensive footage by various directors who had been allowed to film in China to prepare himself for the trip. He claimed that Antonioni had given a naive picture of 'candour and dignity' of the Chinese, while he had found a people 'filled with irony, subtle and profound, proud and, when they set their mind to it, malicious'. Antonioni composed a bad-tempered retort, accusing Fo of oversimplification and of arrogance in claiming to have grasped the nature of China after a visit of twenty-three days. 'The actor was there a few days, and on his return to the West, all the enigmas on Mao's regime have vanished,' wrote Antonioni. Fo countered by berating Antonioni for producing a set of commonplace banalities which had caused gratuitous offence. He pulled from his knowledge of folk wisdom an Italian proverb which ran: 'Someone who goes looking for frogs, will perhaps find frogs; he is not likely to find mushrooms, which do not grow in ponds. Which means that when you want to find something, you should not let chance take you there . . . .'[18] This is good, if Delphic, advice, but it is advice Fo himself could have taken to heart in rethinking his own experiences in China. He had found the frogs he was searching for, but missed the poisonous mushrooms surrounding the pond.

Chapter 10

Dealing with Drugs

The mid-seventies brought no abatement of the turbulence in Milan. 'Between the years '74 and '77, the city experienced difficult hours,' wrote the journalist Giorgio Bocca.

> There were clashes with the Fascists: mile-long marches which paralyse the centre and give foreign tourists the impression of a revolutionary Milan, while it is nothing more than neurotic. Everywhere proletarian circles and free radio stations spring up . . . in Milan more than in other cities the risky interdependence between New Left culture and the Movement appears. In the city and its hinterland the most important extra-parliamentary periodicals are concentrated . . . it is not possible to know how far the professors behind these reviews, in particular those with explicitly revolutionary programmes, realize how much their opinions, their ideas impact on the Movement.[1]

Demonstrations which always threatened to erupt into violence continued apace. In January 1976, during a demonstration against the Shah of Iran, lorries were burned in the centre of Milan. In February, the Central Station was immobilized for hours until the police made a baton charge into the ranks of strikers. More serious, but small-scale, events involving the beating-up of individuals or the throwing of home-made Molotov cocktails were so frequent as scarcely to merit detailed reporting in the press.

New groups began to show their hand and different forms of protest were practised. On 17 January 1976, a group of thirty feminists stormed the cathedral, while in February, violent scuffles lasting several hours followed a 'happening' jointly organized by various alternative magazines to coincide with a religious ceremony. Julian Beck's company, Living Theatre, added to the disruption of day-to-day living during a return visit to Milan in March. Their anti-nuclear show, performed in the Galleria near Piazza Duomo, involved bodies being laid out end to end. The company also appeared, together with Dario and Franca and a left-wing pop group calling themselves Stormy Six, at a factory on the outskirts of Milan occupied by striking workers. Dario and Franca were still subject to threats and harassment, and, though they coped well enough, those surrounding them found it a greater strain. The warehouse of Giorgio Bertani, publisher of Dario's plays, was set on fire on more than one occasion, and he and his family received several anonymous, threatening telephone calls. The accumulated problems proved too much for Bertani. In March, he attempted to take his own life, although the bullet missed his heart and he survived.

Militant action was not limited to Milan. Rome's homeless occupied some of the many empty buildings scattered around the city. The squatters were acting in the spirit of *Can't Pay? Won't Pay!* and expected, and indeed received, full-hearted support from Dario and Franca, who in January 1976, performed in the open area in the centre of occupied flats. In the same month, the couple took part in a midnight demonstration outside San Vittore prison in Milan after word got about that the Red Brigade leader, Renato Curcio, was about to be moved. Curcio had briefly escaped, but was back in captivity after an armed raid on his flat. His stay in San Vittore was brief, since he was moved by the authorities after an mysterious incident inside the prison in which three alleged terrorists were stabbed in the course of disturbances. Six prisoners and a prison guard were charged in connection with the assault. A lawyer, Sergio Spazzali, who had worked for Red Aid, was also among the intended victims, and only escaped injury because he was in the shower when his cell door was broken down by the attackers. The demonstration was concerned with prison conditions as much as with the transfer of Curcio.[2]

The occupation of the Palazzina Liberty was still a matter of political debate in Milan's council chambers, particularly after the return of Massimo De Carolis to active politics after his assault by the Red Brigades. Some socialist councillors had been seen at shows, but officially the council was still intent on repossessing the building. De Carolis raised the question of modifications to the Palazzina interior for which no official permission had been requested, and went on to accuse the new municipal office bearers of not pursuing the action against Fo and La Comune with due diligence. At a council meeting, De Carolis said:

> In the meanwhile, Dario Fo continues to produce his shows (his is the only company in Milan which has its own venue provided gratis, at the expense of the City Council), not to mention the conferences where it is explained that the council drugs children in the nurseries [conference held at Palazzina Liberty on 8 February], or the meeting of Red Aid or the League for abortion.

The complication for the city authorities was that Fo's residency was now viewed as a fixture by the neighbourhood committee as well as by the various groups who used the building as headquarters. La Comune drew its support from the constituency to which the Socialist Party wished to appeal, making it politically impossible for the new council simply to evict Fo. Negotiations were opened in February between Fo and the council, and two months later it seemed that the question had been amicably resolved. The company would end their occupation and take up residence in a new, purpose-built venue near Piazzale Cuoco. The Palazzina would revert to the council, which would not seek retrospective rental but would offer no compensation for the restructuring work undertaken. The proposed new building would take the form of a vast, spherical geodesic structure of glass and steel, of the kind originally devised by Buckminster Fuller and made famous by its use in the Montreal Expo in 1967. When complete, it would hold 1,200 spectators.

Fo's comments were moderately sanguine. 'I have only one regret. When people thought of the Palazzina Liberty, they were by now used to thinking of it as a theatre. Reaching an agreement is positive but having restored Palazzina Liberty, the idea of starting from scratch does not fill me with enthusiasm.' Even De Carolis offered a form of support. 'I am not sorry that Fo will be moving to another council area. I have no problems with Dario Fo as an actor; he is one of the possible components of a pluralistic society. What I did not like was that he had transformed the Palazzina into a kind of Mompracem where he did what he pleased.'[3] Unfortunately, the residents of Piazzale Cuoco did not share the prevailing optimism. The prospect of seeing a quiet, empty space converted into a bustling social centre did not appeal to everyone, particularly since the promised hurly-burly would bring with it heightened police vigilance and the threat of attention from the violent enemies of Fo. In addition, the earmarked area had previously housed an ad-hoc theatre put up by the local community. They declared themselves devastated by the 'decision which fell from on high from the council'.[4] Fo could hardly oppose such expressions of popular culture or of popular democracy, so the agreement was never ratified. La Comune remained at Palazzina Liberty.

There were many other legal cases pending, but their outcome was now more frequently in his favour. The first break had occurred on 1 April 1973, when a judge, Antonio Soda, had referred a case to the Constitutional Court to determine if Fo was justified in his argument that the police had no right to interfere with the operations of a private club. Prosecutions were being brought under a 1931 Fascist law, and the judge asked the Upper Court to decide on the rights, in a democracy, of a citizen whose political philosophy differed from its statutory law. The wheels of Italian justice grind exceedingly slowly, and in March 1976 the Constitutional Court had still not reported, but Dario was acquitted in a court in Pordenone after being charged with having prevented a public official from entering the building where La Comune was performing in May 1970. The celebrations in the Fo camp were short-lived. The prosecution entered an immediate appeal.

While not as yet in a state of disenchantment over the prospect of grand political reform, or revolution, from this period in the mid-seventies the energies of Dario and Franca were channelled into social rather than grand political projects. They both lent full support to the pro-abortion campaign, even if their high-profile presence created difficulties. At one demonstration, several young women appeared on a platform to announce they had undergone abortions, but the following day they were charged by magistrates. The Palazzina housed press conferences and discussion groups on the issue, but Dario cast his public support in the form of semi-theatrical, grotesque satire. The early versions of the bill before the Chamber of Deputies required the doctor to satisfy himself that the woman really wanted an abortion. The real problem, Dario suggested in a spoof dialogue he devised between a doctor and a woman, was that gynaecologists and private clinics had been living for years off the profits of semi-clandestine, illegal abortions and had no interest in seeing a public system established. In addition, he said, the proposed law required the gynaecologist to convert himself into a magistrate or police officer. In the scene, the doctor accuses the girl of two-timing her boyfriend. Since the authorities had to be proactive as regards pregnancy and had to know who was the real father, they had filmed her every sexual or intimate act over recent months. 'There was no other solution,' concludes the doctor.

> This law which lays on the doctor, and on the doctor alone, the responsibility of deciding on abortion is either a nonsense, in which case let's forget it, or else it's serious, and then the doctor who really believes in it and wants to apply it, is obliged to turn to methods which are not exactly democratic. They are an outrage to the privacy of the woman as well as requiring a kind of body-search on her. In other words – More babies and less freedom!

In a fine excess, the doctor climbs on to the window ledge and exclaims – 'Make love, all you women, who cares if you're young, mature or mere girls, because I am filming you and have ways of checking up on you! Don't think you can escape by turning out the lights. We have infra-red film. We see everything! Every hug is checked. Women married or unmarried. Every foetus is filed!'⁵

Dario and Franca began to take greater interest in the drug problem in Italy. They had visited a group in Turin who helped addicts and had been accompanied on the China trip by Hrayr Terzian, a Marxist doctor who was a specialist, if an unorthodox one, in that field. They were concerned that their son Jacopo was mixing in circles in which drugs circulated freely. Years later, Fo recalled the atmosphere of those years.

> Twenty-five years ago, we were at the time of the 'free needle', of the first arrests for possession of 'small quantities' of hashish, even for personal use. Above all these were the days of the petty moralists, of the rigid scientists who pointed their finger at young people and screamed, 'Watch out! Taking grass is the quickest way to end up shooting up with heroin.' Franca and I, together with the whole Comune company, were still performing at the Palazzina Liberty and were constantly engaged, both with agnostic spectators and with friends and comrades who were passionate about the problem, in discussions about the slaughter of youth from overdoses. The most bitter debates exploded among the young, including our son, Jacopo.⁶

On 3 March, a bar in Corso Romano was blown up by a unit which left leaflets claiming that it had been selected because it was a 'centre of heroin dealing'. The document carried the slogan 'All Power to the Armed Proletariat'.⁷ The proletariat, armed or otherwise, may have been waking up to the problem of the use and diffusion of drugs, but their self-appointed, intellectual avant-garde was not quite sure how to react.

Debates concerned threats to health or life but also exposed fissures and stresses in the whole mish-mash of ideas, prejudices, attitudes, poses and affectations which made up the culture of the amorphous Movement. The disputes reflected its dual parentage in unbending 1968, Left-Bank anti-capitalism on the one hand and in the libertarian social and sexual attitudes of the Swinging Sixties on the other. The politicals and the hippies could make common cause on many issues; the same people turned up on demonstrations, the same dress sense made the same statements of non-conformism, the same music appealed to both, the same politicians were hate-figures, but the gulf was wide. 'Drop out' urged the siren voice of Timothy Leary from California, but the injunction was rejected by those who wanted social commitment and political involvement. Drugs offered bliss, escape, ecstasy and the artificial paradise Rimbaud preached, while Marxist doctrine and practice aimed at the creation of a real paradise for all. At this time, a more mournful voice began to make itself heard: the lament of those ordinary working people who simply saw drugs as a scourge which poisoned their neighbourhoods, made their streets unsafe and inflicted disabilities and sometimes death on their children. Dario chose to pay heed to this voice.

'I had two scripts prepared,' he recalled.[8] 'One on China, and the other on a family of shack-dwellers around Piazza Duomo in Milan. I did a reading for workers and people from the neighbourhood. They told me – yes they are fine but there are more urgent problems to discuss, for instance, drugs. So I set to work and have produced this play.' The work, premièred in the Palazzina on 2 March, was eventually given the title *Mum's Marijuana is the best.*[9]

The version of the play published by Giorgio Bertani was furnished with enough material to make a treatise. 'You wanted an essay on the problem of drugs,' wrote Hrayr Terzian,

> to put in the appendix to your extraordinary play and to emphasize that our earlier conversations, during and after the journey to China, provided the opportunity for your imagination to construct this new work . . . the trip to China helped us a great deal to understand, in the incommensurable distances which separate Chinese society from ours, our own problems, and in particular the problem of drugs.[10]

The Chinese experience provided Fo himself with the model approach. 'Look at the Chinese,' he told a representative of the Campaign against the Spread of Drugs.

> They do not put addicts in prison. They didn't even say that after the revolution, hey presto!, no more addicts. Neither did they leave them in the condition of 'cold turkey', the worst thing that can happen to an addict who wants to give up. Your flesh turns all creepy, and your nervous system breaks down. This is what is happening to thousands of young people today in Italy with this new law. They want to give up heroin but have no idea where to go because there is no one there to receive them, neither prisons nor hospitals. The only ones who can save them are the men and women who are there at their side, who give them back interest in life, in politics, because politics are life. In conclusion, for me, the problem is cultural, not abstract, and it must be put in those terms.[11]

With one part of his mind, he believed that the drugs explosion was due to political factors, possibly to CIA action. The bent policeman in *Mum's Marijuana* explains that the CIA

> is inside it to control all movements. Closing here, opening there . . . At the very moment it's bumping up trade and consumption, it's yelling – Help! Help! Help! Wake up, mothers! The Chinese are flooding us with drugs! The red criminals are destroying your children! It's kicking up dust. For example, that story that all drugs are the same, smoking, injecting, sniffing – do you know who put it about? The CIA.

In his more expansive moments, he knew that he was dealing with forces which surpass politics and which go to the very heart of human experience. As he told the campaigners,

> We have to pose again, in correct terms, the question – what is life? what is man? what is woman? leading to the question – what is love, love for your own body, not hatred for your body, not suicide and especially not suicide while staying in a sitting position. If you stay sitting down, as the system wants, what are you doing? You can toss yourself off, but then you get fed up with that. You can drink, but with the rubbishy wine that's going around, you get an ulcer. At that point, drugs are only a tiny step on a path that is already marked out.

Fo conducted many conversations, visited various centres and undertook a programme of research, but it was Dr Terzian who provided him with the perspective through which, at this stage, he viewed the whole problem. He also gave him the slogan which turned the problem into one of class. 'A sentence by Terzian, a real luminary in this field, is significant: in the sub-proletariat, it is the drug which uses the individual, while among the rich it is the individual who uses the drug.' The rehearsals in the Palazzina were open to the inhabitants of the area, who felt free to drop in and make suggestions.

With *Mum's Marijuana*, Dario Fo found himself at odds with many of his youthful audience, still wedded to the view that 'pot is the symbol of a generation in revolt'. Although unswervingly didactic in purpose, it is none the less a confused play, and Dario later admitted that his ideas were not altogether clear in his mind at the time of writing. A lightly dramatized debate intercut with a sequence of jokes and gags, the work is dependent for its impact on a feeling of outrage which has as yet no precise focus. There are three underlying notions being advanced, but none very convincingly: that drugs are a class problem, that the powers-that-be manipulate public attitudes so as to justify wider repressive measures and that everyone is prone to taking an inappropriately moralistic stance on the question. The basic mechanism is the reversal of expectations and roles. While an attachment to drugs was more common among the young, in the play the older generation, played by Franca and Dario, seem set on championing the liberating effects of hashish. When the youthful Luigi comes home from work at midday, he discovers his mother and grandfather guiltily concealing traces of the drug and admitting not only to smoking it but also to growing and dealing in it. The mother, Rosetta, spokesperson for the author's opinions, has the most dynamic part. This role is another indication of the increasingly high profile accorded female characters, although it is striking that Fo can only accord such roles to the mother figure.

The play concludes on an unexpectedly Chekhovian note, with two long speeches from Rosetta which transcend all talk of machiavellian CIA plots to ponder deeper dilemmas pertaining to human beings in a technological society. To some extent, Dario was expressing the alienation from a soulless society which Marx saw as the basis of religious sentiment and which Herbert Marcuse, the ideological brahmin of the sixties, saw as the ultimate condemnation of capitalism, but he was venturing into territory on which he had rarely trespassed previously. The emotional life is not the stuff of his theatre. The speeches were given to Franca, who talks first of loneliness and then tells an allegorical tale of three prisoners in a cell, fed by their captors only on fish and meat so hard that it cannot be chewed or digested. The first prisoner devises a way of beating the food into a mash which can be swallowed, the second files his spoon into a sharp knife with which he cuts the food into tiny segments, while the third sinks into despair and hopelessness, refuses to take any measures and grows so weak that he is on the point of death. At this point, the first prisoner intervenes and prepares a mash for the dying man. After a couple of days, the second prisoner lends a hand and explains why he is scraping away all day at the prison wall with his sharpened spoon. He is cutting a hole in the cement between the bricks of the cell, so as to let in the light and afford hope of escape.

> In other words, this story tells you that everything is all right . . . every effort that we make to live and get by . . . but, put it any way you like, at the end, we've got to bore a hole in the wall if we want to get out. Through the hole, and only that way, we can make our escape. But watch out! A little window with bars won't do, no matter what some people say. 'Let's make do with it .

. . then we'll see.' No, a hole or nothing else, a breach in this bastard wall . . .
maybe we should knock the whole wall down . . . air, air! Keep on burrowing
away . . . doing what we can until they all come flocking to give a hand . . . to
knock down the wall . . . until we see the whole sky . . . all of it, great and deep
as it is!

It is a fine, rousing flourish to bring down the curtain, implying a revolt
as much against heaven as against a society which is askew. Whether it
helped understand the problem of drugs is another matter. The tone must
have jarred with the author himself, since this speech was cut in the greatly
modified version published in 1998, but it remains of significance. There
were none of the rousing certainties and exhortations to rise up against
oppression which had marked the finales of plays with Nuova Scena or La
Comune.

In May, Dario was elected president of the Italian Playwrights' Federation.
The post, though largely honorary, was an indication of regard from
fellow writers. Franca, meanwhile, continued with her Red Aid work, and
took up the case of Umberto Farioli. Farioli was one of those hauntingly
Dostoevskian characters who emerge in any history of terrorism, in Italy
or elsewhere. Pathetically, doggedly bent as much on self-destruction as on
the overthrow of the state, he had been arrested, not for the first time, the
previous November for allegedly planning the kidnapping of Gianni
Agnelli, a situation Dario was to use in a later play. Farioli was a semi-
invalid, with a heavy limp, and the day after his arrest the Red Brigades
had issued a statement saying that he was ill 'and in constant need of
medication'.[12] He was refused this care in prison until Franca took up his
case. She issued her own statement, making it clear that she had no
sympathy with the violence used and advocated by the Red Brigades and
that her involvement was purely humanitarian. Her intervention brought
Fariolo some relief.

The company spent June in Rome, performing in a specially constructed
circus tent. Aware of the criticism of some of his recent work, Dario
decided against producing anything new, preferring a retrospective of productions not previously seen by the Roman public. The programme
included *Mistero buffo*, *The Kidnapping of Fanfani*, *Mum's Marijuana is the
Best* and *Can't Pay? Won't Pay!* He was stung by the response to *Mum's
Marijuana*, especially the criticism from normally well-disposed sources
who feared that he had overstretched himself with the unremitting
demands he had imposed on himself year after year.

Meanwhile, political opinion in Italy continued its swing to the left. The Movement and its terrorist flankers captured the headlines, but the constitutional left-wing parties were growing steadily. The Communist Party increased its membership from 1,496,000 in 1969 to 1,798,000 in 1976,[13] and was generally expected to overtake its opponents in the general elections scheduled for 21 June 1976. The Christian Democrats had been involved in various large-scale scandals in the mid-seventies, the most notable of which was the Lockheed Affair, which led to the resignation of president of the republic, Giovanni Leone. On the other hand, there was still a widespread fear of any party carrying the label 'Communist', and during the campaign the right-wing journalist Indro Montanelli coined the memorable phrase which helped save the DC bacon – 'Hold your nose and vote Christian Democrat!' Many did, so although the Communists succeeded in winning 34.4 per cent, the Christian Democrats recovered to register 38.7 per cent of the vote. The DC knew that they could not govern without PCI support, so they called on the wiliest of their politicians, Giulio Andreotti, to form a government of 'national unity'. Under the agreement, the PCI, while not formal coalition partners, had the right to be consulted before legislation was introduced, and in return offered support, or at any rate non-opposition, from the opposition benches. Both Dario and Franca regarded these moves with undisguised dismay.

After the Roman season, the couple retired to Cesenatico for their annual summer break. Cesenatico, on the Adriatic, had always been a favoured resort of many Milanese, and Dario and Franca had been going there regularly since the early years of their marriage. In the 1960s, they had purchased an old *casa colonica* well away from the hubbub of the beach and the seafront promenades, and some years later were able to buy the adjoining property so as to make one spacious, luxury holiday home. In spite of the substantial amounts they had distributed to assist striking workers, to help out with the legal costs of militants facing trial or to support the various causes they espoused, they were by now a wealthy couple. In addition to income from their own work as actors, they were also in receipt of royalties for performances in Italy and overseas. They built a large, private swimming pool in the land surrounding the house, although privacy was never guaranteed. Children in the immediate locality had free use of the pool and the home was always liable to be invaded by friends from the city, as well as by directors or actors from other countries who wanted an exclusive workshop on how to produce Dario's work. In spite of that, Cesenatico was a haven where they could work and relax, and where they were accepted without fuss by the local people. It is here that Dario still does much of his writing.

They can be a demanding couple. Neither suffers incompetence with any gladness. When he feels he had been let down or cheated, Dario reacts with embittered spleen. His polemical armoury includes a sarcastic wit which he does not reserve for national politicians or internationally famed writers. Occasional correspondents in newspapers who criticized him or the causes he championed were liable to be subjected to sardonic disdain. That August, he was pursued by journalists anxious to find his response to a dispute with Domenico Modugno, the poet and singer now best known for his song 'Volare'. Modugno was recording a series of protest songs for television, and hoped to include some pieces written by Fo both in the programme and on a disc. Modugno's version of the disagreement was that he had proposed a programme on the riots in Bronte, the Sicilian town where, shortly after Garibaldi's landing in 1860, the inhabitants had risen against the landowners and aristocracy. Fo asked him to set some of his verses to music, and while Modugno was enthusiastic, pressure of time meant that the project was not carried to completion. Fo, on the other hand, claimed that a year earlier he and Modugno had explored the possibility of putting on a performance at Palazzina Liberty.

> The production was one of a series of artistic initiatives of ours, with the takings going to help workers who had been laid off by their employers. At the beginning, Modugno seemed enthusiastic, but when the time came for production and performance, he couldn't be traced. Now I hear that that he has made a record, but I am no longer in agreement, and I will do everything in my power to block him. What he has done is very serious and uncivil. It amounts to a form of artistic expropriation. I am sorry but I will not put up with certain kinds of behaviour. He has decided, on his own behalf, to bring to fruition a project which we had tossed about together, and which had quite different origins. I have not the slightest interest in having Modugno sing my songs.[14]

A more acrimonious dispute followed Dario's acceptance of an invitation issued by the Communist Party to take part in a debate on theatre at its national Festa de L'Unità at Prato. Dario was promised that the contributions to the debate would be published in the party's theoretical journal, *Rinascita*. What appeared was a highly partisan mixture of reporting and derogatory comments written by the party's official critic, Alberto Abruzzese.[15] Abruzzese wrote of Fo's theatre with the lofty disdain of a

Moses looking down from a plateau, offering lukewarm praise but conveying an overall impression of amused, patrician tedium. In Fo's words, he
adopted 'the tone of a verdict from the Upper Tribunal of the Cultural
Court, making his sentence beyond all appeal'. The crux of his complaint
was that Fo lacked 'any genuine dramaturgy', that he had never developed
any adequate theory of theatre to explain and justify his activities as writer
and performer. His poor awareness of the relationship between theatre and
class consciousness had caused him to use implements which were too
blunt and unsubtle, meaning that the politics were entrusted to direct
delivery by the chief actor. Normally people who wrote of Fo in these terms
conditioned their criticism of the writer by praise of the actor, but
Abruzzese sneeringly described these skills as those of the 'craftsman'. There
was more than a touch of snobbery in Abruzzese, which was shared by
many Communist intellectuals, apparent in Pasolini's disdain for Fo, and
often expressed as a preference for the avant-garde over popular theatre.
Abruzzese regarded Fo's theatre as simplistic and plainly had no instinctive
sympathy with popular culture. This left him in a dilemma over the theatre
of Brecht and the writings of Antonio Gramsci on this topic. Brecht he left
aside, but since Gramsci occupied for a Communist intellectual in Italy the
place occupied by Aquinas in the Catholic Church, he could not ditch him.
He neatly side-stepped the problem by claiming that Fo had misrepre-
sented and misunderstood Gramsci. And for good measure, he accused Fo
of being 'moralistic'.

Fo's lengthy, outraged reply was polemical in the extreme. His first
appeal was to the authority of Mao. Was Abruzzese familiar with a passage
where Mao attacked 'the stereotyped and sententious language of certain
party bureaucrats? Re-read it, it might be useful to you.' Fo was defensive
towards his own audiences, people 'who understand what we are saying
... who enjoy with their brains even when we say things that do not meet
with their full agreement, because they love the fantasy and imagination we
offer them'. As for the lack of 'dramaturgy', Fo insisted that even reactionary
authors had a theory of drama, clinching the case with a reference to
Ionesco, the man who had been his favourite reactionary dramatist since
the break-up of the Parenti–Durano–Fo group in the 1950s.

> It cannot be denied that even [Ionesco] possesses a clear theory of theatre; it
> might nauseate you, but he had it, as do the authors of a *pochade* and of Grand
> Guignol. Science and theory are not the exclusive heritage of Marxists ... At
> least on this, Albert, you will agree with me. So, how can this be? You concede
> dramaturgy to many people but not to me. 'Why not? That's why not.'

There was a hurt tone to his defence of his record in maintaining his independence from state interference, and to his attack on the 'cultural decentralization' practised by the Piccolo Teatro and supported by the PCI. This he viewed as 'cultural colonialism, a joke and swindle which were at times downright vulgar – a tramps' dinner offered by Ladies of Charity with spumante and cake once a year, at Christmas . . . and for the rest of the time, shit'. However, he astonished many of his followers by his assertion that his model and aspiration was Milan's famous opera house, La Scala, where his audience could sit in well-heated comfort and watch a show where everything worked to perfection and where nothing had to be roughed up. Until that pinnacle of perfection could be attained, Dario told radical theatre practitioners to forge their own path, create their own theatre, find their own public and not sit about waiting for subsidies or state aid. Italy is full of plangent playwrights or frustrated actors who complain about the existing structures and lack the will to take their own initiatives. In Dario's view, it was time for them to display 'the dignity and the courage' which come from enjoying autonomy from control imposed by interested bureaucrats in charge of funds or cultural programmes.

> In the meantime, while struggling to take over the structures which the authorities do not wish to cede, I do not think we are entitled to stand about idly, much less to come to some deal by accepting (with the noble alibi that we 'must get by somehow') shameful blackmail and compromises in return for grants, circuits with a guaranteed minimum or maximum with the powers that be will make you pay dearly by imposing on you its policies and ideas.

The point was clinched with an Arab-African fable which had been told to him by a member of the Fedayn. A lion chased a zebra from dawn to dusk, but could not catch it. Dragging himself home defeated, he struck up a conversation with a lynx which had watched the hunt with amusement. The lynx was derisive, but when the lion invited him to do better, the lynx demurred, saying that the zebra was too fast and too resourceful for one like him. 'But Your Majesty cannot allow himself to be humiliated in this way. You must punish this animal, otherwise what will remain of your dignity?' The lynx summoned all the animals of the forest for a congress, at which he would make a speech in the lion's name.

At the conference, there was also a 'neo-critic, who kept himself to one side'. The lynx proposed that the zebra be severely censured for its contemptible behaviour and banned from the forest. 'Why,' asks the crocodile, 'because you felines cannot manage to catch it?' Not at all, replies the lynx, who insists that his species had always upheld the sacred right of each animal to defend itself in any way it saw fit, but there were ways and ways. The horse or the giraffe knew how to maintain their dignity while fleeing, unlike the zebra, who was prone to exercise its undoubted right to flee in 'an unacceptable, ungainly way, bereft of all style'. The expulsion motion was passed, and the edict scratched into the bark of the trees. The zebra, who was illiterate, had to have the edict read to him by 'a monkey with a hairy bottom, of the species bureaucrat', but he reacted with disdain and anger. 'I'll show them a thing or two about style,' he determined. He took lessons in dance, learned how to walk gracefully on his hindlegs and even attempted a complex *pas de deux*. The watching monkeys went into ecstasies, and even the lion admitted he would have to rethink his objections. 'It would be a real pleasure to chase an animal of such delicacy, so delightfully rhythmical in its steps.' Having uttered these words, he leaped on the zebra and sunk his teeth into his ribs. The zebra tried to run off while maintaining the grace it had acquired, but the lion jumped on to the animal's back and killed it. 'Such a pity,' groaned the monkeys. 'A very noble animal has perished there. He cared more for his style than for his skin. A real artist. Amen.'

In the *Rinascita* piece, Fo said that the moral was evident, but he spelled it out in another journal.

> I am not the zebra who is going to fall into the problem of someone else's model. I have a model and have no need of a science and elegance which are not mine. The concept which they, *Rinascita* or the Communist Party, have of dramaturgy is up to them. Let me say, I have my own dramaturgy, you don't notice it, just as the zebra had. My dramaturgy lies in the relationship with people; my way of making theatre consists of breaking up the play with interventions, with reality. As for being a craftsman, this is an attitude which is a consequence of a dramaturgy. What *Rinascita* is making is an aristocratic, not a progressive, statement. The men of the Renaissance attended a studio before they could be artists. They boasted about their art, and their art was their craft.[16]

There were other, more predictable, matters to be attended to. In November, he faced trial in Reggio on the familiar grounds of having resisted a police officer in the pursuit of his duties on 11 April 1970. The disputed duties involved attendance at a performance from which Dario felt entitled to bar the officer since the company enjoyed private-club status.

Dario won his case on the grounds that the acts in question did not constitute a crime. That same month, works of his were being performed in Malmo, Copenhagen and Stockholm, while Ingmar Bergman's Dramaten theatre in the Swedish capital had taken an option on *Order, by GOOOOOOOOD!* In response to an invitation from the Stadsteater in Copenhagen, he was contemplating doing *Hamlet*; not Shakespeare's tragedy, but a version of a Danish popular play from the late fifteenth century. 'There are the first revolts by the Scandinavian peasants and weavers, and the voice of the ghost is the voice of the people emanating from the mouth of a hanged man. It is a project I am very keen on,' he told the *Corriere della Sera*, but it was a project he never managed to bring to the stage.

There were other offers which he did not feel free to reject. The election results led to a loosening of Christian Democrat control of institutions, especially the broadcasting media. RAI had been a Christian Democrat fiefdom, but the new management now made overtures to Dario to see whether, after fourteen years' exile, he would be interested in returning to the television screen.

Chapter 11

Televised Anathemas

Since the *Canzonissima* fracas, Dario and Franca had shown a certain ambiguity towards television. As would be expected from any strong-minded individuals, they replied to the ban with expressions of robust insouciance, implying, if not quite stating, that television was irrelevant to the task they had set themselves of updating the popular theatre tradition, finding their own audience and talking directly to them in the medium of their own choosing. Dario in particular missed no opportunity of expressing his dismay at the brainless light-entertainment shows broadcast on RAI, and of denouncing the cynical political management of a supposed public service by the Christian Democrats for the Christian Democrats. At the same time, the two were clearly frustrated at their denial of access to the principal medium of communication and entertainment in modern society. Hans Enzenberger once wrote that in a *coup d'état*, the insurgents occupy first the broadcasting station, then the chancelleries. Television is a centre of power from which Dario and Franca were excluded by an act of political will.

After the 1976 elections, the Socialist Party was given *de facto* control of the RAI 2, a newly established channel. Dario responded positively when Massimo Fichera, the channel's director, wondered if he would be willing to let bygones be bygones and return to the television screens. 'It may not be the ideal,' he said,

> but even television has been forced to reflect the collective consciousness of these years. I have seen some broadcasts where it was possible to call a spade a spade. On the other hand, we must take advantage of the contradictions which emerge. These plays of mine have been seen by some 350,000 spectators, *Mistero buffo* by perhaps a million or more, but the chance of reaching 6–10 million viewers is impressive.[1]

The first proposal was to turn back the clock and begin with the episodes of *Canzonissima* which had caused so much controversy fourteen years previously, but a search of the archives revealed that the programmes had been destroyed. The next proposal was for a wide-ranging retrospective of Dario's theatre during the years of his absence from the television screen, but Dario was nervous about introducing his work too abruptly to an unprepared television audience who might be unaware of the controversies these works had aroused.

> I decided to go for my theatre of the sixties, so as to permit a gradual approach by the television audience to our stage language and to our style of putting on shows. If we had offered our more recent work, the impact might have been too violent. Plays like *Accidental Death of an Anarchist, The Kidnapping of Fanfani, Bang! Bang! Who's There? The Police!* might well have been too strong a shock for people brought up on yesterday's school of mind-numbing television.

The series was given the humdrum title *Theatre of Dario Fo*, and would feature *Mistero buffo* in two episodes for a total of five and a half hours' television time, *I Think Things Over and Sing About Them*, which was also to be broadcast in two parts, as well as the plays *Seventh: Steal a Little Less; Isabella, Three Caravels and a Con-man*; *Toss Out the Lady*, and a new piece on the condition of women.

RAI demonstrated the importance they attached to the series by announcing it would be filmed in colour. Colour television was in its infancy in Italy, but the management was aware of the worldwide sales potential of any initiative involving Dario Fo. Dario set his face against special adaptation for the screen and made it a condition that the filming be done in the Palazzina Liberty, not in a television studio,

> first of all, [because] the Palazzina has become a symbol for us. And then what I have in mind is not a television show in the strict sense, but something which conveys the significance of the Palazzina in relation to our theatre, to the debates which take place there, to the participation and intervention of an audience which is not only popular but also, to a large extent, bourgeois. The bourgeois audience pays by experiencing a scandalized emotion, for example when the police arrive to kick us out.[2]

The prospect of RAI, a public corporation, filming inside the Palazzina Liberty caused ructions inside the Milan City Council. Carlo Bianchi, a DC stalwart, raised the question in the council chambers, referring with some indignation to newspaper reports that RAI and Fo had already signed a contract. How could this be, he wondered, since Fo was supposedly on the point of vacating premises he had no right to be occupying? He was assured that Fo would be leaving in a couple of months, and in any case no municipal expenditure would be involved. RAI would put its own generators in place.

Initially the contract envisaged a total of eight or nine hours of broadcast material, but there would appear to have been greater flexibility in broadcasting circles than would be tolerated nowadays, or perhaps accountants had less sway. In any case, those involved were carried away by their own enthusiasm and ended up with a total of eighteen hours of programming. The material was broadcast in two cycles, one in spring and the other in autumn 1977. Curious journalists and people from the neighbourhood turned up to watch the filming, although public access had to be restricted because of the general confusion of wires, reflectors, moving cameras, temperamental technicians and irascible engineers that are part and parcel of filming. Dario was an early casualty; he fell over an extended wire, rolled down the stairs of an emergency exit and ended up with his leg in plaster. The sacred rule that the show must go on was observed. The schedules were altered, and filming began with *I Think Things Over and Sing About Them*, which he was only directing, rather than with *Mistero buffo*.

For the series as a whole, Dario was involved on all fronts, as writer, actor and director. He modified aspects of the plays, reducing the length of *Toss Out the Lady* but introducing into it the dwarf routine he had perfected for the Fanfani play. The *I Think Things Over* piece was a distillation of the three successive productions and allowed Dario the freedom denied him at the first staging to use choreographed movement alongside the songs. There were very few modifications to *Seventh: Steal a Little Less*, neither in the rhythms and development of the plot nor in the central attack on corruption. 'Scandals are always with us,' he said. He also pointed out that what had seemed outrageous flights of fancy, such as the use of lobotomy in dealing with criminals, had been practised on members of the Baader-Meinhof gang in Stammheim prison in Germany. The final programme of broadly feminist sketches and one-act plays, eventually given the title *Let Us Talk About Women*, was completely new.

In the frantic lead-up to the first programme, scheduled for Friday 22 April, Franca found time to accept an invitation to go to Portugal to join in the celebrations for the revolution which toppled the dictatorial regime, but the couple were otherwise fully engaged on a round of interviews and personal appearances in the unnecessary attempt to drum up interest. The press responded with gusto, though in those days of civic unrest, tension and terrorism, there was no shortage of alternative topics. Giorgio Gaber, singer-songwriter and friend of Dario's, announced in Rome that he would be abandoning the stage to return to his earlier career as an accountant. This dramatic announcement followed attempts by left-wing groups, with whom he was in broad sympathy, to behave in accordance with the principles of *Can't Pay? Won't Pay!* They forced their way into a concert, paying only the ticket price they themselves thought fair. Some, offended at the bourgeois distinction between performer and audience, went further. A group tried to storm the stage in Rome, claiming to be admirers of Gaber's who wanted to sing their own songs. 'The stuff about some people being tuneless is a bourgeois invention,' they stated. In the early months of 1977, the University of Rome was occupied by disgruntled students. When the respected trade-union leader and Communist activist, Luciano Lama, went to calm the student body, he was greeted by jeers and mockery. When the police moved to evict the students in April, two police officers were killed by gunfire. Meanwhile, accusations of corruption had reached the highest level of government. Two ministers, Luigi Gui and Mario Tanassi, were impeached in February for their part in the Lockheed affair.

In spite of this flurry of newsworthy activity, it was the return of Fo to television screens which commanded most column inches. 'The Great Return' was a favourite headline, followed by variations on the theme of the 'prodigal son' or the 'heretic readmitted to the fold'. The work chosen to open the series on 22 April was *Mistero buffo*, but the serendipity of scheduling meant that Franco Zeffirelli's film *Jesus of Nazareth*, with Robert Powell in the title role, was serialized on television the same month, with the final episode due for transmission on the evening following Fo's programme. Although personal relations between the two were cordial, Zeffirelli, an ardent Catholic and an enthusiastic supporter of the Christian Democrats, represented everything in Italian artistic life which Fo abominated.

Fo used several of his interviews to denounce Zeffirelli's interpretation of the figure of Christ. He excoriated Zeffirelli with scornful violence, accusing him of having ignored the bacchic joyfulness, the sybaritic eroticism, the delight in sensual appetites, the disdain for the rich and powerful which are integral to the popular reading of the story of Christ.

In *Mistero buffo*, I accepted the popular approach in its totality. I turned back to the popular tradition which is not made up of boorish inventions, as some have always believed. Indeed, the people's way of reading the gospels is much closer to the substance than that of intellectuals and the literary set. What do

I regret in Zeffirelli? That all the moments of grand, generous sexuality, of festivity, of joy, of song, that is of the Dionysiac rite, have been eliminated. It is not a casual mistake, because each time the body should be on stage, when the body has its part, he intervenes to cut it out. The first example is Mary Magdalen. The Magdalen is old, wrinkled, vulgar, ugly, she lives in the dirt. She goes to Jesus and Jesus says to her, 'You have washed my feet in your tears and dried them with your hair.' But we never see her carry out that gesture. Zeffirelli never shows it to us. He is terrified of that gesture, because it is a gesture of great sexuality. In the popular tradition, Mary Magdalen is a sensual woman, always depicted with long hair. In Simone Martini's *Crucifixion*, Mary Magdalen embraces the cross, she embraces Christ by the legs, once again wraps his feet in her hair. Not in Zeffirelli. He cuts, castrates, emasculates. He is ascetic, Platonic, Aristotelian. It is an Aristotelian concept of Christianity. It is blasphemous.[3]

The accusation of blasphemy was to be heard more frequently and stridently in Italy that April than at any time since the heyday of the Holy Inquisition, but it was Fo who was indicted as the blasphemer. If Dario's views on the earthiness of gospel conduct would startle biblical exegetes or moral theologians, his principal charge against Zeffirelli was clear and coherent. Dario is invariably an egocentric critic. The strength of his criticism lies not in the acuteness of his observations on other writers or actors, but in how his criticism clarifies his own artistic and political credo. For him, the gospels were not a source of religious revelation nor a privileged access to moral absolutes, as they were for Zeffirelli, but an integral part of the only tradition he recognized, the people's tradition. He was never more Gramscian than when he discussed religious practices. The value of the Bible for him lies not in the canonical interpretation handed down *ex cathedra* by bishops or scribes, but in the folk vision of it which had been incorporated into the worship, the festivals, carnival rites and workaday lives of the poor and dispossessed. Mandarins might dismiss that vision as mere superstition, but Fo held that the popular vision was the only authentic evangelical interpretation. It was certainly his.[4]

He was equally at odds with Zeffirelli over his the depiction of certain incidents, such as the expulsion of the merchants from the Temple ('because he makes Christ hysterical. He uses the Christ of Fra Angelico . . . The yelling and screaming of Masaccio will never be part of Zeffirelli's vision; it was not by chance that Pasolini turned to Masaccio'). Equally, he found fault with Zeffirelli's portrayal of Judas. Fo made Judas into a member of the upper class, 'the only intellectual among the sons of carpenters

184

and fishermen. Judas knows how to read and write, he knows Greek, Judas is from a wealthy family.' In the popular tradition, Judas was never accorded any respect or forgiveness. 'In *Mistero buffo*, I inserted a sophisticated monologue where Judas . . . tries to save himself with dialectic, overturning the truth. I leave Judas hanging from a tree.'

Presumably that expression of views should have been warning enough of the nature of the vision which would underlie Dario's work. Ignorance was in this case inexcusable. *Mistero buffo* had toured the length and breadth of Italy in performance before coming to the television screen, but seemingly nothing of its contents had permeated the consciousness of Italy's parliamentary or ecclesiastical authorities, or of their representatives in the press. The day after the broadcast, the plain people of Italy were treated to a display of outrage and indignation which would have been excessive even if Fo had advocated dethroning the Pope, demolishing St Peter's basilica and defacing Michelangelo's *Pietà*. The Italian Senate and Chamber of Deputies, the Vatican, the Conference of Italian Bishops, RAI, every newspaper of whatever political slant, every weekly, including those that normally concerned themselves with sport or sex, set aside their normal activities to debate what was immediately dubbed 'the Fo question'.

Normally sane men and women, charged with responsibility for governing the affairs of church and state, lost all sense of equilibrium. 'On Television the Fo Bomb Has Gone Off' thundered Genoa's *Secolo XIX*, and that was one of the more moderate responses. 'Indignation Among Catholics After Fo's Programme' was the expression used in *Il Tempo*. 'The Jesus of Dario Fo' ran the *Corriere d'Informazione* in bold capitals, before adding below, 'The Polemic Explodes on the *Mistero buffo* Broadcast Last Night on Channel Two'. In the article itself, the paper reported that 'this poor Jesus never does finish dying'. Explosions of the type the headline referred to went off all over Italy that week, mainly in the editorial offices of the national dailies. Father Romeo Panciroli, official Vatican press officer, excelled with the sheer intemperance of his comments. 'A disgusting, crass and degrading broadcast,' he opined, 'which offended the Catholic faith and the religious sentiment of the Italian people, and one which,' he added, warming to his task, 'has considerably lowered the level of television transmissions. I believe that this is the first time that a national television network has, in the time that television has existed in the world, broadcast a programme of such blasphemy.' Fo had secured himself a place in history, or at least in that section of history controlled by Fr Panciroli, as the most blasphemous of writers. Fo himself retorted that this was the 'finest compliment the Vatican could pay me, apart from the fact that I do not consider the Vatican sacred'.[5]

The upper echelons of the Vatican hierarchy entered the fray. Cardinal Ugo Poletti, cardinal vicar of Rome, sent a telegram to Italy's prime minister, Giulio Andreotti, expressing his anxiety over the damage this programme had done to Italy's image abroad and voicing deep concern over wounded religious sensibilities.

> Speaking for innumerable citizens and organizations of Rome, I express sadness and protest over the blasphemous and anti-cultural television programme *Mistero buffo* by Dario Fo, to which should be added profound humiliation for the inconceivable vulgarity of a public broadcast which demeans the Italian nation before the whole world.[6]

The Conference of Italian Bishops also sent a telegram to the prime minister, demanding respect for 'the religious sentiments and conscience of a considerable part of the Italian people, in these difficult moments which require not division and anathemas, but the concord and collaboration of all'. There was no shortage of anathemas. The Vatican daily, *Osservatore Romano*, reminded parish priests of their duty to denounce such irreligious talk from the pulpit, and went on to demand a purge at RAI. 'How is it possible', it asked in Latinate prose, 'for the authorities responsible for radio-telecommunications in Italy to permit an operation so clearly destined to wound the consciences of Catholics?'[7] Although consciences among the faithful appeared intact, the Vatican itself was in a state of shock. *Panorama* reported that on the Sunday following the programme, the highest authorities in the government of Vatican City, including Cardinal Jean Villot, the Secretary of State, Cardinal Benelli, Archbishop of Florence and Monsignor Agostino Casaroli, Minister for Foreign Affairs, met to consider an official diplomatic protest to the Italian Republic. They decided instead to encourage the Italian faithful to make their own protests.[8]

This they did in varied ways. Italian law still contained a provision outlawing 'contempt of religion', and the Roman magistrate, Rosario De Mauro announced that he had received dozens of official complaints from private citizens and from such bodies as 'Catholic Parents' or 'Ex-Salesian pupils', inviting him to open proceedings against Fo. De Mauro, clearly a man of some independence of mind, declined to take any action, since he could find no trace of any attack 'on moral values or on the divinity. The figure of Christ, for example, appears clearly contrasted with that of Boniface VIII. The sensation drawn from the work is of respect for the spiritual heritage of the Catholic Church, in contrast to the representation of human behaviour which deviates from the values of that heritage.' His was a whisper in a storm which continued to rage.

The board of RAI was in more or less permanent session, and had to decide whether to screen the second episode. It was hopelessly divided, with one half threatening to resign if the series went ahead, and the other half threatening to resign if it did not. RAI was still not a fully independent body, and the puppetmasters were the party bosses. On the floor of the Chamber of Deputies and in the parliamentary Committee of Vigilance on Radio and Television, protests grew in intensity and shrillness. The committee chairman was the veteran Christian Democrat, Paolo Emilio Taviani, formerly Minister for the Interior and later the subject of a venomous, derisive letter written by Aldo Moro while in captivity with the Red Brigades. The committee itself contained thirty-seven members, of whom fifteen were from the DC, eleven from the Communist Party, three from the Socialists, with one each from the Social Democrats, the Republicans, the Liberals, the Independent left, the Radicals, the neo-Fascist MSI and the Democratic Party of Proletarian Unity (PdUP). Two days after the broadcast, Taviani too received a telegram from the Italian Women's Committee, one of the leading Catholic organizations, demanding that the programmes be immediately suspended. He wished to reply immediately to the Vatican and the Women's Committee but was stymied by procedural wrangles dreamed up by the PdUP, for whom Fo had done a party political broadcast.

Taviani emerged as the most vehement of Fo's denouncers. 'The initiative of the DC group in raising the matter means that the DC is echoing in parliament and elsewhere the bitterness and contempt felt by Catholics and by the millions of citizens whose religious feelings have been outraged,' he intoned. If that was not denunciation enough, he went on to say that 'this programme reminds me of the Nazis who burned books and attacked both the *Osservatore Romano* and the boys from Catholic Action'.[9] He explained that he was speaking from the standpoint of a man 'who had always liked culture', who had been involved in the restoration of the Teatro Argentina and in reforming RAI, therefore as one 'who is entitled to raise [his] voice'. His objection was firstly to the fact that Fo had been granted the privilege of having his entire repertoire shown on television, a privilege not extended even to Eduardo De Filippo, and secondly to 'the contents, a unilateral act of violence against fundamental religious values held by many citizens'. Lest he had missed his target, he accused Fo of 'ideological hooliganism . . . the anti-clericalism of seventy-years ago'. In another interview, he denounced Fo as 'an ideological fraud, a liar, the mongol brother of Jacques Tati'.[10]

Judging by press reports, it would seem that no topic other than *Mistero buffo* was being discussed from the Swiss border to the southernmost tip of Sicily. From the unmanageable mass which *Mistero buffo* had become, Dario had selected four sketches – 'The Grammelot of the Zanni', 'Saint Benedict', 'The Raising of Lazarus' and 'Boniface VIII'. The first two sketches were plainly considered innocuous, leaving two main sources of conflict: Fo versus the DC over Boniface VIII and by implication over political and ecclesiastical power in Italy; and Fo versus Zeffirelli over Lazarus and therefore over religious belief. In the whole incredible business, it was Zeffirelli who conducted himself with most tact and restraint. He was used in the columns of the *Osservatore Romano* as the seraphic counterpoint to the Mephistophelean Fo, but while disagreeing with Fo's use of religious iconography, he continued to express his admiration for Fo as man of theatre. Two newspapers, *Milano Sera* and *La Repubblica*, brought them together for face-to-face confrontations, covering largely the same ground. Zeffirelli defended his own film, saying that he had wanted to emphasize 'pacification and love. My *Jesus* is created so as to enter into people's lives without disturbance', which was the opposite of the effect Fo wished to create. Fo was out to overthrow the altars. Zeffirelli insisted that Fo 'was one of the great Italian theatrical phenomena',[11] and had the subtlety to recognize that he operated in the frolicking goliardic tradition which was offensive and debunking by definition, but he was unhappy at the terrain Fo had chosen. Zeffirelli was upset at the unseemly squabbles which attended the miracle of the raising of Lazarus from the dead and by the introduction into a sacred scene of costermongers, pedlars, hucksters and assorted con-men plying their trade while waiting for Jesus to work the miracle. While claiming to be sophisticated and tolerant himself, Zeffirelli adopted the standpoint of the plain, uneducated Catholic.

> That type of scurrility cannot be proposed to a television mass audience without careful preparation. This is not a question of censorship. Fo can say what he pleases, but he himself performs in one way when he plays for workers and peasants, and in another when he performs for a radical bourgeois audience.

For a moment, Zeffirelli sounded uncannily like the defence advocates in the *Lady Chatterley* obscenity trial in London, worrying about the impact of such literature falling into the hands of 'wives and servants'.

Dario was entitled to his perplexity when he wondered if his work would have been acceptable if it had remained in basements and chamber theatres, where only a select audience had had access to it.[12] Yet the real paradox was that *Mistero buffo* had never been a work written or performed for an élite. Behind this whole discussion of the public reception of the televised version of the play lay the wider question of the power of television. *Mistero buffo* was not a new work premièred in 1977. In the years since the first performance in 1969, the work had been seen by vast numbers of people. Fo put the figure as high as 1.5 million, and even if that is excessive, the numbers of spectators were very high. But television in modern society has a power and a reach which theatre today, *pace* Dario Fo, can never have. The debate over *Mistero buffo*, involving as it did the hierarchies of church and state, was *ipso facto* a debate about power: power over minds, power over the circulation of ideas and thus the power to determine what Gramsci called cultural hegemony. The fracas demonstrated the truth of the charge that censorship on theatre was lifted but retained on television when television replaced theatre as the prime medium for entertainment. Having been spurned by television all these years, Fo was given a dramatic lesson in exactly why he had been ostracized. Television could be used to help develop critical faculties among the ranks of the people. The year 1977, in terms of Italian television, was one of those rare open moments when contentious, rebellious ideas can be aired. It was a brief interval.

The debate over power in church and state focused on the sketch satirizing Pope Boniface VIII. The sketch showed Boniface revelling in the pomp of office, vesting himself with the magnificent robes which proclaimed wealth and influence, all the while bullying the attendant altar boy. Although claiming to be sophisticated and processing in imperial splendour through the streets of Rome, Boniface meets Christ carrying his cross. Christ refuses to recognize his successor in the opulent figure of Boniface, a refusal symbolized by the kick with which he sweeps the Pope aside. The anger and scorn in Fo's portrayal are palpable. The medieval pope was not a straightforward allegory of the contemporary pontiff, but when critics said that his depiction of Boniface represented a challenge to contemporary ways, there could be no denying the charge. Without identifying the two, Fo did, in his preface to this sketch, make fun of the reiging Pope. But Boniface VIII was also an historical character and here Fo's critics faced a situation of some delicacy. The historical Boniface was a contemporary of Dante, whose position as Italy's supreme poet, and indeed as Europe's Catholic poet *par excellence*, could not be placed in doubt. Dante had hated – no milder word will suffice – Pope Boniface with a ferocity Dario Fo could never equal. Dante made it clear that there was a place in hell reserved for Boniface, who was still alive in the year 1300, the year in which *Divina Commedia* was set. When Dante reaches *Paradiso*, St Peter himself berates his successor for desecrating the papal throne with such virulence that the celestial rose of heaven, where the souls of the saved are clustered, turns red with shame. To condemn Fo over his treatment of Boniface is to condemn Dante Alighieri. It would be easier to have people believe that the Sacred College of Cardinals had embraced Calvinism.

There is much innocent fun to be had with the newspaper columns of those days, and even with the reports of parliamentary debates. Daily papers found space, among reports of terrorist attacks or events in Vietnam, for learned articles on medieval history and in literature. Those who had forgotten what they had learned at school found that Boniface had also been a target for the venom of the thirteenth-century Franciscan poet, Jacopone da Todi, who had been left chained to a wall for years on Boniface's orders. 'Boniface VIII in Parliament' ran a headline in the *Corriere della Sera* on 26 April. An absolutist pontiff, some six centuries dead, found himself at the centre of a debate about liberty and libertarianism in twentieth-century Italy. 'Jesus Is a Star' ran another headline. The French medieval historian Jean Chesneaux, commissioned by the *Corriere* to assess Fo's depiction of the Middle Ages, concluded that Fo had a deeper and more accurate knowledge of that epoch than most professional historians.

Fo was now the centre of a national disputation which recalled the controversy aroused a decade earlier when Hochhuth's *The Deputy*, with its accusation that Pius XII had declined to intervene to defend the Jews from Hitler, was staged in Rome. As it developed, the polemics went well beyond the issues raised by *Mistero buffo* itself and quickly degenerated into a debate of the deaf. Fo's more prosaic, political defenders railed against censorship, defended democracy and free speech, while the more aesthetically inclined spoke of the claims of imagination, the freedom of creativity, the necessary offence, the extension of cultural boundaries and challenges to sycophancy of mind. His opponents raised banners proclaiming the rights of religion, denouncing desecration, upholding respect for the sacred and questioning claims for absolute tolerance and free speech. The brilliant cartoonist, Forattini, produced a wicked *vignette* showing Fo crucified, but on a carefully worked rearrangement on the letters 'TV'. His head was positioned at the crook of the *V*, while his arms were stretched out under the upwards-sloping sides of the same letter, allowing his hands to emerge, nailed to the extremities of the *T*.

There were other ironic points which emerged in the course of the controversy. In April, Amintore Fanfani and other DC notables travelled to Florence to speak at a conference in defence of the absolute freedom of painters. The decision to focus on artists rather than writers was dictated by the logic of the Cold War. Some painters in the USSR had exhibited their own work but the exhibition had been disrupted by the KGB, not because their canvases were politically motivated but because they did not conform to prevailing tastes in the upper echelons of the Soviet Communist Party. By supporting the right of artists in the Soviet Union, the right in Italy believed they were embarrassing the Kremlin while also putting their own Communist Party on the defensive. An alert journalist remembered that the Venice Biennale in 1976 had been dedicated to the theme of 'dissent'. The question was obvious. When and where was dissent permitted and indeed encouraged? Did pictorial artists have greater rights than those enjoyed by writers? Was Fo entitled to be regarded as a dissident? Was Italy on a par with the USSR?

Dario had blown apart the silence of servility or of habit which underlay acceptance of the *status quo*, as the ecclesiastical and political right in Italy fully recognized. He was plainly perceived as a threat by Christian Democratic Italy. The threat to religious belief itself was not intentional, but the threat to the established order and hierarchy of church and state was. Transcendental theology held no interest for him, and he steadfastly rebuffed any effort to enlist him among the ranks of the twentieth-century's mystics without a creed. 'I am not even distantly a follower of any religion,' he told *Panorama*. 'I am a convinced atheist, a Marxist, a materialist. These are for me points which cannot be touched.'[13] It is legitimate to doubt this assertion, and perhaps the 'religious element' in Dario Fo has deeper roots than he himself recognizes; perhaps Fo is pursued by his own Hound of Heaven. He is certainly no proselytizer for secularism, nor does he jeer at doctrines or dogmas. Nowhere in his theatre does he pit the religious against the materialist vision of the cosmos. His scorn is reserved for the growth of the institutional church into a centre of power and wealth, and its uncritical cohabitation with oppressive forces in the state. His researches into the history and development of popular theatre, especially of medieval theatre, have convinced him of the centrality of the religious experience in the world-view of ordinary people, and have led him to conclude that there is a subversive element in the popular interpretation of gospel teaching.

> Boniface VIII, what is he? He is the violence of the power of the Church. What happens? Boniface VIII bedecks himself in finery, sacred finery if you like, but today people want a different Church, not the mired-down Church they see . . . I offend power, not religious feeling.[14]

The Fo case was rapidly caught up in the thickets of party politics at a time when Italy was governed by a series of daily deals between the DC Cabinet and the PCI opposition. As such, it rapidly became a nuisance for the respective leaderships, each of whom had reasons to fear the ramifications of the 'Fo affair'. One journalist wrote that the Fo affair presented the most serious risk not only to the continuance of the government in office, but also to the whole process of integralization of the Communists into democratic life and of the normalization of relations between the PCI and the rest of the political parties. The plan was three-pronged: 'to force the Christian Democrats and the Communists to vote against each other in the parliamentary commission, to offer space to those inside the DC who were still prepared to ride the tiger of anti-Communist intransigence, and to turn the remaining fifteen episodes of the *Theatre of Dario Fo* into so many bombs against PCI-DC dialogue'.[15]

Other countries looked on bemused. Fo was invited to France in May to explain on French television exactly what was going on in Italy. He told them that he was aghast to discover that Boniface VIII had his defenders in modern Italy. The rest of the series went ahead undisturbed, watched by more viewers than any other programme in Italian television history. Dario expected *Seventh: Steal a Little Less*, with its mockery of political–commercial corruption, to be controversial, and perhaps it should have been, but in the event it passed off more quietly.

When the first approaches were made to him, Dario was asked why he wanted to return to RAI, which had treated him so appallingly in the past. He replied that he had not changed but that RAI had. This was true enough, but was only a part of a wider truth, as the ecclesiastical–political establishment came to realize in the course of the fracas. Italy was no longer the clerical or confessional state it had been when Alcide De Gasperi and the founding fathers succeeded in making Christian Democracy the natural governing party in the republic. In the 1970s, there was no longer any meaningful sense in which Italy could be described either as a Christian Democratic state or even as a Catholic country. The watershed date in this transformation of Italian society was undoubtedly the 1974 referendum on divorce, when electors rejected the advice of the Church and of the party which was its political arm. There was a wild exaggeration to the entire 'Fo Affair', but the hysteria of the response was also a belated recognition in certain quarters of fading powers. Vatican anxiety and Vatican policies had the advantage of logic, even if it was the logic of *realpolitik*. The working arrangements between the DC and the PCI meant that the PCI was no longer the pariah party, but also that Italy was no longer a monolithic society. Dario Fo, as was shown by the bugging of his phone, the bombing of theatres where he played, the threats issued to collaborators and the persecution he had endured from police and prosecution services, was very much a *persona non grata* both to the official ministries and to the unofficial masonries which held sway in the governance of the republic. He was principally the singer of this process, but he had also played his part as composer and orchestrator. And he was proud of both roles.

Chapter 12

Liberating Franca

The final television programme was given the downbeat title *Let's Talk About Women*, and, although not fully recognized at the time, the interest in women's issues marked the opening of a new phase in the career of Dario and Franca, wherein Franca would assume the dominant role.

According to the new cliché, Italy was in a period of 'ebb-tide', a time of diminished energy after the excitement and optimism of the years of mass political agitation. The Movement, and terrorism, had not yet collapsed, but there was a grudging recognition that the Bastille could not be stormed, perhaps even that there was no Bastille to be stormed. The more opportunistic, those who would in future decades occupy seats in parliament, posts in editorial offices or on court benches, began to distance themselves from what it was convenient to term the excesses of youth. The view more commonly heard was that the days of grand public strategies had passed and that people were entitled to turn their minds to private matters, to culture, to ecology, to agriculture, to self-fulfilment, to hedonism, to warding off disillusion, to cuisine (which enjoyed a boom), to marrying and raising families. Retiring into the private dimension was put forward as a gesture of contempt and an assertion of purity, but it was soon clear that the 'ebb-tide' was part of a process of integration into an unreformed, warts-and-all society. Street action was forgotten: revolutionary socialist theatre too had run its course, as it had in previous generations for Meyerhold, Reinhardt, Piscator, Brecht and Clifford Odets.

Dario and Franca had no sympathy with the proponents of 'ebb-tide', but their stance shifted, perhaps unconsciously. In 1977, the two published an interesting little booklet, whose prosaic title, *The Political Theatre of Dario Fo*, conceals a certain depressed bafflement.[1] The work contained two scripts – *Mistero buffo* and *Isabella, Three Caravels and a Con-man* – a preface by Dario, an article by Franca and a cartoon version by Jacopo Fo of the television theme song 'Who Makes Us Do It?'. The focus and the critical gaze are retrospective. Dario reflects on the theatre he has already

194

produced, defining it in newly discovered Sartrean terms as 'theatre of situation' as opposed to the 'bourgeois theatre of Chekhov or Pirandello. [Theirs was] a theatre of characters who tell each other their own stories, their own moods which are then the key to mechanical conflicts. We were always concerned to take a different approach, the situation approach.' Even the term 'political theatre' now seems to him of dubious validity. 'As far as the works staged by La Comune are concerned, I would have preferred to call them "popular theatre", on account of the discourse they contain, meaning that they succeed in reclaiming a certain type of class theatre.'

> The term 'political theatre' was coined by Piscator, as a polemical provocation to distinguish it from 'digestive' theatre, which is a theatre alienated from all contingent, dramatic, lyrical problems. Piscator's was a political theatre in the decisive fact of being managed directly by the working class.
>
> With the employment today of the term 'political', I would not like to make people's hair stand on end. Perhaps they are right, because 'political theatre' has become a kind of subtitle for tedious theatre, know-all theatre, schematic theatre, non-enjoyable theatre.
>
> Now, as is well known, all theatre is political, all art is political. It is when someone wants to hide the political value, as with Feydeau, that we have the most stridently political theatre, in this case bourgeois-political.
>
> Greek theatre is political theatre, indeed commissioned theatre. The *Oresteian Trilogy* was commissioned by the then hegemonic authorities in the *polis*. By adopting the absolutist, or the mythical and religious, approach, they hoped to make grand-style, great-power propaganda, that is, they hoped to ensure the election of a man to office. This theatre set itself against the archaic, peasant, rural tradition which saw the female as sacred, as the mother not only in the sense of progenitor but also as the source of culture and repository of the values of tradition.

For the first time, Dario chose to highlight the female aspect, but the emphasis on the mother figure is more idiosyncratic, and a foretaste of one of the main strands of the new female theatre Dario and Franca would produce. For some time, Women's Liberation movements had been growing in force, perhaps more strongly in Italy than in any other European country. In the same booklet, Franca contributed a piece which had elements of Maoist self-criticism and feminist consciousness-raising. She looked back over the type of role she had played both in the 1950s as a jobbing actress and in the work she and Dario had produced in the 1960s. These parts were, as she readily admitted, essentially decorative. In the 1950s, the empty head under a blonde hairpiece, atop characterless eyes and an inviting smile, the whole perched above a generous bosom, were the indispensable characteristics for the rising female star. Federico Fellini succeeded in seemingly satirizing this iconic figure, while in reality indulging the frisson it provides, with the scene in *La Dolce Vita* where Anita Ekberg, her body inflated beyond the dreams of any fetishist, wades provocatively in the Trevi Fountain.

Franca now recognized that she had not been a lifelong rebel. When she appeared in the revue *I Fanatici* with the Billi e Riva troupe in the fifties, she was photographed in sultry poses, leaning provocatively against pillars, or bedecked in low-cut dresses and wearing ribbons which resembled the rabbits' ears worn by Playboy Bunnies. Franca's head then was no more empty than Jayne Mansfield's, but she shared the American star's physical attributes and allowed herself, she now believed, to be reduced to sex-symbol status. By the seventies, she had discarded this image. As was noted by a writer in the women's magazine, *Noi Donne*:

> In the years in which she created together with Dario Fo the revue theatre, she entertained people principally by her provocative attractions combined with a 'vamp' style of performance (the 'empty-headed beauty' entertains and induces tenderness at the same time, thereby fully re-establishing the predominant position of the male, who takes from it an additional cause for reassurance): today, in the years of a theatre strongly committed at the level of social, political and ideological militancy, Franca Rame, still attractive though she may be, is more and more prone to refuse to make a display of her still appreciable features. She disguises herself, she makes herself ugly, conceals her profile and acts in such a way as to permit her to set out ideas and facts. She has chosen that style of acting which overrides differences between man and woman, between actor and actress, which eliminates sexual attributes as focus for attention . . .[2]

There is more than a touch of exaggeration in this estimate. The sexual charge in Franca's performances remained strong, but she regretted opportunities lost due to the sexist climate of earlier times:

> In Italy, in the theatre and cinema circuit, a disconcerting superficiality and banality were current. Since, as I have already said, I have certain physical characteristics, in other words those of the dumb blonde (*bellona*), I cannot do anything other than the vamp. This is true today, never mind then. In each and every film, I 'logically' played the vamp (but one who was good-hearted and a bit unlucky), and was never offered the role of an ordinary

woman, who just might have been able to speak and think for herself.

I carried this kind of sexist burden for many years. Even in Dario's plays, I was never, ever asked to display any kind of skill, craft, stage sense . . . well, if it was there, so much the better . . . this, obviously, from critics and not from Dario, who has always tried to create precise and concrete, as well as human, characters. Obviously he could hardly make me hunchbacked, but he gave me at least a minimum of brain. The finest compliment I received came from François Perrier, when he came to see *Isabella, Three Caravels and a Con-man*. 'You are a girl with a head on your shoulders, with a brain.'[3]

In reality, even in the revues, the one-act farces of the fifties and the first comedies of the bourgeois period, she donned revealing costumes and played vacuous women who did not aspire to positions of control over their own lives. This situation changed and evolved over the years. It was Enea, the seeming simpleton of *Seventh: Steal a Little Less*, who revealed the scheming and corruption all around, while Franca had the leading roles in both parts of *Isabella*, first as the dominant queen, and then as the mad Joan. With *Can't Pay? Won't Pay!* the female character took charge and became not the comic 'feed' but the principal comic actor.

The position of women in society was a subject which both Dario and, especially Franca now felt it necessary to address. 'For a theatre like ours,' she wrote, 'which both keeps up with what is going on and is fashioned by it, to have avoided associating ourselves with questions raised by women would have been a serious matter. The woman question is too important nowadays.'[4] The remaining problem was finding the appropriate style. In the discussions following the first production of *Let's Talk About Women*, she stated that 'speaking about women is easy. Everybody does it, perhaps too much. The difficulty is to do it in the theatre, and to say something serious on the condition of women while laughing and entertaining.'[5] Theatrical means had parity of importance with content, but there were problems over content too. Franca was uneasy over aspects of contemporary feminism. In her brief contribution to *The Political Theatre of Dario Fo*, she made a sharp, polemical distinction between her own position and that of 'feminists'. Occasionally, very charily, she would use the term 'feminist' to describe herself, but more commonly 'feminist' was a word applied to other women whose convictions she recognized, whose fervour she admired, but whose ways were not entirely hers. However much she may have been branded an extremist in social and economic politics, Franca was a moderate in sexual politics:

These girls, these women have done extraordinary things even if, as in every movement, there have been negative, mistaken phases. But this happens with all real movements. Were there not mistakes in '68? We can well admit it, since we are paying for them now.

I have a great deal of respect for the feminists, especially for those who do not take up positions of out and out antagonism to men, and for those who are working courageously to change reality, beavering away in their own localities, carrying out abortions, etc. I am not a militant feminist, in the sense that the greater part of my time is already absorbed, apart from the theatre, in other activities such as Red Aid and the thousand and one things needed to 'look after the shop'. But I do follow some initiatives and activities of the feminist movement. I was present, for instance, at the work of a group of young women who carry out abortions, and I must confess I was dumbfounded. I watched them (both those who performed the abortion and those who underwent it), and they were truly . . . heroic.[6]

Feminism which was anti-male in tone was not for her. The manifesto of the American group called SCUM (the Society for Cutting Up Men) filled her with uncomprehending dismay. It is facile to put this down to her age and background, as was done by some women who belonged to the category of 'militant feminists', but her rejection of this stance was determined primarily by her Marxism. Her political thinking was essentially class-based, where the classes were the exploited and the exploiters, or the proletariat and the bourgeoisie. She was never able to afford women the status of an independently exploited class. The compatibility or incompatibility of socialism and feminism was a theme which recurred endlessly on the agenda of the conferences and gatherings of those years, but Franca remained a socialist first. The only revolution to which she gave assent was one which would liberate all proletarians, male and female. In the socialist perspective, men, too, she repeated, were oppressed, and her 'feminism' aimed at a raising of consciousness, male and female. She never swerved from this view. Two years later, in an interview with a Sicilian paper, while on tour with *All Bed, Board and Church*, the final form of the work premièred on television as *Let's Talk About Women*, we find her saying:

I am not a feminist in the sense of militant. In fact I have never been a member of any group. I am a feminist by personal and political choice. I am not a separatist. For women to liberate themselves, it is not sufficient for us to change our heads, or those of men, we must change society. In my play, there is also a pitiless exposure of a society by means of laughter. I have always wanted to make people laugh while thinking, and to make them think while laughing.[7]

Encouraging rethinking by laughter had been the aim of the theatre which Dario and she had produced, and she had no wish to change tack. Leftist intellectuals in Italy had had problems with Fo's humour in the years of political militancy, and now the same attitude of a priori refusal recurred with the broadly feminist theatre the couple created in the late seventies. Humour which was subdued, subtle, dry or pawky was acceptable, but tomfoolery, knockabout, laughter which was festive, full-hearted and open-throated seemed somehow inappropriate or demeaning for serious subjects. In an article which appeared shortly before the broadcast of *Let's Talk About Women*, the novelist Natalia Ginzburg, who had always been prickly on any topic concerning Fo, wrote that he was not a real comic because real comics were 'tragic and ingenuous' and displayed an ability to be 'forgetful, dismayed and alone'.[8] Franca heard the same objections, and grew exasperated with critics who told her that her comic approach was letting women down.

At that time, many women's theatrical collectives were set up, although Franca never considered joining. Her discussions with feminist writers were a rerun of the debates inside Nuova Scena and La Comune. She received plays from women writers which dramatized the condition of women, but these rarely met her professional standards. She rejected any depiction of women as victims, or any pitying or self-pitying portrayal of women.

> I launched a kind of desperate appeal to some feminist comrades: 'Help and Solidarity! Sisters, help!' Some scripts were dispatched to me: tales, autobiographical stories, collections of letters, but all things which it would have been very difficult to transfer to the stage. Anyway, I tried, but what a disaster. Scripts which would never stand up, not even with the support of a crane.[9]

Franca knew that the only works which were likely to be acceptable to her were those written by Dario, or by her and Dario in tandem. At the high noon of feminism, Franca herself grew more noticeably assertive about her own part in the creative partnership. She and Dario had always worked together but her role had been overshadowed or downright neglected. Until the late seventies, the plays were published under Dario's name alone. She received credit neither for her contribution to the reworking of the texts during rehearsal, nor for the rewriting and editing, which she did alone, in preparation for publication. Dario by himself is unlikely to have left any published version of his work. Shakespeare could always be quoted to justify indifference to the printing press, but the truth was that the tedium, the routine, the concentration on unrewarding detail challenged his attention span. The show has always gone on, the plays have always been written, the rehearsals keenly supervised and the post-performance discussions attended to with unswerving attention, but Dario's horizons are marked by the play's run. Once that is over, his interest wanes. Stage directions, for instance, are not his forte; in the published versions of the early plays, they are entirely lacking. It was only when Franca decided they were indispensable that they began to appear. The final script would be an amalgam of the various modifications, rewrites, changes and alterations which had been introduced in the course of rehearsal and performance, so that the editor would find himself, or herself, faced with piles of scribbled pages from which to extract a publishable version. Shakespeare's folios were produced by admirers after his death, but the anonymous scribe-admirer deserves credit, as does Franca. There would be no Fo folio without her.

Franca began to speak of 'our' theatre, and from this period the playbills, programmes and the spines of the books began to accord her due credit. It is worth noting that while Fo is invariably quoted as the world's most performed living playwright, it is the jointly signed works which have been most frequently staged. The question is whether any change in the creative process actually took place at the time of *Let's Talk About Women*, or whether Franca was receiving belated credit for what she had always done. Both in private and in public, Dario and Franca have each given different versions at different times of the contributions each has made to the writing. On one occasion, Franca denied herself any role in the composition of the scripts,[10] saying that Dario was the writer in the house, but on another she said that 'of the hundred comedies by Dario, half were written with me'.[11] Most probably, there was no real change during this 'feminist' period, when the plays began to be jointly credited. The plays begin, in general, as Dario's but end as Franca's. That is not to lessen her importance in the creative partnership. Dario is the writer in the conventional sense, but it is hard to incorporate into that conventional sense the discussions before and after writing, at home and in theatre, between a couple with a unique relationship. It is left to Franca to do the honing and editing of the texts once the run is complete, and her contribution during rehearsals and performance is immense. Dario invariably defers to her sense of theatricality, of timing, of what works on stage. Her demands on other actors can be severe.

She tapes every performance and summons the actor if his or her timing is faulty and a laugh is missed.

Franca was sole author of *The Rape*, which was a very special case, and of some works produced later, but she did not write these first monologues on women. She pestered Dario to write something on the condition of modern women, but then was dismissive of the plays he brought her. He told her to emancipate herself and, since she wanted something specifically female, to go and do her own writing. She tried but, by her own account, without great success.

> At a certain point, Dario came down from his Aventine hill, and gave me a hand, in all truth, fortunately, two hands. He took up the pile of sheets of paper and scribbles and set off to make something of them. Well, I must say that one or two pieces came out more or less as I had always imagined them. They seemed (finally) to have been written by a woman. And there was more of mine left than I expected could be used.

Dario's version was more or less the same. He told an American magazine that *Accidental Death* was his work, but when asked about the monologues played by Franca, he replied: 'they were based on some ideas by Franca, but the definitive writing, the treatment I did. And then in due course Franca adapted them for performance.'[12]

Her collaboration allowed her to ward off certain types of criticism. While prepared to accept that there were deficiencies in the scripts, she would not accept the criticism that the monologues were inferior or unacceptable because they had been written by a male.

> It is a criticism I do not accept. I have always helped Dario in the composition of his theatrical works with suggestions, criticisms, proposals, but this time – I really want this to be understood – everything was completely different. In fact – and I want this to be clear – I even put my name on the title page, because if I did not write it in my own hand, I built it up verbally in long discussions with Dario. Some parts, indeed, I wanted to have redone, because they did not convince me.[13]

Dario had begun work on *Let's Talk About Women* some two years prior to the first performance in 1977, but then put it aside to take up the *Fanfani* and the *Marijuana* plays. Before the television version, the work went on stage at the Palazzina in March in the presence of a patient but frustrated audience. Dario painted special backcloths, one featuring a parody of the traditional *Flight into Egypt* motif. St Joseph was shown seated comfortably on horseback, while the Virgin Mary, in a state of evident exhaustion, walked ahead, holding the lead of the horse in one had and the infant Jesus in the other. Another drape depicted a parody of the *Creation*, with the woman seeing the light as she emerges from the rib of the lordly male and immediately kneeling at his feet.

In this first version, the work was a cabaret-style miscellany of assorted pieces, consisting of one-liners, songs, monologues and sketches, some of which were plundered from earlier works. The protagonist was Franca, with Dario supposedly her straight man, although this was a part he had some difficulty in maintaining. Since Dario was the author, the pieces showed his penchant for history, especially sacred history. One sketch featured a discussion arising from a dilemma enunciated by Erasmus of Rotterdam over whether women have a soul and whether Eve should be regarded as the daughter of darkness; another paraded Elizabethan female figures, including Juliet and Ophelia, all played by bearded men to satirize the contemporary ban on women appearing on stage. Franca performed the monologues of the Resistance heroine, Mamma Togni, and of the mother of Michele Lu Lanzone, the Sicilian trade unionist killed by the Mafia, who was herself confined in an asylum for threatening to denounce his killers. One of the musical interludes had Franca attempting to sing a folk song entitled 'I Am My Own Person', but being drowned out by Dario blaring a blues number into a microphone. Another sketch featured a man whose anti-abortion convictions are put to the test when he himself falls pregnant. The most successful piece was the monologue *Waking Up*, which subsequently became one of the most frequently performed pieces in the Fo–Rame repertoire.

These last two pieces reflected current debates, but it is not hard to see why seventies feminists were mystified by the other sketches. The theological disputations of Erasmus and the debates on women on the Elizabethan stage may have intrigued Dario and were doubtless part of the traditional underpinning to women's subaltern position in history, but they bewildered younger women who had honed their activism on divorce and abortion campaigns, and their critical thinking on the writings of Julia Kristeva and Luce Irigaray. Franca accepted some of the points made in discussions after the performance, while remaining baffled by the aggression of some of her critics. 'It is an old project, some years old,' she told one critic.

> Let me make one point clear. We did not plan, nor have we provided, a feminist work, or a work on the condition of women. We aimed at the construction of some female figures without in any way wanting to exemplify

the problems of women as such. We picked up on some topics – to deal with them all would take a thousand hours.

Post-1968 feminism had set itself a different agenda, and some said that Dario and Franca were out of touch with the times. There is no Italian word which exactly renders the English term 'generation gap', but the reality existed and no previous generation had been so conscious of the facts of ageing. Dario and Franca were among those who made 1968, but the times they were a-changing, as Bob Dylan sang, and the daughters, if not the sons, were beyond their parents' command. In the same number, Dylan also advised people who were not of the younger generation to start swimming, lest 'they sink like a stone'. Dario and Franca were swimming, but to their surprise they found themselves, if not sinking, certainly buffeted by cross-currents. One critic present at the première of *Let's Talk About Women* recorded reactions.

> The gist of the various contributions is that they do not see their themes in the play, because those featured are old, and not of their generation. There is no mention of sexual exploitation, of the black economy, of the authentic liberation of women or of any criticism of the system. Nor did the feminists there recognize themselves in the mother of the murdered trade unionist. In other words, the whole thing did not go down with them in the slightest.

'Authentic liberation', in Franca's eyes, was to be found embedded in the experiences of the women featured, not trumpeted in an abstract discourse on patriarchy. Her theatre was an arena of voices, all speaking of their distress but expressing, however awkwardly, a brave optimism that conditions could be changed. Her characters live lives of emotional and spiritual aridity, represented in tones of mockery and self-mockery. The comedy of the plays is not a rejection of their woeful experiences but a cry that happiness is possible, that human relations can be improved, that life for women, and for men, can be made richer.

Franca was unsettled at this period, and the experience of appearing in plays written for her crystallized her discontent. She had on many occasions expressed her dissatisfaction with life as an actress. Acting gave her no pleasure, she said on more than one occasion over the course of years. 'If I could go back, I would without any question choose another kind of work. The job does not give me any kind of fulfilment.'[14] Having been brought up in a family of travelling actors and entertainers, she was immune to the romance of the stage. The tedium, the chore, the routine of displaying herself in parts which presented no challenge, in a medium which familiarity had led her to despise, had always depressed her. Hovering in the wings before a first entry on a first night may have set the adrenalin coursing through the veins of actors who had joined the profession in adulthood, but having been on stage since her tenderest years, she regarded walking on in front of the footlights as humdrum. Only duffers, she implied, puff out their chests at plaudits for reciting lines and leading someone else's life, or grow fearful at the prospect of making a fool of themselves in public. She gave the impression that she had sleepwalked into the profession. 'To put it very simply, if my father's job had been shoe-making, I would have set out to make shoes. If there were no limitations to one's choice, I think I would have dedicated myself to trade unionism or social work.'[15]

She was already engaged on works of charity or philanthropy with Red Aid, but it was proving too much for her. When asked why she had begun to go her own way in 1977, she replied that it was necessary to look back to the years from 1968, when she and Dario left the established theatre circuit.

> I continued acting, but there was also all the rest. I looked after the administration, sold the tickets, kept things in order and out of 'revolutionary morality' I had no domestic help. Then as an afterthought, there were those ten thousand prisoners that I was involved with. That was how it was then: politics first. If it so happened that there was a good part for an actress in the script, so much the better. If not, 'the political discourse has to work, so you, what the hell do you want?' And in fact I asked for nothing. But I was absolutely ground down.[16]

The new slogan had it that 'the personal is political', so Franca introduced politics into her own life. She went on strike. The event has become part of family and company legend and, as with all legends, there are various versions of how she went about it. In some, she put a notice up in her home alerting her husband and her son that if, from that point on, they wanted clothes washed or ironed, meals prepared, rooms tidied or phone messages passed on, they would have to do it themselves. In another, she informed the company and the groups who used the Palazzina that she would no longer be available for the various services and tasks she had previously performed. In further versions, she announced that she was retiring from the stage. The announcement galvanized those around her. Dario declared that he agreed with Franca. Previous requests for domestic help had been refused on the grounds that it introduced the class system into the home, but now the guardians of revolutionary morality decided that flexibility was in order, that domestic work had no greater or lesser dignity than any other proletarian sale of personal labour, that it was not *ipso facto* exploitative, and that provided a domestic servant was well treated and generously paid, there was no reason why one should not be employed. A woman, later replaced by a Filipino couple, was taken on as cleaner and cook. The number of employees grew, and a decade later Dario and Franca were surrounded by secretaries, agents and personal assistants. They were well treated and well paid, but the demands put on them, especially by Franca, could be high. She works on high-octane energy, and when stressed or fatigued is prone to fits of temperamental intolerance or displays of excitable emotionalism.

Dario was disconcerted at the prospect of Franca abandoning acting. He wrote a further set of monologues, *All Bed, Board and Church*, in eight days, and presented them to her. 'We put it on, with me acting. On my own. After the première, which was a success, I could have given up. I had shown myself that I could do it. And my insecurities vanished.'

> For years and years, I had heard them say nothing about me except 'beautiful and brainless'. I became famous as the Italian Rita Hayworth, but without having done anything. So they all thought of me as the 'dumb blonde'. In addition, I was extremely shy. When I was with someone who interested me, I got myself into such a state that I couldn't even risk going for a pee. I would have stupendous thoughts in my head, but all that came out was 'Chilly tonight, isn't it?'

The new programme was first staged in Milan in December 1977. Initially there were five monologues, one of which, '*Waking Up*', had survived in modified form from the television series. In the first version, an alarm clock wakes up a woman who runs around the house preparing her child for nursery and herself for work, only to realize that all her rushing is unnecessary since it is Sunday. In the amended form, the woman abandons herself to a Utopian dream of peace and harmony, where she can stroll at leisure in a world were work has been humanized, where relations are relaxed and idyllic and where 'there is no egoism, only communism'.[17]

Same Old Story exploits the grotesque to strong effect. Rather than making love to her husband, the narrator is being compelled to copulate. Her fear of pregnancy is swept aside with rough words, and in the course of the monologue the woman takes the part of the gynaecologist, of the woman giving birth, of the new baby and then, with devastating suddenness, of the doll which is the uninhibited doppelgänger of the conventional, repressed woman. To the woman's initial disgust, the doll unleashes a flood of obscenities and scatological, foul language. The woman tells her baby a fairy tale which turns into a grotesque parody of itself, involving a doll with a favourite cat, which is killed when a dwarf pees on it. The dwarf falls in love with the foul-mouthed doll, but his plan to marry her is thwarted by the arrival of a ferocious wolf, who turns out to be an electronic engineer, transformed into a wolf by a wicked witch. The two marry, but fall out of love. The doll is ingested by the man, with only her feet sticking out through the man's arse. From there she is freed by a midwife, but in the process the man explodes, leaving the woman free and in control of her body and being. She walks off into the sunset until she reaches a tree whose branches shelter a group of young women, who agree that they all have the same old story to tell.

The swelling ebullience of the piece is intoxicating, but the most intriguing aspect is the use of the doll as double. The woman is twee, stiff and demure, but the doll can kick over the traces and unshackle herself from the demands put on women in society. If woman's liberation was an aim Franca accepted, release from convention presented a difficulty she found it hard to cope with. She has always stuck to standards of propriety and decorum and responded with a shudder to anything which could be regarded as vulgar, especially in linguistic matters. However incongruous it may be in one of her rebellious views, there has always been something of the mannerly bourgeois about her. Several actresses elsewhere in Europe were objects of her disapproval when their productions of her shows were damned as lacking in taste, or as 'vulgar'. One woman in Finland had the misfortune to trick out the set she was using for her own version of Franca's monologues with outsized phalluses. When Franca got wind of it, she immediately withdrew performing rights. In a translation I did of a later play, *An Ordinary Day*, I grappled with the problem of finding a word to express the part of the male body which an enraged prostitute had a habit of biting off. In the original, the word was the polite *coso*, which is more properly rendered as 'thingummy'. My translation, 'prick', was certainly more direct than the original, and when the English was retranslated into Italian for Franca's approval, the hired hand used the word *cazzo*, which is even more crude than the English. Franca was incensed, and bawled down the phone from Milan that Dario would never use such improprieties. She made the same point in a prologue:

Too many taboos . . . we carry them inside ourselves from birth, or even earlier; inhibitions in behaviour, in language . . . for example, I who am quite
uninhibited, in public, standing here in front of you, I cannot bring myself
to name, explicitly . . . the thingummy . . . the male organ. I cannot do it . . .
really! . . . I do believe that with time we can get to grips with the problem of
language. I am talking of the women of my generation, because the new generations have succeeded, and very successfully I would say, even if sometimes
this heavy language is only a response to the grim conformism of their parents, of society. They believe, we believe that in this way we are emancipated,
autonomous, avant-garde. We fail to realize that once again we are subjected
to the culture of the pr . . . , of the male organ!

A Woman Alone caused Franca to be picketed by English feminists when
she performed it at the Riverside Studios in 1982. The work was a protest
against harassment, but in London the problem was the see-through neg-
ligée which Franca chose to wear. To English eyes, any form of nudity or
semi-nudity was equivalent to the presentation of the woman as sex-object.
Franca reacted with disbelief and regarded the protest as a manifestation of
traditional British puritanism. The Woman Alone was kept locked by her
jealous husband in the home to attend to household chores. The only other
humans were a crippled but sex-crazed brother-in-law and an unseen
female neighbour living opposite. The Woman pours out her frustrations
and her memories of a love affair which had satisfied her emotionally and
physically to this woman. She is also beset by peeping Toms, whom she
wards off with her rifle, but her uninhibited monologue persuades her that
the gun would be better used on her uncaring husband, and the finale
shows her seated quietly, gun across her knee, awaiting his return.

Over the years, the number of monologues grew, so the volume published in 1989 carried the title *Twenty-five Monologues for a Woman*. Their
success all over the world eventually rivalled that of *Mistero buffo*. Like
Dario, Franca came on stage to address the audience in improvised prologue about issues of the day in whichever country she happened to be,
before performing the written script. These pieces represent Franca in her
own right, if not quite in her own write. The underlying demand is not so
much for a rethinking of female identity as for a new deal for women in
their everyday lives. If it is true that Italian feminism has contained in itself
the competing themes of equality with men and of the intrinsic diversity of
women,[18] Franca only really engaged with the first. The language and the
structure have a touch of surreal clowning, but the agenda could not be
more concrete.

These plays dramatize the day-to-day plight of ordinary women, chained to the home but without the means to leave it, of housewives dealing with inflation at the micro level, of wives dealing with emotional neglect and physical overwork, of women hoping for change. 'Franca's theatre is not meta-feminist, in the sense that it doesn't question the sex of God and the existence of the individual,' wrote one critic, somewhat heavily, before adding that the "painful proximity" that characterizes her voice results in a fusion of writer, performer, subject and audience that bypasses the necessity of intellectual argumentation'.[19] It is true that these monologues are never adventures in ideas, which is why they disappointed those who expected more intellectual fare. The fundamental conviction is that human beings, male and female, huddled together for a brief period of consciousness on Earth, must behave towards each other with respect, fairness and decency. This statement has the crystalline banality that, as G. K. Chesterton put it, is the mark of a truism. There is always a need for some alchemy in literature, and Chesterton himself, to escape accusations of triviality, sought to dress his truisms as startling paradoxes. The alchemy in Fo and Rame is a humour which is zany, surreal, adventurous and grotesque, but never merely whimsical. Humour is the artifice which mediates and transforms, and yet, like some of Chekhov's short stories, these sketches impress and disconcert by their seeming lack of art, by their ability to cling close to lived life. 'Gentlemen, you live badly,' Fo had been saying for years, and now Franca's riposte was 'Ladies, do not put up with it.' Both continued to chorus that the fault was in the system, in the structures of power which left both male and female oppressed and alienated.

Franca's feminism was not especially revolutionary. Heterosexual relationships marked by mutual fidelity, love and commitment, all underpinned by a previously unknown equality in every domain, was the ideal. Her Marxism did not persuade her to follow Engels in questioning the family itself, nor did her feminism ever lead her to take an interest in 'separatism'. The witnesses she lined up in her theatre may have experienced misery and dissatisfaction in their married lives but, even in *A Woman Alone*, they craved fulfilment in shared heterosexual life. The passion they expressed was for parity of consideration. There is no ideology of anti-male feeling at any level other than the purely jocose. On one occasion in Rome, a group of twenty female students arrived when the theatre was full and the performance about to commence. They declared themselves to be feminists and demanded entrance. Franca apologized, pointing out that all tickets had been sold, but offered to arrange seats for them on the stage. The leader of the group demurred, saying that there were several men in the audience who could be ejected. Franca refused, saying that her plays were intended for a male audience as well. 'Yes I am a feminist, if it has a political edge, not when it involves a sterile struggle against men. Yes, if it means walking hand in hand. Women need to be helped to liberate themselves.'[20]

The students might have expressed surprise, even shocked dismay, at the recognition that the central figure in Franca's drama was the mother. The stock character of much feminist theatre, the woman, normally youthful, asserting her independence, learning bravely to make her way by herself in a hostile world, is simply not present. Franca's maternal heroine is a figure with deep roots in Mediterranean culture and mythology. She makes her first appearance as the Virgin Mary, standing desolately at the foot of the cross in the sketches from the Passion which were added to *Mistero buffo* in the 1976 summer season. In one, Franca is shown rejecting the Archangel Gabriel's attempts to comfort her while her son hangs on the cross, telling the archangel that only a mother who has suckled her baby, who has sat beside him when he cried as he was teething, can understand her plight; in another, she is shown lamenting that her thirty-three-year-old son will never have a family, and arousing the compassion of a Roman soldier and of the other women at Calvary not because she is a queen or her son divine, but because he is human and she is experiencing a mother's pain. This medieval Madonna returns in the closing vision in *The Kidnapping of Fanfani* as the eternal mother who mourns for all her children, everywhere.

> I am on earth, at every moment I am on earth . . . I am inside all mothers torn apart from suffering and by your violence. I am inside the withered flesh of Vietnamese women, holding in their arms their slaughtered sons . . . I am in the anguished cry of black mothers, embracing the feet of their children lynched by racists . . . it is my tears which fall on the head of a poor Chilean boy, gunned down in the stadium in Santiago . . .

The same figure dominates these new sketches, most obviously *The Mother*, a play based on the experiences of a woman who had contacted Franca through Red Aid. This mother, who has lost touch with her son until she sees television footage of him being arrested for involvement in terrorist activity, is a direct descendant of the *mater dolorosa*. The women in *Same Old Story*, *Waking Up* or *The Freak Mamma* may be facing all the dilemmas of modern women juggling work and home, but they are first and foremost dedicated, sacrificing mothers, whose first thought is for their children. Feminism represents liberation inside the family, not from it.

These plays also revealed Franca's real range as actress. Not being devoid of vanity, she relished the appreciation she received abroad, where she was known for her own achievements and not simply as Dario Fo's wife. She happily reported that she had been listed in France as 'one of the three great, world-class epic actresses'.[21] In Italy, she had only appeared in plays written in Dario's style, and so had made her reputation as a comic actress. The part of Mrs Warren in Shaw's play, on television, in 1981, was one of the few exceptions, but for the most part she had denied herself the opportunity normally given to celebrated actresses – Eleonora Duse, Sarah Bernhardt, or indeed Vanessa Redgrave and Madeleine Renaud – to test themselves on melodrama, modern comedy and classical tragedy. It is always intriguing to speculate on what Franca and Dario might have been had they not known each other, or if, having met, they had formed an antipathy towards each other. How different, wondered Pascal, would history have been if Cleopatra's nose had been longer and if Antony had not been attracted by her? And if Franca Rame's nose had been misshapen, and Dario not drawn to her? There is no sign that Franca wished any such dispensation, but, holding wider speculations at bay, it is reasonable to assume that Franca's acting career would have taken a different turn. She would have done more film and television, and might have had the chance to perform in styles other than the comic. The life she chose gave her no such possibility, but some of these stronger monologues, notably *Medea* and *The Mother*, gave a glimpse of what might have been. They revealed in her an inner force, an integrity, a spiritual quality, a stillness, and a capacity to induce in spectators that reflective and deeply felt silence which is a more profound sign of appreciation in theatre than noisy applause.

Chapter 13

Tiger, Tiger

The 'ebb-tide' mood, with the weariness with politics it implied, was not the only problem facing the Left. The ideology of terror and violence itself, instead of bringing the state to its knees, was producing a disabling malaise among the remaining adherents of the Movement. The reponse to terrorism, not the struggle against the capitalist state, was now the main issue. Political society had closed ranks, with the Communist Party backing the hard line taken by the Christian Democrats in defence of the state and railing against the infantilism of all, be they intellectuals or youthful militants, who dissented from this approach. The authorities, with a range of special laws and newly instituted police units, were now coping with student and industrial dissent. Many of the first-generation terrorists were now in jail.

Like the novelists Leonardo Sciascia and Alberto Moravia, Fo found himself subjected to constant sniping in *L'Unità* for his supposed ambiguity towards terrorism. The televising of the second segment of *Mistero buffo* coincided with the killing of two policemen during the occupation of Rome University, and Antonello Trombadori, Communist member of parliament, veteran of the Resistance and author of some volumes of verse, suggested that Dario should insert a condemnation of these killings in his programmes. Dario's replied that he had no objection in principle, but would prefer it to be part of a wider condemnation of all violence, certainly including 'those who shoot and kill policemen', but taking in 'the poisons from Seveso [the chemical plant which spewed dioxin over northern Italy after an accident in July 1976] and the provocations which have been causing blood to be shed in this country for the past nine years'. Lest this be seen as prevaricating, he added, 'Of course I am opposed to violence, ferociously opposed, firstly because people are killed, a most serious sin. Secondly because in this way, we fall into the traps laid by the authorities.'[1]

Franca was similarly criticized in December 1977 by a correspondent from the *Corriere della Sera* who took exception to the closing scene of *A Woman Alone*, where the woman settles down with a rifle on her lap to await the return of her husband. Fo penned an acid reply, wondering at the selectivity of the correspondent's distaste, pointing out that the heroine could plead self-defence since she was preparing to ward off attacks on her. He emphasized that no violence occurred on stage and wondered why there was no objection to the violence of *Medea*, 'but you can't accuse Euripides of being an instigator of violence or of terrorism. By God, he's a classic!'[2]

The implacable Antonello Trombadori returned to the scene after seeing a petition in the magazine *Cinema Nuovo*, which protested against the treatment in a German jail of Irmgard Moeller, a member of the Baader-Meinhof group who had been found in her cell with stab wounds in the stomach. The signatories, he suggested, were not humanitarians but covert sympathizers with terrorist violence. 'Trombadori is a terrorist,' wrote Fo,

> in the sense that he creates terror. A natural terrorist. No, he does not point a gun, but his index finger . . . I insist in saying that Trombadori is a terrorist because his aim is to terrorize all those who do not accept the logic of the defence of violence offered by any regime, at any cost, against any person guilty of any crime, for the simple reason that that person is a human being.

Fo also took exception to Trombadori's habit of casting aspersions on Franca. 'In each of your writings, you never fail to refer to "the well-known actress, Franca Rame", portraying her as a kind of suffragette who – these are your words – "has certainly never experienced real Fascist violence." (And I am not here to remind you how out of place and in bad taste this expression is.) But where were you, Honourable Vigilante, at the time of the Fascist aggression Franca suffered?'[3]

If criticism from the despised Communist Party could be brushed aside, it was harder to silence doubts from inside the Movement. It was felt on all sides that there was a manifest need for rethinking and regrouping. A grand meeting, to embrace all shades of left-wing thinking, was called to take place in Bologna in September 1977. The official topic was Repression, in itself an acknowledgement, however grudging, that the government's measures against militancy and terrorism were proving effective, but the real agenda was that vague sense that a decade of unrest had produced scant results and that it was time for maps to be redrawn. Dario stated that the Bologna meeting had two urgent tasks: 'to take soundings inside the Movement and to evaluate the weight which an "armed party" ideology has, both quantitatively and qualitatively, in the Movement'.[4]

The choice of Bologna, the traditional stronghold of the Communist Party as venue, was deliberately provocative. The New Left had made a habit of attacking the 'Social Democrats', that is, the Communists, for their abandonment of revolutionary ideals, while in reply PCI leader Enrico Berlinguer dismissed those planning to attending the conference as 'untorelli', a word used in Alessandro Manzoni's novel *I promessi sposi* to describe spreaders of the plague. Conferences, especially those involving such disputatious groups as the Italian left in those years, were always tricky events to manage. The previous year, Lotta Continua had simply disintegrated during its congress in Rimini when constituent parts representing workers and women failed to find sufficient common ground to allow them even to meet in the same room.

In Bologna, the Communist administration of the city smothered its opponents with kindness. It announced that those attending were welcome to roll out their sleeping bags in the city parks, and mobilized the social kitchens of the city to provide meals at give-away prices. The management of the conference itself was a more delicate matter. There were many events billed, and each room or building was occupied by a different faction of the disunited left desperate to proselytize for their own cause. Delegates wandered from building to building at will. Since the various groups kept to themselves, when they did not actually come to blows, there was little meeting of minds. Distinguished visitors had a hard time. Felix Guattari and Gilles Deleuze, two of the leading French leftist opponents of the better-known *nouveaux philosophes*, were in attendance but they were confronted by the Italian press at its most chauvinistic over the insolence of the French in daring to criticize human rights in Italy when the guillotine was still in use in France.[5]

Dario's principal contribution to the proceedings was the première of *The Tale of a Tiger*, on 22 September in the Palasport. The setting is China in the days of the revolutionary war and the tale opens with a soldier who injures his leg on the Long March, holding up the progress of the army. When Brecht at his most Stalinist devised a similar situation in *The Measures Taken*, also set in China, his activist accepted death rather than impede the revolution. Dario's soldier, on the other hand, refuses the 'offer' made by one of his comrades to shoot him, but he is abandoned and takes refuge in a cave, which turns out to be the lair of a tiger and her cub. The tiger heals him by licking his wounds, and the three then form a surrogate family. However, the soldier finds himself relegated to the position of servant and flees to a nearby village. The animals follow him, causing the villagers initially to disperse in panic. They come to appreciate the advantages of having a tiger on their side when they are attacked first by the Japanese and then by the forces of Chiang Kai-shek. As reinforcements, they fabricate false tigers using carnival masks and costumes, and live peacefully until a functionary of the now victorious Communist Party arrives to inform them that tigers must be returned to the forest forthwith since it has been decreed that they are 'anarchistic, lacking a command of dialectics and so cannot be assigned a role in the party'. Instead, the peasants enclose the tiger in a henhouse, allowing them to tell future apparatchiks that instructions have been complied with and that the occupant of the henhouse should be registered as a 'tigered hen'. Later, higher commissars arrive to compliment them on their initiative in disobeying petty officialdom, since they are now regarded as revisionists and counter-revolutionaries, but issue new directives that, in the absence of enemies, tigers are to be confined to a zoo. The only reply is the roar of the tiger, in itself sufficient to keep all placemen in subjection.

This multi-layered tale transcends its allegorical elements. Dario lists the allegories in his prologue, starting with the revolt against passivity and death contained in the soldier's refusal of euthanasia. Unlike Brecht, he found himself every day compelled to express his own disagreement with those 'mistaken comrades' who had chosen the 'armed struggle' and arrogated to themselves the power of life and death. The fable contains a challenge which toned in with the anti-party mood of the Bologna conference. In China, the tiger is, according to Fo, associated with all the qualities which distinguish honest candour from fawning servility, so 'to possess a tiger means never to mandate anything to anyone, never to invite others to resolve problems, not even those people who have previously been given a mandate, not even the most highly esteemed of officials, not even those who have demonstrated their know-how on countless occasions, the most trusted and honest party secretary . . . no, never!'[6]

There is more to this enigmatic tale than veiled politics. The man, female tiger and cub form an idiosyncratic but authentic and even idealized family unit in the forest caverns. The family circle is tight and exclusive and satisfies all the needs and cravings of creatures for shelter, warmth, nutrition, care, comfort and affection. The cave is the home, with the tiger initially unsure whether to invade the privacy of what she takes to be the man's private dwelling-place. The soldier has equal feelings of delicacy towards the tiger, in addition to more evident feelings of fear towards a beast known in legend for its ferocity. The tiger acts as nurse for her injured mate and there

are even fairly explicit sexual overtones to the description of the tiger licking the soldier's wounds, and of the man sucking milk from the tiger's teats.
The man becomes hunter and provider, showing the wild animals the benefits of cooked meats, so when he flees to the village and to civilization, he
leaves behind a feeling of betrayal and disloyalty. The villagers may be ter-
rorized, but the focus is on the mutual recriminations between the partners
as the tiger reproaches the man for ingratitude after all her efforts to nurse
him back to health. The man is driven to explain how the family had been
formed: 'you know, when there is love in a family . . . we made peace. I
stroked her under the chin . . . the tiger gave me a lick on the . . . the cub
gave me a little kick . . . ' The distance between civilization and the jungle
evaporates, but so does the gap between this piece and the monologues
which had preceded it. Both express a demand for continued love and
loyalty. *The Tale of a Tiger* bestrides political commitment and the 'ebb-
tide' culture of Italy in the late 1970s.

Not even in *Mistero buffo* did Dario create for himself such a platform for
his acting talents. Here he gave a demonstration of his own, non-Brechtian
style of epic acting, switching effortlessly from one character to another,
turning lightly to address the audience as though the fourth wall were an
alien imposition to be ignored rather than destroyed, transforming himself
from man to beast and filling the stage with armies which only the crassly
unimaginative could fail to see. He summoned the audience into person-to-
person confidence, wheedled, coaxed and coerced them to see the world
through his eyes. His hands and flailing arms painted pictures of men holding weapons, of wounded soldiers, of menacing tigers, of houses spaced
around a village, of hen houses and cages, and even of precisely positioned
walls. In a Fo performance, the body is king. In *The Tale of a Tiger*, he
crawled like a man in pain, pranced like a child, paced like a feline, ran like
a crowd in terror, all the while producing a flow of sounds which reproduced the roar of animals, the creaking of rusty doors, the cawing of birds,
the crowing of cockerels, the clanging of bars and the scuttling of soldiers
in fear of death. He impersonated a deer captured in a hunt and even a
bullet as it emerges from the barrel of a gun. Nothing was more astonishing
than the lightness and grace of movement this now heftily built, no longer
young, man could achieve. He combined mime, mimicry and ventriloquy
in a bravura style which was a reminder that he had once learned a trade
with Jacques Lecoq, but that he had applied his learning in a way Lecoq had
never intended in order to become, in succession, orator, teacher, performer
and tribune of the plebs. The ideology to which he had dedicated his life

was still detectable in the words that flowed in torrents, but his solitariness as he strutted back and forth spoke of an actor who, as an actor, could not give assent to notions of equality. Some talents cannot be acquired, but, having been inherited, demand display; art leaves no space for democracy. Dario is an instinctive *generalisimo* of the stage, and while he had in other days attempted to rein in his tendency to elbow others aside or to leave them in the shadows, now he strutted as monomaniac and lord.

Even Italian audiences required the guidance of the mime and gestures, since Fo performed in a synthetic dialect with elements taken from Venetian, Lombard or Paduan speech but spoken by no one in the form he employed it. Communication depended on non-linguistic devices; above all, on *grammelot*. *Grammelot* was, he claimed, invented by Italian actors in France in Molière's day as a means of deceiving censors. In essence, it consists of a series of sounds, each plausible but wholly meaningless in itself, which accompany performance. It is an onomatopoeic device where meaning is conveyed not by grammatical speech but by gesture, action, movement and expression. It became the favoured language of his one-man performances.

There is some mystery over the origins of the *The Tale of a Tiger*. The canonical explanation is that the tale is an elaboration of a story Fo had heard recited by a Chinese jester during his visit to China. He gave his own version in his prologue:

> I heard this story recited for the first time years ago, performed rather than recited, in China, at Shanghai. At that time there were many stories of this sort making the rounds over there.
>
> I do not believe that this story is performed in public as I saw it recited, recited before thousands of men, women and children in a field . . . in the countryside around Shanghai. The story-teller expressed himself in the dialect of the Shanghai countryside, a dialect spoken by a minority, a minority of some sixty million people . . .
>
> Unfortunately our guide was from Bejing and did not understand a single word of this dialect, but fortunately we found someone in the locality who spoke the national language, and so we got a translation. I had heard Colotti-Pischel (an astonishing woman, a fount of knowledge on Chinese culture and politics) talk about it, but she was aware only of the outlines of the story. She did not know the whole tale as it was told to me.

However, in none of the many interviews Fo gave on his return from China does he make any mention of the tiger story. He does refer to the history, not of a tiger or a soldier, but of an old woman who liaised with the partisans in the war against the Kuomintang. A boy tries to reach her hide-out, is wounded by pursuing soldiers and is hidden by the woman in a washing basket. When the soldiers rummage about looking for him, the boy coughs, but the woman coughs in unison and confuses the men so deeply that they end up throwing their leader down a well.[7] There is no tiger. Bent Holm, the Danish dramaturg and Fo translator, drew up an alternative, admittedly speculative, genesis of *The Tale of a Tiger*.[8] He points out that it is simply inconceivable that in the conditions prevailing in Maoist China any story-teller could have made the criticisms of the party which are implicit in the closing sections of the tale. His own suggestion is that the book by Colotti-Pischel, overlaid with the tale told by the Shanghai story-teller, could have provided Fo with inspiration for the parts of the story dealing with the march, escape from death and refuge in the village, but that the introduction of the tiger to replace the old woman is an original invention. The closing attack on grey bureaucracy and party apparatus is pure Fo, and the target Italy and Italian Communism. In any case, the tale has, like Shakespeare's comedies, an authenticity and charm independent of any putative sources. Dario is not a reliable guide to his own sources of inspiration.

Franca had to face problems of a purely private nature when, in January 1978, while on tour in Genoa, she was run over by a car. In addition to injuries to the spine, arm and hand, she suffered damage to the central nervous system. She was kept in hospital for several weeks and was subject to strange, troubling bouts of hallucination, when she believed her arms and hands were on fire. The pain was intense and her recovery was never complete. She only regained partial use of her hand and arm. For a long time afterwards, she required painkillers to continue work. Even slight changes of condition or temperature could cause a relapse. During her convalescence, Dario and Jacopo, she said, looked after her like a baby, washing her, dressing her and even at times feeding her.

> It is thanks to them that I did not give way to despair, that I was able to return
> to acting in the autumn, that I did not die. Believe me, I am not exaggerating.
> That's why I say that perhaps it is right that I have suffered so much if this
> suffering has given me the certainty of such great love from my husband and
> my son. It is love we are talking about, not pity. If they had only felt pity, they
> could have hired a nurse or put me in a clinic. I have had proof of love which
> few woman have in their lives, from Dario and Jacopo above all, but also from

the comrades who perform with us, who organize our company.[9]

Franca was still convalescing when, on 16 March 1978, the whole of Italy was thrown into turmoil by the kidnapping of Aldo Moro by the Red Brigades. Andreotti's government had resigned in January, and Moro had been working behind the scenes to stitch together a stronger Christian Democrat–Communist alliance which would give the PCI greater influence while still denying them Cabinet posts. His efforts were successful, and Moro was on his way to parliament to vote on the confidence motion when his car was ambushed. The five men in his escort were slaughtered and Moro himself was dragged away. He was to remain a hostage in the 'people's prison' for fifty-five days while the police searched the length and breadth of Italy for any trace of him. The terrorists threatened to kill him unless their conditions, which included the release of 'political prisoners', were met. The government, supported by the PCI but not by the Socialist Party, replied with assertions of the need for 'firmness' in the face of blackmail. From captivity, Moro wrote a series of anguished letters to his wife, to party colleagues, to political opponents, to civic leaders and to the Pope, begging for their assistance in saving his life. The Italian authorities were unyielding. Moro was assassinated on 9 May and his body left in the boot of a Renault in via Caetani in Rome, halfway between the headquarters of the Christian Democrats and of the Communist Party.

Italy was split over the desirability of negotiating with terrorists. The main argument against doing a deal was that enunciated memorably by Rudyard Kipling – 'If once you pay the danegeld/ Will you ever get rid of the Dane?' Paradoxically, the most forceful advocates of a negotiated settlement to save a human life were those who most abominated all that Moro represented politically. *Lotta Continua*, the extreme-left newspaper which had survived the disappearance of the party, was highly critical of the Red Brigades. Leonardo Sciascia, who had revealed himself in his novels a virulent opponent of Moro and of all the whole Christian Democrat apparatus, came out in favour of negotiations, and was attacked by Giorgio Amendola, a leading Communist, for his trouble. Dario and Franca, in total consistency with their rejection of all violence, criticized the Red Brigades and interceded for Moro's life. They took their stance on the fundamentalist notions of human rights and the sanctity of life which had been the basis of their objections to the use of terror and to the torture or ill-treatment of terrorists. Dario, together with Marco Pannella, leader of the Radical Party, and several dissident Communists and independent bishops, was a signatory to a petition prepared by an ad-hoc 'party of negotiation', which only *Lotta Continua* would publish. Franca was invited by the very authorities who had condemned her mercilessly for her work with Red Aid to use her influence and act as intermediary. She travelled to Turin to meet the imprisoned Red Brigade leaders, including Alberto Franceschini, who were on trial in the city. Franceschini gives his own account of the meeting:

> The last request for intervention was made by Franca Rame. She came to the prison in the name of the Christian Democrat undersecretary for Justice, Renato Dell'Andro, asking for the unconditional release of Moro . . . the conversation with Franca was brief and dramatic, almost a year after her visit to the Asinara. On that occasion I had been struck by her human expression, the expression of a woman sincerely upset by the conditions in which we were forced to live. But now she seemed to have aged, as though more than a year had passed; there were signs of suffering on her face, her arm was in plaster as a result of a road accident. She had difficulty in finding the words she needed, perhaps she was not happy with the role she was called on to play. She weighed attentively every word and began by talking about the accident. She was authorized to talk only to Renato [Curcio], Roberto [Ognibene] and me. We take a hard line. We concede her nothing, not even a smile or a greeting. We tell her we are enraged with her for having agreed to come to make such a proposal to us: Moro's life when they make us live in such inhuman conditions? The Ministry has suspended meetings with our families, while we can freely meet with her without guards or glass partitions. Does not she, who had always been so involved with the problems of the families of inmates, realize what all this means? Instead of making proposals of this sort, she should be trying to modify our living conditions, then we could talk. She replies that there is nothing to be done. All we can do is rise to our feet in the court and say that Moro must be freed. If he is assassinated, things will get worse for us. I read the anxiety on Franca's face as she transmits what they have told her. We do not know what to reply to her, we remain in silence for some seconds, perhaps some minutes, exchanging glances between the three of us, knowing glances. We cannot make a declaration of that sort, not even we who had released Sossi without obtaining practically anything in return. The Moro kidnapping is not the Sossi kidnapping. It was Renato who spoke for all of us. We did not await Franca's reaction. We filed back to our cells.[10]

The Moro kidnapping presented Italy not merely with a dilemma of *realpolitik* but also with a crisis of spiritual vision for which a largely secularized society was unprepared and ill-equipped. Dario was deeply offended by the systematic defamation of Aldo Moro by those who had been friends and acolytes but who now denigrated him for cowardice, or who suggested that the 'real' Moro was already dead and the man writing those letters was the empty shell of a man. He was overwhelmed by the spectacle of a man of power at bay and by the glimpse of his humanity suddenly and unexpectedly revealed, *in extremis.* In the final letters Moro had cast off all false trappings or pretensions, Dario wrote, and spoke as someone who had seen the imposture which had been his life as holder of power.[11]

Moro's murder, preceded by the stripping away of his prestige and dignity, seemed to Dario to constitute the basic matter of tragedy. In the people's prison, Moro found himself facing the primal fear of extinction, the anxieties of human powerlessness and the terror in the face of the irrational which tragic writers had dramatized in *Oedipus* or *King Lear.* Dario set aside his other work and announced that he wished to dramatize the plight of Moro. For the first and only time in his life, he decided that tragedy in the prime, Aristotelian sense of the word offered the appropriate key to understanding the catastrophe which had overtaken Moro himself and Italy as a whole. Tragedy had always obsessed Fo but, like Samuel Beckett, Eugene Ionesco or Eduardo De Filippo, he was convinced that for twentieth-century society, tragedy could be made acceptable only when presented in the garb of farce. When contemplating Ruzzante, Molière or the figure of Harlequin from theatrical history, Dario was intrigued not by the comic devices they employed, or not only by them, but by the layers of tragedy which underpinned their comic vision. He admired Ruzzante's ability to create laughter which eschewed escapism, and to fashion a granite-hard farce which did not soften the realities of hunger, fear, poverty or sexual cravings. In Fo's view, tragedy was an intrinsic part of grotesque humour and satire, and their ultimate justification. 'Satire is nothing other than the comic treatment of tragedy; without tragedy, there is no satire. It provokes the laughter of the conscience, of the intelligence,' he once said.[12]

However, a satirical farce of the *Accidental Death* type would have been an inadequate response to the spiritual and human traumas of the Moro case. The clashes and contrasts between 'the safeguarding of man, his liberty, his dignity, his life', and 'the reasons which we today call *raisons d'état* and which were once called the great law of the gods with, as its base, sacrifice, renewal through the sacrifice of the scapegoat, through bloodshed',[13] lay too deep. Instead, Dario composed an austere, classical tragedy, *The Moro Case,* but he had no experience in the genre and was never satisfied with the final work. He never allowed it to be performed, although he has permitted it to be published.[14] The leading figures in the Christian Democratic Party, including Giulio Andreotti and the then Minister for the Interior (and future president of the republic), Francesco Cossiga, come on to speak the words they uttered at the time, as does Pope Paul VI and Moro himself. The cast is completed by satyrs and Bacchae, a Shakespearean fool, a Tiresias-like elder and a chorus borrowed from the Greeks. Behind Fo's tragedy lay a quasi-theological anxiety, worthy of Dostoevsky, over the mentality and motivations both of the terrorists and of the holders of public office, over the willingness of both sides to weigh human life like a commodity. The distinction between the concepts of destiny in Sophocles and Euripides aided his quest for understanding:

> On the one hand the imponderability of the destiny of men overwhelmed by fate, which determines everything and against which reason has no sway, and on the other the conceptions of Euripides who sets his face against the absolutism of fate, who focuses on the reason of men. There are two key tragedies in this respect, *Philoctetes* and *Iphigenia*. You will recall in particular the terrifying encounter at the moment when Iphigenia was to be sacrificed to the possibility that the Achaeans, the Attics and the Illyrians might find unity, a unity of action which strongly resembles the situation of the coalition between the PCI and the DC. You could also consider the crucifixion of those who preferred to sacrifice the assumptions of the agreement, of the conquest, etc., who considered it preferable to save the life of this woman who was the scapegoat. Finally, all the falseness, the hypocrisy, the madness of this group of men in power, to convince themselves that this sacrifice had to be made. The same could be said of Philoctetes: he is wounded, he could be saved but the word is that his gangrene is incurable. It is easy to make out the meaning of this gangrene, this isolation, this expulsion, this decision to leave him for dead before he really is, but there is the other fact of his bow. What is his bow? It is the allegory of his strength, of his credibility, of his history and could be the pivot of his victory. Therefore it is necessary to sacrifice Philoctetes to take away his bow . . .

The work has the heavy rhythms of oratorio or a Dies Irae, and perhaps could be performed if set to music, although it might need the talents of a Palestrina.

Dario performed an updated and rewritten version of *The Tale of a Tiger* at the Palazzina Liberty in February 1978. It was to be his last appearance there.

Milan City Council's action for his eviction came before Court of Cassation the following year, and this time the council was granted the order. The order did not have automatic effect, but the council had the option of serving it when they chose. Perhaps in deference to their own sense of changed times, perhaps ground down by the dogged perseverance of the council, Dario and Franca decided to abandon the struggle. The council promised not to use force, and announced that the next step was to calculate how much had been spent on restorations as against what was owed in rent. Fo set off on a disillusioned, half-hearted search among ex-cinemas and assorted halls for another venue, giving as his minimum requirement a building with at least a thousand seats. 'I am not interested in subsidies,' he said. 'All I want is compensation for what I have spent.' According to his own estimates, he was owed 100 million lire, plus legal expenses.[15] The company remained in the Palazzina until 1981, when they bowed to the unceasing pressure and left. They did not find another venue, so the Palazzina Liberty was the last theatre Dario and Franca had as their own. The building was subsequently used, officially, as a venue for chamber orchestras, puppet shows and touring companies and, unofficially, as a refuge for drug-takers and the urban destitute.

The days of the 'alternative circuit' were closing. Declining energy and enthusiasm undermine dedication to all causes, and both Dario and Franca began to speak with some nostalgia of the great theatres where they had performed at the beginning of their careers. While rehearsing *Mum's Marijuana*, Dario had spoken longingly of the Piccolo theatre or La Scala opera house, with their superior facilities, properly equipped stage, comfortable green rooms and plush seats for the audience. Maybe, suggested Franca, we have neglected the middle class? Do not they have rights, should their dilemmas not be dramatized, or at least should they not be given the opportunity to face the problems confronting working-class people? Is it really an act of apostasy, the couple asked themselves, to return to the official circuit if we retain faith with our own style of theatre and in our own politics?

Dario was put to the test when, in su§mmer 1978, he was invited by La Scala to direct Stravinsky's *Histoire du Soldat* as part of their bicentenary celebrations. Claudio Abbado was behind the approach and although the production was to be part of the company's official programme, it would be staged not in La Scala itself but in various venues in Milan and northern Italy. The decision to accept was made easier when Dario was able to recall that La Scala had never been the chosen home of the 'conformist bourgeoisie', but had hosted satirical works which undermined the social *status quo*, such as *William Tell*.[16] La Scala hoped this project would be the first of a series of collaborative ventures with Fo. A new opera by Luigi Nono was proposed, but in the event the Stravinsky was the only production brought to completion.

Quite apart from the return to mainstream theatre which acceptance implied, Dario's involvement in the project marked another turning-point. Until this point, he had limited himself almost exclusively to staging his own work. In 1967, he had directed *Sunday Parade*, based on original work by Georges Michel, but from this moment onwards, he would frequently accept invitations to direct the work of other writers. 'Directing' is hardly an adequate term for the kind of transformation and rethinking involved in a Fo production. With Georges Michel, with Stravinsky, and later with Rossini, Molière, Brecht and Ruzzante, puzzled or outraged critics would point out that the script or score had been so comprehensively manhandled as to make it a full part of the Dario Fo canon. Whatever he stated, or even believed, Fo lacked the selflessness to limit himself to releasing an energy in the text as he found it. He imbued, and perhaps enriched, it with his own fantasy, imagination, creativity, vision and personality, so every work Dario directed was done in his own image and likeness. Stravinsky's *Histoire du Soldat* ('Story of *the* Soldier') became *Storia di un soldato* ('Story of *a* Soldier'), and, as one reviewer pointed out in a trenchant but generally favourable notice, Fo's name was mentioned twice in the programme as against the one mention of Stravinsky. Fo was credited with the 'scenic action', as well as with responsibility for 'directing, scenes and costumes'.[17] The original librettist Charles-Ferdinand Ramuz, was written out. Fo explained:

> I love the *Histoire*, I consider Stravinsky to be one of the greats, much greater than is suggested by this scenic and musical action, which had of necessity to be entrusted to few actors. Ramuz's script seems embarrassing, highly dated, full of lines of phoney philosophy with no meaning, like, 'nothingness is all, all is nothingness . . . ' It restricts the action in the tale, nothing happens on stage, everything has already taken place. That's why I tried to have everything recounted, with few words and many gestures . . . Ours is, rather than a means of re-reading a great, exciting author, an act of love towards Stravinsky.[18]

There are conventions and expectations associated with directing, as there are standards and rules which can be applied to a process of translation or adaptation, but 'acts of love' can be executed only in an Erewhon where no laws apply. In this case, love dictated a complete polemical overturning of the Stravinsky–Ramuz work. 'I had two and a half months to get the show ready, with all the work done on stage, and not a word written at home.'[19] Where La Scala had expected a 'chamber piece', Dario chose to give them a 'piazza' piece. He introduced other compositions by Stravinsky, including the *Octet*, composed in 1923, five years after the *Histoire*. He considered inserting *Ragtime* too, but concluded it was not feasible. The orchestra was not concealed in a pit but left in full view on a raised platform in the centre of the stage; the action unfolded around them. Instead of the one dancer which Stravinsky and Ramuz had intended, Dario created an instant collective with thirty unknown young actors from the Piccolo theatre drama school. Dressed in informal but brightly coloured costumes, they performed with riotous, festive *joie de vivre*, waving coloured banners and streamers and creating an infinity of images. Each took it in turn to play the part of the soldier. The plot ended up resembling Ruzzante more than Ramuz. 'The action was completely overturned, in both dramatic and ideological terms,' wrote Dario in his introduction.[20] A poor peasant makes his way to the city, where he arouses the attention of a devil-flatterer, who tries to rob him of his violin, that is, his soul. The peasant is persuaded to enrol for what he believes to be a crusade, but finds it to be a war of profit. On his return, no one recognizes him. In disillusionment, he sets sail in a 'ship of fools', only to be shipwrecked. He escapes to an island, ruled by an enormous skeleton made of reeds. The skeleton, who is king and head of state, is beset by a detachment of hooligans brandishing the P.38 (the favoured weapon of Italian terrorists) and surrounded by argumentative, unscrupulous courtiers, each desperate to grab positions of power. The king has a sickly daughter, represented on stage by a huge puppet, whom the soldier tries to coax back to life by playing his violin. The marriage of the two saves the state, but only for a dubious future of social democracy.

Critical responses were mixed, but the most ferocious came from the novelist Marta Morazzoni. She was no doubt right to conclude that 'almost nothing remains of Stravinsky, his music and his story, except for a musical theme kept as a distant background sound', but her real objection was to 'the evident and flavourless political satire, which recalls television political parodies'.[21] In addition to criticisms from theatre and music critics, Fo found himself yet again engulfed in controversy with the political authorities of the city. His old adversary, Massimo De Carolis, came to see the première in Cremona, but left without a word. Fo paid tribute to his 'intelligence, ability and political wile' but suspected him of employing that wile to foment trouble behind the scenes.[22] There were objections to Fo's employment with a publicly financed company while he was still engaged in unfinished legal business with the Milan City Council, and further complaints that he had overspent his budget. La Scala, like many other theatres and opera houses in Italy, had accumulated a huge debt.

Dario was blamed for adding to the company's deficit, but retorted out that his production was one of the cheapest and most successful that La Scala had mounted for some years. He complained that some sections of the company were anything but enraptured with his work or his presence, and that he was being undermined from within. He was irked that the secretary-general of La Scala had failed to alert Stravinsky's heirs of the plan and to seek due authorisation, and that only his intervention with the agent had prevented the production being aborted. 'I run the risk of losing my percentage,' he said, before turning to other problems. When he required balancing weights to hold the high panels in place, the props department refused to provide them. He resolved this problem by the unlikely expedient of procuring plastic bags from a supermarket and filling them with sand 'which we asked workers on a building site to give us'.[23]

These local difficulties notwithstanding, he had succeeded in his central aim of attracting a mass audience to a work which had previously been regarded as only suitable for an élite. He delightedly gave out detailed financial accounts to anyone who would listen, boasting that they played to 14,000 spectators in two days in Bologna, to 8,000 in Udine and Turin and that the entire run in the Teatro Lirico in Milan was sold out before the first performance. His own estimate was that his production had cost only 25,000 lire per spectator, as against the 40,000 lire which was the company average. He calculated that in a season, La Scala would expect to attract around 20,000 spectators to each production, whereas *Storia di un Soldato* had attracted 60–70,000 in Lombardy alone. He also received invitations to bring the production to London, the Edinburgh Festival, Belgium, Sweden, Holland and Germany. If these invitations had been taken up, it would have been reasonable to expect that all the costs could be recovered. In the event, opposition on the council and inside the company was so intense that none of the invitations were accepted and the run ended in Milan in 1979. It was a storm in a teacup compared to past quarrels, but Dario's problems with official Italy were not over yet.

Chapter 14

On the Defensive

Dario's heightened profile after his return to television in 1977 was the occasion for the appearance of unwelcome articles questioning his account of his conduct in the last days of the war. The fact that several of the journalists responsible for this renewed interest were motivated by political spite did not lessen the gravity of their charges. The basic facts were not in dispute. Dario had joined the army of the Fascist Republic of Salò when called up, but his explanation was that he had done so to protect his father who was engaged in escorting escaped prisoners of war across the border into Switzerland. Members of the Salò army were later called '*repubblichini*', a word which defies exact translation. The meaning is not 'republican' but something more contemptuous, like 'petty republicans', but since it serves to indicate adherents of Mussolini's last republic, the real, unadulterated sense is 'Fascist'. The other damning term from that time is '*rastrellatore*', that is, a member of the anti-partisan death squads. In February 1977, the extreme right-wing periodical, *Il Nord*, which circulated in Piedmont, published an article written by one Angelo Formara, headlined 'The Red Fo Called Dario Once A Fascist'. The language was deliberately offensive, containing accusations that Fo was a 'turncoat, a histrionic, a social-climber, a clown, who turns with every wind, a Fascist, a radical, a Communist, a fool with his snout in every trough'. This was bad enough, but Formara went on to claim that Fo had been a *repubblichino* and a *rastrellatore* and that he had been enrolled in 'the Mazzarino battalion of the National Guard of the Republic of Salò'. This detachment had been active in the region of Romagnano Sesia, and a fear of being recognized explained why, the article continued, Fo had never been able to return to that area. His alleged membership of the Mazzarino unit was the subject of questions in parliament. The Milan daily, *Il Giorno*, repeated the allegations, while the weekly, *Gente*, dispatched journalists to dig more deeply. These two publications later apologized to Fo, but *Il Nord* refused to publish a retraction. Fo raised a case for criminal libel against the writer of the article and the editor of the periodical.

226

The hearing opened in Varese, where the magazine was published, in February 1978 and dragged on for over a year. Even by the standard of libel actions, it was a singularly nasty case and turned on the details of Fo's movements in the confused months of the civil war in 1944–5. Fo's lawyer, Giovanni Cappelli, outlined for the court his client's whereabouts in those months, insisting that his known movements made it impossible for him to have been a participant, as alleged, in massacres perpetrated by Fascist *repubblichini*. Cappelli was able to show that Dario had not belonged to the Mazzarino detachment, but only at the cost of establishing that he had been enrolled in the Folgore (Lightning) detachment, a group whose reputation for pitiless ferocity had passed into legend. The magazine's lawyers produced a grainy photograph of Fo with a group of young recruits, dressed in the uniform and beret of the *repubblichini*.

There was no proof of any of the major allegations, but Dario was compelled to admit to embarrassing exaggerations. He had previously said 'I was always among the partisans', but in the witness box, he modified this statement to the more modest 'I once brought food to some friends'.[1] There were also discrepancies between an account drawn up after the appearance of the *Gente* article and his subsequent deposition in court. Cappelli invited the court to view the early statement as the kind of bragging tale a grandfather might recount to his grandson. Some friends in the Resistance became 'in that kind of dream' partisan leaders, while the fact of having given some assistance would be sufficient 'to transform the Fo home into a refuge for partisans, and indeed into their headquarters'. The accepted history of the Fo family's involvement with the Resistance was also placed in doubt. The most damaging statement came from General Giacinto Lazzarini, a Resistance leader and hero whose credentials were beyond all question. He headed the bands active in the area where the Fo family lived, and in one of his more extravagant moments, Dario had claimed to have searched in the hills and valleys for the Lazzarini group, but to have been unable to locate them. In the witness box, Lazzarini denied having heard of the Fo family as Resistance fighters. This denial included not only Dario but also his father.

The most devastating of the allegations was that Dario had not been a passive and unwilling recruit to Mussolini's army, as he claimed, but that he had actively participated in massacres of partisans and Resistance fighters, especially in Val d'Ossola. A certain Sergeant Milani, who had served with the Folgore, came forward to say that Fo had been at his side in one of the bloodiest and most barbaric of these round-ups. He declared that, in

October 1944, Fo had been with him when the Folgore disembarked at Cannobio, on Lake Maggiore, during an operation against the 'Free Republic' established by the partisans at Val d'Ossola. The Fascist detachment was ambushed at a cemetery near Falmenta by partisans, and several soldiers were killed. Milani said the event occurred in October, Fo insisted it was September but in any case was able to produce documents showing that he had only enrolled with Folgore in November, that is, after the massacre. Prior to that he had been with another *repubblichino* unit, an anti-aircraft detachment at Monza. The two men were brought face to face in court, in accordance with Italian legal practice, and while Fo held to his assertion that he had joined up only to ward off suspicion from his father, he agreed that he had known Milani in that period. Milani continued to insist that Fo could not have known him in early November 1944, since at that time he was on service in Piedmont. The court found unconditionally in Fo's favour on this point and at the end of the case Dario raised a further action for slander against Milani.

The crux of the case was not to establish whether or not Fo had been in the uniform of the *repubblichino* forces, since this was beyond discussion, but the level of commitment he had brought to the cause. This was a difficult case to argue in law. After all the time that had elapsed and given the bad faith that so many displayed in this regard, reliable witnesses were hard to find. It was easier to produce documents to demonstrate an alibi for the period of the massacres. It was shown that Fo enlisted on 3 April 1944, the last time call-up papers were issued, and chose to go to Varese, where he believed there was no military equipment. His movements were complicated, in part because he escaped from one camp but then re-enlisted after being stopped by militiamen in Milan, and in part because he received official passes which allowed him to continue his studies at the Brera. He was able to prove that he could not have been involved in the death squads, but only by producing documents which reminded people that he had been in other military bases with *repubblichini*, not on the mountainside with the freedom fighters.

Cappelli made the point that 'the wish was to haul out the most tragic bitter moment of Fo's life to discredit him in the face of the masses who love him. Fo the 17-year-old boy has been produced with the aim of killing Fo the actor and author of the present day.'[2] In his summing-up, *Il Nord's* lawyer, Leandro De Maio, asked the judges to see in Fo not an unbiased artist, but one who 'dictates to his audience the destruction of the values in which, rightly or wrongly, the majority of people believe'. He wondered if

Fo was entitled to deny freedom of criticism to his client, since he had availed himself of that right to 'criticize God, the saints, the popes, the Madonna and the politicians'.[3] The stance of the Public Prosecutor, who had a role because the case involved a charge of criminal libel against the journalist Angelo Formara, was harder to justify. He went so far as to ask for Formara's acquittal.

The verdict was recorded in Fo's favour, but many saw it as a Pyrrhic victory. Formara was condemned to pay damages of 200,000 lire, a penalty judged mild by the press, and kept so low because the judges found unequivocally in Fo's favour only on one point. They rejected totally the accusation of participation in the raid on Romagnano Sesia. There had been death squads operating in that area, they stated, but there was no proof at all that Fo had any involvement. On the other points, the judgement was more equivocal and the published verdicts reek of prejudice. 'It is certain', the judgement ran,

> that Fo wore the uniform of parachutist in the *repubblichino* ranks of the 'Blue Battalion' of Tradate. He himself recognized this point – indeed could do no other, since there was circumstantial evidence supported by numerous additional documentary and testified grounds – even if he attempted to mitigate his voluntary enlistment, maintaining that he had played the part of an 'infiltrator', engaged on a double bluff. But his mental reservations leave things unchanged.

It is a puzzling assertion. 'Mental reservation' is a Jesuitical category which the court had introduced of its own accord. It was not part of Fo's case. He claimed his enlistment was a gesture to aid to the Resistance and to ward off suspicion from his father. This point was not debated.

The finding over whether Fo could be called a *repubblichino* or even a *rastrellatore* was more harmful. The reasoning was again tortuous, but the verdict was that it was legitimate to use the tag *repubblichino*. 'While it is certain that the Tradate parachutists were employed in some death-squad activities . . . it is not certain, indeed it is debatable, whether Dario Fo was so employed.' To a non-lawyer, the absence of proof would seem conclusive, but the judgement continued:

> this circumstance is, in the view of the court, of negligible value, since there is no need whatsoever of rigorous proof that the plaintiff was physically a member of a death squad to legitimize the adoption in his case of such a qualification. It is the certainty of his membership of the Parachute Group of Tradate (Blue Battalion) which justifies the use in regard of him of an

appellative of which Dario Fo, champion of an art almost entirely dedicated
to the service of a particular kind of political propaganda, is inclined, more
than any other citizen, to complain.

This final judgement flew in the face of all logic and all sense of individual
responsibility. Since Fo had indeed been a member of a *repubblichino* body,
it was decreed that he could be held 'morally co-responsible for all the
activities and all the operational choices of that school which, by free
choice, he had decided to enter'.

Even if there were some columnists who expressed bafflement at the
court's judgement, the terms *repubblichino* and even *rastrellatore* were
carried in the headlines the following day. If criminal law is based on the
principle that a person is responsible only for his own actions and that guilt
by association has no legal force, it is hard to see how it could be right and
lawful to legitimize for Fo a description based on actions which he did not
commit. The notion of 'free choice' was scarcely the appropriate standard
to apply in the conditions of Italy in the closing phase of an all-out war. The
term *repubblichino* would be flung in his face thereafter, even when he won
the Nobel Prize. 'The first *repubblichino* to win a Nobel Prize,' sneered various newspapers when the award was announced in Stockholm. Pier Paolo
Pasolini, no friend of Fo's, delighted in the use of the term.

The verdict pleased no one. *Il Nord* announced, inevitably, that it would
appeal, while Fo announced an action against Milani. He was free of the
slur that he had been a Fascist by conviction, and certainly free of any alle-
gation that he had ambushed partisans or taken part in murderous attacks.
And yet, it was clear that his early accounts of his activities in the days of
the Resistance were embellished and exaggerated. In all his theatre, no
myth, no legend, no call to arms had more strength than the call to revive
and abide by the values of the Resistance, but Dario had not been involved
in that struggle. As De Maio put it, '[Fo's] hero General Lazzarini was operating in the zone where Fo was living, and at the moment the conscription
papers arrived. Why not join him?' No one living in comfort has the right
to judge those who lived in darker days and climes, and Fo was shown by a
hostile court to have committed no enormity. The face in the photograph
was that of a very callow youth. There was no shameful, concealed history
to be compared to that of Martin Heidegger, Paul de Man or Kurt
Waldheim, but there was a less than glorious story of subsequent exaggeration, evasion and disingenuousness.

At the trial's close, Dario and Franca went to Sweden to play *Mistero buffo* and *All Bed, Board and Church* in theatres which had been sold out weeks in advance. Dario proceeded to Jutland to meet up with Eugenio Barba and his Odin Teatret, while Franca went on to Cologne. They spent part of that summer in Umbria with Jacopo, who was now making a career for himself as a cartoonist with a satirical weekly, *Il Male*. With the assistance of his parents, he had bought a large wooded area near Gubbio equipped with abandoned farmhouses and towers. This he transformed into a hippie-cum-cultural compound which he named the Free University of Alcatraz. It hosted many relaxed seminars on a variety of topics, from arts and crafts to psychotherapy and the techniques of cartoon-drawing. Dario and Franca, not to mention many others writers and performers, used the centre to give classes for aspiring actors from all over Europe.

Franca was invited by RAI to front a series of television variety pro-grammes to be broadcast in January 1980 under the title *Buonasera con Franca Rame*. The roles between the couple were reversed, with Franca taking the lead role and Dario guesting as 'feed'. They insisted that the programmes be scheduled for a time when housewives, including both their mothers, would be watching. The new series gave another opportunity for a further settling of accounts. The treatment meted out to them at the time of *Canzonissima*, and the subsequent destruction of the film reels, still ran-kled, so they decided to re-record and broadcast sketches censored in 1962. They also found space for some pieces from the *Let's Talk About Women* of three years previously, topped and tailed with fresh material. All the mate-rial was written by Dario at Cesenatico over the summer. Some of the new sketches, like one featuring the ideal husband who turned out to be a robot of such terrifying efficiency that he was replaced by a flesh-and-blood man, or the piece on a mythical Batman-male, were a continuation of one-act plays Franca had been doing. A one-acter on a nurse tending an ex-minis-ter who had much in common with Mario Tanassi, the politician jailed for his part in the Lockheed scandal, struck the familiar note of political satire. The programmes were among the few occasions when Franca sang solo.

As had happened earlier with Dario, Franca now found herself placed on a pedestal she had no wish to occupy but which she found impossible to vacate. She was the subject of profiles and endless requests for interviews. Occasionally the interviewers wanted to discuss politics, so when asked if she was ever tired of struggling, Franca replied that she was not, but admit-ted that in the present climate she often found herself 'dismayed'. She went on, 'if they were to ask me what I think politically at this moment, I would not know how to reply. We have nothing ahead of us, no Communist or socialist model.'[4] Such moments of serious reflection were rare. The majority of interviewers, especially those writing for women's magazines, sought to satisfy their readers', or their own, curiosity about her private life. For the first time, in some of these interviews, Franca allowed readers a glimpse of dissatisfaction with her private life and relationship with Dario. It was by no means the only, nor even the dominant, note. When asked if she was still proud to have Dario as husband, she replied in breathless tones,

> More than proud! We have been married more than twenty-five years, and there is a beautiful relationship between us, a relationship of absolute regard the one for the other, of respect, of love, love in the deepest sense of the word. We cannot do without each other, this is undeniable. You have no idea of how marvellous it is to have a man like Dario at your side.[5]

However, in the same month, when asked if she of all women had been successful in attaining equality in her marriage, she expressed herself in more assertive and troubled terms:

> Yes, now I have, because with *All Bed, Board and Church* I have shown other people that I can walk by myself, but it has taken me a lifetime to get here, and I have had to overcome so many conflicts, so many mortifications. This show has had for me the value of a wager. I said to myself: 'If it does not go well, I will close it down after three days and open an orphanage.' (An orphanage has always been an obsession of mine.) It has gone well, so now I can tell you that my relationship with Dario is on an equal footing.

Franca was now fifty-one, and had been working on the stage all her life. Her position as one of Italy's leading actresses and most prominent public figures was well established, yet she felt that only with the rise of feminism and with her own solo performances had she won a position of parity with Dario. Even then, the equality was restricted to professional matters. When she switched to the personal level, she gave voice, perhaps unconsciously, to a different kind of resentment:

> Or nearly, because there is always a substantial difference: the judgement of your neighbours. For instance, if Dario were to come to Spoleto and happened to meet up with a fascinating young girl, and were to spend the night with her, no one would think twice about it.[6]

It was an ancient complaint, made by women in Shakespeare or Ariosto, dramatized by Madame Bovary or Anna Karenina. Feminism, Franca implied, could not change men's conduct or society's judgement. An older man involved in an affair with a younger woman will be congratulated, while society will 'condemn, invariably and inexorably, the relationship between a woman who is, let's say, more than 40 years old, and a man who is younger than her, even by very little'. She gave vent to feelings which were obviously more than political:

> A woman over 40 is seen as an old lady, and she herself will be filled with complexes. She no longer has the right to fall in love at all, let alone with a man younger than herself. This is the proof that we still live in a society made for the benefit of men. It seems to me that there is nothing squalid about the relationship between an adult woman and a boy if it is lived with dignity, conscience and straightforwardness. On the contrary, if the woman is profoundly woman, it cannot but be positive. An adult woman knows how to love completely: and when she loves completely, she gives everything, she is more patient, more understanding than younger women, more maternal, more loving. In addition to this, the act of love with a womanly woman is extremely important for a young man, it helps him discover what sex is.

The quest to help youthful males to discover what sex is can turn sour. There is a touch of exasperation as Franca went on:

> The only problem is that then you can't get rid of him. Even if they are relationships with no future, even if they are tortured relationships, they are still lovely and rich relationships and when they end they leave a good memory, do they not? Both for the man and the woman, a relationship between people of unequal age can have as its support little presents or major gifts from the party who, precisely because of their age, has better economic prospects. I do not allow myself moralistic judgements. At the end of the day, with money you can buy anything, so why not buy yourself a little bit of an illusion?[7]

These complaints over an inequality which cannot be remedied by financial status and which transcend political action would appear in the future plays performed, and to some extent co-written, by Franca. There is a higher level of autobiographical reflection in the 'feminist' plays than had ever been permitted in the directly political plays. If Franca puts herself forward as Everywoman, she also explores, in lightly disguised form, experiences of her own. The perspective is frequently that of a woman whose salad days have passed and whose life is neither totally satisfying nor totally frustrating. There is a vein of deeper sadness to her self-portrayal, explicitly so in the interviews, and implicitly, on a careful reading, in the monologues. 'The problem with escape,' as Theodore Zeldin put it, 'is knowing where to escape to.'[8] Franca had no clearer answer than Zeldin. She was and is an accomplished, successful woman, whose career is enviable, whose talents are diverse and yet who was nagged by a persistent sense of dissatisfaction, based on a feeling of persisting inequality. Professionally, she had known only success, but personally she wanted more. Franca isolated herself from new-wave feminists by seeing some form of resolution not in 'separatism' but in a non-revolutionary language of love and loyalty. It was something she feared was now missing in her marriage.

She said that for the first eighteen years, Dario had been unswervingly faithful to her. Another intrusive interviewer was told that sex no longer played the role in their life that it once did. 'It was highly important for the first eighteen years, and that seems quite a lot to me. Then, little by little, Dario and I found that we did not desire each other any longer. We love each other a lot, but we no longer make love.'[9] With the availability of the Pill, women, especially young women, enjoyed a sexual liberation women of Franca's generation had never known and to which she could not entirely adjust. Franca blamed, no doubt rightly, inner complexes and outer social judgements for her own predicament. 'In making love, I saw only "Sin", and every time I sinned, there was my mother staring at me unsmiling, severe, at the foot of the bed, even when the act of love was totally legal.'

Dario, on the other hand, found himself surrounded by liberated and admiring younger women who had cast off the shackles of restraint and inhibition. He emerged blinking into a new landscape changed utterly by the sexual politics of early feminism, and he cheerfully adjusted. The Italian press does not pry into private lives in the way the British or American press does, but photographs of young women alongside Dario began to appear in various publications. Franca began to receive phone calls not meant for her, and even to take receipt of presents sent for Dario. She later said she set aside a trunk marked 'Gifts Girls Dario' to contain the 'belts, scarves, socks, gloves, books, perfumes' he received from female admirers.[10]

Something of her resentments, and perhaps even of his guilt, are apparent in the subtext to The Open Couple, a work which is an anomalous part of their output. The play was premièred in Stockholm in 1983, the only one of their works to receive its first staging outside Italy. It was also the only time, leaving aside the politically determined decisions made by the cooperatives of the later 1960s and early 1970s, that Dario declined to take the leading role in his own work. The reason, paradoxical as it may seem, was that this play did have autobiographical overtones, albeit veiled behind the surface irony, and he had no wish to be publicly identified with the character.[11] The play was written by Dario as a private gesture to pacify Franca after a quarrel over his affairs with other women. It was meant to be read by a few close friends and not intended for the stage, but was picked up in their house by Carlo Barsotti, who was impressed by its potential and who, together with his wife, Anna, translated and produced it in Stockholm's Pistol theatre. Dario recalled meeting an Italian journalist in an airport who requested an impromptu interview about his recent success. He assumed she was referring to *The Tale of a Tiger*, but she was on her way back from Stockholm, where *The Open Couple* was playing to packed houses. On the back of this success, Dario directed Franca in an Italian production.

The play faces the contradictions, complications and, from a woman's perspective, the inadequacy of the 'open couple' relationship. It tackles the unequal power balance that such relationships involve while also probing, with a seriousness belied by laughter, the delicate emotional complexity of all relationships. The militants of previous decades had now settled down with families but retained the libertarian philosophy of their salad, or hashish, days. The recommendation in the play, even if it clashed with Dario or Franca's personal conduct, was to live in fidelity and mutual respect. The supposedly adult agreement allowing the married couple in the script to indulge in casual affairs begins to grate first on the wife, who realizes she is passing an increasing number of evenings alone, but then, in a comic overturning of expectations, on the husband when the wife casually announces over a game of cards that she has initiated a relationship with a fascinating man, a nuclear physicist who is also a rock star. The husband becomes increasingly frantic at this turning of tables, initially scoffing, then pleading and finally threatening to kill himself. He is left to choose his own catastrophic end as the wife strolls off with her fabulous Prince Charming. This was one of Fo's most successful comedies, made all the more striking because of its dark, or tragic, undercurrent of sadness and poignancy.

The play was taken as an assertion of the woman's right to equality of sexual fulfilment and freedom, but in the intention of the authors, and in Franca's own convictions, the underlying moral was one which would satisfy the most rigid of traditional monogamists. It gave a modern twist to old questions on mutual trust, on the force of jealousy and the capacity for manipulation by the powerful partner in any couple. The 'open couple' ideology was, Franca believed, a fraudulent front for egocentric male behaviour, advocated by men of all sides of the political spectrum because it satisfied their purposes.

> The 'open couple', if it means the belief that a couple can have affairs without the relationship being damaged is simply impossible, because there are feelings involved, feelings of love, and one of the two always suffers. Normally it is the woman who comes off worse, but that is not the main point of the play . . . For couples of my age, it is much worse, because men do not look for mother figures, or run off with women of 80. They go off with young girls, and for the wives it can be traumatic.[12]

Dario and Franca were now receiving invitations from all around the world, both individually and jointly. In 1980, they were invited to the USA to perform at a Festival of Italian Theater in New York. Their manager, Pietro Sciotto, was dispatched a month in advance to make preparations, but the American authorities denied them visas on the grounds that they were terrorist sympathizers. Faced with their protests, the American consul in Milan produced a huge file relating to the work of Red Aid. Franca was outraged, not least because Red Aid was entirely her business and Dario had little to do with it. The deeper grounds for their outrage were that the two had invariably set their faces against terrorist violence. Their sponsors in America appealed, but the State Department refused to budge.

Their hosts had the wit to organize, on 25 May, *An Evening Without Dario Fo and Franca Rame*. Sciotto remembers that before the refusal of the visa, the visit was awaited in theatre circles with a measure of polite interest, but was hardly a burning issue for society at large. 'Afterwards, they all reacted as though they were old schoolfriends of Dario, devastated at being deprived of his company.'[13] The evening attracted the support of the foremost names of American literature and theatre. Martin Scorsese, Arthur Miller, Joe Chaikin, Sol Yurick and Bernard Malamud were all in attendance. Norman Mailer promised to be there but crashed his car en route. Students put on a production of *Can't Pay? Won't Pay!*, a letter from Dario and Franca was read out, and the two received more publicity than if they had been there in person.

That summer, Fo finally found the appropriate means to dramatize the thoughts that had been circling in his mind since the Moro assassination. He had written various scripts which did not, in his own view, stand up, and he had not produced any full-length play since *Mum's Marijuana* in 1976. 'The tragic paradoxes which [I] kept on inventing were outdone by even more tragic and paradoxical events.'[14] In the summer of 1980, the ideal approach occurred to him, and *Trumpets and Raspberries* was completed in ten days and premièred at the Cinema Cristallo in January the following year. Although inspired by an event which had occurred only two years previously, the play was stylistically and ideologically something of a throwback to the kind of work he had performed in the seventies. The production even brought back the good old days of questions in parliament, objections from the PCI and complaints to the police about the reading on stage of letters written by prisoners in Trani jail, where there had been prison riots. This reading was taken as further proof of support for violence and terrorism.

Dario would write many more plays, and have many more successes, but this was the last of the noisy, rumbustious, didactic political farces for which he is best known. The basic elements of the plot were borrowed from Plautus' *Menaechmi*, and the inspiration was to treat the Moro case obliquely, by supposing that the kidnap victim was not a politician but Italy's leading industrialist, Gianni Agnelli, owner of Fiat and of Juventus Football Club. A worker in Fiat, Antonio, happens to be in the vicinity when the car in which Agnelli is travelling is attacked by would-be kidnappers. Antonio covers the disfigured body of Agnelli with his jacket and takes him to hospital. The doctors find in the jacket a photograph, which is actually that of Antonio, and use it to reconstruct Agnelli's appearance. Fo played both of the now identical characters with a variety of quick-change routines and unrestrained comic horseplay. The Agnelli/Antonio character is suspected of involvement in the original kidnapping, causing secret police to swarm around the home of Antonio's divorced wife, played by Franca. The character is taken hostage, a scene which led to press attacks on Dario for tastelessness. Shortly before the opening night, a judge, Giovanni D'Urso, was kidnapped by the Red Brigades, and in the play, Dario had his Antonio/Agnelli recite words from the letters written by Moro in captivity. In the fiction, the hostage is released. Moro was only a politician, but Agnelli represents capital, so the state bows to the kidnappers' demands.

The play was received coolly in Italy. The English translation, a substantially revised piece shorn of the many references to Italian politics, worked well. With so many translations and adaptations of his work being staged in so many countries, the problem of how to present Fo abroad was by now an acute one for directors and translators. The balance between political commitment and farce was difficult to attain on stages outside Italy, especially when translators had to face the added difficulty of clarifying events which were well known to Italian audiences. Fo's brand of didactic farce was unique, so the temptation of inexpert directors was either to exaggerate the clowning or to step up the political thrust. Fo himself winced at many of the versions of his work. 'I have seen few good works,' he wrote. 'Some were respectable, others appalling, either on account of the actors, the director or the text itself which had been supposedly corrected but often cheapened.'[15]

Dario had an opportunity to appreciate the dilemmas of translation from the other side later that year when the Teatro Stabile in Turin put on a work of his entitled *L'opera dello sghignazzo* (The Opera of Guffaws). In the programme and in the subsequent published version,[16] it was described as being based on 'John Gay's *Beggar's Opera*, and on some ideas from my son Jacopo'. Acknowledgement was also made of the contribution of poets and rock singers including Allen Ginsburg, Patti Smith, Donovan and Frank Zappa. There was no reference to Bertolt Brecht or to *Threepenny Opera*. In fact, the project was initiated by the Berliner Ensemble who invited Fo to direct a new production of Brecht's play. When they saw the modifications Dario intended to introduce, they recoiled in horror and refused him permission to make any use of Brechtian material for any production anywhere. Fo professed himself mystified by this elevation of a theatrical work into untouchable sacred text, and devised a strategy to circumvent the legal veto. Brecht's play is itself a reworking of John Gay's original, but John Gay is dead and has no heirs to threaten recourse to law. Dario did what Brecht had done: he went back to Gay's *Beggar's Opera* and recast it in his own way. Or so he said, and no one could challenge him.

In his introduction to the published version of *L'opera dello sghignazzo*, Dario justified his intervention by reference to Brecht's own theories, and went on to provide what reads like a manifesto for *laissez-faire* translations:

From the moment I first received an invitation from the Berliner Ensemble to stage *Threepenny Opera*, it seemed to me essential to set to work on Brecht's text with that open-minded irreverence Brecht had himself recommended. 'When you find yourself faced with the task of producing some work by an illustrious author flee from the terrorism of the classics,' he insisted. 'If you wish to display the slightest regard for the ideas which classic works contain, treat them without respect.' Personally, since Bertolt Brecht has been himself reduced to the status of a classic, I took him at his word and threw myself at him (his text, naturally) feet first, boots on.

This principle is radical enough in itself, but Dario goes on to state that some operation of updating is not only desirable but indispensable.

Another tricky piece of advice from Brecht was his repeated invitation to transfer the script into the space and time of the present, 'especially since ours are times of tragic and desperate dejection' . . . Certainly Brecht, if he were alive today and had to produce this play, would introduce into the script the tragically urgent problem of drugs, of kidnapping, of the internationalized, industrialized organization of terrorism, of crime, of the robotic sex market, of widespread, worthless psychoanalysis, the mass media, etc., not to mention the question of the somewhat trivial level to which the political world has sunk . . . everywhere.

This was certainly the principle which guided Dario's own forays into the field of directing. With *Histoire d'un Soldat* for La Scala, Molière's *Le médecin malgré lui* for the Comédie-Française or Rossini's *Il Barbiere di Siviglia* for the Pesaro Festival, he behaved not as a Stanislavskian servant of the author's text but as an exponent of director's theatre. He reinterpreted freely, rewriting, reordering, introducing mime and imposing his own vision. The resultant stage versions have produced in critics exactly the doubts and hesitations – or even the frustrated rage – which Fo himself has experienced over foreign adaptations of or directorial interventions in his own work. It is hard to reconcile what he wrote about responsibilities towards original work *vis-à-vis* Brecht with what he expects in his own case. While as director or interpreter of the work of other playwrights, Fo takes to himself the role of liberating contributor to the creative process, he expects his own directors and translators to be his hewers of wood and drawers of water. This inconsistency may be brushed aside by reference to the superior claims of 'genius', but the further difficulty is that it is anything but clear that Fo's translators or directors would be doing his theatre justice by assuming the workaday role he requests of them. Dario's works are often, as he believed true drama ought to be, dull on the page.[17] Fo the actor best translates and enlivens Fo the author, but in his absence the job still needs to be done. Translation of Fo requires audience-centred techniques, which do not necessarily coincide with the author-centred translation he advocates – for his own work.

Chapter 15

Separations and Reconciliations

No observer of Italian society, and especially of the Movement, in the 1980s could doubt that a sea-change had occurred in the attitudes of the hopeful pilgrims who had, a decade previously, set off on a march towards brighter tomorrows. No longer fortified by the conviction that they were in tune with history, they saw the Cold War resumed, Ronald Reagan in the White House, Mrs Thatcher in Downing Street, the Christian Democrats dominant in Italy, the Communist Party in frustrated opposition and the extra-parliamentary left dispirited. The new forces which would, for good or ill, convulse Italy at the end of the decade were hardly glimpsed. Umberto Bossi and his Lombard League were still the object of scornful jokes, the Milanese magistrates still did not dare inquire into the doings of politicians or businessmen and Silvio Berlusconi was still fully occupied with his business empire.

The theatre of Dario and Franca continued to be dissident, but it was political only in a wide sense, and now performed in the grand, bourgeois palaces they had spurned with such contempt years before. *Obscene Fables*, a series of three one-man narratives by Dario, plus a reprise of *I Ulrike* by Franca were staged in early 1982 in the Cinema Cristallo. The tales were reworked *fabliaux* of Franco-Provençal origin, originally told by a jester. The main innovation was the introduction of the 'obscene' to a repertoire which would not previously have offended the most puritanical con-science:

> The subjects dealt with in these fables are, as the title suggests, obscene in character and nature. I emphasize – obscene, not salacious or prurient. In other words, the principal aim of the story-tellers was to reverse by the use of eroticism the sense of guilt which had been imposed, almost as an act of terrorism, by the authorities. Erotic obscenity is used as a weapon of libera-tion. Nowadays, we could reduce the whole thing to a slogan: 'obscene is beautiful!'[1]

Beautiful was not the description people would instinctively have used for *The Tumult of Bologna*, a story based on an incident which had been ignored by 'university professors, or by anthologies of ancient writings. Complete censorship . . . And yet we are dealing with a stupendous page of our history. Stupendous indeed, but slightly indecent.' The events concerned a siege in the late Middle Ages, when the people of Bologna attacked papal forces who had holed up in the citadel of their city. Locked out, facing starvation, some defeatists spoke of surrender, but one man had the inspired idea of collecting all the human and animal shit available and catapulting it into the enclosure. Victory was guaranteed.

The other two tales were richly obscene in a more conventional sense, the one focusing on the vagina, given the nickname 'butterfly mouse' and the second on the penis, given no nickname. *The Butterfly Mouse*, a tale of unexpected tenderness, told with a wholly new lyricism, featured a simple man, Giavan Pietro, who falls on good times and in love almost simultaneously. Being simple-minded, he is easily gulled by the woman he loves and by a devious priest, Father Weasel, who wants to keep the woman as his mistress even after he has married her off to Giavan Pietro. The woman persuades Giavan Pietro that she has left her 'butterfly mouse' in her mother's house, and sends him off through the forest to collect it while she sleeps with her priest. In his performance, Dario reproduces every noise in the forest, every puff in the run through the woods, but the final twist, when the woman is moved to pity and affection by the spectacle of her deluded admirer, is one of the few occasions in Fo's theatre when human warmth for its own sake is allowed to appear.

The final story, *Lucius and the Ass*, a magical tale of a man turned into an ass when a spell goes wrong, is taken from Lucian of Samosata, not from the better-known version by Apuleius.

> Anyone who knows both versions cannot fail to notice the great difference of style and taste. Where Lucian satirizes eroticism, the other falls often into mere, gratuitous scurrility . . . given the development of this work we are about to hear, we are entitled to suspect that the original author was a woman. So, in this story, which may be pre-Lucian, we are invited to listen to the doings of a character stricken with a fantasy phallocracy.

The ass is involved, to its evident delight, in various erotic adventures, but when he resumes human shape the woman who had been so taken by him in animal form has him thrown off her land. This is Dario the native of Lake Maggiore, dusting down the story-teller's craft he had learned as a boy, focusing on episodes of alternative history but discovering for the first time the liberating power of Eros. The talk is not of political liberation but, in the tones of a follower of Wilhelm Reich or Herbert Marcuse, of the liberation from suffocating complexes and from repression. The personal is not political, but the personal is all that remains.

Dario and Franca were still enveloped in a seductive cloud of notoriety and viewed in certain quarters as individuals likely to kick over the traces in all manner of unspeakable ways. They were dismayed when the Italian Ministry for Entertainment, who plainly had no grasp of the sense of the play, slapped a ban on a revival of *The Open Couple*, forbidding access to the under-eighteens. The State Department in Washington once again refused them a visa when, in 1983, they were invited to perform at Joseph Papp's free theatre in New York's Central Park, but they spent a highly successful period in London, doing workshops and performances at the Riverside Studios. Franca went on her own to Quebec, and at the beginning of 1984 they went together to a theatre festival in Havana, where Franca performed some of her monologues. Springtime took them to Buenos Aires, where they received graphic proof that their power to shock was undimmed. In Argentina, the military were in control and the Church still a force in the land. Franca was due to perform some of her feminist pieces and Dario *Mistero buffo*, but even before the first performance the theatre where they were to perform was the target for whistle-blowing, flag-waving and stone-throwing demonstrators. The so-called Mothers of Plaza de Mayo, who met each day to demand information on the '*desparecidos*', expressed their support for them, but they were no match for the Archbishop of Buenos Aires who denounced *Mistero buffo* in the local press. Members of the Church Militant took him at his word and crowded into the theatre foyer, clutching pictures of the Sacred Heart of Jesus and kneeling in the doorways to recite decades of the rosary. Others made their way into the theatre itself, rising to their feet to scream in outrage each time the word 'pope' was mentioned. Some patrons had to be dragged forcibly from the stalls. This was unpleasant but bearable, but one evening a youth threw a tear-gas bomb at the stage, causing panic. Dario leaped from the stage to seize hold of him, as much to defend him from the police as to prevent him causing further havoc. Before the man was dragged off, Dario had time to note how young he was, and to conclude there and then that someone had put him up to it.

Edinburgh during the International Festival in August did not present the excitement of Argentina, but uninteresting times can be preferable. There were several productions of Dario's works being staged in the church halls, closes and Masonic lodges which are pressed into service during the festival, and Dario toured them all to see what had been made of his writing. Having Dario or Franca in the audience can be a daunting experience for directors or performers. Dario himself is unlikely to be overtly dismissive in public, but Franca can be much more cutting. She does not suffer fools gladly, a Shakespearean euphemism which conceals a bluntness which can draw blood. At times, her recognition of shortcomings in plays she has done herself takes the form of an offer of private rehearsal sessions, which are physically taxing and psychologically draining for the women who are the object of such attention, but on other occasions, she can rise majestically to her feet to issue loud and uncompromising denunciations. Once, a young student actress from England, performing at a Fringe show in Edinburgh, was reduced to tears when her performance as Queen Elizabeth, in an admittedly appalling production, drew audible comments of '*vergogna*' from Franca. The word means 'shameful', but there was no need of a command of Italian to grasp the sense.

In autumn that year, they were finally granted a six-day visa to allow them to see the Broadway production of *Accidental Death*. The production itself was freely adapted and stylized, and had required the services of literal translator, adaptor and script doctors before being passed on to director and actors. Jonathan Pryce played the part of the madman and although his performance was much admired, several reviewers wrote that he had made the piece a vehicle for his own talents. An especially trenchant review in *Village Voice* suggested that the process of transformation to suit American tastes and American expectations had made *Accidental Death* resemble a Neil Simon comedy. In an interview when he returned home, Dario spoke with his customary civility about Pryce's acting abilities, but lamented the absence of the 'aggressive passages', and their substitution by 'euphemistically innocuous material'.[2]

Back in Italy, Dario and Franca set to work on *Almost by Chance a Woman: Elizabeth*, a complex, multi-layered historical farce set in an imprecise land, halfway between Elizabethan England and contemporary Italy. Initially, Franca had great reservations over the piece, and told a sulky Dario that while the play was an excellent essay on Shakespeare, it lacked all dramatic qualities. Even after it was rewritten, she was never happy with the part of Queen Elizabeth, which she described as requiring the strength of an ox. In addition to giving expression to his highly idiosyncratic fascination with Shakespeare, Dario used the piece to discuss the birth of the modern state, to return to the theme of commitment and the intellectual and even to refer to the Moro kidnapping. He told an interviewer that it was 'both a pamphlet and a theatrical manifesto . . . but also, I hope, a comic work'.[3] He had little interest in Shakespeare the great universal poet who inhabits spheres common mortals could not attain, and has on several occasions offered interpretations of Shakespeare's plots as reflections and comments on current events in his society. Fo's Shakespeare was, rather like Fo himself, a writer whose work illustrated his relationship with contemporary society.

The relationship between Elizabeth and Shakespeare was intended as the crux of the play, but there was so much bustle in the acting, and so many criss-crossing threads in the writing, that no single theme could ever command exclusive attention. Dario took on the mock-female role of a vulgar, quack beautician who babbles in a pseudo-popular idiom and trades in such eccentric beauty aids as bee stings which help the nipples stay upright. Elizabeth's urge to enhance her attractiveness is part female foible and part political stratagem, for she is facing a *putsch* led by her ex-lover, Essex, and numbering Southampton, Shakespeare's patron, among the plotters. Some lords loyal to the queen are kidnapped, in a deliberate parallel with the Moro case. Elizabeth maintains the hard line taken by the Italian establishment, but the killing of Essex was also her own death as a woman, if not yet as queen. The burlesque elements in the plot, the echoes of *commedia dell'arte* and even of the Shakespearean fool in the part Fo wrote for himself ensured that the comedy was always amusing, but it was more soft-centred and less hard-hitting than Fo intended.

This work was quickly translated and performed in several countries. Dario received many requests to direct his plays in translation, and accepted such a request from Arturo Corso, who had appeared in many Fo productions in Italy and who was then working with a Finnish company. The company wanted to stage *Elizabeth*, and in summer 1985 they arrived in Alcatraz, where Dario was to direct, with Corso as assistant and a Finnish director also helping in some unspecified capacity. As is his invariable custom, Dario found it necessary to rewrite as he went along, so the rehearsals were a confused, multi-linguistic babble of shouts, retakes, stops and starts, backtracks and instructions given and countermanded. It was a particularly hot summer and the strain proved too much for the unfortunate interpreter, whose stamina gave out and who collapsed on the set. She had to be carried from the camp on a stretcher, babbling incoherently in a mixture of

Finnish and Italian. The hospital diagnosed her as suffering from 'non-specific stress', although her condition would appear to a non-medic extremely specific. She returned home before the company, made a good recovery but shunned the theatre thereafter.

In October that year, at the invitation of the Venice Biennale, Fo revisited history in a more personal way. He was now almost sixty, an age when successful men commonly take to composing memoirs as a hedge against mortality, but conventional autobiography, detailing childhood, adolescence and formative influences, was not for him. He did, however, feel a need to order his affairs, arrange his legacy, examine his origins and pay homage to his household gods. *Hellequin, Harlekin, Arlecchino*, a stage history of the Harlequin, was the first of a series of works which may be regarded as repayment of artistic debts, or as acts of deference to the authors, actors and even stage characters who people his own private pantheon. Molière and Ruzzante would receive similar veneration in future years, while Rossini, as previously Stravinsky, would be subjected to procrustean treatment to ensure that he too would fit into the niche in that pantheon reserved for his revered predecessors.

Following T. S. Eliot, it could be said that every great writer re-orders the past, and creates from the chaos of inheritance a coherence termed tradition. As Harold Bloom has argued, every tradition is founded on a 'principle of selectivity', and not by some pseudo-natural process. From the Harlequin show in 1985, Fo was manufacturing his own tradition, stressing his own, very personal, relations with each individual in it. Harlequin was his twin. 'I have always played Harlequin, whether I wanted to or not. Without necessarily skipping about or doing double turns, my characters have always been in this key.'[4]

The Harlequin show could have been regarded as safely mainstream had he not aimed simultaneously to encourage a revision of received wisdom on *commedia dell'arte*, which he believes has been neutered by theatre historians and contemporary directors. The surprise, or outrage, which greeted the production in some quarters was occasioned by the clash between the preconception that *commedia dell'arte* required an elegant, elaborately stylized display of delicately devised movement techniques and Fo's belief that it involved the clowning, horseplay, acrobatic tumbles and vulgarity which are associated in the twentieth century with low farce. Other critics were disconcerted to discover that they were being offered a standard Fo piece rather than a more rigorous work on Harlequin in history. He decided not to wear the famous mask associated with the character and so, whether intentionally or not, emphasized the continuity between the medieval jester, Fo's fundamental model and the Harlequin of *commedia dell'arte*.

Franca spent two springtime months in 1986 in London, attempting to learn English. She was still having trouble with the arm she had injured in the car crash in 1977, and had planned to go to Ischia to rest and recuperate. At the last moment she changed her mind. 'What am I going to Ischia for? To die?'[5] She rented a flat in Piccadilly, attended classes at a language school in the morning and went to the theatre in the evening. Dario's plays were now being performed regularly in Britain, with productions of *Elizabeth* and *Trumpets and Raspberries* both mounted in London about that time, so she spent some time overseeing the British end of the operation. Dario joined her over Easter, and Franca later described those two months as being 'absolutely the happiest two months of my life'. She never did learn English.

Meanwhile, there were moves afoot to persuade the American government to grant them a visa which would allow them to perform in the USA. Ron Jenkins, a circus clown turned academic, received a grant from Harvard University which would allow him to travel anywhere in the world to study theatre, and chose to spend his year observing Dario's theatre. He showed Robert Brustein, the celebrated critic and theatre historian, tapes of Dario's work, and, together with Joel Schechter and Peter Sellers, he arranged an invitation. The backing of a prestigious institution like Harvard facilitated the grant of a visa. Jenkins also speculates that Dario's having a show on Broadway helped. 'With an investment of $500,000 in that production, Fo was automatically recategorized from terrorist to businessman.'[6] It was agreed that Jenkins would appear as his on stage interpreter but since he had never done that kind of work before, Dario invited him to Brussels, where he was performing, to observe the techniques of stage translation. When he arrived, he discovered that Dario had decided to do the performance in French himself and dispense with the interpreter, but he asked Jenkins if he would like to accompany him to Vienna. Since Jenkins had no knowledge of German, this was of limited use, but he went anyway, and came away impressed by the need to aim for a certain rhythm as much as for accuracy if Dario's improvised humour was to be communicated to an audience.

Arriving in America in June 1986, Dario and Franca embarked on a tour which took in Cambridge, Boston, New York, Washington and Baltimore. They appeared on successive nights, playing *Mistero buffo* and *Female Parts*.

Dario was uncertain of the reception awaiting him, but was quickly reassured.

> You can joke about them, their power, their society . . . People went wild. I did not expect it, because in other countries, like Britain, irony on certain domestic problems does not work. You are in trouble if you mock the English. They just don't laugh. In America, I could bring up everything, Vietnam, Watergate, blacks, Italo-Americans, Republicans, veterans.

Matters sexual were an exception. 'A fear of sex. An incredible prudery. They blushed. They dried up at the jokes.'[7] Any reference to the American flag which was not totally respectful was strictly off-limits. Once, in his improvised prologue to the 'Lazarus' sketch, he delivered a one-liner about the miniature version of the Stars and Stripes at each place at a dinner he attended. It was just the right size for wiping the cutlery, he quipped, but before he had spoken the line, he felt his audience drift away from him. He did not repeat the joke. One of Jenkins's tasks was to read the daily press to him, so he could incorporate up-to-date gags about President Reagan into each evening's routine. On one occasion, Reagan opined that there was no hunger in America, only people who did not know where to find assistance. Dario's retort, that the problem of the poor was that they did not know where to find the garbage cans, was, to his surprise carried by the *New York Times*. For the rest of the tour, Reagan's words were put into the mouth of the Doge of Venice in 'The Hunger of the Zanni' sketch.

Franca was accompanied by her brother Enrico, a theatre manager, and her sister Pia, a costumier. Enrico was impressed by her progress and at her confidence in solo performance after a lifetime on stage with Dario. On the night before her opening at the Lincoln Center in New York, the whole troupe dined together. Enrico complained of feeling unwell and left early. The following morning, he was found dead in his hotel. Franca was awakened by a call from the receptionist who announced casually that her brother had just died. The rest of the day was spent in preparations for having the body flown home, but Franca was determined that, in the best traditions of the trade, 'the show must go on'. She insisted that the news be withheld from the audience, and made only a veiled reference to it at the end when she was called back on stage by enthusiastic applause.

In August, after a brief tour in Denmark and Germany, Franca returned to the Edinburgh Fringe Festival with a programme consisting of *The Open Couple* and the monologues *Medea* and the *The Rape*. Although he was not performing himself, Dario accompanied her, and took the opportunity to see various shows, including Tilda Swinton in a one-woman performance at the Traverse. He does not speak English, but returned to the hotel that night in a state of excitement, fired by enthusiasm for an idea which had occurred to him while watching. At a party the following evening, he spoke of his developing idea with growing fervour, and at an increasing volume. Franca, seated with her back to him, turned round repeatedly to tell him to be quiet as he was disturbing the other guests. Suppose there were a woman in a flat, he told the group who gathered round him, making a video as her last testament to her ex-husband before she kills herself, but she is continually interrupted by phone calls from other women who are experiencing problems and undergoing suffering much like hers. Why would they be phoning, he wondered? A wrong number, obviously, but whose? He was initially unsure but began to devise possible problems. By the following morning, the idea was even clearer, and over breakfast he began to write out notes. He had little paper and no patience with the idea of going to a shop to buy some. He wrote furiously on napkins, talking as he wrote, the emerging script spilling off the napkins on to the white tablecloth. The management was magnanimous towards the demands of creativity. The head waiter rolled up the cloth with a fine flourish and presented it to Dario as though it were an Egyptian papyrus. He left Edinburgh for Milan on Friday, and phoned on Monday to say that the play, now entitled *An Ordinary Day*, was fully written.

Rehearsals were completed in twelve days in the autumn, and the new play, twinned with *The Open Couple*, opened in October as part of a double bill entitled *Female Parts*. The couple re-formed the Fo–Rame company they had disbanded in 1968, and sought readmittance to ETI, the Italian Theatre Board, which they had abandoned the same year and whose responsibilities included organizing the official touring circuit in Italy. The theatre was the Nuovo, where Franca had last appeared in a variety show in 1952 at the beginning of her career. The symbolism of their return to one of Milan's most stately, bourgeois theatres was laboured by several critics, who seemingly had not been aware of Fo's cooperation with La Scala. 'The days of the Palazzina Liberty, of the anoraks and of slogans are far-off now that Franca Rame is at the Nuovo, the most middle-class and traditional of the theatres in the city centre,' wrote the *Corriere della Sera*.[8] Even if *An Ordinary Day* did not arise from the life of Dario and Franca as directly as did *The Open Couple*, it is impossible to overlook the fact that it takes the fictional couple further down the same path. Now the separation has occurred and Giulia is seated in front of a camera, intent on suicide and recording last thoughts and memories which are transmitted on to a large video screen. The phone calls are caused by a confusion between her number and that of a quack Japanese analyst who offers 'psycho-respiratory' cures based on Indonesian lore to women in distress. The callers are other women oppressed by the chauvinism to which they are exposed, or by the unmanageable problems of their married life. Some cases, like that of the prostitute whose trade suffers when she develops a propensity for biting off the testicles of her clients, have a surreal quality, but a call from another woman causes Giulia to abandon her plans for suicide when the two become aware of the uncanny similarity of their complaints. Fo's delight in incongruity and grotesque is kept in check as he traces Giulia's descent into panic and misery and ascent into a state of determination which is still short of optimism. The ending is limp, but the play bounds along with Fo's zany momentum, even if it gives further evidence of a newer, introspective tone and a subdued, mellow mood.

In real life, the relationship between Dario and Franca was still unsettled. Dario had had a variety of affairs of greater or lesser levels of commitment. The annual gatherings at Alcatraz brought young women from all over Europe, and Dario had had brief encounters with several of them, even when Franca was on the premises. Newspapers carried reports of a more serious relationship with a young actress, Maria Passamonti, and some journalists speculated that she was about to replace Franca. Dario had been working with Passamonti on a book, but the relationship was more than professional. The woman's parents in a village in the Marche were besieged by photographers and reporters, while Franca herself received phone calls from journalists anxious for her reaction. Franca phoned her lawyer on various occasions to request him to draw up papers for a separation, but then backed off. She began to talk of relationships of her own. She told readers of *Marie Claire* that 'like Jean Cocteau', she considered any love affair between 'a man or a woman in their twilight and a younger person to be an act of turpitude', but she also spoke of a young actor who had fallen in love with her and deprived himself of meals so as to buy her chocolates and flowers.[9]

Working relations were largely unimpaired. This was not due to Herculean efforts to control emotion, but because in any relationship of that standing, there was much that could be entrusted, in every sphere, to habit and custom. Dario wrote and directed Franca in *The Kidnapping of Francesca*,[10] which opened in Trieste at the end of the year. Dario and Franca insisted that nothing was to be read into the decision to give her name to the protagonist, a banker kidnapped while engaged in an adulterous liaison with a young employee of her company.

Dario went alone to Amsterdam in early 1987 to begin work on a production of Rossini's *Barber of Seville* for the Amsterdam Musiktheater. It was his first venture into the grand tradition of Italian opera, and it can hardly come as a surprise that he viewed the work as 'a continuation of my researches on *commedia dell'arte*, a logical widening of the field to take in *opera buffa*'. Seen from this perspective, Figaro was 'a bourgeois Harlequin, a young man who could equally be Don Giovanni or Tartuffe. Don Bartolo is a Pantaloon, Don Basilio a knowing Doctor or a Balanzone . . . the whole of Italy or Spain could be on the stage, in the atmosphere. There are quotes from Goya, an unmistakable Mediterranean air.'[11] The production had the witty panache which Dario brought to all productions and the unruly exuberance which was part of his vision of *commedia*, but he was less successful in releasing the energy in the work than in imposing an interpretation on it. For all the ingenuity and jocularity of his inventiveness in devising situations and gags, much of it was irrelevant to the opera. Perhaps Dario was more attracted to the Beaumarchais play on which the opera was based than to the opera itself, and several critics complained that the production was not an ideal marriage of music and on stage business. 'Fo will do anything,' wrote one, 'fly a kite, paddle a gondola, sit on a swing, toss a doll in a blanket, anything to distract his audience from Rossini.'[12]

Franca remained in Italy, performing *The Kidnapping of Francesca* in Rome. She was invited to make what should have been a routine appearance on a Sunday afternoon television chat show, *Domenica In*, hosted by Raffaella Carrà. After performing an extract from the play, she sat down for the celebrity chatter which is a staple of such programmes. Carrà asked about marriage in general, then about her marriage. Franca casually replied that it was over. What followed provided one of the most memorable moments ever recorded on Italian television, rivalling the couple's walk-out from *Canzonissima* decades before. The boundaries between private and public had long eroded in the life of Dario and Franca, but now their life became theatre, or even soap opera. Viewers recalled Carrà turning pale and gawking in disbelief. 'Does he know?' she stuttered. Franca replied: 'No, but now that I have said it in front of your ten thousand viewers, he'll soon find out.' Carrà was not quite equal to the moment, and must have been later conscious of the bathos of her reply, 'In fact, my viewers come to ten million.' Franca was unmoved: 'So much the better. Dario will be informed more easily.'[13]

One of the ten million was Jacopo, then aged thirty-one, who learned of his parents' separation at the same time as the rest of Italy. Franca's sister Pia was another, and she told reporters that she felt as though a 'tile had fallen on her head'. Dario did not find out until some time later. Messages were left for him in various parts of Amsterdam as Italian newsmen on the spot and his son at a distance rushed to reach him first. He was at the house of his Dutch interpreter, Franz Roth, and the two read the reports in the next morning's paper. If he was surprised, so was Franca. She had had no prior intention of making this announcement, nor even any certainty that she wished to take this step. There was some ribald laughter in Italy over this couple who said in public things they were too shy to say in private, but tension had been high in the Fo–Rame household for some time and she was living in a state of personal anxiety and uncertainty. No set of intellectual beliefs, not even ones bound up under the heading 'women's lib', was really of any emotional service to Franca at that time. The idea of separation had been on her mind, but the declaration was very much a spur-of-the-moment response to insistent questioning. Talking of the programme shortly afterwards, Franca herself said: 'You must understand what happened,' and it was far from clear that she understood herself. 'I had been invited on to the programme and was expecting questions about my work but – it was a bit funny – the presenter started with a barrage of personal questions. It was as though she was provoking me. Anyway, it just came out spontaneously. I told them – it's all over between me and Dario.'[14]

The news made the front pages all over Italy the following day, and gave rise to a series of retrospective articles, some written in the obituary tone. Franca spoke of the humdrum life of any married couple after years together, of the poison of habit, the lack of sparkle induced by familiarity, and was also driven to the apocalyptic conclusion that

> marriage should be prohibited by law. Of course there is the will to sleep and waken up together, but then there comes the morning when you wake up and find that it is not working any more. It is the fault of life which grinds down relationships, of the fact that a man and a woman married for many years no longer make love, or if they do, make love two or three times a year ... then a relationship with people outwith the couple becomes indispensable. And then the troubles begin.[15]

In her case, however, the troubles had not begun with a normal sequence of familiarity-breeding-neglect, but with complex complaints of being under-appreciated in public, and of having to endure Dario's infidelities. Franca was hardly the ground-down, home-ridden housewife, and she had had her own relationships outside the marriage, but a sense of anger and humiliation was apparent in her statements. There was one image which recurred, the image of male sexuality being like instant coffee.

> If there are a thousand women in the stalls, at least nine hundred and ninety-nine are ready to faint if he looks at them . . . What am I to do? If women go along with it, why not? It is well known that men, even the most intelligent, are always ready, like Nescafé. It is the fate of every wife of a famous man. Every so often, someone asks me, how many women has Dario had? I would not know how to answer. I have not counted. Yes, sometimes, I have gone off my head, I have certainly suffered, but now, from the height of my years, I ask myself: Was the suffering worthwhile? I have a laugh to myself. I have put away the gifts they gave him.[16]

Dario was contrite. He fully understood why Franca had taken this step, he was a swine to have forced her to it.

> The more I think about it, the more I am convinced that Franca was quite right to bring all this out into the open. Indeed, I admired her, I found in her that ability to give things a kick which I have always liked in her. At the end of the day, what Franca said was – I am fed up playing the wife who sees nothing and feels nothing, the cheery, dumb blonde who spends her time with stages and prisons, pretending not to notice that her husband is one enormous bastard.[17]

This interview was the beginning of a strange campaign which saw Dario publishing public letters to Franca asking for a reconciliation. In private, he dispatched Franz Roth to Milan with a letter for Franca. Roth went into the green room in the theatre where Franca was performing. She took the letter, tore it to pieces and told Roth to tell Dario that she wanted nothing more to do with him and that if he wanted to return to Milan, he could sleep in the flat upstairs. Roth watched the show and went backstage afterwards to find her on her knees, picking the pieces of the ripped letter out of the basket and reassembling them on her dressing-table. Two days later, when he was about to leave Milan, she called to say that it must be cold in Amsterdam and that she had packed a case of warm clothes for Dario.

In newspapers and magazines, both made declarations of love and esteem with a profusion and frankness they had not used since the time of their courtship. In a newspaper article on his forthcoming book, *Manuale minimo dell'attore* (published in English as *Tricks of the Trade*), Dario drew attention to the sections written by Franca and wished that they could be together again, 'not only within the covers of a book'. Each was protective of the other. In later years, although the story of their bizarre separation was one of the things which people remembered most clearly about them, Franca herself appeared to have erased the matter from her memory and would deny that they had ever left each other. At the time, she considered going her own way professionally, and thought about starting up a company of her own. She circulated her various agents in Europe to see if they had any script on their books which would be suitable for a fifty-seven-year-old actress with wide experience of comic theatre but willing to try her hand at anything. Nothing came of it. Dario stayed in Amsterdam for the period of the rehearsals and opening nights, but during that time, he phoned, Franca estimated, five to seven times a day. When he returned to Milan, one of them did stay in the spacious attic flat which was part of their property, but they met for breakfast and continued life as usual. There had never really been any question of anything else. Franca was there at his side when Dario's mother died that spring.

Chapter 16

Debts and Homage

Tricks of the Trade,[1] published in spring 1987 at the height of the public and private turmoil affecting Dario and Franca, can seen as part of Fo's effort to elucidate his ideas on popular theatre and to stake his own claim for inclusion in that tradition. The individual sections first saw the light as occasional writings and ad-hoc contributions to myriad workshops held in various parts of the world from Jutland, London and Bogotà to the Teatro Argentina in Rome. Once again, it was Franca who taped, deciphered, transcribed and edited the individual pieces for publication, guaranteeing their survival.

The Italian title, *The Actor's Mini-Manual*, gives, correctly enough, the impression of a pedagogic handbook, but its range is much wider than any workbook. The focus on the actor rather than the author is a reflection of how Dario saw himself, but both receive equal consideration. Initially, Dario toyed with the idea of giving the volume an anti-Diderot slant by entitling it *The Anti-paradox of the Actor*, but he was persuaded this was too recondite. Since *Tricks of the Trade* was never conceived as a unitary treatise, anyone hoping for an equivalent of the writings of Stanislavsky or Brecht will be disappointed, but it is reasonable to regard the book as one of the component parts of the manifesto he has never written. He makes fun of adversaries from past and present, pays homage to fellow spirits and thus clears the ground for some possible, more systematic definition of what constitutes 'popular theatre'. The refusal to be bound by too rigid a method is reflected in the structure of the book, which is divided, in a parody of Boccaccio, into six 'days'. Included in the pages are discussions of the popular tradition from *commedia dell'arte* onwards; an account of the origins of the Harlequin; a demonstration of the problems of wearing masks on stage; an analysis of Greek tragedy; a proposal for the revival of the jeering monologues from Greek comedy; a polemical attack on Diderot, Jacques Lecoq and Louis Jouvet; a range of idiosyncratic judgements on Brecht, Chekhov, Shakespeare and Stanislavsky; as well as accounts of individual workshops where dialogues were improvised and some of his own works dissected. The final section is Franca's contribution to discussions on women's theatre.

One essential element of Dario's poetics is his distinction between 'theatre' and dramatic literature. Those who produce the latter, including Pier Paolo Pasolini, or who praise it, as does Benedetto Croce, are banished from his Eden. Approval of Brecht and his ideas of 'alienation' is guarded, but Dario subscribes wholeheartedly to a doubt Brecht once expressed on Shakespeare. The only problem, he wrote, was that his works were 'too beautiful on the page. It is his only defect, but a great one.' Fo shared the belief that a work of theatre, as distinct from a mere work of dramatic literature, should give limited pleasure when read, since its worth should be apparent only in performance. The actor-author, the lynchpin of the Italian tradition of theatre, is his ideal. He encouraged actors to convert themselves into playwrights, but laid down demanding conditions. The dilettante could expect no kind words. The dramatist had to master the craft and not trust to instinct; a knowledge of history and tradition were indispensable, but so too was a deeper form of commitment.

> The moral problem is fundamental for the actor in particular. It is a guarantee of equilibrium and verve, a reserve of creativity, of life. If they said to me – 'Is there anything to which you would never submit yourself?' I would reply 'To doing something in which I do not believe' . . . I wish to wage war on the jobbing actor, a greater affliction in theatre than any other calamity.[2]

Aged sixty-one, he was now conscious of generational differences, and complaints against his younger contemporaries began to appear with a certain frequency in his public statements. The indolence and reluctance of a new breed of actors to apply themselves with due diligence to mastering all aspects of theatre-making dismayed him. 'We were ignorant, but we were aware of it,' he wrote, referring to the condition of his generation as they emerged from the war. 'Today we are just ignorant and nobody cares . . . As I look around me, all this chatter about research seems to me only so much bluff . . . quite apart from the fact that they scarcely ever manage to break away from the usual mannered clichés.'

Looking back over theatre history, Dario reverses conventional assessments and hierarchies, awarding pride of place to authors who worked in styles of theatre normally regarded as minor, or those performers more frequently regarded as purveyors of mere entertainment – clowns, variety artistes, *farceurs* and the nameless scribes of popular festivities of carnival exhibitions. His exemplars are as likely to come from Iran or Bali as from Slovenia or Sardinia, but all operate inside the boundaries of 'popular theatre'. To be worthy of that name, it is not sufficient to create accessible theatre or agit-prop. It must be theatre which has roots in history and society, which grows from the experience of one class and instinctively or consciously expresses the attitudes, humour and resentments of that class. The basic polarity was patrician versus popular, hegemonic versus subaltern, not didactic versus escapist. Fo's ideal was the combination of entertainment plus education; each in isolation fell short of his notion of theatre. His supreme models were the carnival and the characters who could be associated with the carnival spirit – principally Harlequin and the jester. They displayed the impish or Puckish spirit, but transcended it to give voice to the satiric, the tragic or the subversive.

Dario was never a critic *de métier*, and has little use for consistency. On individual authors, he will happily contradict himself according to the needs of the moment. There are, however, some constants. Ruzzante, the sixteenth-century actor–author from Padua, is his *alter ego* and supreme model. He invariably writes of him with passion and love, he always revered the Greeks, always venerated Molière and esteemed, somewhat idiosyncratically, Shakespeare and the Elizabethans. But remember, he says, to glance from these grand monuments at the more ramshackle tombs commemorating a motley crew who sang cruder songs, were more given to ribaldry, cavorted in the public squares, but were on the alert since they knew that at any moment they would have to pick up their jackets and run if the constabulary were sighted. There is a Fo-land, as much as there is a Greene-land, situated somewhere between the wasteland and Wonderland, and the sounds most frequently heard are the rage of indignant denunciation and the cackle of laughter. The lord of misrule is on the throne, and comedy is his servant, but the laughter is not necessarily the laughter of blasphemous derision. Laughter can be a response to elements normally identified as tragic. Dario was fond of quoting Molière to the effect that tragedy was emotionally comforting but laughter defiant. Nothing characterizes his own thinking on theatre more than this quest for a synthesis of laughter and tragedy. Laughter is the identifying mark of humanity. In laughter, the human being becomes fully conscious of his own potential, of his individuality and his ability to assert his autonomy from convention and rule. 'Laughter denotes a critical awareness; it signifies imagination, intelligence and a rejection of all fanaticism. In the scale of human evolution, we have first *Homo sapiens*, then *Homo faber* and then finally *Homo ridens*, and this last is always the most difficult to subdue or make conform.'[3] In his youth, Fo had learned from Feydeau; his farce had long since outstripped his old master in its depth and subtlety.

Having overseen the publication of the book, Dario left for Boston to direct his 1959 play, *Archangels Don't Play Pinball*, for the American Repertory Theatre. It was an odd choice. Perhaps he thought that the play which had set them on the road to success in Italy would do the same in America. If so, he was disappointed. His on-set rewriting and modifications to the original text created difficulties for the actors, who found the demands put on them excessive. The revised work did not quite cohere, but his presence there gave a boost to the popularity of his theatre in the USA. Franca was with him in America, but she went to the West Coast on her own, and received the heightened appreciation invariably accorded her when she was able to appear in her own right.

They appeared together at a demonstration to oppose a decision by the Milan City Council to remove the plaque marking the spot at the police station where Pino Pinelli had fallen to his death. As part of the protest, Dario did a dramatized reading of *Accidental Death of an Anarchist*. The reactions from some critics read less like reviews than premature obituaries, for the actor if not yet for the man. 'Fo is a somewhat tired maestro, with an ever more detached look, who now rarely descends into the arena,' wrote Franco Quadri, a critic who had followed his whole career with sympathetic interest. When invited to retort, Dario, ever the gentleman, demurred gently, saying only that he had not lost the passion of earlier years but that he had acquired a technique which allowed him to work on stage without wearying himself.[4] Nevertheless, the impression was put about that the old ardour was spent and that since the Movement had crumbled, Dario and Franca had been eclipsed. In December 1987, journalists were preparing special supplements and documentaries to celebrate the twentieth anniversary of the student revolts in Paris in 1968, and saw Dario and Franca as belonging to a mood and culture which could safely be consigned to history. That month, Dario was reminded that in an interview he had given in April 1973 he had said that the revolution would come if they succeeded in 'managing the people's rage'. He agreed that earlier he had been 'guilty of ingenuousness' but added he had remained immune from the 'loss of irony' which had affected many of their contemporaries. Nevertheless, they were aware that the climate had changed profoundly. Said Franca:

For me today, doing theatre means above all speaking of people's lives. On the political level, there is a great deal of despair and aimlessness about. Some words like 'struggle' or 'commitment' make me shudder; I can't bring myself to pronounce them. It's not because things in Italy are getting better, in fact they're getting worse. There are two million unemployed now, and the only difference is that nobody wants to hear about them. But some ways of doing politics are over and done with, and there's no point in trying to revive them. But it is much easier to communicate if you talk to people about their existence, about everyday problems.[5]

Lest she be taken as one of the renegades appearing on television screens to deplore the errors of their youth and express the hope that they could now settle down to a career and domesticity, Franca added that she was happy to have lived those years as she had, and would do it all again. However, neither could any longer put trust in the certainties of previous decades. John Osborne's Angry Young Man regretted that there were no 'great brave causes' for his generation. Dario and Franca had fought for their 'great brave cause', but saw those who had shared their beliefs deserting the field. They at least would still ruffle feathers with further plays and with the stances they would take in political and social affairs, but the days of danger were over. Drama would be confined to their activities in theatre.

They could still stir up controversy, as they did towards the end of 1987 when they appeared on successive weeks on a Sunday afternoon television variety show. Franca performed her autobiographical monologue *The Rape*, while Dario followed with a new piece, *The Miracle of the Child Jesus*, based on an episode in the apocryphal gospels. Although Franca's monologue had been seen many times in theatre, the television performance created renewed controversy over the appropriateness of showing such a work at prime time. The Vatican followed with an attack on Dario for giving credence to a tale which was not part of canonical scriptures. For most Italians, the surprise was to discover that, after all the brouhaha surrounding the separation, they were back together. Franca's explanation was gnomic:

> for me, it's as though he was my father or my mother. Maybe I was wrong to take it so badly, not to accept the inevitable contradictions of life as a couple. I have come to understand that in times like these, when you hardly have time to say hello to your friends, you cannot lose a relationship like ours; you cannot bankrupt an undertaking to which you have dedicated your whole life.[6]

They were back on the screen early in 1988 with an eight-part series entitled *Forced Transmission*, which included many clips and extracts from work completed in previous years. Dario wrote a *Letter from China* at the time of the Tiananmen Square repression, a slightly melancholy corrective to what he had written years before on Mao. Unexpected corners of the world showed interest in their work. Companies in Sri Lanka found that the events chronicled in *Accidental Death of an Anarchist* paralleled experiences on an island divided by long, internecine warfare. In 1989, Dario's production of *Barber of Seville* was presented in Rio de Janeiro, while both he and Franca toured the country with their own works. Later that year, he wrote a new farce, *The Pope and the Witch*, which opened in Novara in October, with him and Franca in the title roles. While the Pope in question, who is not some generalized pontiff but John Paul II, is constrained by the magic of the Witch to rethink various dogmas, the main focus is on birth control, drug use and public policy towards addicts. Their interest in these questions had led Dario and Franca to advocate decriminalisation. The play attracted more spectators in the 1989–90 season than any other in Italy.

The following year, Dario was invited to direct Molière at the Comédie-Française, an irresistible opportunity to repay accumulated debts to the greatest of comic playwrights. Typically, he chose two of the farces normally viewed as minor, *The Doctor in Spite of Himself* and *The Flying Doctor,* and, as was his wont, set about restructuring them. Experts agreed that the extant texts were defective, and since they were based on the *commedia dell'arte* tradition, Fo had full authority to digest and rework the plays in the style he knew best. Molière had been, Fo said, a friend of Domenico Biancolelli, the proto-Harlequin and had himself played the part. For *The Flying Doctor*, Dario had the great good fortune to find an original script with a list of props, including a mysterious reference to a rope for which there was no obvious need. It was known that the same actor had played both doctor and the servant in Molière's original production, and that his entrances had at times been made via the window. Dario concluded that the entrances could have been effected, Tarzan-style, by leaping in through a window, scaling down the rope to be met at the foot by an actor with one of two coats, a great coat for the doctor and a livery for the servant. Thus costumed, the actor could perform both roles. Dario was fortunate to find a French actor of considerable acrobatic ability. As rehearsals progressed, he pressed into service an entire troupe of acrobats and trapeze artists. Dario decided that a flame-thrower was indispensable and was impressed when one of the cast said that he had done fire-eating as a student. The man gave a creditable performance but later admitted that he had never actually attempted the feat before in his life. As usual, the demands made on actors were enormous, but Dario was repaid with intense loyalty. There were other curios in the production. The rediscovered script made reference to a sheep which Molière had apparently allowed to wander about on stage. Had he succeeded in taming a sheep, Dario wondered? For the modern production, they contented themselves with a dog in sheep's clothing. Molière received the approval of the king, while Dario had to make do with a commendation from President Mitterrand, who wrote a letter of appreciation.

There was no let-up in the output of plays now jointly signed by both Franca and Dario, nor any reduction in their touring schedules. *Quiet, We're Falling* took the Aids epidemic as its subject, while the following year, 1991, the couple produced a double bill of plays for Franca, both focusing again on the mother figure. In *Fat Is Beautiful*, she is a woman who, in her struggles to come to terms with desertion by her husband and the indifference of her daughter, gorges herself with gargantuan quantities of food, before finding comfort with a virtual lover. The more substantial piece, *Heroine/Heroin*, while repeating the demand for the decriminalization of drugs, is the blackest play in the Fo canon. Grotesque comedy is discarded and the action allowed to unfold in a bleak, Beckettian urban wasteland, where acts of savage, gratuitous violence are commonplace. The protagonist has already seen two of her children die, one of Aids and the other of an overdose. She declaims against an unseen God, and explains to Him that her determination to save her third daughter, also an addict, has led her to lock her up at home. In the meantime, she herself has turned to prostitution to raise the funds to take the daughter to Liverpool, where, according to an article Dario had read, enlightened detoxification and therapeutic policies were practised.

Dario was meanwhile engaged in writing a new extended monologue, commissioned by the Expo in Seville, to mark the fifth centennial anniversary of the European discovery of America. The general theme was to be Christopher Columbus's exploits, although in the changed climate created by multi-culturalism and the heightened awareness of the impact of Columbus's landing on the Native American population, it was no longer acceptable simply to celebrate Columbus. Even so, *Johan Padan Discovers America*[7] was judged dangerously iconoclastic by the Expo authorities, who rejected it. The première took place in the small northern Italian town of

Trento in December 1991. Columbus himself was sidelined in favour of an anti-hero, whose forename is a corruption of the *zanni* character from *commedia dell'arte*, and whose surname denotes the Padua region, the source of the dialect Fo employed in the work. Johan is the quintessential 'poor devil', whose lover is believed to be a witch, a misfortune which arouses the attention of the Inquisition in Venice. A scoundrel without principle or honour, intent on survival at any cost, he stows away on board a ship which he believes is making its way round the Italian coast, but which is actually bound for Seville. Here he meets up with Columbus, just returned from the Americas with a booty which the royal court judges insufficient. When he hears that the Inquisition is in pursuit, Johan joins Columbus's crew for the next voyage.

The tale itself has the dramatic momentum of a picaresque epic, featuring shipwrecks, battles, cannibalism, threats of execution and the encounter of Europeans and Indios with each other. From the early shipwreck off Santo Domingo through various captures and escapades, Johan is never at peace. On mainland South America, he and his companions are first given hospitality by a tribe which then sells them to cannibals. His life is a whirlwind of unpredictable events. Johan himself is saved from the pot because he has jaundice; he uses the knowledge of astronomy he gained from his former lover to predict a hurricane and finds himself worshipped as a son of the moon. With the tribe now in his power, he uses his influence to persuade them to lead him to an encampment of Christians. Although his only thought is to escape back to Europe, he is obliged to teach them something of the mysteries of Christianity, from the Trinity to the relationship between Christ and Mary Magdalen.

The play has a Rabelaisian bawdiness and racy vigour which Fo in this later phase preferred to the bilious satire of his earlier work. He eschews any depiction of Native Americans either as noble savages or as victims. Dario had read deeply in contemporary chronicles and was impressed by an unknown history of the success of the Indios in campaigns and battles. His main source was the work of one Michele Da Cuneo, who also provided him with the pastiche dialect employed in *Johan Padan*. Or so Dario claims in the prologue. In fact, Da Cuneo did no such thing; he wrote in clear, standard Italian.[8] The synthetic dialect, inaccessible even to Italians, is an invention of Fo's. The use of impenetrable dialect causes spectators to focus on the actor's voice and body as it recreates storms, dances, horse-riding, wading though water, tramping through jungles, tending animals and attempting to make love in a hammock. The published text is accompanied by a translation into Italian by Franca, but is embellished by designs and drawings which Dario used as an *aide-memoire* during performance.

Back in Milan, the couple could not fail to respond to Clean Hands, the anti-corruption campaign initiated by the city's magistrates and taken up enthusiastically by magistrates elsewhere. The first move occurred in February 1992, with the arrest in Milan on a charge of bribery of Mario Chiesa, a socialist functionary in charge of a rest home in the city. The campaign snowballed and soon the magistrates had uncovered the existence of what was dubbed Tangentopoli, Bribesville, a massive network of corruption which embraced the overlapping worlds of politics and industry. The Italian political system, which had remained impregnable when faced with the assaults of the Movement, crumbled, taking with it the Christian Democrat and Communist parties. New political forces began to emerge, with Milan once again in the front line. The most significant of these forces was the Lombard League, led by the charismatic Umberto Bossi. The platform of the League, wobbling between federalist and separatist demands, was imprecise and opportunistic, but always included rhetoric hostile to the poorer South of the country.

Dario was implacably opposed to the League from its inception and, like many left-wingers, found himself giving the support to the Italian state that he had withheld during the terrorist crisis. During one demonstration in Piazza Duomo in Milan, the scene of the great trade-union and leftist demonstrations in the sixties, he was to be seen on the platform waving the tricolour vigorously in the face of League hecklers. He was an enthusiastic supporter of Clean Hands, and delighted in retelling tales of socialist ex-premier Bettino Craxi facing jeers and boos from outraged crowds. Franca and Dario dusted down the title of an anti-corruption play from 1964, *Seventh: Steal a Little Less*, but rewrote it and transformed it into a one-woman show which Franca toured around Italy.

Dario Fo Meets Ruzzante, premièred at Spoleto in 1993, represented the repaying of Dario's deepest debt. Angelo Beolco (1495/6–1542), known as Ruzzante, after the peasant character he invented and played, was, like Dario, an actor-author. His plays were precisely the hard-edged farces dealing with the tragic realities of hunger, sexual appetites, violence and the experience of warfare which Fo aspired to write. His theatre was rooted in history, and provided a worm's-eye view of the Renaissance Venice of Titian, Tintoretto and Bellini. In its original conception, Fo's work was to be entitled *The Dialogues of Ruzzante*, directed by him and performed by a fifteen-strong cast drawn from the (private) Fo–Rame troupe and the (public) Teatro degli Incamminati. Even at this stage in his career, Fo still suffered vexations from bureaucrats. A ministerial communiqué, only circulated when rehearsals were at an advanced stage, uncovered, or invented, an obscure law forbidding co-productions between public and private companies. The actors employed by the publicly funded company were required to withdraw, but the work was renamed and recast to include Franca and Dario himself, who both performed in some individual pieces by Ruzzante and provided the overall continuity and introductions. Ruzzante enthusiasts were appalled at the freedom Fo took with the original plays, but it was a sell-out success with festival audiences, and Fo revived it in modified form the following year under the title *Fo Performs Ruzzante*. For the revival, the rest of the cast was eliminated and the show became a monologue, part performance and part lecture, in the style of *Mistero buffo*. On this occasion, Dario incorporated a newly discovered one-act play by Galileo, an admirer of Ruzzante.

Franca encountered problems with her own next work, given the saucy title *Sex? Thank You! Don't Mind If I Do*. The monologue was intended as a sex-instruction piece, based on a book written by Jacopo Fo with the title *Zen and the Art of Screwing*,[9] but the Ministry stepped in to ban the work to under-eighteens. Outraged at this act of censorship, Franca reverted to campaign mode. The Ministry backed down, and even issued a special edict saying that the work was 'imbued with maternal love', and could therefore be *recommended* to minors. Sex was good, decent, clean and could be made fun and an adjunct to love, provided men and especially women understood their bodies.

Dario directed another Rossini opera, *L'Italiana in Algeri* for the 1994 Pesaro Festival. There was no let-up in his workload, and later that year he took the opera to Amsterdam. There were plans for a grand international tour, taking in France, Germany, Britain and the USA in autumn 1995, in which Dario would have performed *Johan Padan* and Franca her most recent piece, but these plans had to abandoned when on 17 July 1995, at their summer house in Cesenatico, he suffered a stroke. He had been working long hours with his American translator, Ron Jenkins, on the English-language surtitles for his plays, while also drafting a series of lectures for Florence. Jacopo was in the house at the time and he and Franca became concerned when Dario started complaining of severe headaches. In the evening, he began babbling incoherently and then collapsed. The local doctor was summoned, but he diagnosed a detached retina and said Dario should be kept at home until the morning. Franca was unconvinced, and the following day packed Dario into the car and took him on a nightmare journey, in the heat of midsummer, to Milan. He had in fact suffered a stroke. He was sick several times along the way, and doctors later told Franca that the stress of the journey could have made him go into fibrillation or even suffer a second stroke. They arrived at the neurological unit in Milan, where he was put into intensive care.

He made a good recovery and although the attack left no trace on his mind or speech, he lost 80 per cent of his sight and his memory suffered. He had difficulty calling to mind the names of people or movements with whom he had worked all his life. Sometimes a name would come to him freely, only for him to forget it in the following sentence. A lengthy period of convalescence was prescribed, but Dario, wracked by anxieties and desperate to get back to writing and acting, was a poor patient. With his impaired vision, he could no longer read, nor could he write as before. His ability to draw and sketch was not impaired, and he did more artwork than he done for decades. He also used this ability to compensate for what he had lost. He covered pages with series of designs and enlarged cartoons which contained outlines of scripts, plots and speeches, and which he planned to use as prompts in future performance. He was now more than ever dependent on Franca. They developed a system whereby he wrote as best he could, in large lettering or sketches, and she then collected the pieces together and put them into coherent form on the computer.

Collaborating in this way, they produced a body of work, starting with *Peasants' Bible*, staged in September 1996, which was surprising both in volume and variety. A monologue on Leonardo da Vinci was broadcast on television, and Dario made a tentative return to the stage in May the following year in Copenhagen, as part of a celebration of his and Franca's work which included an exhibition of paintings, costumes and puppets. On stage, there was little sign of any weakness or fatigue. The laughter of the audience acted as a transfusion of some life-force and his rapport with the audience was again total; he was jumping and dancing on the boards, but as soon as the lights went down, his energy drained. He insisted on setting up a new touring schedule in Italy, but tackling a new work was beyond him. *Mistero buffo* was the agreed choice of play, but he required an hour's interval, during which Franca performed a reduced version of *Sex? Thank You! Don't Mind If I Do*. The touring schedules required military precision. The two arrived with their suite a day before performance so that Dario could settle, go for a walk and rest before going on stage. His prologues no longer had the up-to-date freshness which had been their distinguishing mark. His introduction to the sketch on Pope Boniface still used material relating to the attempted assassination of Pope John Paul II in 1981.

While on the road, the two were writing a new full-length play, *The Devil in Drag*. Franca was performing in the evening and rising early in the morning to type up the previous day's work so that Dario could make corrections or alterations when he arose. This enhanced workload took its toll. During a stop in Udine, they were working on sections of the play where the female lead would speak in Neapolitan dialect. Franca was exhausted, and discovered that she had lost her command of Italian and could only speak in pure Neapolitan. The doctor diagnosed panic attacks and told her to suspend performances until she could regain her balance and her command of standard Italian. *The Devil in Drag* was premièred in August 1997 in the Sicilian town of Messina, and played that summer in the Greek theatre in nearby Taormina. Dario agreed that he could not perform himself, so Giorgio Albertazzi appeared opposite Franca. The Milanese magistrates' Clean Hands campaign was at its height, and so although the play featured a judge conducting an inquiry into corruption at the time of the Counter-Reformation and the Inquisition, it was easy to see parallels with Antonio Di Pietro, the leading magistrate in Milan, and the situation of contemporary Italy.

Meanwhile, the case which had dogged Dario since 1969, and which was the basis of *Accidental Death of an Anarchist*, returned unexpectedly to the headlines. Dario took up cudgels against a further act of injustice. Ever since the murder of Luigi Calabresi on 17 May 1972, some officers and magistrates had viewed Adriano Sofri, one of the leading lights in Lotta Continua, as the principal suspect. In 1988, Sofri, together with Ovidio Bompressi and Giorgio Pietrostefani, two other ex-members of the same organisation, were arrested and charged with the murder of Calabresi. The news caused consternation, not least because Sofri, like many other sixties revolutionaries, had in the intervening years become a writer and journalist, a supporter and apologist for Bettino Craxi's moderate, reformist brand of socialism and a familiar, well-connected figure in the best salons of Milan and Rome. His case became a *cause célèbre*, and was taken up by writers and intellectuals including Vincenzo Consolo, Umberto Eco, Dacia Maraini and the historian Carlo Ginzburg as well as Dario Fo and Franca Rame. Some were motivated by friendship, but others were moved to indignation by what seemed to them one of the most outrageous miscarriages of justice in twentieth-century Italy.

It transpired that the *carabinieri* relied on the testimony of an informer,

Leonardo Marino, who had also been in Lotta Continua in the seventies but who in the eighties was under police investigation for alleged criminal activity. Marino accused himself of having driven the vehicle at the time of the killing, although contemporary eyewitnesses all agreed that the driver was a woman. According to police accounts, Marino only made his confession on 20 July 1988, but it transpired that Marino had been in touch with the *carabinieri* since 2 July. The accounts given by Marino in the course of the various trials were contradictory on many details, and differed from the accounts provided by eyewitnesses. He suggested, for instance, that he had been overwhelmed by an onrush of guilt, especially after a conversation with a Salesian priest. In the witness box, the priest denied having ever set eyes on him.

The judicial history of the Sofri case has been a disgrace to Italian justice. There were seven trials in nine years. In the first, in Milan, on 2 May 1990, Sofri, Pietrostefani and Bompressi were condemned to twenty-two years, and Marino to eleven years. This was upheld by the Appeal Court the following year, but overruled by the Cassation Court in October 1992 because of defects 'of form'. The case was referred back to the initial court, who found all the accused not guilty, but this verdict was again overturned by the Cassation for the same reason as before. The case came back before the Appeal Court in 1995, who this time found the three guilty and sentenced them again to twenty-two years, but acquitted Marino. Finally, on 22 January 1997, the Cassation confirmed the finding and sentence of the Appeal Court. Sofri and Pietrostefani were found guilty of being the instigators, and Bompressi the actual killer. The men finally began a twenty-two-year sentence in 1998, only to be released for yet another trial the following year. In 2000, Sofri, Bompressi and Pietrostefani were again found guilty, although this time on grounds of moral responsibility, and Sofri was sent back to continue his sentence. The other two had gone into hiding.

It is not surprising that the historian Carlo Ginzburg, an expert on witchcraft trials, concluded that the 'logic which led to the condemnation of the three men is that of the witch trials'. Dario and Franca had long known Sofri, and gave full support to the campaign for the release of the three accused, but it was 1998, when the legal process seemed to be finally exhausted – in fact there were several more rounds to come – and the men committed to prison, before Dario wrote his one-man piece on the affair, *Free Mario! Mario Is Innocent!* This work can hardly be subjected to normal critical scrutiny. Dario relied on pages of drawings to aid him through the lecture-cum-performance, but he subjected the hapless Marino to a barrage of ridicule and scorn such as few men have endured.

Although his involvement in the Sofri campaign was altruistic and humanitarian, Dario found himself retracing his own steps through the 'years of lead' as the Italians called them, and drawing up balance sheets. Franca wrote of the dismay both of them experienced when they saw 'comrades' from the days of militant campaigns appear on television as lawyers or PR representatives for multinational corporations. The Sofri case made them wonder whether much had changed in the 'system'. Power resided where it always had and behaved as it always did. But Dario and Franca stood where they had stood. They had never medised, but the days of 'struggle' were over. In 1997, both were well over sixty and unsure of their future course.

Chapter 17

The Actor Vindicated

In early 1997, an Italian television company came up with a bright idea for a series to be called *Roma–Milano*. The formula was simple: hire a couple of instantly recognizable celebrities who have never previously met, put them in a car furnished with three cameras, set them on the *autostrada* between Milan and Rome and film their every word and gesture. On the assumption that they would hold comfortably clashing views about television and society, Dario Fo and Ambra Angiolini, a teenage singer and television personality, were chosen to inaugurate the series. The date for the filming was fixed as 11 October.

By chance, 11 October was also the date scheduled for the announcement of the winner of the 1997 Nobel Prize for Literature, and Rome had been rife with rumours over Dario's inclusion among the candidates. Dario played down his prospects, and officially the reports were discounted in editors' offices but, when the car containing Dario and Ambra set off, it was accompanied by a task force of press vehicles.

Near Orvieto, there was a commotion. A journalist from *La Repubblica* got the news and made frantic but unsuccessful signals to attract Dario's attention. Eventually, he scribbled a message on a piece on cardboard and held it up to the window. It read: 'You've won the Nobel.' Ambra, who was at the wheel, drew over at the first service area, where champagne was produced. Some children in the vicinity restored a sense of proportion. They rushed over for an autograph, not of the new Nobel laureate, but of Ambra.

Surrounded by journalists and television lights, Dario had to make an on-the-spot declaration. 'I'm terrified,' was his first response. 'I'd had some vague hint, but I'd put my chances at no more than 10 per cent.' The correspondents crowded in on him but he asked them first to contact Franca. 'A good half of this prize is hers.' He did a series of immediate radio interviews by phone and, ever the professional, got back into the car to finish the journey to Milan and the programme. 'I left Rome with a great actor and

269

arrived in Milan with a Nobel Prize-winner,' remarked Ambra, who had a sense of occasion.

In the meantime, a Swedish journalist phoned Franca, who was alone in the flat in Milan, and screamed, 'It's him, it's him!' before breaking down. Franca too burst into tears. She had little time to compose herself before the phone started ringing from around the world as the news media everywhere sought to record first impressions.

The Academy's official citation stated that Fo

> emulates the jesters of the Middle Ages in scourging authority and upholding the dignity of the downtrodden. For many years, Fo has been performed all over the world, perhaps more than any other contemporary dramatist, and his influence has been considerable. He if anyone merits the description of jester in the true meaning of the word. With a blend of laughter and gravity he opens our eyes to abuses and injustices in society, and also to the wider historical perspective in which they can be placed. Fo is an extremely serious satirist with a multifaceted oeuvre. His independence and clear-sightedness have led him to take great risks, whose consequences he has been made to feel while at the same time experiencing enormous response from widely differing quarters.

The citation also identified the 'non-institutional tradition' as vital to his development, and added that medieval jesters, *commedia dell'arte* and 'twentieth-century writers such as Mayakovsky and Brecht had provided him with important impulses'. The statement concluded:

> Fo's strength is in the creation of texts that simultaneously amuse, engage and provide perspectives. As in *commedia dell'arte*, they are always open for additions and dislocations, continually encouraging the actors to improvise, which means that the audience is activated in a remarkable way. His is an oeuvre of impressive artistic vitality and range.

That same day in Italy, Communist Refoundation voted with the right to bring down the moderately leftist coalition headed by Romano Prodi, whose government Dario and Franca supported. The two events shared headlines round the world the following day. Internationally, a creative Italy was juxtaposed to a political Italy whose ways were judged simply incomprehensible. Domestically, for every expression of delight over the award, there were many more of gawking disbelief, of outrage, envy or curmudgeonly gracelessness. The politicians, unsurprisingly, divided along party lines. Gianfranco Fini, leader of the neo-Fascist National Alliance, spluttered that the whole business was a disgrace. 'I can't understand the motivation for this prize. What has Fo given to Italian or world literature?' Others on the right took the opportunity to snigger over Dario's member-ship of the Salò militia. 'The first veteran of Mussolini's republic to be celebrated by the highest honour for Literature', ran the headline in *Il Giornale*. The Vatican's daily, *L'Osservatore Romano* was equally hostile. 'Fo is Italy's sixth Nobel Prize-winner after Carducci, Deledda, Pirandello, Quasimodo and Montale; after such wealth, a jester', it wrote, shaking its patrician head. Whatever the Swedish Academy thought, the term 'jester' was no compliment in the eyes of the Vatican. The mayor of Milan declared himself unable to deliver congratulations in person because of a prior com-mitment to attend a fashion parade.

Many representatives from the world of culture and the arts found it equally hard to be magnanimous. There had been a widespread feeling that it was 'Italy's turn' for the Nobel, and one man who had set his heart on receiving the Nobel Prize was the poet Mario Luzi. Florence had even pre-pared a reception for him. When the press phoned him, he attempted an Olympian disdain: 'I am glad for this new acquisition and knowledge offered us. As an author I do not know him. I have never read him. I can-not give an appreciation.' It was a hard pose to sustain, and his next com-ment had the spareness and purity of poetry: 'All I have to say is I've got a pain in the balls'. Rita Levi Montalcini, who had herself won the Nobel Prize for Medicine in 1989, was asked for a reaction but claimed never to have heard of Dario Fo and not even to know if he was Italian. Reactions among theatre people were mixed. Franco Zeffirelli said he had always viewed Fo as a genius, the actor Carmelo Bene said he was outraged, and Giorgio Strehler's comment was scarcely categorizable: 'We are honoured as Europeans and actors. This more and more "virtual" world needs a grand, vitalizing chuckle.'

Alongside personal spleen, the announcement gave rise to a more seri-ous debate about theatre and literature, about the qualities of playwriting in itself and whether such writing, however estimable in itself, should be eligible for the world's supreme literary award. From Peru, Mario Vargas Llosa added his voice to the dissent, wondering whether Fo's writings were of a quality to merit that level of recognition. Not everyone in Italy was able to detect the 'vitality and range' that so impressed the 'immortals' of the Royal Academy in Stockholm. Giulio Ferroni, author of a much-admired history of Italian literature, was left perplexed, and returned to a familiar refrain: 'I have a high regard for Fo the actor, but where is the literature?' he asked. Fo still had many prestigious defenders, including the novelists

Dacia Maraini and Vincenzo Consolo, as well as Umberto Eco, who stated unequivocally that Fo deserved the prize for his literary achievements.

> I am delighted by the fact that they gave the prize to an author who does not belong to the traditional academic world. What I find impressive is his enormous popularity abroad. For us in Italy it is very difficult to separate the power of Fo as a theatrical character from the scripts he writes. We are mistaken if we allow ourselves to be conditioned by the character, great as he is. His plays are of great importance in our literature.

These debates over Dario Fo had been rumbling on for years in Italy. Political judgements and personal spleen aside, there had been always a certain perplexity over his rank as writer. Is Fo an actor who writes rather than a writer who acts? Are his texts merely what *commedia dell'arte* performers would have termed a *canovaccio*, in other words, an outline script or a pretext, and often a very flimsy pretext, for a display of his bravura as actor? Do the scripts he has produced have any depth and vitality independent of his on stage presence, or are they a fraud perpetrated on a gullible theatre public but easily exposed by the more alert reading public? Is theatre really literature?

The debate is rendered more difficult in Fo's case by the fact that the critical instruments employed to judge a playwright of his stamp are inadequate. He claims to be a popular playwright, so the question could be reformulated to ask whether a comparison between Fo and George Bernard Shaw or Luigi Pirandello, two other Nobel Prize-winning playwrights, is of any greater worth than a comparison of, say, Conan Doyle and Dostoevsky? They both write novels, but the genre in which they operate and the critical criteria to be applied are *toto coelo* different. What answer can be given to a questioner who asks if an igloo is better than an adobe, or a whale stronger than a lion? An adobe is of little value in the Arctic, or an igloo in Mexico. Fo operates in what were conventionally considered the lesser trodden paths of the Western tradition, ignored by theatre historians. The distance between writing and performance is in his case minimal. In his theatre, listening, seeing and enjoying the spectacle have the same importance as weighing ideas. Farce, his favourite medium, is viewed as of lesser value than comedy, and of virtually no standing if set beside tragedy. His plays may be performance scripts, or *canovacci*, but he himself is unsure whether or not that is a compliment. At times he was irritated at the dismissiveness of that term, at others he said that Shakespeare's plays were *canovacci*, and that all theatre scripts were *canovacci*.

Fo does not beguile academic critics by inviting their participation in the erudite dissection of psychic wounds or individual dilemmas. He has no interest in investigating fractured psyches, in portraying the plight of the human animal in a world made barren by the death of God or in delving into the adequacy of language for communicating emotional dilemmas. There are no subtexts to be uncovered, no hidden ambiguities to be revealed, no delicate psychology of character to be probed, no curiosities of flawed personality to be dissected and analysed, no alternative world of the fantasy to be contemplated. Further, he does not construct a philosophy, as does Pirandello, or offer a portrait of a bourgeoisie in thrall to a claustro-phobic malaise as does Ibsen, or of a regime in terminal decline like Chekhov. Critics will search in vain for the metaphysical dimension con-structed by fellow *farceurs* like Beckett or Ionesco. Nor does his theatre, unlike that of Artaud or early Strindberg, display neurotic symptoms of the creative mind which could be taken as a warped illumination of the sense-less world in which men and women have their daily being. Fo stands with the buskers at the theatre door, singing and joking of matters of impor-tance to the queues seeking admission to the gods. But who remembers a busker?

Obviously, the comparison with the busker is in its own way demeaning, for beneath Fo's theatre there is a rich tradition. His written and performed theatre can be appreciated only if seen robustly 'out of context', out of the context created by his contemporaries. He himself gambles and plays in the amphitheatres where the Atellan *farceurs*, the medieval *giullari* or the late Renaissance Harlequins perform. His theatre speaks to and of the needs of the powerless in a world they do not control. He looks towards Utopian horizons, and invites his audiences to join in liberating laughter at the spec-tacle of dishonesty and power. It is odd and inconsistent that the Harlequin of times past is now an object of reverential study, but a Harlequin of today like Fo is treated with condescension. His real success can be gauged by the way he made theatre dangerous again. His Stockholm speech touched on the perils faced by performers in other times, but he too was the object of official harassment and persecution. He was hounded not by douce critics, but by censors, politicians, magistrates, police and, ultimately, by terrorists in cahoots with ministries.

Fo fashioned a theatre as a public arena where values – mainly, but not exclusively, political values – could be aired and discussed. He was the first to attempt to weld this seriousness of purpose on to the supposedly light-weight genre which is farce, and he is not to blame if followers allowed his style of theatre to degenerate into 'didactic farce'. His comedy, or farce, has an underlay of a seriousness which tragedy cannot attain, or at least cannot attain for a contemporary audience. Like Molière and Ruzzante, he lacks refinement of taste and is wholly free of the urge to conform to canons of aesthetics sanctioned by the better salons of the day. Like them, his wish is to create an upside-down world in which it is normal to flay the practices of those who wield power in the hope that these practices will be shown as preposterous, and committed by people who, whatever status they have arrogated to themselves, are themselves preposterous.

Fo's own preference during the polemics following the award was to identify himself as an actor, and to see the prize as a 'vindication' of the acting profession. It was not Fo alone who was being justified but generations of actors. 'I am pleased about this prize because it represents the vindication of the actor, because it goes to an actor and not only to a writer, to the jester and not to the man of letters. It will be first time an actor has shaken a king's hand.' Only when pressed would he defend his own writing and the writing of all who had written for the stage. When one journalist put to him the apocalyptic scenario that the award marked the end of literature as such, he distinguished between the standards needed in theatre and those required of literature. Traditional theatre, he said, had never relied entirely on the written text. 'Improvisation has always been important, and then there is what we could call the lesson of Molière. The actor who wrote was always taken as a fool. In the case of Molière, the word was put about that he couldn't have written his own works. This prize is a vindication of poor Molière as well.'

With the authoritative backing of the Swedish Academy, Fo could now reiterate his deepest-held conviction that theatre writing was an independent branch of literature, different in kind from novel-writing or poetry, with distinct merits and qualities but of equal dignity. It could not afford to be fey and meandering, any verbal magic had to be subordinate to action and incorporated into a vivid whole. Ambiguity was not necessarily a value in itself, while a playwright had to bear in mind that cooperation with actors was of the essence, that action and immediate impact was what theatre had to aim for. Those who wished to tease out new depths and to subject a work to successive interpretations were free to do so, but there were qualities which lay on the surface and the great playwrights had always given the immediate, surface attractions pride of place. Unlike his apologists, Fo himself did not claim any special concessions for writers in the popular tradition. In all the debates and discussions in those days, he never used the term. He spoke of himself as the actor-author, revelled in the description 'jester' that had appeared in the official commendation but insisted that his writing was in the theatrical mainstream. The names he produced to back up his claims for the autonomy of theatre writing were Ruzzante, Shakespeare and, above all, Molière. The debate about his own scripts could and should be rephrased so that it becomes not a writing-versus-performance dispute but a recognition that writing-plus-performance, or writing with a view to performance, provides the only standard by which drama can be judged. When it was put to him that the great playwrights were also *littérateurs*, he replied:

> Those who reason in this way show that they have never understood what theatre is. These gentlemen who go into ecstasies over the reading of Shakespeare forget that his scripts too were *canovacci*. 'The word is the theatre,' said Shakespeare. And I believe that this Nobel Prize is indeed a recognition of the value of the word on the stage. The word can become written only after it has been used, after it has been chewed many times on the set. That's the way it was for many famous authors. Half of what we know of Ruzzante was printed only after his death. The scripts of Molière were *canovacci* until some traditional authors encouraged him to have them published.[1]

There would be little point in attempting to trace the Shakespearean quotation. Nor is it clear how it coheres with his other assertion that one of the most important aspects of his break with conventional theatre in 1968 was liberation from the slavery of the script. 'We rejected the law according to which "the script is theatre", we put a bomb under its bum.' In any case, for Dario, theatre was the word made flesh and brought to life. Many of his opponents would have agreed with his ability to give life even to banal words, would have conceded him any theatrical prize he coveted, but contended that the world's supreme literary prize should be based on qualities of the page alone. Fo saw the prize principally as giving new but overdue dignity to the totality of page plus stage.

Dario insisted from the moment the news was broken that half the prize was Franca's, but she refused all merit, ironically claiming to be content with the status of 'pedestal beneath the feet of the monument'. Many others were surprised that the prize was not made in their joint names. Fo found himself at odds with friends and admirers who feared him joining 'them' and becoming the lost leader. The question put on the left was not whether he was worthy of the Nobel, but whether the Nobel was worthy of him. Establishments had always tamed opponents by distributing baubles or giving them ribbons to stick in their coat, and how could Dario Fo, the anarcho-Marxist-subversive justify taking from the king's hand a bagatelle sponsored by a dealer in dynamite? The example of Jean-Paul Sartre, who had refused the offer of the Nobel, was used as a reproach to Fo, who had never entertained for a moment the possibility of turning down the award.

> Remember that those were different times. There were terrible things going on. The conflict between culture, our 'culture' and the bourgeoisie could not have been more clear-cut. And those were the years of the great conflicts, the Vietnam War was beginning, people were still afraid of America. Sartre's gesture was part of the choice made in the all-out struggles of those years.

Right up until the last moment, the Academy was fearful that Dario would 'do a Sartre on them', or pull some trick to show that his compliance had been part of some elaborate hoax on authority. They could have set their minds at rest. He was enchanted at the honour, and threw himself into discussions on appropriate dress and fashions needs with the enthusiasm of a young dandy. He hired one of Italy's most prestigious dress designers, Gianfranco Ferrè, to design the formal wear both he and Franca would require. Initially, Franca declared she would be unable to go to Stockholm, since she had a touring schedule and the show must go on, but Dario declared he would not go without her. He hired a private jet to fly her from Genoa. The preparation of the official Nobel Lecture presented difficulties for a man who had not been able to write in the normal way since his stroke. To facilitate translation, the Academy requested that the lecture be in their hands at least three weeks before delivery, and were disconcerted when three days before the due day the fax machine spilled out a mere three pages of highly coloured drawings and doodles. He brought with him the rest of the pages, similarly bedecked but almost completely unfurnished with any conventional text which could be distributed to the world's media. The drawings, with some large words at the top, were his prompts. He forgot to bring a tie which etiquette required for the ceremonial delivery of the speech and had to borrow one in Stockholm. The speech was performed rather than delivered in the bravura style Fo habitually employed on stage, but it did respect the traditional requirements of such occasions. Malraux, Camus, Shaw and Beckett had used the occasion to give a statement of the basic poetics which informed their work, and those among the elegantly dressed audience in the surprisingly dingy rooms of the Swedish Academy who could see beyond the extravagance of style, would have recognized that Dario's speech had a similar aim. The speech was a mini-manifesto, a statement of belief in the capacities of theatre.

The imposing Latin title, 'Contra Jugularores Obloquentes' ('Against Jesters of Irreverent Speech'), was taken from the law passed in 1221 by the Holy Roman Emperor and King of Sicily, Frederick II. The speech was a carefully structured venture in literary autobiography, opening with a heretical examination of passages from history, continuing with homage to acknowledged masters, known and unknown, who had contributed to Dario's formation as writer, and ending with a denunciation of injustices perpetrated in his own day. The recipe was the same as in many of his plays: laughter with anger, farce with denunciation, history and topicality, and always theatre as the universal fulcrum. He paid homage to *fabulatori* from his home village on the shores of Lake Maggiore, from whom he had learned the techniques of story-telling and the value of irony. 'We laughed, but, but . . . we stopped to appreciate the irony'. His praise of his predecessors – not Brecht and Mayakovsky, but Ruzzante and Molière – was equally fulsome. 'Ruzzante remains too little known, but this man who lived seventy years before Shakespeare is the greatest playwright of the Italian Renaissance. Together with Molière, he is my master.' In the course of his speech, Fo performed an extract from Ruzzante and a poem by Mayakovsky. He somewhat spoiled the effect the following day by admitting that he had made up the poem on the spot, but suggested that Mayakovsky would have been pleased with it. No doubt he would.

The core of the speech was dedicated to the nature of laughter and the topicality of theatre. Laughter had become as serious a subject for him as it had been for Henri Bergson, and while never denying the value of laughter as relaxation, he also saw it in more transcendental terms.

> The ancients regarded the moment when man laughs as the moment he comes to awareness of his own humanity. In the south of Italy, during a baby's first forty days, everyone speaks in funny, clowning voices so as to make it laugh. A baby's first smile is viewed as the birth of intelligence, or even as the moment of the infusion of the soul. Laughter is sacred.

Theatre, on the other hand, is of today. 'A theatre which does not talk of its own time has no right to existence,' he said, before referring to the slaughter by Muslim fundamentalists of a group of intellectuals in Sivas, in Turkey, raising the question of genetic engineering, and returning to the case of Adriano Sofri and his colleagues languishing in jail in Italy.

The following day, he filled the city's Royal Dramatic Theatre for what was billed as a dialogue with Swedish actors and public, but which turned out to be another one-man performance by Fo. No one paid much heed to a figure who stood silently in the doorway and put no questions. He was Ingmar Bergman, who had previously held seminars for actors on Fo's drama and acting methods. Those who were with him said he laughed uproariously during Fo's exhibition in a way not typical of him. On leaving, he told a local journalist they had been in the presence of a genius. To Fo's regret, the two did not meet.

On this occasion, Dario spoke at length of the nature of the political and moral commitment required of the actor. Acting is portrayed by him as a vocation, whose mission consists not of providing a celebration of living, but of spreading awareness of social reality. His actor, or writer, must not allow himself to become a mere professional or a master of technique, capable of arousing any reaction by acquired skill, nor can he allow himself the indulgence of objectivity. His obligation is to temper his capacity for arousing indignation, hilarity or rage by a willed decision to direct these emotions towards a cause which is worthwhile. The luxury of moral neutrality cannot be justified in the actor, a point which has kept Fo at odds with his friend and one-time master, Jacques Lecoq. Fo told his audience that he had recently visited Lecoq in Spain and found what he had invariably found each time he had watched young actors trained by the Lecoq method – an enviable expertise in technique, a command of mime and gesture, a perfection of agility and acrobatics, but no sense of any greater finality. 'Lecoq teaches his actors to walk, stand, use their hands, impersonate, hold their breath and deliver a joke, to talk endlessly but to say nothing.' Lecoq's method, he said, encourages performers to exist in a historical vacuum, to take no responsibility for the effects they create. For Fo, the impact created by performance is central, and to exemplify his point, he acted out a scene from *commedia dell'arte* involving the Magnifico and Harlequin from the point of view of both parties. The Magnifico was overseeing the preparation of a table for a banquet, watching as the waiters came in and out with dishes of greater and greater opulence, casually carrying on a conversation with a famished Harlequin, whose attention was so taken by the procession of dishes that he was incapable of concentrating on his master's words. Fo was devastatingly amusing in both roles, but he insisted that the failure to choose between them is dangerous and morally indefensible. The sketch of the poor devil can be made pitilessly humorous, hunger can be portrayed as amusing greed, the offhand cynicism of the upper crust can be the stuff of brittle comedy, but makers of theatre, in Fo's terms, are not permitted to be bewitched by notions of pure art or pure professionalism. When discussing acting, Fo is motivated by the wary moralism of Einstein on the duties of scientists.

There was no laughter at the official ceremony itself in the grand Stockholm Concert Hall on 10 December. Fo paraded in with due solemnity with the other Laureates, dressed in the evening attire which was *de rigueur*. The last time he had worn such dress was in 1958, for one of his early one-act farces, *One Was Nude and One Wore Tails*. The Royal Stockholm Philharmonic Orchestra plays a suitable piece of music as each Laureate is introduced, and while the others were introduced by stately pieces from Berlioz or Mahler, Fo was introduced by the playful music of Stravinsky's *Circus Polka for a Young Elephant*. There was nothing of the lord of misrule about him that day. He came forward to receive the medal from His Majesty of Sweden, and made the regulation triple bow to king, Academy and audience. At the official dinner that evening, he was seated beside the king, who spoke for two hours on the joys of deer-hunting.

Chapter 18

New Enthusiasms

Dario and Franca decided to give away the prize money received from the Nobel Foundation. There was no shortage of deserving causes, but after long discussions they chose to distribute it to people with disabilities or to charities working in that field. Franca took charge of the actual disbursement and found the task both inspiring and dispiriting. To offer assistance was inspiring, but to deal with the crooks and con-men who wrote plausible letters but suffered from no known ailment was less so.

Both of them were now showered with awards and decorations, and could have spent their time moving from city to city receiving honorary degrees or medals. Spain gave Franca the Leon Felipe Prize for Human Rights, the Province of Milan awarded her the Gold Medal for her initia-tives in prisons and against drugs and Siracusa gave her the Vittorini Prize for her work in theatre and society. Dario accepted an honorary degree from the University of Rome, although not without some resistance from certain quarters who were still uncertain whether he had produced work of a quality which merited academic recognition. The French Ministry of Culture made him Commandeur de L'Ordre des Arts et des Lettres, Mantua gave him the Golden Harlequin Award.

Late in life, Pirandello wrote a wry, introspective play entitled *When You are Somebody*, on the perils of fame. Dario was now unquestionably Somebody. The award of the Nobel Prize meant that he routinely received a kind of respect, even if dull respect, in the Italian media, and any state-ment he made on any subject was guaranteed coverage. Neither he nor Franca had moved on to a plateau where all dissent was stilled, especially since ecology and green politics became Dario's new enthusiasm. Trends in bioengineering and genetic technology, a subject he had mentioned in his Stockholm speech, caused him dismay. The prospect of human cloning particularly shocked him. In Stockholm, he voiced his horror on hearing of an American researcher who was experimenting on the possibility of producing a humanoid clone without a brain which could be used as a source of spare parts in transplant surgery. He was invited by a specialist committee of the European Parliament in Strasbourg to give evidence, and shortly afterwards delivered a speech at a conference in Milan entitled 'Ten Nobel Prize-Winners: For the Future'. A scientist wrote in the *Corriere della Sera*, asking if Dario believed that 'anyone who has once received the Nobel Prize has the right to deliver opinions on any topic at all', and went on to remind Dario of his obligation not to misuse his gifts as entertainer and satirist to stir up public opinion against scientific research in delicate areas.[1] Dario replied that he had the same right to attack genetic engineering now as he had had to attack nuclear technology in the past, and that his concerns were shared by scientists.

Green politics are not his only interest. In autumn 2000, he announced his candidature for the position of mayor of Milan. His hope was to become the agreed candidate of the centre-left alliance grouped together under the denomination Olive Tree. The Greens and Communist Refoundation declared support immediately, but he declared he would not stand if his candidature were to threaten the precarious unity of the left. After a few weeks of public debate, he withdrew his candidacy. Other campaigns, notably the movement in Italy against the death penalty in the USA, have drawn his support. When he arrived in Boston in September 2000 at the beginning of a lecture and performance tour, he held a press conference to denounce the execution of an Italo-American in the state of Virginia. His intervention had no impact, and the man was sent to the electric chair. In Italy, he has continued to lend support to the campaign to have Adriano Sofri and his colleagues released.

One of the main shifts in perception has been the increased recognition accorded to his painting. His problems with his reading induced him to devote more time to art, and at the same time various galleries and public bodies offered to exhibit his work. The most complete retrospective, *Pupazzi con rabbia e sentimento* ('Puppets with Rage and Feeling'), was mounted in Cesenatico in 1998, and has subsequently toured to various other venues in Italy and abroad. The exhibition took in his work both as stage designer and painter. Dario's canvases display a wide diversity of styles and subjects, as is to be expected of any artist who has been active over a span of fifty years. He came close to many currents and schools, was influenced at times by many artists without ever throwing in his lot with any one, and without losing his own individuality. From the outset he preferred figurative, not abstract, art, and already at the age of sixteen, as a self-portrait in pencil and watercolour dated 1942 shows, he showed a remarkable sureness of touch.

It would be easy for the professional critic to isolate echoes of Picasso, Gauguin, Chagall or de Kooning, but whether reproducing landscapes of his native villages, female nudes or cartoon treatments of scenes from Tolstoy, the freshness of eye, the clarity of line, the boldness of colour, the impeccable pictorial resolution and fidelity of representation are characteristic of all his work. At times his strokes are understated, at times they have a strength which causes them to explode in riotous exuberance. 'I am an amateur actor and a professional painter,' he wrote. 'The image aids me to fix an idea which will then be developed in the written word, in a script,' he declared at the opening of the exhibition.

This assertion could be reversed. If his theatre has been conditioned by his painterly eye, his artwork – and not only those works which began life as preparatory work for productions – is dramatic in conception and execution. His figures are in constant movement. They may be nymphs fleeing the unwanted attention of satyrs, young men and women in uninhibited, improbable gymnastic romps, fantastic figures rolling and gyrating in incomprehensible and unarrestable motion, but there is the sense that some drama, perhaps unseen by the viewer, is being played out. Nothing is more disconcerting than the sheer erotic excess of much of his work. The female nude is not exactly an unfamiliar figure in the Western art, but the priapic, sensual, carnival carnality and joyousness of Fo's nudes, both those painted when he was a young student at the Brera and those rings of Grecian dancing girls drawn for theatre works of later years, are overwhelming. There is no trace of guilt or self-questioning detectable in these pagan, corybantic depictions of sexual exhilaration. The absence of Christian symbolism is striking. Fo used Christian tales in his theatre but when he needs a framework of myth, he turns to the Greeks or to the epics of the late Middle Ages. His irony is not absent here. The exhibition contained a mural which had initially decorated the walls of Fo's Vatican for *The Pope and the Witch*, featuring unusually roguish, extremely naked women cavorting in the woods.

Dario has continued writing and performing. At the promptings of a group of art students, who turned up at his holiday home in Cesenatico to ask his help with a project they were engaged on, he became engrossed in the history of Ravenna. He joined in their work, and was so carried away that he ended up producing a book, *The Real History of Ravenna*.[2] Ravenna was once the capital of a part of the divided Roman Empire, and in a series of brief chapters, the book provides an alternative history of the city. Dario painted the remarkable illustrations, some of which are totally original and others pastiches of the mosaics in the city or of the works of the great masters. In a sign of changed times, the volume received the commendation of the cardinal archbishop of the city.

These interests in ecology and religion merged in the principal work produced after the Nobel Prize, *The Holy Jester Francis*, a one-man play on Francis of Assisi, premièred at Spoleto in July 1999. St Francis had identified himself as God's *giullare*, the term Dario has used of himself all his career. He was also gratified to find that Francis had taken part in a peasants' revolt in Assisi and had received a prison sentence as a result. His researches revealed that while St Francis was a crusader for peace, he was also given to use, principally in an anti-war speech in Bologna, verbal violence of a scurrility far removed from any cliché of the meek and mild saint.

The opening speech, a sermon in a *grammelot* which was a mixture of dialects, was followed by scenes retracing well-known episodes such as the encounter with the wolf of Gubbio or the sermon to the birds, but the play as a whole is a very contemporary call to respect nature and distrust science. St Francis dies as a result of maltreatment by doctors who disregard his wishes and treat him according to the pseudo-scientific knowledge of the age. Controversy was inevitable, but this time Dario found unexpected allies. Certain Catholic writers were ready to condemn the work before the first performance, particularly since advance publicity spoke of St Francis as a revolutionary. This was true, but the revolution in question was not political but evangelical and philosophical. However, a Franciscan priest, Fr Tommaso Toschi, leaped in to accuse Fo of misrepresentation and of making Francis 'a Marxist leader'. For good measure, he added that the anti-war speech in Bologna was an unhistorical invention because the war between Bologna and Imola which supposedly gave rise to it never occurred.[3] Fo produced the original chronicles and Fr Toschi found himself abandoned by other historians. More significantly, he found himself deserted by the Church. Italy's leading Catholic newspaper, *L'Avvenire*, wrote that there was nothing heretical about Fo's Francis, and that the Church should be 'grateful' to Dario Fo.[4] Their critic wrote that he had gone to Spoleto expecting to find 'a heretical Fo, intent on transforming Francis into a heretic'. Instead, he wrote, the Church owed Fo a debt of gratitude since he was 'one of the few writers, in Italy or elsewhere, to continue talking of Jesus Christ. In the Middle Ages, Fo would perhaps have been a heretic, but today with new religions raising a technological, computerized, empty, abstract God, cannot this man who talks of a historical God be viewed, leaving aside all the differences which divide us, with a friendly and even grateful eye?' Fo the jester, satirist, blasphemer, Marxist, iconoclast of the sixties and seventies had now become, at the turn of the century, Fo the quasi-believer and stimulus to faith in a godless age. No plaudit could have been more unexpected than an expression of benevolent regard for Dario Fo from the Catholic Church, but little in the lives of Dario Fo and Franca Rame has been safe or predictable.

Notes

Chapter 1 Childhood and War

1. Unpublished article, 1960?, quoted by Lanfranco Binni in *Attento te . . . !*, Verona, Bertani, 1975, p. 193.
2. Pina Rota Fo, *Il paese della rane*, Turin, Einaudi, 1978, pp. 21–2.
3. Ibid., 10.
4. Quoted in *Fabulazzo*, edited by Lorenzo Ruggieri, Milan, Kaos, 1992, p. 52.
5. *La Repubblica*, 14 August 1996.
6. Pina Rota Fo, op. cit., p. 92.
7. Enzo Colombo and Orlando Piraccini (eds), *Pupazzi con rabbia e sentimento*, Milan, Scheiwiller, 1998, p. 16.
8. *Fabulazzo*, p. 27.
9. Interview with Dario Fo in *Corriere della Sera*, 2 July1993.
10. Lanfranco Binni, op. cit., p. 193.
11. Op. cit., p. 194.
12. Pina Rota, op. cit., p. 107.
13. Italo Calvino, *The Path to the Spiders' Nests*, London, Jonathan Cape, 1998, p. 22.
14. Document preserved as folder 25 in the Fo–Rame Archive in Milan. Some sections are reproduced in Claudio Meldolesi, *Su un comico in rivolta*, Rome, Bulzoni, 1978.
15. Chiara Valentini, *La storia di Dario Fo*, Milan, Feltrinelli, 1977, p. 24.
16. Roberto Vivarelli, *La fine di una stagione*, Milan, Il Mulino, 2000; interview in *Corriere della Sera*, 6 November 2000, p. 17.
17. *Corriere*, op. cit.
18. Dario Fo, *Ballate e canzoni*, Rome, Newton Compton, 1976, p. 140.
19. Primo Levi, *Conversazioni e interviste 1963–87*, edited by Marco Belpoliti, Turin, Einaudi, 1997.
20. Quoted by David Ward, in *Antifascisms*, Cranbury, NJ, Associated University Presses, 1996, p. 165.
21. Bianca Fo Garambois, *La ringhiera dei miei vent'anni*, Turin, Einaudi, 1981, p. 11.
22. Claudio Meldolesi, op. cit., p. 33.

23. Interview with Pietro Landi, in *Dario Fo: il teatro nell'occhio*, Florence, Casa Usher, 1984, p. 17.
24. Pietro Landi, op. cit., p. 18.

Chapter 2 First Ventures in Theatre

1. Franco Parenti, *Di me stesso*, in pamphlet entitled 'Franco Parenti', Rome, Armando Curcio editore, 1981, p. 30.
2. Bianca Fo Garambois, op. cit., p. 64.
3. For information on her life, and the experiences of her family, I am grateful to Franca Rame for a long interview she gave me in 1998. She also allowed me to see pages of an autobiography she planned to write, but has, at least for the moment, abandoned. I am also grateful to Professor Ferruccio Marotti of the University of Rome for letting me watch a video recording of an interview he had recorded with Franca.
4. Serena Anderlini, 'Franca Rame: Her Life and Works', in *Theater*, Winter, 1985, p. 34.
5. Franca Rame, autobiographical pages, op. cit.
6. Dario Fo, *Fabulazzo*, op. cit., p. 72.
7. Interview in *Donna*, April 1991.

Chapter 3 The Absurd at Work

1. Enzo Jannacci, *Canzoni*, Rome, Lato Side, 1980, p. 66.
2. Private interview with Enzo Jannacci in Udine, January 2000.
3. Interview with Marco Mangiarotti, in *Doppiovu*, February 1978.
4. Umberto Eco, in 'Sipario', December, 1963, p. 29
5. 'Dario Fo Explains', interview with Luigi Ballerini and Giuseppe Risso, in *Drama Review*, March 1977, p. 36.
6. Interview with Enzo Magri, included in *Fabulazzo*, op. cit., p. 40.
7. Jacques Lecoq, *The Moving Body*, London, Methuen, 2000, p. 8.
8. Chiara Valentini, op. cit., p. 45.
9. Lecoq, op. cit., p. 8.
10. Luciano Lucignani (ed.), *Franco Parenti*, Milan, Armando Curcio, 1981, p. 33.
11. Dario Fo, *Fabulazzo*, op. cit., p. 22.
12. *Il Giorno*, 27 May 1958.

Chapter 4 Being Bourgeois

1. Miriam Mafai, *Il sorpasso*, Milan, Mondadori, 1997, p. 50.
2. Miriam Mafai, op. cit., p. 56.
3. Bent Holm, 'Dario Fo's Bourgeois Period: Carnival and Criticism', in *Dario Fo: Stage, Text, and Tradition*, edited by Joseph Farrell and Antonio Scuderi, Southern Illinois University Press, 2000.

4. Erminia Artese, *Dario Fo parla di Dario Fo*, Cosenza, Lerici, 1977, p. 40.

5. Paolo Puppa, *Il teatro di Dario Fo*, Venice, Marsili, 1978.

6. *Sipario*, no. 164, September, 1959, p. 37.

7. Dario Fo, *Aveva due pistole e occhi bianchi e neri*, in *Commedie*, vol. 1, Turin, Einaudi, 1966, p. 97.

8. Dario Fo, *Ballate e canzoni*, Rome, Newton Compton, 1976. p. 49.

9. *Ballate e canzoni*, op. cit., p. 50, and the episode recounted in Chiara Valentini, op. cit., p. 80.

10. This analysis is made by Paolo Puppa, op. cit., and by Bent Holm.

11. *Le commedie di Dario Fo*, vol. 2, p. 207.

12. *Le commedie*, op. cit., p. 214.

13. Dario Fo, *Tricks of the Trade*, op. cit., pp. 22–3.

14. *Le commedie*, op. cit., p. 246.

15. I am grateful to Nanni Ricordi for his recollections of this period. I have also made use of the history of the NCI by Cesare Bermani, *Una storia cantata*, Milan, Jaca Book, 1997.

16. Bermani, op. cit., p. 87.

17. Quoted in Cesare Bermani, op. cit., p. 87.

18. Cesare Bermani, *Il nuovo canzoniere italiano dal 1962 al 1968*, Milan, Mazzotta, 1978, p. 17.

19. Lanfranco Binni, *Dario Fo*, Florence, La Nuova Italia, 1977, p. 44.

20. Michele L. Straniero, *Giullari & Fo*, Rome, Lato Side, 1978.

Chapter 5 Viva la Rivoluzione!

1. Gianfranco Manfredi, introduction to Enzo Jannacci, op. cit., p. 30.

2. Dario Fo, *Tricks of the Trade*, op. cit., pp. 171–2.

3. David L. Hirst, *Giorgio Strehler*, Cambridge University Press, 1987, p. 14.

4. Dario Fo, *Le commedie di Dario Fo*, vol. 1, 1966, p. 26.

5. From interview in *Liberation*, 9 January 1974, quoted by Lanfranco Binni, *Attento te . . . !*, Verona, Bertani, 1975, p. 227.

6. Dario Fo, lecture on Popular Theatre. Quoted by Lanfranco Binni, op. cit., p. 147.

7. Binni, op. cit., p. 146.

8. Franceschi's speech is quoted in *Giullari & Fo*, op. cit., p. 150.

9. *Giullari & Fo*, op. cit., p. 151.

10. Philip Willem, *Puppet Masters*, London, Constable, 1991.

11. Italo Moscati, in *Sipario*, December, 1970.

12. Michele L. Straniero, op. cit., p. 44.

13. Dario Fo con Luigi Allegri, *Dialogo provocatorio sul comico, il tragico e la ragione*, Bari, Laterza, pp. 140–1.

14. Dario Fo, op. cit., p. 94.

15. Dario Fo, *Commedie*, vol. 5, p. 66.

Chapter 6 On the Road Again

1. Quoted by Lanfranco Binni, op. cit., p. 263.
2. Dario Fo, *Fabulazzo*, op. cit., p. 76.
3. Dario Fo, *Compagni senza censura*, Milan, Mazzotta, 1973, vol. 2, p. 189.
4. Dario Fo, introduction to the third edition of *Bang! Bang! Who's There? The Police!*, Verona, Bertani, 1974.
5. Dario Fo and Luigi Allegri, op. cit., pp. 149–50.
6. Interview with Gianni Giolo, in *Il Lombardo*, 8 September 1973.
7. These dates and figures are taken from Tullio Barbato, *Il terrorismo in Italian*, Milan, Editrice Bibliografica, 1980.
8. *L'Europeo*, 16 February 1981.
9. *L'Europeo*, 3 June 1980.
10. *L'Europeo*, op. cit.
11. Franca Rame, in *Non parlarmi degli archi parlami delle tue galere*, Milan, F.R. edizioni, 1984, pp. 133–4.
12. Alberto Franceschini, *Mara, Renato e io*, Milan, Mondadori, pp. 143–4.

Chapter 7 1973: *Annus horribilis*

1. *Il Giorno*, 21 February 1973.
2. Interview with Natalia Aspesi, *Corriere della Sera*, 15 February 1998.
3. Based on interview of Franca with the author, and with Natalia Aspesi, op. cit.
4. Translation by Gillian Hanna, in Dario Fo and Franca Rame, *A Woman Alone & Other Plays*, London, Methuen, 1991, p. 86.
5. Article in *La Repubblica*, 11 February 1998.
6. Natalia Aspesi, op. cit.
7. Introduction to *Ci ragiono e canto 3*, Verona, Bertani, 1973, p. 7.
8. Interview with Gianni Giolo, *Il Lombardo*, 8 September 1973.
9. Franca Rame, op. cit., p. XI–XII.
10. Epilogue to volume quoted, p. 89.
11. The document is quoted in full in Lanfranco Binni, op. cit., pp. 67–84.
12. This document too is given in full in Binni, pp. 85–96.
13. Franca Rame, Introduction to *Le commedie di Dario Fo*, vol. III, Turin, Einaudi, 1975, p. XI.
14. *Avanguardia Operaia*, 26 October 1973.
15. *Avanguardia Operaia*, 19 October 1973.
16. Quoted by Chiara Valentini, op. cit, p. 147.
17. Dario Fo in Artese, op. cit., pp. 124–5.
18. This account is based on Chiara Valentini, *Panorama*, 22 November 1973.
19. Dario Fo, *Guerra di popolo in Cile*, Verona, Bertani, 1974.
20. Franca Rame in *Il teatro politico di Dario Fo*, op. cit., p. 148.
21. *Panorama*, 22 November 1973.

Chapter 8 Occupations

1. Lanfranco Binni, op. cit., 1975, pp. 127–75, provides a detailed account of this conference, with verbatim reports of Fo's speeches.
2. Binni, op. cit., pp. 137–8.
3. Binni, op. cit., pp. 155–7.
4. Binni, op. cit., p. 153.
5. Dario Fo, in a note to the first edition of *Non si paga, non si paga!*, Milan, 1974.
6. Paolo Prato, *Tradition, Exoticism, Cosmopolitanism in Differentia*, no 2, Spring 1988, p. 212.
7. Interview in *Nordest, Venezia-Mestre*, 26 December 1974.
8. *Non si paga, Non si paga!*, op. cit, p. 4.
9. *Non si paga, Non si paga!* in *le commedie di Dario Fo*, vol. XII, Turin, Einaudi, 1998, p. 11. The version given here is the version revised for the 1980 production.

Chapter 9 Politicians Revered and Reviled

1. Interview with Paolo Calcagna, in *Corriere d'Informazione*, Quoted in *Fabulazzo*, cit., p. 273, February 1975.
2. *Panorama*, 12 June 1975, p. 144.
3. *Panorama*, op. cit., p.147.
4. Franco Quadri, *La politica del regista*, Milan, Edizioni il Formichiere, p. 219.
5. *Corriere della Sera*, 7 September 1975.
6. Autobiographical writing by Franca Rame. Unpublished.
7. Philip Short, *Mao: A Life*, London, Hodder & Stoughton, 1999; Jonathan Spence, *Mao*, London, Weidenfeld & Nicolson, 1999.
8. *Corriere d'Informazione*, 6 September 1975.
9. *Il Mondo*, 25 September 1975.
10. *Espresso*, 25 September, 1975.
11. Interview in *La Gazzetta Sportiva*, February 1986.
12. *Panorama*, 25 September 1975.
13. Conference proceedings published in Lanfranco Binni, *Dario Fo*, op. cit., p. 83.
14. Proceedings, op. cit., p. 87.
15. *Corriere d'Informazione*, 6 September 1975.
16. *L'Espresso*, op. cit.
17. *L'Espresso*, op. cit.
18. Article in *L'Espresso*, republished in *Fabulazzo*, op. cit., pp. 301–3.

Chapter 10 Dealing with Drugs

1. Giorgio Bocca, *Il caso 7 Aprile*, Milan, Feltrinelli, 1980, pp. 97–8.
2. Tullio Barbato, *Il terrorismo in Italia*, Milan, Editrice Biblioteca, 1980, p. 123.

3. Quotes from an article by Guido Passalacqua, in *La Repubblica*, 1 April 1976.
4. Wladimiro Greco, in *Il Giorno*, 15 April 1976.
5. Dario Fo, in *L'Espresso*, December 1975.
6. *Le commedie di Dario Fo*, volume XII, edited by Franca Rame, Turin, Einaudi, 1998, p. 87.
7. Tullio Barbato, op. cit., p. 126.
8. Carlo Brusati, *Corriere d'Informazione*, 28 April 1976.
9. Dario Fo, *La Marjuana della madre è la più bella*, Verona, Bertani editore, 1976.
10. Introduction, op. cit., p. 12.
11. Interview in *Fronte Popolare*, 22 February 1976.
12. Tullio Barbato, op. cit., p. 117.
13. Grant Amyot, *The Italian Communist Party*, London, Croom Helm, 1981, p. 208.
14. *Corriere d'Informazione*, 26 July 1976.
15. The articles by Abruzzese and Fo, as well as contributions by other directors such as Mario Missiroli, appeared in *Rinascita*, nos 42, 43, 44, October 1976. Fo's article was republished in *Fabulazzo*, op. cit., pp. 275–80.
16. Corrado Stajano, article in *Il Messaggero*, 12 October 1976.

Chapter 11 Televised Anathemas

1. Corrado Stajano, *Il Messaggero*, 12 November 1976.
2. *Radiocorriere*, 6 November 1976.
3. Interview with Ettore Mo, *Corriere della Sera*, 22 April 1977.
4. Antonio Scuderi, *Dario Fo and Popular Performance*, Ottawa, Legas, 1998, pp. 68–77.
5. *La Repubblica*, 24 April 1977.
6. *La Repubblica*, op. cit.
7. *La Repubblica*, 28 April 1977
8. *Panorama*, 30 April 1977.
9. *La Repubblica*, 26 April 1977.
10. *Panorama*, op. cit.
11. *La Repubblica*, 26 April 1977.
12. *Milano Sera*, 26 April 1977
13. *Panorama*, op. cit.
14. *Milano Sera*, op. cit.
15. Luigi Accattoli, *La Repubblica*, 28 April 1977.

Chapter 12 Liberating Franca

1. *Il teatro politico di Dario Fo*, Milan, Mazzotta, 1977.
2. *Noi Donne*, 13 March 1977.
3. Ibid.
4. *Il teatro politico*, op. cit., p. 144.

5. Chiara Valentini, *Panorama*, March 1977.

6. *Il teatro politico di Dario Fo*, op. cit., pp. 144–5.

7. *La Sicilia*, 6 March 1979.

8. Natalia Ginzburg, in *Corriere della Sera*, 10 May 1977.

9. *Il teatro politico di Dario Fo*, p. 143.

10. Interview with the author, in the *Scotsman*, 28 August 1986.

11. Interview with Giuseppina Manin, *Corriere della Sera*, 8 December 1999.

12. 'Contaminated Art', interview with Matthew Fleury, in *Bomb*, 1985; quoted in *Fabulazzo*, op. cit.

13. Interview with Marisa Fumagalli, *Noi Donne*, 16 April 1977.

14. Interview with the author in the *Scotsman*, 28 August 1986.

15. Serena Anderlini, 'Franca Rame: Her Life and Work', in *Theater Studies*, Winter, 1985, p. 34.

16. Interview with Rosella Simone, in *Marie Claire*, August 1988.

17. *Le Commedie di Dario Fo*, vol. viii, Turin, Einaudi, p. 6.

18. This point is made by the historian Anna Rossi-Doria, quoted by Paul Ginsborg, *A History of Contemporary Italy*, London, Penguin, 1990, p. 368.

19. Anderlini, op. cit, p. 39.

20. *Brescia Oggi*, 12 May 1978.

21. Rosella Simone, op. cit.

Chapter 13 Tiger, Tiger

1. *La Repubblica*, 24 April 1977.

2. Quoted in *Fabulazzo*, op. cit., pp. 208–9.

3. Quoted in *Fabulazzo*, op. cit., pp. 209–14.

4. *Corriere della Sera*, 29 September 1977.

5. Eugenio Scalfari, *La Repubblica*, 15 September 1977.

6. Dario Fo, *Storia della tigre*, Milan, edizioni F. R. La Comune, 1980, p. 6.

7. Interview in *Il Manifesto*, republished in *Fabulazzo*, op. cit., p. 298.

8. Bent Holm, *Fo, the Story-Teller*, lecture delivered at University of Copenhagen, 12 December 1997. I am grateful to Bent for providing me with a translation of his talk.

9. Interview in *Bolero Teletutto*, 18 January 1988.

10. Franceschini, op. cit., p. 161.

11. Interview with Roberto Sciubba, in *L'Europeo*.

12. Interview in *L'Europeo*, 19 January, 1981.

13. Ibid

14. In *Fabulazzo*, op. cit., pp. 174–89.

15. *Corriere della Sera*, 5 April 1979.

16. *Panorama*, 14 March 1978.

17. *L'Espresso*, 14 October 1978.

18. Dario Fo, in *Panorama*, 7 March 1978.

19. Interview in *Ottobre*, 22 February 1979.

20. Dario Fo, *Storia di un soldato*, Milan, Electa, 1979, p. 22.
21. Marta Morazzoni, in *Il Sipario*, January 1979.
22. *Corriere della Sera*, 5 April 1979.
23. Ibid.

Chapter 14 On the Defensive

1. *Il Nord*, 8 January 1979. In successive numbers, the magazine gave detailed accounts of the trial, with lengthy quotations from the various parties to the action. The case was covered by other newspapers and periodicals. I have compared and contrasted various reports of the case.
2. *Il Giorno*, 28 January 1979.
3. *Il Nord*, 22 February 1979.
4. Anna Pensotti in interview with Franca Rame, *Oggi*, January 1980.
5. Interview with Cristina Mazza, *Bolero Teletutto*, 18 January 1980.
6. Interview with Pensotti, *Oggi*, op. cit.
7. Interview with Lalla Mori, *L'occhio*, January 1980.
8. Theodore Zeldin, *An Intimate History of Humanity*, London, Sinclair-Stevenson, 1994, p. 233.
9. Mori, op. cit.
10. *La Repubblica*, 11 March 1987.
11. This information is based on a discussion with Dario Fo in 1984.
12. Franca Rame in interview with the author, *Scotsman*, 28 August 1986.
13. Private interview with Piero Sciotto.
14. Interview with Ferdinando Scianna, *L'Europeo*, 19 January 1981.
15. *Sipario*, August–September, 1985, quoted by David L. Hirst, op. cit., p. 74 (translation mine).
16. Dario Fo, *L'opera dello sghignazzo*, Milan, Edizioni La Comune, 1982, p. 5.
17. *Tricks of the Trade*, op. cit, p. 92.

Chapter 15 Separations and Reconciliations

1. Dario Fo, *Fabulazzo osceno*, Milan, Kaos 1982, p. 3.
2. *Oggi*, 5 December 1984.
3. Interview with Ugo Volli, *La Repubblica*, 6 December, 1984.
4. *Il volo* (inflight magazine of Alitalia), November, 1985, p. 35.
5. Interview in *Marie Claire*, August 1988.
6. Private interview with Ron Jenkins.
7. Interview in *Panorama*, 17 August 1986.
8. Renato Palazzi in *Corriere della Sera*, 17 October 1986.
9. *Marie Claire*, op. cit.
10. Dario Fo, *Il ratto della Francesca*, Milan, Edizioni La Comune, 1986.
11. Interview in *Il Messaggero*, 16 April 1987.
12. Gerald Larner, *Guardian*, 26 March 1987.

13. Dialogue reported verbatim in Carlo Verdelli, 'Sono solo nozze di Rame,' in *Epoca*, 16 February 1987.

14. Interview with the author, in *Plays and Players*, June, 1987.

15. *Panorama*, 15 February 1987.

16. *Corriere della Sera*, 11 March 1987.

17. *Panorama*, op. cit.

Chapter 16 Debts and Homage

1. Dario Fo, *Manuale minimo dell'attore*, Turin, Einaudi, 1987; *Tricks of the Trade*, (translated by Joseph Farrell), London, Methuen, 1991.

2. Interview on *Tricks of the Trade* in *Il Messaggero*, 16 April 1987.

3. *Tricks*, op. cit., p. 109.

4. Inteview in *Panorama*, 20 December 1987.

5. Ibid.

6. Ibid.

7. Dario Fo, *Johan Padan a la Descoverta de le Americhe*, Florence, Giunti, 1992.

8. Antonio Scuderi, *Dario Fo and Popular Performance*, New York, Legas, 1998, pp. 42–3.

9. Jacopo Fo, *Lo Zen e l'arte di scopare*, Bussolengo, Demetra, 1995. The playscript is given as an appendix.

Chapter 17 The Actor Vindicated

1. Chiara Valentini, *Espresso*, 23 October 1997, p. 80.

Chapter 18 New Enthusiasms

1. *Corriere della Sera*, 15 December 1998.

2. Dario Fo, *La vera storia di Ravenna*, Modena, Panini, 1999.

3. *Corriere della Sera*, 2 August 1999.

4. *L'Avvenire*, 11 July 1999.

Bibliography

The theatrical works of Dario Fo and Franca Rame have gone through various editions and publishers. It is hard to talk of a definitive form of a Fo script, but Franca Rame has edited the Einaudi edition, of which there are so far thirteen volumes. This is as close to a canonical text as there will be:

Vol. I: *Gli arcangeli non giocano a flipper, Aveva due pistole con gli occhi bianchi e neri, Chi ruba un piede è fortunato in amore*

Vol. II: *Isabella, tre caravelle e un cacciaballe, La colpa è sempre del diavolo*

Vol. III: *Grande pantomima con pupazzi piccoli e medi, L'operaio conosce trecento parole, il padrone mille: per questo lui è il padrone, Legami pure che tanto spacco tutto lo stesso*

Vol. IV: *Vorrei morire anche stasera se dovessi sapere che non è servito a niente, Tutti uniti, tutti insieme, ma scusa, quello non è il padrone?, Fedayn*

Vol. V: *Mistero buffo, Ci ragiono e canto*

Vol. VI: *La Marcolfa, Gli imbianchini non hanno ricordi, I tre bravi, Non tutti i ladri vengono per nuocere, Un morto da vendere, I cadaveri si spediscono e le donne si spogliano, L'uomo nudo e l'uomo in frack, Canzoni e ballate*

Vol. VII: *Morte accidentale di un anarchico, La signora è da buttare*

Vol. VIII: *25 monologhi per una donna*

Vol. IX *Coppia aperta, quasi spalancata, Una giornata qualunque, La casellante, Il pupazzo giapponese, L'uomo incinto, I piatti, Il problema dei vecchi, Il blackout, Previsioni meteorologiche movimenti di stupro in Italia, Voce amica, Ho fatto la plastica, La nonna incinta, Il figlio in provetta, Parigi-Dakar, Lettera dalla Cina*

Vol. X: *Il Fanfani rapito, Clacson, trombette e pernacchi, Il ratto della Francesca, Il Papa e la strega*

Vol. XI: *Storia vera di Piero D, Angera che alla crociata non c'era, L'opera dello sghignazzo, Quasi per caso una donna: Elisabetta*

Vol. XII: *Non si paga! Non si paga!, La marijuana della mamma è la più bella, Dio li fa e poi li accoppa, Il braccato, Zitti! Stiamo precipitando!, Mamma! I Sanculotti!*

Vol. XIII: *L'eroina, Grasso è bello!, Sesso? Grazie, tanto per gradire*

Other Plays

Compagni Senza Censura (2 volumes), Milan, Mazzotta, 1970
Storia di un Soldato, Milan, Electa, 1979
Arlecchino, in Cacao no. 1, Alcatraz News, Perugia, 1985
Johan Padan a la descoverta de le Americhe, Florence, Giunti, 1992
Marino Innocente! Marino Libero! Turin, Einaudi, 1998

Other Works by Dario Fo

Ballate e canzoni (introduced by Lanfranco Binni), Rome, Newton Compton, 1976
Il teatro politico di Dario Fo, Milan, Mazzotta,1977
Dario Fo parla di Dario Fo (with Erminia Artese), Cosenza, Lerici, 1977
Manuale minimo dell'attore, Milan, Einaudi,1987
Dialogo provocatorio sul comico, il tragico, la follia e la ragione (with Luigi Allegri), Bari, Laterza, 1990
Totò: Manuale dell'attor comico, Turin, Aleph, 1991 (second edition: Florence, Vallecchi, 1995)
Fabulazzo (edited by Lorenzo Ruggiero and Walter Valeri), Milan, Kaos, 1991
Vladimir Majakovski: Messaggi ai posteri selezionati e condivisi da Dario Fo, Rome, Editori Riuniti, 1994
La vera storia di Ravenna, Modena, Franco Cosimo Panini, 1999

Works by Franca Rame

Non parlarmi degli archi, parlami della tue galere, Milan, F. R. Edizioni, 1984
Parliamo di donne, Milan, Kaos, 1992

Catalogues and Anthologies

Il teatro dell'occhio/The Theatre of the Eye, Florence, La Casa Usher, 1984
Pupazzi con rabbia e sentimento, Milan, Libri Schweiller, 1998
Disegni geniali di Federico Fellini e Dario Fo, Milan, Mazzotta, 1999

Selected Plays in English

Can't Pay? Won't Pay! translated by Lino Pertile, adapted by Bill Colville and Robert Walker, London, Pluto Press, 1978. Second edition, London, Methuen, 1988
Accidental Death of an Anarchist, translated by Gillian Hanna, adapted by Gavin Richards, London, Pluto Press, 1980
Accidental Death of an Anarchist, translated by Ed Emery, in Plays: One, London Methuen, 1992
Accidental Death of an Anarchist, adapted by Alan Cumming and Tim Supple,

London, Methuen, 1991

Coming Home, translated by Ed Emery, London, Theatretexts, 1984

The Mother, translated by Ed Emery, London, Theatretexts, 1984

The Open Couple, translated by Ed Emery, London, Theatretexts, 1984

The Rape, translated by Ed Emery, London, Theatretexts, 1984

The Tale of a Tiger, translated by Ed Emery, London, Theatretexts, 1984

One Was Nude and One Wore Tails, translated by Ed Emery, London, Theatretexts, 1985

Archangels Don't Play Pinball, translated by R.C. McAvoy and Anna-Maria Giugni, London, Methuen, 1987

Trumpets and Raspberries, translated by R.C. McAvoy and Anna-Maria Giugni, London, Methuen, 1986

Elizabeth: Almost by Chance a Woman, translated by Gillian Hanna, London, Methuen, 1987

Mistero Buffo, translated by Ed Emery, Methuen, 1988

Archangels Don't Play Pinball, translated by Ron Jenkins, New York, Samuel French, 1989

The Open Couple and *An Ordinary Day*, translated by Joseph Farrell and Stuart Hood, London, Methuen, 1990

The Tale of a Tiger, translated by Ron Jenkins, *Theater*, vol. 21, Winter 1990

A Woman Alone & Other Plays, translated by Ed Emery, Gillian Hanna, Christopher Cairns, London, Methuen, 1991

The Pope and the Witch, translated by Ed Emery, adapted by Andy de la Tour, London, Methuen, 1992

Plays: One (contains *Mistero Buffo, Accidental Death of an Anarchist, Trumpets and Raspberries, The Virtuous Burglar, One Was Nude and One Wore Tails*), London, Methuen, 1992

Plays: Two (contains *Can't pay? Won't Pay!, Elizabeth, The Open Couple, An Ordinary Day*) London, Methuen, 1994

Abducting Diana, translated by Rupert Lowe, adapted by Stephen Stenning, Bath, Oberon, 1996

The Devil in Drag, translated by Ed Emery, in *New Connections 99*, London, Faber and Faber, 1999

Also in English

Tricks of the Trade, translated by Joseph Farrell, London, Methuen, 1987

Secondary Sources

Angelini, Franca, *Il teatro del Novecento da Pirandello a Fo*, Bari, Laterza, 1976

Behan, Tom, *Dario Fo: Revolutionary Theatre*, London, Pluto Press, 2000

Bermani, Cesare, *Una storia Cantata*, Milan, Jaca Book, 1997

Binni, Lanfranco, *Attento te! Il teatro politico di Dario Fo*, Verona, Bertani Editore,

1975

Binni, Lanfranco, *Dario Fo*, Florence, La Nuova Italia, 1977

Cairns, Christopher, *Dario Fo: E La "Pittura Scenica": Arte Teatro Regie 1977–1997*, Naples, Edizioni Scientifiche Italiane, 2000

Cairns, Christopher (editor) *The commedia dell'arte from the Renaissance to Dario Fo*, Queenstown/Lampeter, Edwin Mellen, 1989

Cappa, Marina, and Nepoti, Roberto, *Dario Fo*, Rome, Gremese, 1982

Emery, Ed (editor) *Dario Fo and Franca Rame: Theatre Workshops at Riverside Studios, April–May 1983*, London, Red Notes, 1983

Farrell, Joseph and Scuderi, Antonio (editors) *Dario Fo: Stage, Text, and Tradition*, Carbondale, Southern Illinois University Press, 2000

Fo Garambois, Bianca, *La ringhiera dei miei vent'anni*, Turin, Einaudi, 1981

Fo Rota, Pina, *Il paese delle rane*, Turin, Einaudi, 1978

Hirst, David, *Dario Fo and Franca Rame*, London, MacMillan, 1989

Hirst, David, *Giorgio Strehler*, Cambridge University Press, 1987

Holm, Bent, *Il mondo rovesciato. Dario Fo e la fantasia popolare*, Stockholm, Drama, 1980

Jannaci, Enzo, *Canzoni* (introduced by Gianfranco Manfredi), Rome, Lato Side, 1980

Jenkins, Ron, *Subversive Laughter*, New York, Free Press, 1994

Lecoq, Jacques, *The Moving Body*, London, Methuen, 2000

Maraini, Dacia, *Fare teatro*, Milan, Bompiani, 1974

Marfai, Miriam, *Il sorpasso*, Milan, Mondadori, 1997

Meldolesi, Claudio, *Su un comico in rivolta: Dario Fo il bufalo il bambino*, Rome, Bulzoni, 1978

Mitchell, Tony, *Dario Fo: People's Court Jester*, London, Methuen, 1999

Pizza, Marina, *Il gesto, la parola, l'azione. Poetica, drammaturgia e storia dei monologhi di Dario Fo*, Rome, Bulzoni, 1996

Puppa, Paolo, *Il teatro di Dario Fo: dalla scena alla piazza*, Venice, Marsilio, 1978

Quadri, Franco, *Il teatro del regime*, Milan, Mazzotta, 1976

Quadri, Franco, *La politica del regista*, Milan, Edizioni Il Formichiere, 1980

Scuderi, Antonio, *Dario Fo and Popular Performance*, New York, Legas, 1998

Straniero, Michele, *Giullari e Fo*, Rome, Lato Side, 1978

Valentini, Chiara, *La storia di Dario Fo*, Milan, Feltrinelli, 1977

Index

Ginsburg, Allen, 238
Ginzburg, Carlo, 266
Ginzburg, Natalia, 199
Il Giornale, 271
Girotto, Silvano, 155
giullari, 26, 77, 143, 257, 273, 283
Golden Harlequin award, Mantua, 280
Goldoni, Carlo, 28
Good Soldier Schweik, 40
Gorki, Maxim, *Lower Depths*, 23
grammelot, 216, 283
Gramsci, Antonio, 17–18, 70, 92, 136, 176, 184, 189; *Prison Notebooks*, 17
Grass, Gunther, 109
Grassi, Paolo, 19, 23, 39, 46, 115, 131
Greco, Juliette, 37
Green party, 281
Gruppo Abele, 154
Gruppo Teatro e Azione, 76
Guattari, Felix, 213
Gui, Luigi, 183
Guinness, Alec, 42

Halliwell, Kenneth, 124
Hannah, Gillian, 238
Harlequin, 44, 74, 100, 146, 220, 246–7, 251, 255, 257, 260, 273, 278
Harrison, George, 155
Hepburn, Audrey, 53
'historic compromise', 127
Hobsbawm, Eric, 75
Hochhuth, Rolf, *The Deputy*, 190
Holm, Bent, 57, 217
Hood, Stuart, 103, 238
The Hunchbacks, 37
Hussein, King, 97

Ibsen, Henrik, 29, 273
Invernizzi, Irene, 112
Ionesco, Eugene, 37, 47, 48, 176, 220, 273; *The Bald Prima Donna*, 43; *The Chairs*, 43
Irigaray, Luce, 202
Isabella, Queen, 65
Italia Nostra, 133

Italian Playwrights' Federation, 173
Italian Recreational and Cultural Associations (ARCI), 80, 81, 83, 84, 88, 92, 93, 94, 95
Italian Theatre Board (ETI), 249
Italian Women's Committee, 187
Izzo, Angelo, 119–20

Jacopone da Todi, 190
Janacci, Enzo, 35, 36–7, 73; 'The Dog With the Hair', 36
Jara, Victor, 128
Jenkins, Ron, 247, 248, 264
jesters *see giullari*
Jinan Artistic Company, 162
John Paul II, Pope, 260, 266
John XXIII, Pope, 58
Jouvet, Louis, 255
Judas, 184–5

Kennedy, J.F., 74
Kind Hearts and Coronets, 42
Kipling, Rudyard, 218
Kraus, Karl, *The Last Days of Humanity*, 39
Kristeva, Julia, 202

Labiche, Eugène-Marin, 47
Lake Maggiore, 1, 4, 5, 7, 10, 277
Lama, Luciano, 183
Lu Lanzone, Michele, 202
De Laurentiis, Dino, 45
Lawrence, D.H., 4
Lazagna, Giambattista, 155–6
Lazzarini, Giacinto, 227, 230
Leary, Timothy, 155, 169
Lecoq, Jacques, 39–40, 41, 43, 47, 215, 255, 278
Led Zeppelin, 145
Léger, Ferdinand, 18
Lenin, V.I., 140
Leon Felipe Prize for Human Rights, 280
Leone, Giovanni, 174
Let's Talk About Women, 182, 194, 197,